The Cuba Wars

The Cuba Wars

Fidel Castro, the United States,
and the Next Revolution

Daniel P. Erikson

BLOOMSBURY PRESS
New York   Berlin   London

Published by Bloomsbury Press, New York

All papers used by Bloomsbury Press are natural, recyclable products made from wood grown in well-managed forests. The manufacturing processes conform to the environmental regulations of the country of origin.

LIBRARY OF CONGRESS CATALOGING-IN-PUBLICATION DATA

Erikson, Daniel P.
    The Cuba wars : Fidel Castro, the United States, and the next revolution / by Daniel P. Erikson.
        p.   cm.
    Includes bibliographical references and index.
    ISBN 978-1-59691-434-6 (alk. paper)
    1. Castro, Fidel, 1926—Influence. 2. Cuba—History—1990– 3. United States—Relations—Cuba. 4. Cuba—Relations—United States. I. Title.

F1788.E65 2008
972.9106'4–dc22
2008015816

First U.S. Edition 2008

1 3 5 7 9 10 8 6 4 2

Typeset by Westchester Book Group
Printed in the United States of America by Quebecor World Fairfield

For Eliza

Contents

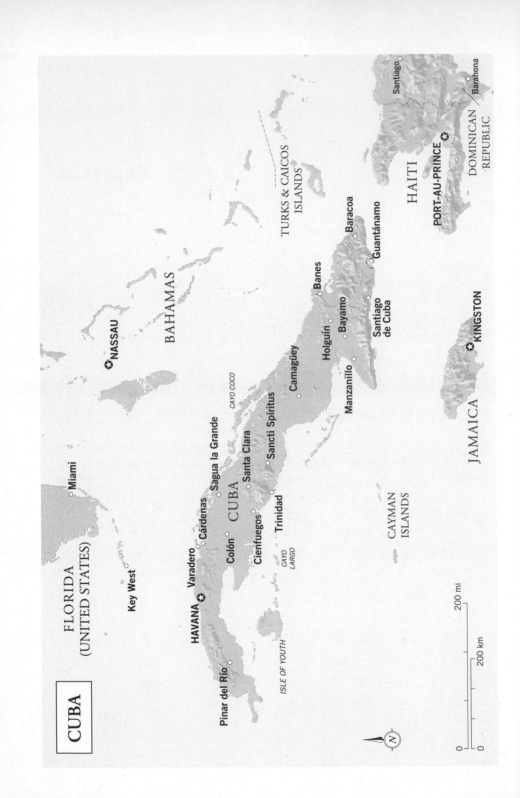

Preface

On the eve of the fiftieth anniversary of the Cuban Revolution, the United States and Cuba remain locked in a long cold war that seems likely to persist, in some fashion, irrespective of which presidential candidate has seized the White House or how boldly or timidly the new Cuban leadership seeks to govern the island. Fidel Castro, the legendary revolutionary figure who took power in Cuba in January 1959, has bequeathed this battle to his successors, and they have signaled a readiness to continue the fight. The United States government, for its part, has internalized its allergic reaction to Cuban socialism to such a large degree that any attempt to change course and seek a rapprochement with Cuba will be the equivalent of making a train jump off its tracks. By all appearances, the United States and Cuba will continue in a cycle of mutual hostility for the foreseeable future, although the possibility remains that the U.S. may lift its embargo on Cuba if the island's new government moves markedly toward democracy.

From Washington's perspective, it had long been hoped that the difficulties in resolving the U.S.-Cuba conflict held the promise of an easy answer: the death of Fidel. This event, sometimes referred to inelegantly as "the biological solution," was supposed to trigger major changes in Cuba that could pave the way for the return of democracy to the island and the normalization of relations with the United States. In the early 1960s, the United States actively sought to bring it about through covert operations against Cuba, but in more recent decades the U.S. approach was based on patiently waiting for Castro's demise. The actuarial timetables, it was thought, would bring about the desired result without the need for greater contact and engagement with Havana that was politically unpopular among Cuban exiles in South

Florida. The events of the past two years show just how flawed that thinking was. Fidel did indeed grow old and fall seriously ill in July 2006 at the age of seventy-nine, and his illness was a shock to Cuba's political system. But it also paved the way for his communist government's rusty succession process gradually to swing into gear under the leadership of his younger brother, Raúl. Nineteen months later, when Fidel formally penned his resignation letter in February 2008, the Cuban government consummated a smooth leadership transition that left Raúl and other members of the country's old guard fully in charge. Still, the temptation persists for the United States to wait until Raúl has passed away before shifting course or seeking to engage with the new government. Since there are other communist leaders poised to take charge after Raúl, this process could take a very long time indeed. Furthermore, while the death of Fidel will remain an extraordinarily significant political moment when it finally occurs, its impact will necessarily be diluted by the simple fact that he is no longer Cuba's president.

As the presidency of George W. Bush recedes into history, there is likely to be a wide range of retrospective analysis on the legacy of his foreign policies, much of which will focus on his handling of the September 11 terrorist attacks and the subsequent war in Iraq. Far less will be written about Bush's impact on Latin America, but one suspects that there will be some renewed attention to Cuba, given the country's leadership transition and its salience in U.S. domestic politics. Indeed, it is difficult to underestimate how deeply the policies of the Bush White House influenced Cuban perceptions of the United States at all levels, and not for the better. Bush's declarations of a global "war on terror" deeply rattled the Cuban government, which has long been deemed by the State Department to be a "state sponsor of terrorism," and Cuba was specifically accused by top U.S. officials of having a developmental biological weapons program. The Cuban people, like most citizens across the globe, were alarmed by the preventive war launched on Iraq, and some grew to believe their government's claim that their country could be a potential future target. The Guantánamo Bay Naval Base, located on Cuba's easternmost tip, became the warehouse for suspected Al Qaeda operatives held beyond the reach of U.S. or international law. At the same time, the Bush administration's decision to shelter Luis Posada Carriles, an aging anti-Castro militant accused of committing serious terrorist acts against Cuba, belied the seriousness of the U.S. anti-terror campaign. Meanwhile, new sanctions implemented in 2004 cut back sharply on the ability of Cuban Americans to visit their families on the island. In addition, the Bush administration allowed Venezuelan president Hugo Chávez to evolve from a regional nuisance to a full-blown adversary of U.S. interests in the hemisphere, and become one of Cuba's closest allies. These policies and outcomes are all part of the legacy bequeathed by President Bush to his successor in the White House.

During his final years in power, Castro also engaged in numerous actions that were severely detrimental to both the people of Cuba and the U.S.-Cuba relationship. At home, he maintained his staunch resistance to economic reforms that could have improved the livelihoods of Cuba's struggling citizens, who were attempting to make ends meet in a climate of pervasive scarcity. In 2003, he implemented a sweeping crackdown on internal dissent that dramatically expanded the number of political prisoners held in Cuban jails. He supervised acts of espionage against the United States that extended to a top official in the Pentagon and a spy network, including the "Cuban Five," intended to keep tabs on exile groups in Miami. His mentorship no doubt played an important role in turning Chávez against the United States, and he remained a fierce critic of what he termed "the American empire" in all its forms.

In South Florida, the Cuban American community has held enormous sway over U.S.-Cuba policy, and in recent years, it tightened its grip on both the executive and the legislative branches of the U.S. government. Strongly supported by President Bush, heavily influential on Capitol Hill (with the help of two Cuban American senators, four representatives, and one of the best lobbying games in Washington), and a political and financial force in Miami, the Cuban exile community reached new heights of political power during the Bush years. Yet it still remained powerless to achieve what it claimed to seek—a transition to democracy in Cuba—because its leadership had so fully renounced the diplomatic tools and economic leverage required to meet that objective. In the absence of political dialogue, economic engagement, communication, and contact, the Cuban exiles rely almost wholly on the bureaucratic tools of the U.S. government to force a change in Cuba.

The obvious failure of this approach has prompted some leaders in Miami to question anew whether the United States' commitment to sanctions, federally funded broadcasts of Radio and TV Martí, and democracy assistance programs can ever achieve the democratization of Cuba. The bad news is that there is little evidence to suggest that this approach will ever succeed. The good news is that Miami's Cuban exile groups have largely rejected the idea that armed intervention against Cuba will lead to anything positive. However, the vast majority of the community's elected leaders still believe that "the road back to Havana leads through Washington," when they could instead be fighting to get U.S. restrictions out of the way and empower their own constituents to engage with Cuba on the community and individual level. More broadly, the same dynamic is true for the American people, who are ready to trade with, travel to, and engage with Cuba as soon as their government will let them.

It has become a truism in U.S. foreign policy circles, and even among Cuba experts, that Cuba is not important. It is, after all, a small island nation of eleven million people, crippled by the twin (and related) scourges of poverty and communism, that matters little in the global economy and only occasionally makes a splash in the world of international diplomacy. True, it produced in Fidel Castro one of the great icons of the cold war, and its famous exports include fine cigars and rum and world-class music and baseball, but that is about as far as it goes. In foreign policy terms, Cuba is an afterthought or a punch line, or maybe a political football: interesting perhaps, but it does not intrinsically *matter*. This line of argument is seductive, and it reflects a certain logic, but it fails on the merits. The truth is that Cuba matters a great deal, and it should matter a great deal to the United States.

Cuba is one of the world's last remaining communist strongholds, located merely ninety miles from the shores of Florida. The U.S. embargo of Cuba is the most comprehensive, far-reaching, and long-lasting policy of its kind in the world. Since Castro took power, more than one million exiles have fled Cuba to make new lives in the United States, and they have left an indelible imprint on the life and politics of our nation. Thousands more have perished attempting to cross the Straits of Florida, and hundreds of political prisoners remain in Cuban jails. The domestic political impact of Cuba policy reverberates deeply in Florida, with the potential to shift U.S. presidential election outcomes via this pivotal swing state. Cuba bears the brunt of soaring American rhetoric about democracy and human rights while at the same time serving as the involuntary host for the globally condemned

Guantánamo Bay detention facility. Over fifty years, U.S.-Cuban relations have become a densely knotted web that encompasses issues of communism and democracy, domestic politics and foreign policy, and diplomacy and security. The scope, intensity, and duration of the standoff reveals a great deal about both nations.

There is a reason this book is titled *The Cuba Wars: Fidel Castro, the United States, and the Next Revolution.* The Cuba wars are the intersecting conflicts that drive the United States and Cuba apart even as they are bound together by political, economic, and cultural linkages that are a fact of life for both countries. Fidel Castro and the United States are the two great adversaries who suspiciously eyed each other across the Straits of Florida for the past half century. The "next revolution" will be the revolution of expectations that is slowly being unleashed in Cuba by the unfolding leadership transition, and it will undoubtedly be matched by rising expectations for a change in U.S. policy when the next American president—the eleventh to confront a Castro at the helm of Cuba—steps into the White House in January 2009.

Indeed, the fiftieth anniversary of the Cuban Revolution on January 1, 2009, presents an auspicious moment to reexamine this contentious relationship. After a half-century of antipathy, it is clear there is no magic solution that will yield a Cuba that is prosperous, democratic, and treated as a valued partner by the United States. But there are steps that can be taken by both sides. In order to envision a more promising future, we must first understand the present, and that will require taking a hard look at the reality as it is, not as we would like it to be.

Daniel P. Erikson
August 1, 2008
Washington, D.C.

CHAPTER 1

Die Another Day

Fidel Castro was accustomed to keeping his country immersed in a state of feverish speculation, but now the time for a decision loomed. Nearly nineteen months had passed while he tried to battle back from the illness that had forced him to relinquish power in July 2006. His health had collapsed during the early months, leaving him at death's door, but he had been gradually gaining strength and weight, and it was possible that he would live for some time more. His brother Raúl, who had assumed the provisional powers of government in Fidel's absence, had proved to be a competent administrator, but he was also growing restless. Moreover, Fidel was aware that his precarious health had ushered his nation into a strange twilight zone that had left him at the mercy of his successors, not the other way around.

Fidel had not been seen publicly in Cuba since his health crisis began, but he remained a prominent voice by writing periodic "reflections" in the national press about international issues that grabbed his attention. His first essay, published on March 28, 2007, attacked a new ethanol initiative planned by President George W. Bush and Brazilian president Luiz Inácio Lula da Silva, which Fidel decried as a "sinister plan for turning foodstuffs into fuel" that would leave "more than three billion people condemned to premature death from hunger and thirst." A steady stream of more than fifty op-eds followed, pondering topics including global warming, the price of oil, the political travails of Venezuelan president Hugo Chávez, the recent death of Raúl's wife, Vilma Espín, and the complicated legal dramas of Luis Posada Carriles and the Cuban Five. The most important function of these "reflections," however, was to signal that Fidel Castro was still alive.

In the waning weeks of 2007, though, Fidel began to drop hints that his days as the formal president of Cuba were drawing to a close. On December 17, he sent a message to be read aloud on Cuban television by the host of the political discussion show *Mesa Redonda* (Round Table). "My deepest conviction is that the answers to current problems in Cuban society," Fidel wrote, "require more varied responses for each concrete problem than the contents of a chessboard." He then added, "My essential duty is to not cling to posts, much less block the way for younger people, but to contribute experiences and ideas whose modest value comes from the exceptional era in which it was my destiny to live. I think . . . that one must be consistent until the end."

Eleven days later, Fidel conveyed a similar message at the ritual year-end session of Cuba's National Assembly, even though the Cuban leader himself was nowhere to be seen. It was December 28, 2007, and Raúl presided over the meeting while seated next to a chair left empty in honor of his ailing brother. He read aloud from a letter Fidel had written to clarify his position further. Referring to his past as a "utopian socialist," Fidel reflected on the fact that "what the foreign press in Cuba have most reported in recent days has been the phrase where I expressed . . . that I am not a person who clings to power. I could add that I was once, for the excesses of youth and lack of conscience. What changed me? Life itself." When Raúl finished reading the letter, the more than five hundred Communist Party delegates present rose and burst into applause. Still, Raúl insisted that his brother remained politically viable, noting that Fidel had been exercising, gaining weight, and meditating and writing regularly. "His powerful mind is healthier," Raúl said as he scoffed at the chances of political reform. "We could say in Cuba we have two parties: one led by Fidel and one led by Raúl. What would be the difference?" he asked. "That's the same thing that happens in the United States . . . both are the same. Fidel is a little taller than me; he has a beard and I don't."[1] It had long been thought that Raúl Castro would be a short-lived transitional leader in Cuba—a simple man who played "checkers" whereas his brother, the master strategist, played "chess." In those terms, Fidel Castro was now paradoxically both one move away from being checkmated and still in full control of the chessboard.

In February 2008, the National Assembly was scheduled to meet to ratify a new Council of State, which is the island's highest governing body. The president of the Council of State is the top role in Cuba's government—and the person who holds the position is also the president of Cuba—although it is arguably a less powerful post than the head of the Cuban Communist Party, which is described in the constitution as "the highest directing force of the society and state." The meeting to choose a new Council of State takes place every five years, and in the past Fidel's selection as president was a foregone conclusion. The Cuban leader's poor health and cryptic writings had raised the possibility that he would seize the opportunity to formally pass the presidency to his brother and end the provisional arrangement that had endured since the summer of 2006. Still, many doubted that Fidel Castro, the most Machiavellian leader in Cuban history, would relinquish his grip on power before he drew his last breath.

On February 19, 2008, he delivered his verdict. The Cuban newspaper *Granma* published a message from Fidel that rendered his decision in no uncertain terms. "There were those overseas who, aware of my critical health condition, thought that my provisional resignation, on July 31, 2006, to the position of President of the State Council, which I left to First Vice-President Raúl Castro Ruz, was final," Fidel wrote. "Later, in my necessary retreat, I was able to recover the full command of my mind as well as the possibility for much reading and meditation. I had enough physical strength to write for many hours, which I shared with the corresponding rehabilitation and recovery programs . . . When referring to my health I was extremely careful to avoid raising expectations since I felt that an adverse ending would bring traumatic news to our people in the midst of the battle. Thus, my first duty was to prepare our people both politically and psychologically for my absence after so many years of struggle. I kept saying that my recovery 'was not without risks.' My wishes have always been to discharge my duties to my last breath. That's all I can offer." Fidel concluded with the words that, after forty-nine years, brought his tenure as Cuba's unrivaled leader to its much-anticipated end. "I will neither aspire to nor accept, I repeat, I will neither aspire to nor accept the positions of President of the State Council and Commander in Chief." Fidel Castro's long reign as Cuba's supreme ruler was over.

Five days later, on February 24, the National Assembly confirmed Raúl Castro as the president of Cuba. The awkward provisional arrangement that had been speedily implemented in the summer of 2006 was no more. Cuba had a new leader, but also a familiar one, who had been joined at the hip with his older brother since their initial triumph in the Cuban Revolution in 1959. It was both a historic moment and a strangely anticlimactic one. Raúl's ascension merely finalized the transfer of power that had occurred many months earlier. Not only was Fidel still alive, defying the gloomiest predictions about his health, but he even retained his seat in the assembly and the powerful post of executive secretary of the Communist Party. While the event received significant media attention overseas, there were no celebrations in Miami, as had occurred when Fidel's sickness was first reported. A spokesman for the U.S. State Department merely dismissed the change as "a transfer of authority and power from one dictator to a dictator-lite, from Fidel to Raúl." Bush, who was caught off guard by the news while on a stop in Rwanda during a tour through Africa, announced that "the United States will help the people of Cuba realize the blessings of liberty" and voiced his support for the U.S. embargo. Even without Fidel Castro at the helm, the struggle between the United States and Cuba showed few signs of fading.

"I die just about every day," Fidel Castro told a television interviewer several weeks before reaching his eightieth birthday in 2006. "But it's really a lot of fun for me, and it makes me feel healthier." Indeed, the aging bearded leader who had ruled Cuba for decades appeared to be in fighting form during that long, hot summer. Hundreds of thousands of Cubans gathered in Havana's Plaza of the Revolution to see him speak at the country's annual May Day celebrations, where he peppered his remarks with statistics about Cuba's health, education, and energy programs and sarcastically thanked the United States for its long-standing embargo of Cuba. After more than forty-seven years in power, Castro still provoked deep and conflicting emotions within the Cuban population, where he was adored, feared, and despised— sometimes all at once. But no one doubted that he remained fully in charge of his country, a picturesque island just off the coast of the United States that was one of the world's last remaining communist regimes.

Castro loved to bask in the limelight, and controversy followed him throughout the spring and summer. In May, he became entangled in a surreal sparring match with *Forbes* magazine, which featured him in a special survey of the world's richest "Kings, Queens and Dictators" and ranked him as the seventh richest, with an estimated wealth of nine hundred million dollars, nearly double the estimated wealth of the queen of England. The claim sent Castro into a state of apoplexy, prompting him to make a special appearance on Cuban television in which he pounded the table and denounced his presence on the *Forbes* list as "repugnant slander." The magazine admitted its back-of-the-envelope calculations were "more art than science," but Castro was incensed. Accusations of illicit wealth threatened to undermine his carefully cultivated image as an international defender of the downtrodden and dispossessed, and he dismissed the *Forbes* statistic as a smear campaign engineered by the Bush administration and the Central Intelligence Agency. Castro then issued a challenge: "If they can prove that I have one single dollar, I will resign from all my responsibilities and the duties I am carrying out. They won't need any more plans of transitions!"[2]

In July, Castro remained an active force in Cuba, presiding over high-level government discussions, approving a series of new joint ventures with Canadian and Spanish companies, and overseeing plans to celebrate his eightieth birthday on August 13. Toward the end of the month, Castro made a snap decision to attend a South American summit meeting in Argentina at the invitation of his close friend and ally Hugo Chávez. Castro always enjoyed the element of surprise, and it was his custom to leave his travel plans unannounced until the last minute, in part for security reasons. Some of the most brazen assassination attempts against him had occurred at international gatherings in Latin America, and this trip marked his first overseas venture since a short visit to Barbados the previous December.

Besides, Castro was a popular figure in Argentina, a country still suffering from the scars of a brutal economic collapse in 2001 triggered in part by the "neoliberal" economic policies that the Cuban leader never tired of railing against. Castro had been greeted like a rock star during a visit three years earlier, and cries of "Viva Fidel!" followed him as he arrived in the country anew on July 21. "Sometimes I have to misinform even my own friends. Not even I knew I was going to come," he told a crowd at an "anti-imperialist" rally in Argentina's second city, Córdoba. He joined with Hugo Chávez the next day to visit the boyhood home of Ernesto "Che" Guevara, the Argentine medical student who went on to become one of the most iconic figures of the Cuban Revolution. It was an emotional event for the two leaders, especially Chávez, who explained, "Fidel invited me to come and get to know the house. For me, it's a real honor being here." Their celebrity tour left some nearby neighbors reeling from the experience, including one Argentine housewife who commented that the uproar "has thrown the whole city into a state of shock."[3]

Castro's Argentine tour ended on a sour note, however, when an enterprising journalist provoked him into an angry tirade by asking about a sensitive case involving one of Cuba's most noted dissidents. Hilda Molina was one of Cuba's top neurosurgeons and had been a medical superstar until the island's economy started to unravel following the collapse of the Soviet Union in the early 1990s. During the resulting crisis, Cuban medical care facilities were ordered to turn away needy Cubans and instead set aside beds for foreign patients who could pay in hard currency. Molina protested the new policies, which ended her glittering career in the communist system. In 1994, her son fled abroad to Argentina, but the Cuban government refused to allow her to leave, arguing that "your brain is the patrimony of the nation." Molina was unable to even meet her grandchildren, who were later born in Argentina, a situation she decried as "supreme cruelty." The plight of a grandmother separated from her grandchildren turned the case into a cause célèbre, and Argentine president Néstor Kirchner had repeatedly tried to use his cordial relationship with Castro to help Molina gain her coveted exit visa, to no avail.

In Argentina, Juan Manuel Cao, a Cuban American television reporter from Miami, dogged the official Cuban delegation with questions about Molina. When Castro joined the South American presidents at the summit for an official photo ceremony, the scene consisted of barely constrained chaos as photographers, journalists, and spectators jockeyed for the best view of the Cuban leader. Sensing his opportunity, the Miami reporter cried out to Castro, "Why don't you free Dr. Hilda Molina? Why don't you let her come see her grandchildren?" Fidel Castro immediately fixated on the journalist, asking, "What's your name? Who is paying you to come and ask questions like this?" The reporter volunteered that he was from Cuba, and Castro nearly flipped with rage. "I already asked you who paid you," he shouted. "Why don't you look for Bush and ask him about Posada Carriles and the crimes they have committed in his country? Cuban?! You are not Cuban. Che is Cuban. You are an intruder that is living like a mercenary. That's what you are." Most of the exchange was captured on videotape, with photographers' flashbulbs erupting in rapid succession. The stray question had clearly provoked Castro.

The fearsome Cuban dictator was getting pretty thin-skinned in his old age.

Castro arrived back in Havana on July 23, and several days later he traveled down to Bayamo, a sleepy provincial capital located about seventy miles west of Santiago de Cuba, his hometown and the city where his initial assault on the established order of Cuba unfolded on July 26, 1953. On that date, Castro led a group of 150 rebels in a surprise attack on a military garrison in Santiago with the intention of igniting a movement to unseat the dictatorship of Fulgencio Batista. The attack was a military debacle that resulted in the deaths of dozens of rebels, but it succeeded in launching Castro as a major national figure at the tender age of twenty-six, and he later defended himself in a famous speech titled "History Will Absolve Me." He spent nearly two years in a Cuban prison before winning early release in 1955 and leaving for exile in Mexico, and in December 1956, he captained a barely seaworthy vessel named the *Granma* from Mexico to the southern shore of Cuba to relaunch the revolution that would eventually bring him to power on January 1, 1959. Castro christened his revolutionary organization the 26th of July Movement, in honor of the date that marked his first military excursion. As president, he made that date a national holiday in Cuba, and he commemorated it with a major speech annually.

On July 26, 2006, Castro arrived in Bayamo, which is located in the province of Granma, named after the boat he piloted back from exile. The two-lane road to the city is marked by a billboard featuring a sketch of his beloved boat next to the words WHO COULD WRITE THE HISTORY OF CUBA WITHOUT THE HISTORY OF GRANMA? That day marked the fifty-third anniversary of his first attempt to seize power, and Castro's rousing address lasted nearly three hours before one hundred thousand flag-waving Cubans. Dressed in his trademark olive uniform, he boasted of how Cuba's health care system resulted in long life expectancy. "I don't know how many thousands of citizens of this nation have even reached their one hundredth birthday," Castro declared, "but our little northern neighbors shouldn't get scared: I'm not thinking of working at that age." Castro meant it as a joke, but he was in fact delivering his final public speech.

On the verge of his eightieth birthday, Castro turned in a bravura performance, riveting international audiences, antagonizing his foes in the United States, and demonstrating his unrivaled dominance at home. But on July 31, he finally granted the wish that many had long hoped for both inside and outside of Cuba: He gave up power. It was a sweltering Monday evening when Castro's thirty-three-year-old executive assistant, Carlos Valenciaga, appeared on Cuban television to break the historic news. Valenciaga, a bespectacled former student leader, bowed his head and haltingly delivered the somber message. "Days and nights of continuous work with hardly any sleep have caused my health, which has withstood all tests, to fall victim to extreme stress and be ruined," Castro wrote. "This has caused in me an acute intestinal crisis with sustained bleeding that has obliged me to undergo a complicated surgical operation. All the details of this health accident can be seen in X-rays, endoscopies, and filmed material." Then came the bombshell news that Cuba's most power-hungry leader since independence was going to step back from the levers of government: "The operation will force me to take several weeks of rest, away from my responsibilities and duties."

While Castro's dominating and charismatic personality held the key to his long rule in Cuba, he also formally occupied all of the top posts in the country's multiple, overlapping power structures. He was president of the Council of State (the 31-member ruling leadership group), president of the Council of Ministers (the executive leadership and cabinet), executive secretary of the Politburo (the top committee of the Cuban Communist Party), and the commander in chief of the Cuban military (known as the Revolutionary Armed Forces). Castro also represented Santiago as a delegate in the 614-member National Assembly, which basically served as a rubber-stamp parliament to ratify his decisions. His sudden absence would leave a gaping hole at the top of the Cuban power structure. Now faced with disabling illness, Castro stopped short of abdicating his role at the helm of Cuba's government. Instead, he issued an edict authorizing a provisional transfer of power that left him with the option of reassuming his duties once his health had stabilized. As jaws dropped across Cuba, Castro's letter reader announced on national television the bureaucratic reshuffling that would accompany the leader's respite from power. In the space of six neat bullet points read out over a few minutes, Fidel Castro created a set of winners and losers, determining who would wield power during this new transitional phase.

Raúl Castro quickly emerged as the biggest winner. Having fought alongside Fidel during the Cuban Revolution, Raúl had been appointed the head of the army during the government's earliest days. During his decades of service as Fidel's right-hand man, he had accumulated an impressive array of titles, including first vice president of the Council of State, vice president of the Council of Ministers, and second secretary of the Cuban Communist Party. Most important, he was the head of Cuba's powerful military and had earned the peculiar honor of being the world's longest-serving minister of defense. Now the seventy-five-year-old heir to the throne quickly racked up an expansive new set of responsibilities previously reserved for Fidel, including the presidencies of the Council of State and Council of Ministers, head of the Communist Party, and commander in chief of the Cuban armed forces. Still, his older brother had pointedly described the promotion as "provisional." Even in the grip of the most serious health crisis he had ever faced, Fidel left the door open for his future return to power.

In addition to Raúl, a team of six other ministers were explicitly named to take on new responsibilities in Fidel's absence. All of the men chosen by Fidel were part of his inner circle, but their ages spanned nearly three decades, and they came from diverse backgrounds. Seventy-four-year-old health minister José Ramón Balaguer and seventy-six-year-old vice president José Ramón Machado Ventura had both fought with Fidel's rebel army in the late 1950s. Now they were responsible respectively for Cuba's health and education programs. Esteban Lazo, the sixty-two-year-old vice president, the chief of ideology for the Communist Party, and the highest-ranking black man in the Cuban government, was also tasked as a chief promoter of education. Carlos Lage, the fifty-four-year-old doctor who served as vice president and economic czar, was among the few potential reformers who had remained in Fidel's good graces. He was charged with supervising the island's energy programs and overseeing "cooperation with other countries in this field," and thereby elevated to key point man in managing Cuba's crucial relationship with Hugo Chávez in oil-rich Venezuela. In addition, Fidel named a troika of individuals to administer state funds: Lage; the sixty-two-year-old president of the Central Bank, Francisco Soberón; and the forty-one-year-old foreign minister, Felipe Pérez Roque. One name that was notably missing was Ricardo Alarcón, the sixty-nine-year-old president of the National Assembly, who was a major public figure both in Cuba and abroad. The absence of Cuba's top legislator may simply have resulted from a desire to preserve the fiction of a separation of powers between the executive and legislative branches of government. In practice, most top government officials were also National Assembly delegates, and Alarcón remained a prominent voice in the months ahead.

The torch of power in Cuba had been passed, if not to the next generation, then at least to a group of men whose average age was more than a decade younger than Fidel's. The Cuban leader also decreed that his August 13 birthday celebrations would be postponed until December 2, 2006, the fiftieth anniversary of the day Fidel's ragtag band of youthful revolutionaries came ashore at the island's eastern tip aboard the *Granma*. He concluded with a pugnacious sign-off: "I do not have the slightest doubt that our people and our revolution will fight to the last drop of blood to defend these and other ideas and measures that are necessary to safeguard this historic process. Imperialism will never be able to crush Cuba."

Fidel's sudden illness that summer was more than just a shock to Cuba's political system. It also posed a direct challenge to a series of assumptions that had, over the years, become the bedrock foundation of U.S. policy toward Cuba. Almost like a religion, the U.S.-Cuba relationship was guided by several central tenets that had been widely accepted on faith: The death of Fidel Castro would trigger major changes in Cuba. Raúl Castro was incapable of maintaining his grip on power without embracing major reforms. Cuba's political opposition figures would be at the vanguard of a democratic revolution in Cuba, and once Fidel was dead, his legacy would be repudiated by the Cuban people, who were longing to be free. Cuban exiles in the United States would rush back to the island to reclaim their expropriated properties. Deprived of its number-one bogeyman in the hemisphere, the United States would tilt toward a process of engagement in Cuba and inevitably play a major role in the island's future as the two countries' long cold war drew to a close. Fidel's surprise handoff of power was about to subject Washington's untested assumptions about Cuba to a harsh reality check.

The revelation that Fidel Castro was gravely ill hit Miami like a bombshell. Minutes after the announcement was televised in Havana, the news traveled across phone lines from Cubans on the island to their relatives in South Florida. Castro's declaration would be the lead news story in the United States the following day, preempting the round-the-clock coverage of the military conflict in Lebanon and news of Mel

Gibson's drunken anti-Semitic escapades in Hollywood that had dominated the airwaves in the final days of July. U.S. newspapers anxiously dusted off and updated obituaries for Castro that had been drafted long ago. In some cases, reporters found themselves revising work first written by journalists who had already died years before, even as Castro lived on.

In Washington and Miami, the BlackBerries of Cuban American power brokers buzzed with alerts that the moment they had long been awaiting appeared to have arrived at last. Within hours, crowds of people gathered to celebrate in Miami's Little Havana, the cultural epicenter for the more than one million Cuban exiles who had fled Castro's rule for a better life in the United States. The city's Spanish-language radio stations were flooded with elated callers, including one woman who exclaimed, "This is the happiest day of my life!" Carlos Alvarez, the Cuban-born mayor of Miami-Dade County, urged residents to indulge in their merriment safely: "It is a cause for celebration. We certainly don't want to hinder in any way, shape or form the enthusiasm we all feel."[4] Outside, the cars continued honking as people banged pots and pans, waved Cuban flags, and came together to cheer, sing, and dance on Fidel Castro's proverbial grave. Television cameras swarmed around the ecstatic crowds. One sweaty celebrant bluntly summed up the prevailing mood: "We hope to God that bastard is dead!"

This sense of enthusiasm was echoed in Washington by the several Cuban American members of Congress who represented South Florida. Ileana Ros-Lehtinen, their most senior member in the House of Representatives, proclaimed "a great day for the Cuban people and their brothers and sisters in exile," adding that "Fidel Castro has only brought ruin and misery to Cuba so if he's incapacitated, even for a short period of time, it is a marvelous moment for the millions of Cubans who live under his iron-fisted rule and oppressive state machinery. I hope this is the beginning of the end for his despised regime."[5] Florida senator Mel Martinez described his reaction to Castro's illness as "intensely emotional" and predicted that "there's a possibility that he may be very, very ill or dead." He told reporters, "My hope is that there will be an opportunity for voices of freedom to be heard in Cuba, that this could begin a moment of transformation and transition to a better life and a better day."[6] Lincoln Diaz-Balart, another Florida representative, sought to repudiate any suggestion that the United States reach out to Cuba's new provisional government, arguing, "You would have to be really blind or really stupid to think that Fidel or Raúl Castro are anything but bloody, torturing killing machines."[7] He later called for Cubans to launch a campaign of civil disobedience against their government, while other exile leaders in Miami urged the Cuban military to reject the transfer of power to Raúl Castro and rise up for democracy.

By contrast, the White House's reaction to Castro's handover was strangely subdued, especially given that just days earlier Bush had visited Miami promoting the findings of the second version of a high-level Commission for Assistance to a Free Cuba, chaired by Secretary of State Condoleezza Rice and Commerce Secretary Carlos Gutierrez. The ninety-three-page report, released in early July, described Cuba's succession process as "intrinsically unstable" and warned that after Castro the United States would face "a critical 180 day period [that] could mean the difference between a successful transition and the stumbles and missteps that slowed other states as they moved towards democracy."[8] Although its classified annex gave the report an air of mystery, its most substantive public recommendation was to create an eighty-million-dollar fund to support Cuban dissidents and expand Internet access on the island—and none of the money had yet been set aside. Two days before Castro's announcement, Bush told a Miami radio station, "If Fidel Castro were to move on because of natural causes, we've got a plan in place to help the people of Cuba understand there's a better way than the system in which they've been living under."[9] He also touted the report by saying, "We are actively working for change in Cuba, not simply waiting for change." But when the moment finally arrived, the waiting game continued.

U.S. rhetoric about democracy flowed freely in the days after Castro's handover, but a second message to the Cuban people was equally evident: Whatever you do, don't get in a boat and try to come here. As the coast guard was placed on standby to counter a possible refugee crisis, White House press secretary Tony Snow urged Cubans on both sides of the Straits of Florida, "Stay where you are. This is not a time for people to try to be getting in the water and going either way."[10] Rice echoed these words several days later when she read a brief statement on U.S.-funded Radio Martí telling the Cubans on the island, "You have no greater friend than the United States of America," and adding some friendly advice: "Work at home for positive change."

Meanwhile, as U.S. intelligence agencies monitored Cuba as best they could, they also kept a watchful eye on Miami. Indeed, the U.S. government had long been concerned that flotillas of Cuban exiles trying to return to the island could prove even more destabilizing than a refugee crisis emanating from Cuba itself. Retired army colonel Larry Wilkerson, who worked as a top aide to former secretary of state Colin Powell for many years, participated in planning exercises in the 1990s. "I remember vividly conducting war games when I was in the military, where we became quickly embroiled in this war game of cordoning off Florida, if you will, and keeping these boats and these Cuban Americans from going to Cuba and invading the island," he recalled. "Because we saw what was happening. They were collecting small arms in Florida . . . I mean machine guns, ammunition for those machine guns, they had boats that were ready to go, and that were targeted to go, lists of who owned those boats, and what piers they were at and so forth." But times had changed in the intervening decade. Any eagerness in the Cuban exile community to take matters into their own hands had dulled with the passing years. Meanwhile, the Cuban people living on the island, despite all of their frustrations, lacked the resources and perhaps the desire to challenge their government at the moment that their leader's mortality was laid bare. Fidel Castro's decision to relinquish power for the first time since 1959 represented the climactic moment of a generation, but it came and went in the blink of an eye, and the bitter divisions between the United States and Cuba remained as entrenched as ever.

Once I was on the edge of a plaza in Old Havana talking with two teenage boys about life in Cuba. It was several years before Castro fell ill, and his seemingly never-ending rule cast a long shadow over his country. "We can't wait until the old man goes," they told me. "Everything here needs to change." By sheer coincidence, an official convoy pulled up across the street in the middle of our conversation, and Castro stepped out of one of the vehicles. It was a spur-of-the-moment visit to a local school, and a crowd immediately surrounded him. The two teenagers pivoted—almost in mid-sentence—and began to chant, "Viva Fidel! Viva Fidel!" with a starstruck look in their eyes. Later I recounted this story to an older Cuban man from the generation that helped thrust Castro into the center of power. He told me, "It's true—he's a hero, but we hate him." When I suggested that he would probably cry on the day that Castro died, he smiled and murmured, "Of course I will. But they will be tears of joy."

Fidel Castro has been Cuba's indispensable man for nearly fifty years, but rumors of his eternal life were greatly exaggerated. It is true that he has survived a remarkable number of assassination attempts (over six hundred by one count), and several of the most colorful were planned by the United States itself. His relentless stamina, hours-long speeches, exacting memory, and workaholic tendencies added to the overall perception that he was a force of nature. According to one popular tale, Castro once declined to accept a long-lived Galápagos tortoise as a pet, explaining that "the problem is that just when you get attached to them, they die on you." In fact, Castro is a hypochondriac obsessed with his own physical well-being, to the point that in the 1980s, the cigar-chomping revolutionary quit smoking.

Still, even before he fell ill, the strains of old age had begun to show in increasingly dramatic ways. In June 2001, he fainted for the first time during a public speech, forcing his younger foreign minister to try to calm the shocked audience. After that moment, the myth of Castro's invincibility began to come apart. He later skipped a Cuban parliamentary meeting for the first time in twenty-five years, reportedly to recover from a bug bite on his leg. Two years later, during his visit to Argentina in 2003, he swooned again and almost collapsed in public. Spooked by his public display of frailty, Castro tried to capitalize on his political celebrity to refute rumors about his fragile health. While showing movie director Oliver Stone a Cuban hospital as part of a documentary film shoot, the fearsome dictator stripped off his shirt and hopped on a hospital bed for an impromptu electrocardiogram. His own doctor has announced that Castro may live until 140—a prediction that a small group of Cubans in the ruling party would love to see come true, but that many others would deem their worst nightmare.

Even in his late seventies, Castro remained a dominant presence in Cuban life as he entertained foreign dignitaries, visited schools and clinics, and delivered frequent speeches to rev up the party faithful. Typically he would arrive at official functions late in the evening, and his entrance at large gathering places like Havana's Convention Palace was always greeted with thunderous applause. Castro would speak for five or six hours without resting, with his top aides seated at a long table behind him, rocking back and forth on their swivel chairs without daring to step outside for a bathroom break. If some attendees began to nod off in the early-morning hours, Castro would abruptly interrupt his speech and jolt them awake: "What? You're sleeping? You need coffee! *¡Café cubano!*" Immediately there would be scurrying in the front of the large conference hall, and then clearly agitated waiters would appear to serve the audience from trays of Cuban coffee in small plastic cups almost too hot to touch. Castro himself favored a cool glass of water. Once he became satisfied that the caffeine level of his audience had been sufficiently elevated, he would continue his sermon with even more energy than before.

Castro's most dramatic show of weakness before the summer of 2006 occurred on October 20, 2004, after he completed a fiery speech in the city of Santa Clara in central Cuba to commemorate the Day of Cuban Culture. It was already evening when he concluded with the cry of "Towards victory forever!," setting off a wave of rhythmic clapping by the large audience that swayed to chants of "Fidel! Fidel!" Castro stepped gingerly back from the wooden podium and began to walk down toward the crowd, but he missed a step, pitched forward, and landed hard. His face and shoulder smacked against the stage, and his body careened forward until his head hit a line of empty folding chairs in the front row. A dozen people from the audience immediately surrounded him and helped him back on his feet. Ever the performer, Castro quickly regained his composure, but his right arm was crunched in a painful position and he held the mike with his left hand. "I ask forgiveness for having fallen," he intoned, provoking coos of sympathy from the crowd. He then smiled and said, "I am very interested to see the photos of how I fell. The international press is going to rush to show this around the world." Castro's injuries included a broken left knee and right arm, but he refused to undergo anesthesia as the bones were set—in case the United States decided to seize the moment for a "provocation," he reasoned. Still, the video clip of the accident was excruciatingly embarrassing, and he was temporarily left to govern Cuba from a wheelchair.

Of course, the top Cuban officials who worked most closely with Castro were well aware that his legendary vigor was fading, and they began to voice concerns about planning for the next phase of the Cuban Revolution. In recent years, Ricardo Alarcón, the president of the National Assembly, began to wonder aloud about the topic of succession. "The fact is that the generation which took power 45 years ago is retiring and dying off. People like Fidel, Raúl, and myself are getting older every year," he told an American interviewer in 2004. "Unfortunately, I haven't found a way out of that one yet."[11] In May 2006, just weeks before Castro fell ill, he repeated the point, saying, "I don't think any human being is irreplaceable," and warning that succession planning should no longer be a taboo topic. "In Cuba there are thousands of leaders much younger than Fidel that were born with or after the revolution and who already have 20 years' worth of practical leadership experience," he said. "We know who they are, although there's no mention of them in the foreign press."[12] In June, Raúl Castro declared in a speech that "only the Communist Party—as the institution that brings together the revolutionary vanguard and will always guarantee the unity of Cubans—can be the worthy heir of the trust deposited by the people in their leader."[13] The Communist Party, however, was a faltering and increasingly embattled institution in a country exhausted by politics, and it would be a flimsy substitute for the charismatic leadership represented by Fidel.

Fidel Castro is still an icon within Cuba, but his legacy will be complex and ambiguous at best, or bitterly divisive at worst. Many people prefer not to mention his name at all, but instead invoke his presence by motioning in front of their chins as if they were stroking an invisible beard. More than 70 percent of the country's citizens were born after he came to power, and nearly every Cuban feels that he or she possesses a personal relationship with Fidel. Some are guided by love and respect, and others are filled with fear and loathing. But even those who deeply despise Fidel Castro cannot help but reveal their awe of how thoroughly he has controlled the country and how deeply he has impacted their lives. Meanwhile, even many of his most loyal and obsequious followers harbor seeds of doubt about whether his leadership has brought their society to the edge of the cliff. Several years ago, the CIA publicly diagnosed the Cuban leader as suffering from Parkinson's disease, but he laughed off the rumors, saying, "The day that I die, nobody is going to believe it."[14] Yet his letter in July 2006 described his health as "ruined." In the minds of many Cubans, Fidel Castro's immortal stature had been irrevocably punctured—and their eyes turned with fear and hope to his enigmatic younger brother.

Raúl Castro had been his older brother's second in command since the earliest days of the Cuban Revolution, and he had long been Fidel's designated successor. Behind the scenes, however, the Cuban government was poorly equipped to deal with the aftermath of Fidel's illness, due to the uncertainty of the situation as well as the latent competing tensions between civilian and military factions within the regime. Thus, the announcement on July 31 was followed by a long period of conflicting and overlapping messages from top officials, with no one figure clearly in charge. Ricardo Alarcón publicly insisted that the leader's "final moment is still very far away." Fidel himself chimed in with a second letter that said, "The most I can say is that the situation will remain stable for many days before a verdict can be given. In spirits, I find myself perfectly fine." He also warned about the possibility of U.S. intervention, writing that "the country is prepared for its defense by the Revolutionary Armed Forces and the people. In the case of Cuba, because of the plans of the empire, my state of health has become a state secret that cannot be continually divulged, and compatriots should understand this."[15] When Fidel's eightieth birthday arrived on August 13, the Cuban newspaper *Juventud Rebelde* (Rebel Youth) ran the first photos of him since the surgery, seated in a red, white, and blue tracksuit. In an accompanying note, he warned, "I ask you all to be optimistic, and at the same time to be ready to face any adverse news."

Raúl Castro waited more than two weeks (until August 18) before making his first public statement to the Cuban people, in the form of a published interview in *Granma*, the official state newspaper. In keeping with his army role, he boasted of mobilizing tens of thousands of reservists with "rifle in hand" to defend against any military intervention launched by the United States. "We could not rule out the risk of somebody going crazy, or even crazier, within the U.S. government," Raúl said, although he wryly noted that "so far the attacks have only been rhetorical." Cuba's provisional president also sought to explain his reticent public persona. "In reality, I'm not accustomed to appearing in public with frequency, except for the moments when it is required. Many of the tasks related to the defense of the country should not be public. I've always been discreet, that is my way of being."

Fidel's absence had left a vacuum that his little brother was only partially capable of filling, and the effect was to lull the Cuban government into a state of suspended animation. Faced with the challenge of proving that Fidel was still alive but things were going just fine without him, Cuban officials soon fell into a peculiar pattern. Weeks of silence on Fidel's health matters were punctuated by occasional public reassurances and the strategic deployment of "proof of life" videos. The first aired on Cuban state television shortly after Fidel's eightieth birthday, showing him lying in bed in red pajamas, speaking and gesturing during a visit with President Chávez. The official image of Fidel seemed to suggest that he was an ill but convalescing grandfather receiving a visit from a favorite nephew. Further photographs of Fidel chatting with a visiting congressman from Argentina in mid-September, while Cuba was hosting an international summit of developing countries known as the Non-Aligned Movement, seemed to hint at the leader's recovery.

But if these early pictures were a tonic for the regime, then the second video, released on October 28, had all the soothing effect of a bucket of ice water. Fidel appeared conducting walking exercises in a red tracksuit with a blue-and-white collar and read aloud an article from the weekend edition of *Granma*. His motions seemed pained and he read slowly and without feeling. Later, seated in a chair, he stated, "They've declared me moribund prematurely. But it pleases me to send my compatriots and friends this small video." He expressed faith in his continued recovery and vowed that he was still participating in important government decisions, saying, "I feel whole. I'm not the least bit afraid of what will occur." Fidel may not have been worried, but his gaunt, frail image in the video sparked widespread concern that the end was near. Rumors swirled around the purpose of the video. Were Raúl Castro and other leaders trying to prepare the Cuban public for Fidel's death? Or had Fidel himself authorized the video against the wishes of his handlers, thus demonstrating that he was still in charge?

Then Fidel literally dropped out of sight for the next two months as it became clear that he was too ill to attend the December 2 celebration to mark the fiftieth anniversary of Cuba's Revolutionary Armed Forces. Back in August, Fidel's letter had indicated that he planned to return in time to preside over this major military event, which would double as his birthday party. On December 2, the weather in Havana was warm and humid, with the blue winter sky streaked by clouds. In the early-morning hours, many Cubans began to make their way toward the Plaza of the Revolution, the broad and majestic epicenter of the public platforms on which Fidel had endlessly performed during his many years in power. Flocks of young people in their late teens and early twenties waved Cuban flags and held up banners and signs proclaiming their support for the revolution and its fading icon, Fidel

Castro. The largest military parade in over a decade unfolded across Havana, including a replica of the *Granma* yacht, Soviet-era tanks that snorted and rumbled down the streets, and fighter jets that streaked through the skies overhead. Raúl Castro had been there in those early-morning hours of December 2, 1956, and during the intervening fifty years he had overseen the development of the Revolutionary Armed Forces into one of the leanest, meanest fighting forces ever produced by a Latin American country. But the days when Cuba was able to project its military power halfway across the globe had receded into the distant past, and Raúl's task this morning was to honor Fidel's legacy, hold his own before the assembled throngs, and use the moment to send a message to the United States.

Raúl appeared on the stage in his green military uniform and cap and surveyed the crowd. Long thought to be the timid brother who pre-ferred to eschew the limelight, he looked like he could almost get used to it. After paying respects to Fidel's eightieth birthday, Raúl reached back to quote words that his brother had spoken thirty-one years earlier in his report to the First Congress of the Communist Party. "The rebel army was the soul of the revolution. Its soldiers vindicated the blood generously shed in all the struggles for independence and with their own blood laid the foundations of Cuba's socialist presence." Raúl knew that his tenure in office would depend, in part, on claiming Fidel's revolutionary legitimacy through the two powerful institu-tions that formed the motor of the Castro regime: the Communist Party and the military. "In the context of the fiftieth anniversary of the Revolutionary Armed Forces, it is fitting to ratify the monolithic unity between the People, the Army, and the Party. This unity is our main strategic weapon, which has made it possible for this small island to resist and overcome so many aggressions from imperialism and its allies."

As these words echoed across the plaza, the crowds continued to stand and watch, flags waving, cheers breaking out when the speech hit a high note. Raúl Castro was no Fidel, but for a moment it seemed that it did not matter. Raúl Castro was enough to guarantee that the system would hold. He then turned his rhetorical attention to Cuba's nemesis to the north and made an appeal for reconciliation with the United States. "We take this opportunity to once again state that we are willing to resolve at the negotiating table the long-standing dispute between the

United States and Cuba," he said. "In the meantime, after almost half a century, we are willing to wait patiently until the moment when common sense prevails in Washington power circles." He anticipated that the United States would bat down the offer, and he was not disappointed.

Fidel Castro was a terrible patient. The old man was cooperative one moment and unruly the next, and even in illness he had the capacity to intimidate the top Cuban doctors who were in charge of his care. Moreover, Castro's sense of pride was wounded by the unpleasant nature of his ailment. He was suffering from diverticulitis, an inflamed bulge in the intestine that often afflicts the elderly. When the affliction became severe the previous summer, Castro underwent an operation to remove part of his large intestine, but he resisted the customary treatment of a colostomy bag, a temporary measure to allow stool to exit the body through an opening in the abdomen. Instead, Cuban surgeons decided to connect the colon directly to the rectum, but the shortcut failed and released feces into the aging leader's stomach, causing peritonitis, a severe inflammation of the abdominal cavity that required emergency surgical intervention. A second operation to cleanse and drain the infection and carry out a colostomy, which the Spanish newspaper that broke the story referred to as an "artificial anus," also ended in failure. Castro then suffered another dangerous medical setback when he was hit with an inflammation of the bile duct and gallbladder. A third attempt to treat the problem with a prosthetic device encountered more turbulence when one purchased from Korea failed to work properly and was later replaced by a Spanish version.[16]

Thereafter Castro needed to be fed intravenously, but the ailing dictator was losing nutrients through a massive loss of fluid. His stitches healed poorly. The problem eventually became so acute that once he was transported to the operating room seven times in a single day.[17] Cuban officials quickly realized that the whirlwind of intrigue about Castro's declining health required a response, but a public statement by Castro himself was not in the cards. As a last resort, the Cuban government chartered a plane to bring in a respected Spanish physician, José Luis García Sabrido, the chief of surgery at a public hospital in Madrid. In his early sixties and with more than three decades of medical experience, García Sabrido met several crucial criteria: He had the surgical expertise to review Castro's condition, his public statements carried the weight of an expert from the Western world, and he had close ties to the Cuban medical community. The plane also carried medicine and medical equipment not readily available in Cuba.

Upon his arrival in Havana, García Sabrido was extensively briefed by Castro's physicians on the top-secret health situation. After returning to Madrid, he held a press conference on December 26, where he proclaimed that the Cuban leader had experienced "a series of complications." He added that Castro's "intellectual activity is excellent and fantastic" and that he could "completely recover."[18] In the course of a few days, the Cuban leadership had cleverly inoculated itself against rumors that its supreme leader was at death's door. Against the odds, an outside expert had given credence to the notion that Fidel Castro's survival instinct remained intact.

This was especially striking given that the death of the Chilean dictator Augusto Pinochet on December 10 had produced an avalanche of comparisons to Castro. After taking power in a bloody coup that left Chile's democratically elected socialist president dead by his own hand (the deposed leader, Salvador Allende, apparently shot himself in the head with a rifle given to him by Castro), Pinochet ruled Chile with an iron fist from 1973 to 1990. If Latin America's iconic right-wing dictator from the cold war era had finally lost his lease on life, could his left-wing counterpart be far behind? One popular political cartoon in Latin America showed Pinochet and Castro standing by a flaming door that led to the gates of hell. "After you," the Chilean general gestured to his Cuban comrade. "No, no," Fidel Castro replied. "I must insist, after you!"

It was an argument that Castro won. In a statement released on December 31, the Cuban leader described his recovery as "far from being a lost battle." While Pinochet was buried in his native Chile without even a state funeral, Castro pulled off a Houdini-like escape from the grave and lived to ring in the New Year.

George W. Bush was the tenth U.S. president to spar with Fidel Castro, and during the summer of 2006 it appeared that he might be the first to outlast (if not outwit) the Cuban leader. As a presidential candidate in 2000, Bush had pledged to hold a tough line against Castro's government. Once in office, he repeatedly vowed to bring democracy to Cuba and reaffirmed his administration's commitment to the U.S. embargo of the island that had been in place since the early 1960s. Like many of his predecessors', however, Bush's plans for Cuba were largely based on waiting for Castro to die, but many of Bush's important allies in South Florida's Cuban American community demanded a more proactive approach. The Bush administration responded to these pressures by setting into motion an extensive array of planning exercises to prepare the United States to hasten democracy in a post-Castro Cuba. These included two high-level reports from the Commission for Assistance to a Free Cuba that were released in May 2004 and July 2006, new sanctions on U.S. travel to Cuba, the establishment of a CIA "mission manager" to collect intelligence on Cuba and Venezuela, and increased foreign aid to dissident groups within Cuba. In the halls of the U.S. government, waiting for Castro to die had been elevated to an art form.

Perhaps the most controversial decision was to create a new senior-level position in the State Department to coordinate the Cuban transition. This post was established in the summer of 2004 but left vacant for a year, until it was filled in July 2005 by Caleb McCarry, a long-time Republican staffer on Capitol Hill with an extensive background in Latin American affairs. In announcing his appointment at the State Department, Secretary of State Condoleezza Rice described the mission "to accelerate the demise of Castro's tyranny" as a top U.S. priority. "With Caleb's help," she said, "the United States is going to hasten the coming of the day when a free Cuba is no longer a dream, but a reality."[19]

McCarry was generally well regarded in conservative circles in Washington, but the role that he was tapped to play was a political lightning rod, criticized as interventionist on the one hand and fanciful on the other. At the time of McCarry's appointment, José Miguel Insulza, the Chilean secretary general of the Organization of American States, chided the Bush administration, saying, "There is no transition—and it's not your country." Insulza's sentiment was widely shared by other Latin American leaders from across the political spectrum, but his statement left many U.S. officials privately fuming. He later told me that "I said something that some of my friends did not like and they complained that I shouldn't repeat it. But I just didn't see the logic of creating a coordinator for a transition in another country." The reality was that the United States was preparing to both stimulate and react to a democratic transition that showed few signs of unfolding in Cuba, with or without Fidel Castro at the helm. Although Cuban exiles were strongly supportive of creating a U.S. point man to undermine Castro, those still living on the island were mystified by the move.

Cuban foreign minister Felipe Pérez Roque quickly christened McCarry as a "Paul Bremer for Cuba," in reference to the former U.S. administrator who ran Iraq after the ouster of Saddam Hussein, telling reporters, "I'm sure he will receive a juicy salary in his new post, but I assure you he will retire without ever setting foot in Cuba."[20] Meanwhile, a number of leading Cuban opposition figures also criticized the new post. Oswaldo Payá of the Christian Liberation Movement insisted that "any transition in Cuba is for Cubans to define, lead, organize and coordinate," while human rights monitor Elizardo Sánchez worried that "it will allow the Cuban government to raise the specter of foreign interference in the internal affairs of our country."[21] If nothing else, the Bush administration's decision to appoint a transition coordinator for Cuba created a rare moment of unity among the island's divided political actors.

McCarry was unfazed by the criticism. He is a bearded, soft-spoken man in his mid-forties, the son of a CIA agent turned novelist, and the top official overseeing U.S. policy regarding Cuba at one of the most sensitive moments in the history of the two countries. He likes to say that he's learned "never to speak in hypotheticals," even though his job title of Cuba transition coordinator is arguably itself a hypothetical. When Castro fell ill in the summer of 2006, both the significance and the limits of U.S. efforts to push Cuba toward democracy became increasingly apparent, but McCarry remained philosophical in his approach. "I actually don't believe that U.S. policy is waiting for any single event to happen. The core objective is to support a process of change in Cuba that all Cubans can participate in that leads to the restoration of sovereignty and rights to the Cuban people," he told me during an extended conversation in his State Department office several months after Castro stepped back from power. "My own view is that something changed last July . . . For the first time in decades the future of Cuba is not entirely clear to Cubans themselves. More importantly, there has been over time a significant increase, particularly in the provinces, of opposition and dissident activity." McCarry refused to contemplate a scenario where the United States would engage in dialogue with Cuba's provisional government, instead insisting, "Our point is that the dialogue that needs to take place is not between anyone but the current, unelected regime in Havana and the Cuban people. What needs to happen here is that Cubans need to talk to each other about their future. That's our view."

McCarry characterized the substantial planning efforts of the U.S. government as a "respectful offer to help a process of genuine, democratic change" and said that "Cubans who want democratic change, and that includes those in the current regime, need to understand they have nothing to fear from us." He added, "I actually believe that Cubans want to avoid violence. I'm convinced that Cubans want peaceful change in their country." Still, he described the United States as extremely well prepared to address a possible migration crisis. Toward the end of our conversation, McCarry asserted, "I truly believe that helping to get to a process of genuine change in Cuba is the right thing to do for the Cuban people and for our country, but I also think it's the right thing to do for the region." When I asked if he thought democratic change would come to Cuba in his lifetime, McCarry smiled broadly and cryptically quipped, "Cubans are extraordinary people." Then he seemed to search for words. "Well, you know, it's, um, I'm hopeful," he said, before describing how Cuba had recently begun celebrating the religious, Christmas-related holiday Three Kings Day, which had been purged by Cuba's atheist state decades earlier. "That's actually very encouraging to me," McCarry concluded.

The State Department's Cuba transition coordinator may not have been waiting for any single event to happen, but for most top U.S. officials the prospective death of Fidel Castro remained an anticipated and pivotal event. On December 14, 2006, Director of National Intelligence John Negroponte predicted that Castro was on his deathbed, telling a group of *Washington Post* reporters, "Everything we see indicates it will not be much longer . . . months, not years."[22] Weeks later, Negroponte quit his intelligence post for the number-two job at the State Department, and a new video was released on January 30 that showed Castro standing up and talking with Hugo Chávez. The Cuban leader had clearly gained weight since his last videotaped appearance, and he seemed in good spirits. The men pored over an article from the Argentine daily newspaper *Clarín* with a headline that described climate change as a health hazard. When Chávez commented, "Wow, what could be more important than your health?" Castro nodded soberly in agreement.

The following month, on February 27, the United States' new

director of national intelligence, Mike McConnell, testified before the Senate: "In Cuba, this year will mark the end of the long domination of that country by Fidel Castro."[23] Later that day, Castro called Chávez's radio talk show in Venezuela to make his first live public statement since his health crisis began. Castro reassured his ally, "I feel good and I'm happy," and added, "I can't promise that I'll go over there soon, but I feel more energetic and stronger." In June, Bush told an audience at the U.S. Naval War College, "One day the good Lord will take Fidel Castro away," prompting Castro to respond, "Now I understand why I survived the plans of Bush and the presidents who ordered my assassination: The good Lord protected me."

On December 2, 2007, a year after Negroponte forecast Castro's imminent demise, the Cuban leader was nominated to run again for his seat representing the eastern city of Santiago in Cuba's National Assembly. Nearly eighteen months had passed since he had announced his illness and stepped back from power, but he nominally remained Cuba's president while Raúl Castro and other top ministers fulfilled his roles on a "provisional" basis. The short bio accompanying Fidel's candidacy stated, "During his convalescence he has continued to be actively involved in the country's most important strategic decisions." Cuba's top officials acclaimed his candidacy. "I am sure he will win," predicted vice president Carlos Lage, while National Assembly president Ricardo Alarcón pledged to vote for Fidel with both hands. Indeed, Fidel's reelection to the National Assembly raised the possibility that he could even be reconfirmed as president if he so chose, although he later declined the post.

As 2008 commenced, Fidel Castro had once more confounded the ominous predictions about the end of his life. By resigning several days before the National Assembly meeting held on February 24, he positioned himself to oversee the very transition of power to his brother Raúl that many of his enemies outside of Cuba had vowed to prevent at all costs. His success guaranteed that nearly half a century of struggle between the United States and Cuba would be inherited by both the next generation of Cuban leaders and Bush's successor in the White House. That fact alone enabled Fidel to escape a fate worse than death: irrelevance. Still, even in his weakened state and bereft of the presidency that he had occupied for forty-nine years, he pledged to remain engaged in the struggle. In the concluding paragraph of his resignation letter, Fidel wrote, "This is not my farewell to you. My only wish is to fight as a soldier in the battle of ideas. I shall continue to write under the title 'Reflections of Comrade Fidel.' It will be another weapon you can count on. Perhaps my voice will be heard. I will be careful." Raúl Castro might have taken charge of Cuba, but it was Fidel whose image, voice, and ideas were still deeply seared into the national consciousness.

CHAPTER 2

War of Nerves

With Fidel Castro's illness and subsequent retirement, the tormented relationship between the United States and Cuba entered a new and uncertain stage. In truth, both countries had spent decades preparing for the moment when Cuba's historic leader would leave the scene, yet in many ways both were fundamentally unprepared. The island's political life under Castro had been deeply defined by the unrelenting antagonism between Cuba's communist government and the United States, which had proved nearly impossible to defuse during ten successive U.S. presidential administrations.

Indeed, Cuba has played an outsize role in U.S. foreign policy since Teddy Roosevelt's Rough Riders stormed San Juan Hill in Cuba to repel Spanish forces during the Spanish-American War in 1898. Cuba formally gained independence in 1902, but the Platt Amendment, inserted into the Cuban constitution by American authorities, gave the United States the right to intervene in the island's domestic affairs until 1934. Then, for the next twenty-five years, a series of elected Cuban governments fell prey to military strongmen. In the 1950s, popular disgust with the corrupt and dictatorial rule of Fulgencio Batista created the political opportunity for Castro to lead a small band of rebels to triumph during the 1959 Cuban Revolution. In the United States, the administration of Dwight D. Eisenhower looked askance at Castro's early moves to expropriate U.S. property and forge an alliance with the Soviet Union. In the early 1960s, Castro's embrace of communism and close ties to the Soviet Union horrified the United States, which responded by imposing economic sanctions in 1960 and then breaking off diplomatic relations with Cuba in January 1961. In April of that year, President John F. Kennedy supported the Cuban-exile-led Bay of Pigs invasion, which boomeranged painfully when Castro's forces easily crushed the poorly organized effort. In early 1962, Kennedy placed a comprehensive U.S. embargo on the island that remains the centerpiece of U.S. policy toward Cuba to this day.

In October 1962, the Cuban Missile Crisis erupted when Kennedy learned that Castro had entered into a secret agreement with Soviet premier Nikita Khrushchev to install nuclear missiles in Cuba. U.S. intelligence sources were already aware that the Soviet Union was engaging in a military buildup in Cuba intended to help defend the island against another American attack. However, the Kennedy administration had strongly warned the Soviets against placing offensive ballistic missiles on the island and believed that Khrushchev would not risk provoking a confrontation with the United States over Cuba. On October 14, however, an American U-2 spy plane spotted a nuclear missile installation in Cuba. The discovery launched the Cuban Missile Crisis, a highly charged standoff between the United States and the Soviet Union that remains the closest that the world has come to a nuclear war. Over thirteen days, Kennedy and Khrushchev engaged in a dangerous game of nuclear brinkmanship that ended only when the Soviet Union agreed to remove the missiles in exchange for an agreement by the United States not to invade Cuba. Castro was only thirty-six years old at the time and had been in power for less than four years, but he had envisioned Cuba playing a major role on the world stage, on equal footing with the larger cold war powers. Instead, the American and Soviet leaders brokered a resolution without even consulting him, and the experience badly burned his ego, although it meant that the risk of a second Bay of Pigs was vastly diminished as long as he remained in the Soviet Union's good graces. Still, Castro's role in bringing the world to the edge of nuclear holocaust left a vivid imprint in the American consciousness.

The botched invasion of Cuba and the subsequent peaceful resolution of the missile crisis stand as the two pivotal moments of Kennedy's foreign policy legacy before an assassin's bullet cut him down in 1963. The dramatic events of the 1960s proved to be only the beginning. In the years that followed, the Cuban Revolution upended U.S. priorities in Latin America. During much of the cold war, the Castro government actively supported wars of liberation in Latin America and Africa, and its fingerprints were found on events across the globe. In complete control of Cuba and promoting a global foreign policy in opposition to the United States, Castro sparred with a string of Kennedy's successors, including Lyndon Johnson, Richard

Nixon, and Gerald Ford. In the late 1970s, efforts by Jimmy Carter to engage with Cuba led to a slight thaw, including the decision by the two countries to open diplomatic missions known as "interest sections" in their respective capitals, but the desire to normalize relations with Cuba ultimately came to naught. During the 1980s Ronald Reagan continued to promote a hard-line sanctions policy. Wayne Smith, who served as the top U.S. diplomat in Havana in the 1980s, famously remarked that "Cuba seems to have the same effect on American administrations as the full moon has on werewolves"—but the reverse was just as often true. Despite occasional expressions of interest in reconciling, the United States and Cuba were never able to capitalize on the available opportunities, instead littering their history with diplomatic failures.

In the early 1990s, the collapse of the Soviet Union and the end of the cold war appeared to create a brief moment of opportunity for the United States and Cuba to set their relationship on a new path. By 1992, the Cuban economy was reeling from the loss of nearly four billion dollars in annual Soviet subsidies, and the country was teetering on the brink of disaster. Instead of reaching out to Cuba, however, the United States responded by tightening the screws further when Congress passed the Cuban Democracy Act, which codified the embargo and increased the economic stranglehold on the island. The bill was signed by President George H. W. Bush, who initially opposed the measure but then switched positions when his Democratic challenger, Arkansas governor Bill Clinton, campaigned in its favor. Castro's government managed to weather this dire crisis by implementing a range of small-scale economic reforms that represented loathed but necessary baby steps toward capitalism.

By this time, the cold war politics that had spawned the Cuban embargo had faded into history. The sanctions were initially put in place in the 1960s to contain Cuba as a potential security threat, but this argument had lost steam with the disappearance of the Soviet Union. Rather than shifting gears, however, the United States instead recast the embargo as a policy intended to restore democracy in Cuba, a goal that it was ill equipped to achieve and that was far removed from the embargo's original rationale. Frustrated that the tightened sanctions had failed to dislodge Castro at his moment of greatest vulnerability, anti-Castro advocates in Congress went back to the drawing board to come up with an even more draconian series of measures intended to drive Cuba's communists from power. Formally titled the Cuban Liberty and Democratic Solidarity Act of 1996, the bill came to be known as the Helms-Burton Act after its two chief sponsors, Senator Jesse Helms, the powerful seventy-five-year-old Republican from North Carolina who chaired the Senate Foreign Relations Committee, and the Republican congressman Dan Burton, who represented a rural district in Indiana. The bill's strongest backing came from Cuban American exile groups who insisted that even stronger economic sanctions were needed to bring Castro down. President Clinton initially threatened to veto the bill owing to the fact that many of its sweeping provisions— such as penalizing non-U.S. individuals and companies for trading with Cuba—were illegal under international law. But the political climate in Washington irrevocably changed on February 24, 1996, when the Cuban government shot down two civilian aircraft affiliated with a Miami-based activist group known as Brothers to the Rescue, killing four Cuban Americans: three U.S. citizens and one naturalized resident. The repercussions were quickly felt in Congress, which turned on a dime to pass the Helms-Burton legislation overwhelmingly, leaving Clinton no choice politically but to sign the bill, which he did to great fanfare on March 12, 1996.

Helms-Burton represented a crucial victory for supporters of the U.S. embargo of Cuba because it constrained both Clinton and any future U.S. president from repealing the embargo without congressional approval. More immediately, it abruptly halted efforts by Clinton to normalize relations with Cuba, a fact that he looked back on with regret when he gave a rare interview about Cuba at the end of his presidency: "I believe if Castro hadn't shot those planes down, and the Congress hadn't passed a law which prohibits me from doing anything about the embargo, then we might have had some real progress there." Clinton's disappointment with the turn that U.S.-Cuba policy took was clear: "I do believe that the Cuban people have suffered because of the embargo, and we should do more in the area of food, in the area of medicine, in the area of people-to-people contact. I believe that it is just a question of time to when the United States and Cuba are reconciled, and I think the situation is tragic."[1]

The strange saga of Elián González marked the last time that Cuba made a major mark on the American consciousness until Castro's recent decision to leave power. Two fishermen found five-year-old Elián floating alone on an inner tube off the coast of Florida on Thanksgiving

Day in 1999. He was one of only three survivors of a journey to escape from Cuba that claimed his mother and ten other passengers. His father, Juan Miguel González, was separated from his wife and remained in Cuba, unaware of her attempt to escape with Elián. The raft that had been carrying the group capsized, and most of the travelers quickly drowned. The very fact of Elián's survival was greeted as a miracle by many in Miami. He was brought to a local hospital for examination, and after a cursory and unsuccessful attempt to contact his father in Cuba, U.S. immigration officials released him into the temporary custody of Lázaro González, the boy's great-uncle. When Juan Miguel was eventually notified of what had occurred and asked for his son to be returned to him in Cuba, his uncle refused to comply. If the custody dispute had occurred between virtually any two countries but the United States and Cuba, it would have been a quiet legal matter. Once the case became public, however, it transformed from a private family drama into a major contest of wills between Miami's Cuban exile leadership, who fought to keep the child in the United States, and Castro, who launched a public relations blitzkrieg in an effort to bring Elián back to his father in Cuba.

Vicki Huddleston was the top American diplomat in Cuba from 1999 to 2002, serving as chief of the U.S. Interests Section, which performs the functions of an embassy but without an ambassador, since the United States does not diplomatically recognize the Castro government. Huddleston was informed about the Elián González issue when a phone call from a Cuban official arrived out of the blue in late November 1999. "We were like, 'Huh?'" she recalled with a laugh. "Because I was waiting to be called up to be told that Fidel was going to the World Trade Organization summit in Seattle, and the [Clinton] administration was kind of in a twitter about that. So the Cubans called me up and said, 'We have a very serious issue. You picked up this child at sea and we want him back now.' So I called Washington and said, 'Nothing on Fidel, but there's this kid and they want him back.' Washington was sort of like, 'Oh, OK.' None of us were even taking it very seriously. Then, of course, it went right through the roof!"

As the legal dispute in Miami dragged on, Castro began to lead marches of hundreds of thousands of Cubans past the U.S. mission in Havana, demanding Elián's return to Cuba, and a massive tribunal was constructed in front of the building as a rallying point. Huddleston thought that Castro had spotted an opportunity and exploited it masterfully. "What was absolutely incredible was that he used it to revitalize the Cuban Revolution and consolidate control. No loyal Cubans could be against Elián coming back . . . Every night on the TV there was a roundtable to talk about the latest travesty of the dysfunctional family that Elián was staying with in Miami. It was pretty funny. I mean, it was just absolutely a wonderful, wonderful propaganda tool for the revolution." Huddleston also thought the case touched a chord in Cuba that went deeper than just its fodder for propaganda. "A lot of Cubans understood that Cuba was not a great place to live. But the idea that the United States would take away or keep their child was just not acceptable."

In Miami, the Elián González spectacle snowballed into a complicated legal and emotional soap opera as Cuban exile leaders sought to fight a court battle to get permanent custody of the boy granted to Lázaro González, while at the same time pushing congressional bills to supersede any court decision and drumming up a public relations campaign opposed to returning Elián to Cuba. When the congressional efforts floundered and American public opinion soured on the exiles' protests, the legal battle became the central front. Attorney General Janet Reno had decided that both the letter and the spirit of U.S. immigration law mandated that Elián belonged to his father in Cuba, but she initially wanted to negotiate this outcome with the Miami relatives. When the federal courts agreed with Reno and dismissed the Miami relatives' claim to Elián, they vowed to defy the order and appeal the verdict. In April 2000, having been granted visas to travel to the United States, Juan Miguel González and his new wife arrived in Washington and waited to be reunited with Elián. Reno then ordered the boy to be handed over to U.S. immigration officials by April 13, to pave the way for his return to his father. When Lázaro González refused to comply (his defiance was supported by Miami's political and civic leaders), Reno ordered a predawn raid on April 22, to extract Elián from the home of his Miami relatives. The boy then joined his father in Washington as the final, and ultimately futile, appeals by his family in Miami wound through the courts, and they returned to Cuba on June 28, 2000. Now a teenager, Elián González lives in the small town of Cárdenas, and he receives a phone call from Fidel Castro every year on his birthday.

Back in Florida, Miami's Cuban American community seethed at the Clinton administration's handling of the Elián González episode, which it viewed as U.S. complicity in delivering a valuable victory to Castro. Reno became more despised than the Cuban leader. Following the initial uproar, the Cuban exiles decided that revenge is a dish best served cold. In the November 2000 presidential elections, they abandoned Vice President Al Gore, the Democratic nominee, and voted en masse for the Republican candidate, George W. Bush. (Earlier in the spring, Gore tried to defuse this bomb by backing legislation to keep Elián in the United States until his case was resolved in family court. The bill later fizzled, and Miami voters gave him no points for his efforts.) When the U.S. Supreme Court ratified that Bush had won Florida by 537 votes, his triumph in the Electoral College delivered him the presidency, despite his having lost the national popular vote. While Bush's victory over Gore can be attributed to a range of factors, the impact of the Elián González crisis on the Florida electorate was undoubtedly a key variable, and perhaps the decisive one.

Once Bush entered the White House in January 2001, the relationship between the two countries initially remained stable. Bush had pledged to hold a tough line against Cuba during his presidential campaign, but so had every other major-party candidate since the end of the cold war. During the early months of his presidency, Bush mainly continued the Clinton-era policies of allowing Americans to travel to Cuba for family, educational, or cultural purposes. His rhetoric on Cuba was perfunctory rather than inspired, and he evinced little interest in reigniting the passions that frequently buffeted the Clinton administration during dramatic episodes like the Brothers to the Rescue shoot-down and the Elián González custody battle. The main initial difference between Clinton and Bush was that the former president appointed relatively few anti-Castro hard-liners to top Latin America policy positions, while Bush made them the heart and soul of his foreign policy team for the region.

The long-simmering conflict between the United States and Cuba heated up when the dramatic 9/11 terrorist attacks prompted the Bush administration to announce a sweeping "war on terror" against rogue regimes across the globe. Even as Cuba was caught up in this new international context, overlapping struggles were playing out between the governments of Fidel Castro and George W. Bush, between the Cuban regime and its domestic opponents, and within the American government and Congress over the future of the U.S. embargo of Cuba. These battles would eventually leak into every aspect of the U.S.-Cuba relationship, including politics, trade, sports, music, and culture. They encompassed a world of spies and sanctions, exiles and diplomats, brinkmanship and intrigue, all provoked by the competing desires to sustain or unravel Castro's communist government. The little-known confrontations that unfolded in Havana, Miami, and Washington were all part of an epic conflict that can be collectively defined as the Cuba wars. During the previous four decades, the friction between the United States and Cuba had simmered to a boil in episodes ranging from the nuclear standoff of the Cuban Missile Crisis to the overheated custody dispute over Elián González. The next skirmish involved a tense war of nerves.

The September 11 terrorist attacks on the World Trade Center and the Pentagon sent powerful shock waves through the U.S.-Cuba relationship. At first, most signs were conciliatory. In the early hours of the tragedy, Castro offered U.S. airplanes that were still in flight the right to enter Cuban airspace for emergency landings. Soon thereafter, Cuba ratified all twelve United Nations conventions for counterterrorism. Cuba also backed the declaration against terrorism set forth by the group of Ibero-American countries at their annual summit, a gathering where, just the year before, in Panama, a plot to kill Castro had been disrupted as deliberations were taking place. When Cuba was hit by Hurricane Michelle, a Category 4 storm in November, the United States offered humanitarian aid to the island. Cuba opted to purchase the goods, as was now allowed under legislation that Clinton had signed during his final year in office, and the two countries became trading partners for the first time in thirty-eight years.

Still, as the Bush administration set its sights on an invasion of Afghanistan in the fall of 2001, the traditional frost crept back into the U.S.-Cuba relationship. The U.S. military's response to the attacks, known in the first few weeks as Operation Infinite Justice, clearly sent a chill up the Cuban leader's spine. Nine days after the fall of the Twin Towers, Bush stood before Congress in a moment of great drama and import and established the broad outlines of the U.S. response: "Americans should not expect one battle, but a lengthy campaign, unlike any other we have ever seen. It may include dramatic strikes, visible on TV, and covert operations, secret even in success. We will starve terrorists of funding, turn them one against another, drive them from place to place, until there is no refuge or no rest. And we will pursue nations that provide aid or safe haven to terrorism. Every nation, in every region, now has a decision to make. Either you are with us, or you are with the terrorists." While the focus was clearly on Osama bin Laden and the Taliban, the wider impact of Bush's words sparked deep fears in Cuba about whether the long-standing animosity in the U.S.-Cuba relationship would inevitably lead to the island getting caught up in the riptide of an administration that was justifiably enraged by the bloody surprise attack on American soil.

Shortly after Bush's declaration, Castro launched an opening broadside against the war on terror. Speaking in Havana, he established the link between the U.S. response to the September 11 attacks and the potential threat that the United States posed to Cuba. When Bush declared before Congress that after September 11 "night fell on a different world," this was true for Cuba too. Castro began by advising the Bush administration to practice restraint, saying, "An objective and calm friend should advise the United States government against throwing the young American soldiers into an uncertain war in remote, isolated, and inaccessible places, like a fight against ghosts, not knowing where they are or even if they exist or not, or whether the people they kill are or are not responsible for the death of their innocent fellow countrymen killed in the United States . . . One day they will admit we were right." But, the aging Cuban leader warned, the United States should also beware of setting its island neighbor in its sights: "Our independence, our principles, and our social achievements we will defend with honor to the last drop of blood if we are attacked!"[2] The words of conciliation were already giving way to a strident view that Cuba's need to defend itself from the United States would be the island's primary response to the war on terror.

In the months and years that followed, Castro's warnings fell on deaf ears abroad but recast his relevance at home, as the possibility of U.S. military actions toward Cuba, however inconceivable in Washington, gained new credibility among a watchful Cuban public. When U.S. forces toppled the Taliban in Afghanistan in the fall of 2001, visitors to Havana could witness the stark difference in perspectives by flipping between the international and local television channels. On CNN, international correspondent Christiane Amanpour breathlessly reported that men were shaving off their beards and women were casting off their burkas to celebrate their liberation from Taliban rule. On Cuban state television (which was all that most Cubans could receive), the screen showed bearded men and traditionally dressed Afghan women fearfully passing by bombed-out buildings, while the voice-over explained that the proud Afghan people were determined to preserve their traditional culture in defiance of "U.S. imperialist aggression." Furthermore, Cuba was one of only seven countries deemed to be a "state sponsor of terrorism" by the U.S. State Department, along with Iraq, Iran, Libya, Syria, Sudan, and North Korea. That determination had been made by the Reagan administration in 1982, owing to Cuba's history of supporting liberation movements in Latin America and Africa. But the designation took on new weight in the post-9/11 context, and the fears of many Cubans were exacerbated by officials in Washington and exiles in Miami who sought to recast Cuba as a relevant security threat to the United States.

In May 2002, John Bolton delivered a speech titled "Beyond the Axis of Evil: Additional Threats from Weapons of Mass Destruction" at the Heritage Foundation, a conservative think tank with stately offices located just a stone's throw from Capitol Hill.[3] Bolton, who was then serving as the State Department's undersecretary for arms control, was a prominent hawk on defense issues in the Bush administration. It was less than a year after the September 11 attacks and six months since U.S. forces had routed the Taliban in Afghanistan, and the room was packed with an influential audience seeking clues to where America's war on terror would lead in the coming months. "America," Bolton declared, "is determined to prevent the next wave of terror. States that sponsor terror and pursue WMD must stop. States that renounce terror and abandon WMD can become part of our effort. But those that do not can expect to become our targets."

Most of Bolton's speech focused on the typical rogue states: Iraq, Iran, North Korea, Syria, and Libya. But then he dwelt extensively on a potential threat located just off our shores. "There is a threat coming from another Bio-Weapons Convention signatory, and one that lies just ninety miles from the U.S. mainland, namely Cuba," he declared. After citing the suspicions that some Cuban defectors have raised about Cuba's sophisticated biomedical industry, Bolton made clear that the U.S. government had resolved its doubts about Cuba's capacity and intentions: "Here is what we now know: The United States believes that Cuba has at least a limited offensive biological warfare research and development effort." Cuba had officially been placed on the waiting list to join the Bush administration's "axis of evil."

Robert Menendez of New Jersey was among the Cuban American members of Congress to express pleasure with Bolton's findings. "I am happy to see that the administration has finally come forth with an acknowledgment of Cuba's capabilities," he said. "Cuba's biotechnology industry is not just for medical reasons . . . I think they could be making a variety of things, from anthrax to smallpox to other agents."[4] Indeed, allegations that Cuba was a biological weapons threat had long been embraced by Cuban exiles and tepidly accepted by official U.S. intelligence assessments, but never before had they been so publicly promoted by the U.S. State Department. Even influential journalists like the *New York Times*' Judith Miller, whose reporting was later found to have exaggerated the threat of nuclear weapons in Iraq, latched onto the story and amplified Bolton's claims by citing "other administration officials" who told her that "Cuba has been experimenting with anthrax, as well as a small number of other deadly pathogens."[5]

It later became known that a fierce debate had raged within the U.S. State Department's intelligence unit about the language that Bolton used in the speech regarding Cuba's bio-weapons programs. In fact, when the aftermath of the Iraq War failed to produce evidence of Saddam Hussein's weapons programs, the Senate conducted an in-depth assessment to examine whether intelligence analysts had been pressured to change their judgments. Senator Pat Roberts of Kansas called for analysts to come forward if they had felt pressured by policy makers in the Bush administration to change their intelligence assessments, but the only analyst who testified to having been pressured by political appointees was the one charged with making judgments on Cuba.[6] (In the spring of 2005, Bolton's assertions about Cuba played a role in prompting Democratic senator Chris Dodd to block his nomination as the U.S. ambassador to the United Nations.) But in the tense moments of 2002, as the United States prepared for war in Iraq, Cuba feared that it was being drawn into the sights of an America on war footing with its enemies. In a subsequent interview with a French journalist, Castro described his perspective clearly: "The war in Iraq hadn't broken out yet, but Cuba was one of the possible targets of the surprise preventative attack announced by Bush, because they had classified Cuba as a terrorist state. Not long before, we'd heard the outrageous accusations by Bolton that we were carrying out research aimed at producing biological weapons . . . We were in a political conflict with the United States, and at risk of a military conflict with them. Our mind was on nothing else—for us the main thing, the essential, fundamental thing, the vital thing, a question of life and death, really, was the conflict with them."[7] The combination of U.S. saber rattling and Cuba's sense of insecurity would soon result in a politically explosive cocktail that left no side unscathed.

It was a warm fall morning in early November 2002 when a single-engine Russian plane appeared over the runway at Key West International Airport, located on the southernmost of the islands that curve southwest off the tip of Florida. The yellow-and-white crop duster was flanked by two U.S. Air Force F-15 fighter jets that had been scrambled from a nearby base in Homestead, Florida, to guide the plane toward its final destination. The plane's cargo included seven adults and a baby who had crammed themselves into the two-seater to escape from the rural Cuban province of Pinar del Río only hours before. The pilot, forty-eight-year-old Nemencio Carlos Alonso Guerra, had been a stalwart member of the Communist Party in Cuba. Now he was on the verge of becoming the first airplane pilot to successfully steer a stolen Cuban craft to a safe landing on U.S. territory in more than a decade. His wife, who had been left behind in Cuba, was stunned, telling the local media, "No one is more revolutionary than he is. We've always been against those who leave. What drove him to this, no one knows."[8]

The crop duster's eight passengers were quickly granted permanent asylum by U.S. immigration authorities, under rules that treated all Cubans as refugees upon their arrival on American shores. Unbeknownst to all but his closest friends, Guerra had agreed to a spur-of-the-moment plot to steal the plane from an airstrip owned by the Cuban government and leave the island for the United States. He had risked everything to bring himself and several family members to safety, but it was a gamble that he had won. The strange saga of the yellow-and-white plane that had brought them to America continued for weeks. In an otherwise unrelated incident, lawyers for Ana Margarita Martínez, the ex-wife of a Cuban spy, had won a twenty-seven-million-dollar judgment against the Cuban government for her pain and suffering. This had given her the right to lay claim to Cuban assets in the United States, and her lawyers filed suit to seize the newly arrived plane as part of her compensation. When the plane's auction produced only lowball bids, she bought it herself for seven thousand dollars, saying that after the legal wrangling over the plane, "by this time, it feels like it's almost my child."[9] (The crop duster was eventually acquired by a local artist, who painted it with brightly colored open mouths to symbolize the lack of freedom of speech in Cuba, and surrounded the plane with more than forty suitcases and trunks that marked each year of exile since 1959. The exhibit was christened the *Cuban Monument to Freedom* and unveiled at a reception in Miami in December 2004.) The early-morning flight of Nemencio Carlos Alonso Guerra had cost the Cuban government one plane, and a good chunk of its pride. But from the perspective of Miami, this successful airplane adventure had produced winners all around.

The year was closing on a sour note for Americans and Cubans alike. A flurry of apparent outreach to the United States in the early months of 2002 had provoked commentary that Castro had launched a "charm offensive" aimed at warming U.S.-Cuba relations. The Cuban leader had hosted a succession of U.S. congressional delegations, encouraged American food companies to trade with Cuba, and kept mum about the transformation of the U.S. naval base at Guantánamo Bay into a detention center for suspected Al Qaeda members. In May, Jimmy Carter became the first former U.S. president to visit Cuba since 1959. Castro greeted him in his finest suit, but at the end of the visit he accompanied Carter to the tarmac dressed in his olive green uniform, looking ready for a fight. Deeply irritated by Carter's public meetings with and support for pro-democracy activists, Castro soon responded by mobilizing millions of Cubans in a nationwide referendum to declare that the socialist nature of the Cuban system was "irreversible."

By the fall, a confluence of factors was setting Castro increasingly on edge. The Bush administration's relentless buildup to the war in Iraq was generating unease throughout the world and leaving Cuban officials deeply unsettled about U.S. intentions toward the island. Top U.S. officials like John Bolton had characterized Cuba as a bio-weapons threat. Carter had helped to defuse these allegations by revealing that during his pre-trip briefings by Bush administration officials, they had never mentioned such a possibility. ("I asked them specifically on more than one occasion: 'Is there any evidence that Cuba has been involved in sharing any information with any other country on Earth that could be used for terrorist purposes?'" Carter had told reporters in Havana. "And the answer from our experts on intelligence was 'no.'")[10] Castro was irritated, however, that Carter's visit had helped to legitimize Cuba's internal democracy movement. Cuban officials had long regarded dissidents like Oswaldo Payá of the Christian Liberation Movement, independent economists like Marta Beatriz Roque and Oscar Espinosa Chepe, and highly critical writers like Raúl Rivero to be principally a nuisance that could be easily controlled. But Carter's visit had elevated the status of Cuban dissidents and raised their international and domestic profile. In October, the European Parliament even awarded the Sakharov Prize for Freedom of Thought to Payá, a triumph for the island's democracy advocates but a slap in the face for the Castro regime.

The successful attempt by Guerra, the crop duster pilot, to escape Cuba for Key West in November was another source of anger and concern. The fact that a Cuban pilot could steal a plane and be warmly welcomed in Miami infuriated the Cuban government, but even worse, the escape itself hinted that the levels of economic desperation on the island remained intense. The deep decline in tourism following the September 11 attacks was still being felt in the Caribbean, and especially in Cuba. Moreover, the island's sugar industry was in free fall, and the government had recently decided to close more than half its mills. The possibility of a mass exodus from Cuba hung heavily in the air, but the Cuban government perceived the potential cost of a migration crisis to be far greater in the age of preemptive war. In June, Florida governor Jeb Bush had said that a flood of refugees leaving Cuba would be considered by the United States to be an "act of aggression" perpetrated by Cuba. The Castro government had a history of launching refugee crises as a safety valve to defuse political discontent on the island, but Cuban officials were deeply concerned by the tough words coming from the brother of President Bush. Lincoln Diaz-Balart later confirmed that a flood of refugees from Cuba at that time could have led the United States to take action. "You notice Castro doesn't create mass exoduses with Bush," he said, "because he knows it would mean his end, literally. This president has told the Cuban regime that it would be considered an aggressive act . . . that would be met in unspecified ways by the American president." When asked whether this would result in U.S. military intervention toward Cuba, Diaz-Balart replied, "Events can unfold in different ways . . . If there were a serious miscalculation by Fidel Castro, then that would have been a possibility." If a mass-migration crisis began while the United States was preparing for war, the possibility lingered that anti-Castro hawks in the U.S. government would seize the moment to provoke the Cuban regime's undoing.

In the midst of this pervasive uncertainty, Washington had dispatched a new diplomat to take over the sensitive post of chief of the U.S. Interests Section in Havana. James Cason arrived in Cuba as a career foreign service officer with more than thirty years of experience in some of the most challenging posts in Latin America. A plain-speaking New Jersey native with neatly parted gray hair and stylish round eyeglasses, Cason came from a policy-planning position at State Department headquarters in Foggy Bottom to replace Vicki Huddleston, who had run the U.S. mission for three years and served as a key point person during the Elián González crisis. Although all top U.S. diplomats in Havana are officially detested by the Cubans, Huddleston had won some grudging respect for her ability to maintain ties with both government and opposition leaders in Cuba, as well as important cultural and intellectual figures. As a Clinton appointee, however, her diplomatic finesse had won her few fans among the anti-Castro hard-liners that now ruled the roost under Bush, and the new Latin American policy team wanted to embrace a tougher approach.

James Cason arrived in Cuba on September 10, 2002, but his tenure had already gotten off to a rocky start when the Cuban government delayed his diplomatic visa for fifty days, leaving him to cool his heels in Washington with all his bags packed. His paperwork came through only when the State Department threatened to pull the visa of Dagoberto Rodríguez, the top Cuban diplomat in Washington. Meanwhile, Miami's Spanish-language talk radio was briefly electrified by the rumor that Cason planned to dock his twenty-four-foot motorboat at Marina Hemingway, prompting State Department officials to offer reassurances that the boat would remain in storage. While he had not been given specific marching orders by Washington, he arrived in Havana with no doubt about what he was there to do.

After completing his tour in Cuba, Cason recalled, "I was told, 'You are not at a mission; you are on a mission.' I never got instructions. My first priority was to meet with the opposition and the dissidents, and I thought I would send a clear signal to the government about what I was there for, and it was not to be a nice guy. The mission was to support the democracy movement." The U.S. Interests Section is the largest diplomatic office in Cuba, with a staff of fifty American diplomats. The office also employs about two hundred Cubans, although none are allowed above the third floor of the building as a precaution against spying. By contrast, most European and Latin American embassies have a handful of professional diplomats and perhaps a dozen Cuban employees. Upon arriving in Havana, Cason met immediately with Cuba's leading dissidents, and within weeks he began traveling around the island to speak with dozens of political party activists, independent journalists and librarians, and virtually anyone who was known to have declared opposition to the Castro government. By Christmas, he had logged more than seven thousand miles traveling to the farthest corners of Cuba with books, shortwave radios, and a message of moral support for the island's beleaguered opposition figures. His official relationship with the Cuban government was frosty from the start and soon plunged into deep freeze. Requested meetings were denied, American contacts with Cuban academics and intellectuals affiliated with state institutions dried up, and the U.S. Interests Section became a diplomat island with few contacts outside of the dissident groups it had pledged to support.

Cason could not have cared less about what Cuban officials thought of him. His focus was wholly on supporting Cuba's nascent opposition movement: "Anybody who is a dissident in Cuba is a really courageous person, because the price you're paying is so great, especially for your family," he said. "I mean, you are screwed. You are not going to be able to get a job. Your kids are going to be taken out of school; your neighbors are going to harass you. They are going to repudiate you, throw rocks at your windows. They are going to beat you up in the street. It takes a lot to be a dissident in a totalitarian system, so I respect them all." During his tenure, the U.S. Interests Section was transformed into a wide-ranging dissident outreach program that included meetings, workshops, and training programs for independent journalists, youth groups, and political party leaders. The United States also provided free access to the Internet and disseminated thousands of publications to average Cubans, including books on Martin

Luther King Jr., Mahatma Gandhi, and the Universal Declaration of Human Rights. The vigorous official outreach to citizens who were disaffected with the regime, or perhaps simply curious about the United States, infuriated the Cuban government, but Cason did not mind: "We knew they weren't going to approve of it, but fuck them. The point is that this was for the Cuban people who were desperate for this. I mean, it was a treasure to get any of this stuff."

In addition, Cason engaged in a war of words with Cuban officials through the press. During a U.S. trade fair in Cuba, he dismissed the country's potential as a trading partner, instead calling it a "Jurassic economy" led by "a totalitarian dictator who runs a repressive regime increasingly reliant on the military." Cason's outspoken taunting of the Castro government won him plaudits in Washington and enthusiastic support in Miami, but the responses in Havana were more complicated. Castro and his top ministers despised Cason, but they also found his overt support for Cuban dissidents to be politically useful, because it helped them to make the argument that opposition to the regime depended on overseas sponsors. Many Cubans in the system with reformist instincts found that the U.S. Interests Section had become such a hot potato that they were forced to give it a wide berth. The dissidents themselves were flattered and impressed to have become the focus of such high-level attention from the United States, and many were grateful for the moral and logistical support. But some were worried about being co-opted by the United States, or worse, used as a way to provoke Castro's government. What is clear is that James Cason helped reshape the rules of the game between Washington and Havana. While the Castro government had testy relationships with every head of the U.S. Interests Section, none had veered so quickly into open conflict with the regime as Cason, whose enthusiastic support of Cuban dissidents was fueling deep tensions on the island.

In January 2003, Cuban voters cast their ballots for the more than six hundred seats in the National Assembly, and nearly twelve hundred delegations to provincial assemblies gathered in regions across the country. Most candidates were members of the Cuban Communist Party, and all had been nominated for their posts by mass organizations controlled by the single party. Castro handily won his seat as the incumbent deputy for Santiago, as did all other nominated candidates. The official newspaper *Granma* reported that more than 97 percent of the voting population—totaling more than 8.1 million Cubans—had participated in the election and overwhelmingly approved the entire slate of candidates backed by the government.[11]

But Castro's gloating over the Cuban Communist Party's ability to deliver millions of votes en masse disguised a contentious debate that had taken root within the Cuban government. The feisty James Cason had succeeded in getting himself noticed. Although he had been in Havana for only several months, he had become a preoccupation deep within the halls of the Cuban regime. Most top Cuban officials were unconcerned with the dissidents themselves, a group that was still small, divided, and deeply penetrated by Cuban state security. But Cason's flamboyant and provocative style had captured their attention. His predecessor, Huddleston, had also met frequently with opposition groups and even introduced a program to distribute shortwave radios on the island to improve people's reception of the anti-Castro programming of Radio Martí, broadcast from Miami at U.S. taxpayer expense. But she had also operated with a certain sense of decorum and cultivated her relationships with counterparts in the Cuban government. Cason, by contrast, flaunted his distaste for Castro at every turn. If he had been a private U.S. citizen, he would have been deported. As a Cuban citizen, he would have been jailed. But he was a U.S. official operating with diplomatic immunity, and his behavior offered no easy solution. Fidel Castro was a man driven by obsessions, and how to handle James Cason was now one of them.

But there were other signs of trouble. The increasing outspokenness on the part of Cuba's timid Catholic Church had also gotten Castro's dander up. On February 24, Cardinal Jaime Ortega Alamino, the archbishop of Havana, released a pastoral letter to mark the 150th anniversary of the death of Father Félix Varela, a national hero in Cuba whose name has been claimed by both supporters and opponents of the Castro regime. Ortega, who was briefly floated as a possible successor to Pope John Paul II in 2005, was widely seen as a source of wisdom in Cuba whose potential was undermined by an excessive sense of caution. Unlike in many of the formerly communist countries of Eastern Europe, where the Catholic Church played a crucial role in creating space for democratic political activity, the Cuban Catholic Church moved incrementally and lacked bold leadership.

Ortega's new pastoral letter marked a stark departure from previous protocol. In a pronouncement titled "There Is No Homeland

Without Virtue," Ortega declared, "The time has come to go from the avenging state that demands sacrifices and settles accounts to the merciful state that is ready to lend a compassionate hand before it controls and punishes infractions." He outlined the range of severe economic and social problems facing Cuban society and concluded by saying, "Only free men can build the homeland of their dreams."[12] Ortega's pastoral letter was uncharacteristically blunt and was viewed by the Cuban government as an open challenge to the political system.

During the first few weeks of 2003, world attention was consumed by the Bush administration's decision to move toward war with Iraq. Cuba was barely a blip on the U.S. radar, but the potential implications of the war were deeply felt in Havana. After all, the island had been formally classified by the U.S. government as a "state sponsor of terrorism" since 1982 and had been targeted with "regime change" policies for decades. A steady stream of invective flowed from Spanish-language radio in Miami, as callers vowed that after Iraq, Cuba would be next. Indeed, the most pro-intervention Cuban American groups in Miami became known as "los chalabitos," or "the little Chalabis," after Ahmed Chalabi, the famed Iraqi exile and head of the Iraqi National Congress who played a leading role in convincing the Bush administration to go to war. With Cuban exile groups screening defectors in search of their own curveball—an insider who would vouch for the existence of Cuba's biological weapons program—Castro feared that his enemies in Miami were preparing to repeat the trick as a way to gain entry to Havana.

Moreover, there were signs of growing tension within Cuba itself. In early January, an official Cuban panel rejected a dissident constitutional reform proposal known as the Varela Project, which had been spearheaded by Oswaldo Payá of the Christian Liberation Movement. Soon thereafter, Cuban officials declared a new war on drug trafficking and began to mobilize neighborhood block committees to monitor the streets with greater vigilance. It quickly became clear, however, that the purported clampdown on drug activity was in fact an excuse to crack down on Cuba's many self-employed workers who were attempting to earn an honest living outside the communist system. During this period, Cuban dissidents also became more vocal, meeting with visiting U.S. congressmen and organizing several public events to express their views. This included an event held in the home of opposition economist Marta Beatriz Roque and attended by Cason that commemorated the seventh anniversary of the Brothers to the Rescue shoot-down of 1996, when Cuban fighter jets attacked two civilian aircraft piloted by Cuban exiles.

On March 6, Fidel Castro was reelected to a sixth term as the president of Cuba's Council of State by the members of the National Assembly. He began his lengthy address by remarking that "you cannot take everything too seriously in this world today. If you did, you would run the risk of heart attack or a nervous breakdown." He then launched into a long-winded tirade against the activities of the U.S. Interests Section. "This past February 24 . . . a gentleman named James Cason, head of the United States Interests Section in Cuba, met in an apartment in Havana with a group of counterrevolutionaries paid by the U.S. government . . . Other diplomats received invitations, but only this illustrious character attended the event. However, he would not limit himself to discreetly attending. Asked by a journalist if his presence there did not in fact confirm the accusations made by the Cuban government, Cason replied, 'No, because I believe they have invited the whole diplomatic corps, and we as a country always support democracy and people who fight for a better life. I am here as a guest.' "

Castro recounted Cason's actions: " 'I am not afraid,' [Cason] answered simply in response to a question from another reporter, as to whether his presence at the oppositionist activity could not be taken as an unfriendly gesture towards the Cuban government, which denounces dissidents as subversive groups. Then, rudely and offensively, he added in perfect Spanish, 'Sadly, the Cuban government is afraid, afraid of freedom of conscience, afraid of freedom of expression, afraid of human rights. This group is demonstrating that there are Cubans who are not afraid. They know that the transition to democracy is already under way. We want them to know that they are not alone, that the whole world supports them. We as a country support democracy, and people who fight for a better life and for justice . . . I am here as a guest, and I am going to go around the whole country visiting all the people who do want freedom and justice.' "

Castro was incensed by the statement: "Anyone can see that this is a shameless and defiant provocation. It would appear that both he and those who ordered the offensive performance by this bully with diplomatic immunity were revealing that they are in fact afraid. Otherwise, his behavior was so odd that anyone could rightly be wondering how much alcohol was served at that 'patriotic' event. Actually, Cuba is so much afraid that it will calmly take all the time needed to decide on its course of action regarding this bizarre official. Perhaps the numerous U.S. intelligence agents working at the Interests Section could explain to him that Cuba can easily do without this office, a breeding ground for counterrevolutionaries and a command post for the most offensive subversive actions against our country."[13]

Castro's fulmination against Cason's support for Cuban dissidents was wrong in its particulars. Cuban opposition figures did not receive direct funding from the U.S. government (although that restriction was later rescinded), but they did benefit from in-kind support such as digital cameras and fax machines. Some of the most prominent dissidents were economists, writers, and librarians—hardly the threatening or violent figures evoked by the word "mercenaries" that Castro often used to describe these groups. Moreover, both U.S. and Cuban officials knew that threats to close the U.S. Interests Section in Cuba were essentially empty. Such a move in Havana would simply result in prompt "eye for an eye" retaliation by the United States, and Havana considered the Cuban Interests Section in Washington to be far too valuable an asset to risk losing it altogether. But Cason's activities had clearly transfixed the Cuban leader, prompting him to signal that squashing U.S. outreach to Cuban dissidents had become a top priority.

On the morning of March 18, Cuban poet Raúl Rivero was taken aback when several police officers arrived at his house and began to interrogate him. He was then arrested and squired away by a squadron of police cars, leaving his wife, Blanca Reyes, in shock. Soon news of additional arrests swept through the dissident community, and brief wire reports were filed by the few independent journalists operating within Cuba. Castro's government was implementing the most sweeping crackdown in recent memory on Cuba's fragile opposition movement. Only over the course of several days did the scope of the mass detentions become clear, with more than eighty known opposition figures detained and the vast majority placed under arrest. While Oswaldo Payá was left untouched, most of the leadership of the Varela Project was taken into custody, as were independent economists Marta Beatriz Roque (the only woman detained) and Oscar Espinosa Chepe and independent writers and journalists such as Rivero and Manuel Vásquez

Portal. Several other opposition figures, such as Oscar Elías Biscet, a prominent Afro-Cuban doctor who was already in prison, had their cases processed together with the seventy-five new arrests.

In an official statement, the Cuban government blamed the arrests squarely on the activities of Cason, decrying "the shameful and repeated attitude by the chief of Washington's diplomatic mission in Havana, James Cason, to foment the internal counterrevolution." The statement added, "No nation, no matter how powerful, has the right to organize, finance and serve as a central barracks for subverting the constitutional order and violating the law by conspiring, threatening security and destroying the independence of another country." A spokesman for the Cuban diplomatic office in Washington, D.C., dismissed the significance of the arrests: "These groups are a minority in Cuba and represent nobody. They were not arrested for what they thought, but for acting against and threatening national security."[14]

But for the first several days, the crackdown on dissidents was buried under the global news coverage of much greater significance: The United States had launched its invasion of Iraq on March 19. Even *El Nuevo Herald*, the Miami-based Spanish-language daily that focuses obsessively on Cuba, placed news of the arrests below the fold on its front page. Fidel Castro had orchestrated his latest wave of repression with a masterful sense of timing: News from Iraq simply dominated everything else that was happening across the globe. Before their arrest, most of Cuba's dissidents were barely known to the outside world. By the time the video of euphoric Iraqis pulling down a statue of Saddam Hussein swept across the world several weeks later, seventy-five Cubans had been sentenced to prison terms ranging from fifteen to twenty-five years—collectively totaling more than fourteen hundred years in prison. Castro had skillfully, if harshly, dealt a strong rebuke to the opposition movement that had been the focus of U.S. policy, but the area of conflict was about to shift to the desperate wave of hijackings that threatened to engulf the island.

Located southwest of Cuba, the Isle of Youth is the largest island off of Cuba's shores and, politically speaking, it is a special municipality administered directly by the central government. Its residents, who number about one hundred thousand, earn their livelihoods primarily through agriculture, timber, and fishing, although in recent years the island has also become a tourist destination for scuba divers and beachgoers. In Cuban lore, the Isle of Youth is famous for its prison system, which for two years during the 1950s held the country's most famous ex-prisoner, Fidel Castro himself. After being released by the Batista regime in 1955, and subsequently claiming power four years later, Castro converted his former prison into a national monument, while using the other prisons to house common criminals and, increasingly, his political opponents. During the 1990s and early 2000s, when the Cuban economy suffered a severe decline, the population of the Isle of Youth became increasingly restive. Cut off from the rest of Cuba, many of its citizens resented the central government's lack of attention, and they faced economic deprivation as dire as anywhere else in the country.

In the spring of 2003, however, the Isle of Youth became the epicenter of a series of airplane hijackings that thrust this sleepy territory to the front burner of U.S.-Cuba relations. It was a moment filled with the extraordinary global tension that accompanied the first days of the U.S. invasion of Iraq, as well as the extreme stress in U.S.-Cuba relations caused by Castro's roundup of dissidents close to the U.S. diplomatic mission in Havana. Soon the two countries were drawn even closer to conflict. It began on March 19, when a group of six men ranging in age from mid-twenties to early thirties hijacked a Douglas DC-3 plane that was scheduled to depart from the Isle of Youth for Havana. Armed with knives, the hijackers restrained the plane's crew with tape and rope and forced the craft to be diverted to Key West, carrying more than two dozen terrified passengers, including five children. With their country now in the midst of a war, U.S. officials were in no mood to reward this latest hijacking with the leniency that greeted Nemencio Carlos Alonso Guerra when his crop duster appeared in the Florida skies the previous November. The U.S. courts convicted the six men of committing a conspiracy to seize an airplane by force and sentenced them to prison terms of twenty years each. However, fourteen passengers—more than half of the plane's total—elected to stay in the United States after landing in their surprise destination. As in the previous case, the plane was seized by U.S. authorities, a move that Castro viewed as both disrespectful and an instance of what he described as "the economic war against Cuba." During a television roundtable held on March 22, Castro denounced the American decision to keep the Cuban plane, saying that "if there is one country in the world where a hijacking with a knife at the throat of a pilot should cause indignation and horror, it's the United States. Returning the plane is the least they can do."[15]

But the onslaught of plane hijackings had not yet run its course. On the evening of March 31, thirty-three-year-old Aldemis Wilson González boarded a Soviet-made AN-24 plane on the Isle of Youth for its regularly scheduled flight to Havana. He was accompanied by his wife, his son, and two fake hand grenades that he brandished in front of the airplane's pilots shortly after liftoff. His demand was simple: Take him and his family to the United States. However, faced with the reality that the small, twin-engine propeller plane lacked the fuel to travel all the way to South Florida, he allowed the pilots to make a fueling stop in Havana's José Martí International Airport at nine thirty P.M. Alerted to the unfolding crisis by the air traffic controller, Cuban officials were concerned that the arrival of another hijacked plane in South Florida would stoke tensions with the Bush administration even higher. In an act of desperation, the Cubans reached out to their American nemesis James Cason to try to persuade the hijacker to abandon his plans.

Cason's phone rang suddenly at two A.M. On the other end of the line was Rafael Dausá, then the head of North American affairs at the Cuban foreign ministry, who apprised him of the hijacking and their desire to negotiate an end to the standoff now taking place at the Havana airport. The two traveled together to the scene, which was blocked off, and Cason was greeted by Cuba's feared minister of the interior, General Abelardo Colomé Ibarra, and several high-ranking army generals. "It was the first time I had ever met any of these people," Cason recalled. They ushered him into the control tower, where he began to talk González into surrendering. The conversation was fraught with tension. Cason told the man, "If you hurt anybody, you are going to get the death penalty, and if you continue on this, then you are going to get at least twenty years." The hijacker was incredulous: "You're not Cason. The government doesn't talk to him. I don't believe you." Cason volunteered to go down to the plane and speak directly to the hijacker, while offering his *carnet*—his official photo identification badge—to prove that he was indeed the top American diplomat in Havana, who was on the scene to deliver a stern warning in person.

On the tarmac, Cason offered his identification badge to the pilot, who passed it on to González, who was visibly surprised. "OK, now I know you are Cason," he said. "Don't do it," Cason replied. "You're going to get twenty years. Let them go. The Cubans said they'll give you something like six and a half years if you don't hurt anybody. And you are much better off." González was unconvinced, retorting, "I'd rather spend the rest of my life in prison. I've got my family on the plane and they'll be free. I'm getting out of here; for me this is the worst thing that could happen. I'm not going to stay in this country. I'll take what's coming." For Cason, it was a moving moment. "It was very poignant," he concluded. "But he kept my damned *carnet*. I didn't have it for two months. The FBI took it when he landed in Key West, and then he was arrested."

Castro had also tried to personally negotiate with the hijacker during the twelve-hour ordeal that ensued. Twenty people were eventually released from the back hatch of the airplane, but González, having already taken enormous risks, was determined to see his adventure through to the bitter end. At ten forty-five A.M. on the following morning, April 1, the plane departed with its crew, González and his family, and twenty-one hostages in tow. The U.S. military scrambled two F-16 fighter jets to accompany the plane to Key West International. Vacationers attempting to fly to the southernmost Florida Key to spend spring break on the beach found that their flights were diverted, while awaiting friends and relatives gaped outside the airport at the U.S. Black Hawk helicopter swooping overhead. FBI agents and SWAT team snipers took up positions around the airport. González emerged from the plane wearing a red jacket lettered with the word AMERICA, and was quickly separated from the other passengers and taken into custody. Like the hijackers whom he copied, he was denied bond and ultimately sentenced to twenty years in prison by the U.S. courts. Although unable to save himself, he did partially achieve his goal: His family still resides in South Florida.

This saga had barely concluded in Key West when Cuba was faced with a new hijacking crisis at sea. On the morning of April 2, a group of eleven Cubans, mainly in their early twenties, armed themselves with knives and took control of a passenger ferry in Havana Bay. The captain was ordered to set sail for Florida, with nearly fifty petrified passengers aboard. The incident began when Lorenzo Copello pulled out a gun and fired a shot into the air while yelling, "This fucking boat goes away for *la Yuma!*"—a common slang term for the United States. (The nickname comes from the 1957 western film *3:10 to Yuma*, which has long been a cult hit in Cuba.) Copello and an accomplice then burst into the ferry's control room, put a gun to the captain's head, and held a knife to the first mate's torso.[16] The boat quickly ran out of fuel in worsening weather conditions, prompting the perpetrators to become agitated and threaten to throw people overboard. The Cuban coast guard eventually caught the ferry and towed it thirty miles back to the port of Mariel, but the standoff continued. Cuban officials regained control of the boat only when a French tourist held captive jumped into the ocean, creating confusion that allowed Cuban security forces to storm aboard and rescue the passengers.[17]

On April 10, the Cuban government was forced to contend with yet another attempt to hijack a plane taking off from the Isle of Youth. Five men snatched a Kalashnikov rifle from a local soldier and then appeared at the airport two hours later brandishing the gun, along with knives and small exercise weights that they apparently intended to use to break a glass wall in the airport lounge that would give them direct access to the tarmac. The men were arrested by Cuban authorities in the airport before their plan could be implemented. But it was the ferryboat hijackers from Havana who paid the ultimate price. Earlier that week the entire group involved had been charged with "very grave acts of terrorism." Four men received life sentences, another received a thirty-year sentence, the three women involved were given between two and five years in prison—and the three ringleaders were sentenced to death in summary trials. In the quiet early-morning hours of April 11, the three men were executed by firing squad. Lorenzo Copello, age thirty-one, Bárbaro Sevilla, age twenty-two, and Jorge Luis Martínez, age forty, were the first people to be executed by the Cuban government in more than two years, and the first to be executed for terrorism-related charges in more than a decade.

The events of the spring of 2003 were wrenching by any measure. Castro's regime had survived the cold war, and even persisted through the economic collapse of the 1990s, but the post–September 11 era and the context of America's "war on terror" had thrust the island into new and uncharted terrain. Tensions within Cuba had reached a fever pitch and provoked a costly war of nerves between the United States and Cuba that had spread collateral damage far and wide. The U.S. effort to reach out to Cuban dissidents had prompted Castro to order that scores of innocent individuals be rounded up and placed in prison for lengthy sentences. With many leading dissidents in their fifties and sixties, it appeared likely that they would spend the rest of their lives behind bars.

The Bush administration had framed its support of Cuban opposition groups as a moral imperative, but its tactics had backfired badly. In this climate of hostility and suspicion, James Cason now had a new cause: to make sure that the world remembered the seventy-five dissidents who had been locked up during his watch. As a practical matter, Cuba's dissident movement had been decimated and would take years to rebuild.

The rash of hijackings by Cubans attempting to escape the island had come to a similarly tragic end. The Castro government, desperate to ward off a mass-migration crisis that risked provoking a hostile Bush administration firmly on war footing, had resorted to summary executions of three hijackers that scandalized the Cuban public and deeply disturbed many of its allies. As the international media's Iraq war fervor faded slightly, Cuba's seventy-five new "prisoners of conscience" and the sudden executions of three hijackers dealt a severe blow to the island's already tarnished image overseas.

In early March, just before the chaotic series of arrests and hijackings nearly turned Cuba upside down, Fidel Castro had given some clues to his state of mind. He knew that difficult days lay ahead, and that the sand was running through the hourglass of his own time in power. At the conclusion of his inauguration speech before the National Assembly, he gave voice to the concerns that were encircling his rule: "We all know that time passes and energy is running out. Perhaps the endless struggle trained us for such a long battle. I think that the secret may lie in the power of a great dream, of endless enthusiasm, and of a love for our noble cause that has grown with every day of life. But life has its own inexorable laws. I promise that I will be with you, if you so wish, for as long as I feel that I can be useful, and if it is not decided by nature before. Not a minute less, and not a second more. Now I understand that it was not my destiny to rest at the end of my life."[18] The old warrior had lost some prestige and pride during the war of nerves that played out within Cuba and across the Straits of Florida in the shadow of the Iraq invasion that transfixed most of the rest of the world. But his determination to resist the external aggression of the United States as well as the democratic desires of his own people remained fully intact. Fidel Castro and his regime had lived to fight another day.

CHAPTER 3

The Dissenters

It was a cool fall day in Madrid when I stopped by the apartment of Raúl Rivero, the celebrated Cuban writer, who had fled to Spain after spending nearly two years in prison for the crime of "betraying the homeland." As a prolific journalist, poet, and author, Rivero was one of the few dissidents arrested in the spring 2003 roundup who had achieved international stature, and his case quickly became a cause célèbre among press-freedom advocates overseas. Rivero was sentenced to twenty years behind bars during a one-day trial and then was sent to a maximum security prison in central Cuba more than 250 miles away from his home in Havana. In his late fifties at the time of his arrest, Rivero found his health quickly deteriorating in Cuba's squalid prison system, which provoked especially strong alarm in Spain, where he had many deep ties. As occurred in a number of especially high-profile cases, the Cuban government granted Rivero an early release for health reasons in November 2004. In the spring of 2005, he and his family were given permission to leave for exile in Spain. His new home was located in a smart business district north of Madrid's city center, in a modest apartment building on a quiet street with occasional traffic but few pedestrians. It felt very far from the steamy barrios of Havana.

Rivero greeted me warmly and ushered me into his sparsely furnished living room. With his longish gray hair and circular-rimmed eyeglasses, wearing a blue-and-white-striped shirt that was unbuttoned at the neck, he looked every bit the part of a seasoned journalist who still had more than a few story ideas tucked away in his head, waiting to be written. He was of medium height and heavy build, having apparently regained the weight that had slipped off him during nearly a year in solitary confinement in prison. His wife, Blanca

Reyes, greeted me briefly at the door and then disappeared into the kitchen to brew some coffee. Reyes had achieved acclaim in her own right as one of the leading voices of the Damas de Blanco, the "ladies in white" who held silent marches in Havana each Sunday to protest the jailing of their husbands, brothers, and sons. The plight of the Damas de Blanco, founded shortly after the crackdown in 2003, drew widespread sympathy among democracy activists overseas, and in 2005 the European Parliament awarded the group the Sakharov Prize for Freedom of Thought, its top human rights prize, named for the famed Soviet dissident. Reyes now served as the group's representative in Madrid, but tonight she was evidently content to leave the political discussions to her husband.

In an earlier part of his life, in the 1970s, Rivero served as the Moscow bureau chief for Cuba's official press agency, and he went on to head the island's National Union of Cuban Writers and Artists. In 1995, he founded an independent press agency called CubaPress, and he remained a forceful, if peaceful, opponent of Fidel Castro's regime. Rivero first broke with the Cuban government in 1991, when he joined a group of ten intellectuals who sent a letter of protest to Castro calling for the release of all "prisoners of conscience." At the time of his arrest in 2003, Rivero was the only signatory of that letter who had not yet fled Cuba. With his departure, none remain.

Rivero's manner is courtly and avuncular, even when he is dealing with harsh truths. "The regime lives on confrontation," he told me with a tone of conviction. "It needs the confrontation—this sense of crisis—in order to justify its survival. Because of that, it sees dialogue as a threat, and it has no use for trying to reach common ground with its opponents." After forty years of communist oppression, Rivero said, "Cuba is suffering a material deterioration and a spiritual deterioration, and I fear that the spiritual deterioration is worse. Cuba today has lost its sense of balance and its value scale. The system cannot exist without crime"—a reference to the hundreds of small delinquencies that most families must commit to get through each week. "It's a Robin Hood system where people rob the state to survive." As Rivero spoke, he worked his way steadily through a pack of Marlboro Reds that sat on the table.

When I asked if he was surprised when the police came to arrest him during the spring of 2003, he replied, "I had a suspicion that they would come for me. The first detentions had already occurred, and I had given an interview to the international press commenting on the arrests. The police arrived shortly afterwards." He laughed quietly. "I was mixed in with the general prison population—some very tough black criminals—drug traffickers, robbers, assassins. They did not know what to make of me, but we managed to get along OK." Rivero was later sent to solitary confinement, where he spent most of a year alone in his cell. Reflecting back on his stay in prison, Rivero told me about a brief but memorable conversation with the prison's head warden, who managed the facility keeping the Cuban poet in lockdown. Rivero was allowed outside to walk on a patio, and the prison warden, while supervising his sojourn, asked him how the prison would be affected by the types of changes that Cuba's dissidents had taken such risks to advocate. "I told him that I was in favor of diverse political parties and free elections, and that Cubans should have the right to open small businesses, et cetera. So the warden asked me, 'But how will all this affect how the prison is managed?' And I replied, 'Well, it wouldn't affect your job at all. You are a technical expert in running prisons, and your expertise will still be needed even if the type of government changes.' "

Rivero recalled that the prison warden was in his late fifties and wore Ray-Ban sunglasses, a subtle class marker in Cuba. The warden had spoken once of how he cherished his 1955 Chevy Pontiac, and he probably kept a younger mistress, as was common among top Cuban bureaucrats of that age. The warden was silent as he led Rivero back to his solitary confinement and the two men left the sunlight behind. But as he escorted the Cuban writer back to his cell, he briefly looked up at his charge and said, "I like this idea." Now half a world away in his unassuming Madrid apartment, palatial by Cuban standards, Rivero nodded at me from across the simple wooden table. "I realized then that this person could be an ally of change in the future. He was a well-read man and a fanatic of Hemingway. All he wanted was to keep his Ray-Ban sunglasses and his Chevy vehicle and know that his style of living wouldn't be jeopardized. He could accept democratic change if he knew that it wouldn't put the things he cherished at risk."

As light faded from the sky and his apartment grew dimmer, Rivero rebuffed the suggestion that he missed Cuba at all. "No, not now," he replied. "You have to remember that I was in prison before I came to Spain, and the community here has been very welcoming of me. The journalistic community has embraced me, and I have been so busy writing my column and other articles that I have not had time to miss Cuba." He pulled one last cigarette from the box of Marlboro Reds and set the box down with the large health warning FUMAR PUEDE MATAR (Smoking can kill) facing upward. He expressed regret that he had spent so much time writing articles for the various contracts that he had accepted that he hadn't had time to finish editing a book of poems that he'd written while in prison. Rivero chuckled as he reflected on the busy new life that he was leading in Madrid, and he gave a good-natured shrug: "Capitalism is cruel."

The jailing of Raúl Rivero and his subsequent exile in Spain was just one of the many far-reaching effects of the Cuban government's massive crackdown on the opposition in the spring of 2003. As one of the world's few remaining communist states, Cuba has a long and dirty history of political oppression that extends back to the Castro government's first days in power, when many of the new regime's political opponents were executed, jailed, or driven into exile. Over the years, Cuba has committed a lengthy list of human rights violations that it has justified as necessary for defending the revolution—ranging from the extreme measures of the 1960s to the purges against artists and homosexuals in the 1970s to the ongoing pattern of harassment, abuse, and imprisonment of regime opponents that has endured for the past several decades. In an authoritative 1999 report surveying the island's human rights situation on the fortieth anniversary of the Cuban Revolution, Human Rights Watch concluded, "Over the past forty years, Cuba has developed a highly effective machinery of repression. The denial of basic civil and political liberties is written into Cuban law. In the name of legality, armed security forces, aided by state-controlled mass organizations, silence dissent with heavy prison terms, threats of prosecution, harassment, or exile."[1] During 2002 and early 2003, it had appeared that the Cuban government was permitting more independent activity, and more dissent, than had been tolerated in years. With the dramatic series of arrests, it was now clear that any such signs of political opening were merely a mirage.

It is only possible to understand Cuba's modern dissident movement in the context of the political environment in which its members live and work. The Communist Party is the only legally recognized political party in Cuba, and opposition leaders cannot run for seats in the National Assembly. There are no competitive, multiparty elections.

The vast majority of the population has access only to Cuban state television, which reflects government views (some Cubans have erected illegal satellite dishes that pick up international channels, but these mainly belong to the government elite). The two main news publications, *Granma* and *Juventud Rebelde*, are official organs of the Communist Party. Many of the elderly still read the broadsheets faithfully, but younger Cubans often refer to them as "toilet paper." (One captive audience consists of the American diplomats and reporters in Cuba who scrutinize every word in an effort to divine the intentions of Fidel and Raúl Castro.) Most of Castro's fiercest opponents fled the country, beginning with a large wave of exiles in the 1960s, but the exodus continues through the present day. Others have languished for years in Cuban prisons. Membership in the Communist Party is a requirement for career advancement, and the state holds a monopoly on most forms of employment, the exceptions being a limited private sector and the sprawling informal economy. Neighborhood watch groups, known as Committees for the Defense of the Revolution (CDRs), exist on virtually every block, and one of their purposes is to guard against activities that are deemed to be "counterrevolutionary."

Unlike many Eastern European countries prior to the fall of the Berlin Wall, Cuba lacks independent trade unions, and the Catholic Church is weak and largely averse to confrontation. Linkages with international partners are severely hampered by the U.S. ban on travel to Cuba and the Cuban government's efforts to monitor individuals' movements and prevent them from entering or leaving the country without prior authorization. Political organization outside of official channels is hampered by poor phone connections, lack of transportation, and extremely limited Internet access. Moreover, any independent political activity must contend with two overarching factors: the sweeping cult of personality created by Fidel Castro that equates his leadership with Cuba's national identity and the existence of an external threat (both real and perceived) in the form of the Miami exile community and, more broadly, the U.S. government. This has proved to be extremely rocky soil for the flowering of a genuinely independent and democratic civil society in Cuba. In particular, the Cuban government closely monitors any interactions between dissident groups and U.S. officials or U.S.-funded organizations working to promote democracy in Cuba—something that Castro has determined to be a provocation of the highest order.

Cuba's emerging opposition leaders come from a mix of backgrounds: They include disenchanted former Communist Party officials who broke with the government, activists guided by religious faith, people genuinely motivated by democratic desires, and opportunists who are betting that the communist system will fall and want to position themselves to play a role in whatever comes next. Although united in their goal of opening up greater democratic space in Cuba through peaceful pressure (as opposed to armed intervention or violent uprising), they are often divided over the practicalities of how to achieve that objective. The differences include ideological cleavages between social democrats and free market reformers as well as conflicts over whether to seek allies in the Cuban government, the desired pace of democratic and economic reforms, and, in particular, what stance to adopt regarding the Cuban exile community and the United States. Moreover, efforts to unify the dissident movement have often been undermined by competition among the prickly personalities of many of the leaders. The independent economist Marta Beatriz Roque and Varela Project leader Oswaldo Payá, for example, spent years sniping at each other, then attempted to reconcile, only to see the old animosities reemerge. In short, Cuba's democracy movement is a fragile coalition of the heroic, the foolish, the righteous, the brave, the caddish, and the just plain frustrated that has emerged in the context of totalitarian society. The miracle is that it exists at all.

Still, Cuba's opposition groups were clearly achieving substantial progress during the months before the crackdown. A network of independent libraries had sprung up around the island where Cubans could swap and share books that were banned by the government, ranging from critiques of totalitarianism by George Orwell to popular literature about adapting to change, like the U.S. bestseller *Who Moved My Cheese?* Although their work was considered untouchable by the official state media, independent journalists were regularly filing stories for Web sites overseas and sometimes landing opinion articles in major U.S. publications. In 2001, a new society for independent journalists was established, and by early 2003 it had published its first two issues of *De Cuba* (From Cuba), which featured poetry, photographs, and hard-hitting essays about the darker edges of Cuban reality. Cuban opposition figures began to meet openly in restaurants to discuss their activities as political party leaders, independent librarians, and journalists, even sharing their samizdat-type magazines with outside guests. Once a waitress, who could not help but overhear a conversation among opposition leaders in a mostly empty restaurant, gave them a fascinated look and asked, "Where are you from—it can't be Cuba!"

Most important, however, was the success of the Varela Project. In an effort to exploit a loophole in the Cuban constitution that allowed for citizens to call a national referendum with a petition that held ten thousand signatures, Oswaldo Payá and his colleagues in the Christian Liberation Movement collected more than eleven thousand signatures supporting a referendum on reforming the Cuban system, opening up the economy to free enterprise, and holding multiparty elections. The Varela Project was notable because it represented a peaceful effort to reform Cuba from within the existing legal framework, rather than an attempt to topple the regime through force or threats. It was transparent, asking Cuban citizens to voluntarily sign their names and identification numbers to a form to be submitted to the government, often at great personal risk. The signatures were collected by more than one hundred teams spread throughout the island, which indicated a level of organizational ability that the dissidents had not previously demonstrated. While eleven thousand people represented just a tiny fraction of the eleven million on the island, it also undercut the Cuban government's claims that only a handful of disaffected troublemakers disliked the communist system. When former U.S. president Jimmy Carter praised the Varela Project during his visit to Cuba in May 2002, it gave Payá and a vast swath of Cuban dissidents an aura of significance and international legitimacy that they had long struggled to attain.

Ultimately, the Varela Project faced a predictable end: It died in committee. In January 2003, Miguel Álvarez, the spokesman for National Assembly president Ricardo Alarcón, announced, "The Constitution and Legal Affairs Committee carefully studied the petition and decided not to move it forward because it went against the very foundation of the Constitution, amongst other reasons. It has already been shelved."[2] But the mild legal language masked the intense skirmishes that were already taking place between the Cuban government and its opponents, as the regime began to methodically notch up the pressure on the dissidents and wider Cuban society under the guise of cracking down on economic illegality.

In early March, two U.S. congressmen, Representatives Jim Davis (a Democrat from Florida) and Jim Kolbe (a Republican from Arizona), became the first American legislators to meet with Payá in his home.[3] Payá assembled his team and displayed copies of the signatures that had been submitted. Labor activist Pedro Pablo Álvarez welcomed them by saying, "You come at a moment of great repression and great hope," while Payá, speaking with seriousness and deliberation, explained the importance of the initiative: "For many years, people have said that you will only see change in Cuba when Fidel dies, but that is a narcotic that must be resisted. The regime is worried and today we are facing another repressive campaign. People have been fired, visited house by house, and faced harassment, but even in the middle of this repression we are collecting more signatures. We are in a full campaign, because the Cuban regime does not have a future project. We are only demanding rights that are recognized throughout the world, and we are going to continue until we reach those rights. The regime is desperate because there are people who don't have fear, but the Varela Project has strong social dimensions, and we do not want to go into the neoliberal abyss. Now it is not the United States that is going to change Cuba—we Cubans will change Cuba ourselves."[4]

When the congressmen emerged from Payá's house, they were surprised to be greeted by the foreign press, which had learned of their visit. Referring to Payá, Kolbe announced, "We are in the presence of an individual who has truly moved ahead the dialogue in Cuba. Anyone in the world with aspirations for liberty and democracy would support this project." Davis, who represented Tampa and was the first sitting congressperson from Florida to make an official visit to Cuba, added, "This is democracy at its best: people expressing their voice to their government and others. We are looking for signs of willingness to change on the part of the Cuban government."[5] While the Cuban government is usually eager to host visiting members of Congress, it also tries to stage-manage these visits as carefully as possible. The visit with Payá marked a clear deviation from the official tour arranged for the congressmen, and the group soon received word that a scheduled dinner with National Assembly president Ricardo Alarcón was canceled.

But a day later, Alarcón reconsidered, and the Cuban government arranged a dinner meeting at a sumptuous guesthouse in Havana's upscale Miramar neighborhood. The delegation had been seated only a few minutes before the congressman from Florida announced that he was "concerned by the fact that so many people in Cuba live in fear." Alarcón, the wily old fox of the Castro regime, slunk into his chair and calmly lit a cigarette. "Oh," he finally retorted, "you learned that after spending three days here, speaking your *perfect* Spanish?" When the conversation moved on to the perilous status of Cuba's pro-democracy activists, Alarcón went into one of his trademark rants, leaving the congressmen stunned. Regarding the Varela Project, he said, "We have no way of verifying the signatures or even knowing if the signatures represent anyone. Still, I forwarded them to the constitutional committee instead of rejecting them out of hand. But in what country can a petition of ten thousand people ask for a referendum to change a fundamental tenet of the constitution of the country? In what country can you do this? And then we have CNN, Reuters, Associated Press, the *Miami Herald*—do they get to decide? Do you really think that we have not penetrated every one of these dissident groups? We have agents in each of these groups, and they report to us."

In response to a question about the mistreatment of political opponents, Alarcón retorted, "The dissidents? We boiled them and ate them for dinner." He then digressed into a critique of NAFTA, the trade pact between the United States, Mexico, and Canada, referring to an article he read "in this subversive paper, the *New York Times*." He lit a cigarette and leaned back in his chair. "In Mexico, corn farmers go hungry. Mexico—a country where they have grown corn for two thousand years, as Mexico now imports its corn from the U.S. Michigan is the number-one exporter of black beans to Mexico. Michigan! So I ask you, who represented the Mexican farmers during the NAFTA negotiations in this great democracy called Mexico? Did anyone tell them that ten years after NAFTA entered into force, they would be hungry?" He then proceeded to lambaste what he described as the "culture of fear" in the United States. The conversation eventually grew so heated that at one point a congressional aide leaned over to his colleagues and whispered, "Do you think we will still get dessert?"

Ricardo Alarcón's tirade was just one indication that the government's ire toward the nascent pro-democracy movement was about to boil over. Fidel Castro spent the first week of March visiting with allies in China and Vietnam, but when he returned, the decision was made to hammer the dissidents hard. Castro and his allies in government decided that the looming U.S. invasion of Iraq presented a tailor-made backdrop for what would be Cuba's most dramatic crackdown on dissidents in decades. Not only did the Iraq invasion ensure that Cuba's new wave of repression would be ignored by the international media, but it also provoked a global upsurge in anti-Americanism that played to Fidel Castro's favor as he accused the dissidents of being "U.S.-funded mercenaries." On March 18, as bombs began to fall over Iraq, Cuba implemented its campaign with military precision, arresting about thirty people. Another thirty were rounded up the next day, and within a week more than eighty were being held in detention.

The stories that emerged from those days were a grim reminder that Cuba's brand of "tropical totalitarianism" still deployed tactics reminiscent of the Gestapo police. In each case, the nightmare began with an unexpected knock on the door, an efficient intrusion into the privacy of family life, and the ultimate arrest and detention of the suspected offender. Squad cars blocked off entire streets as dozens of security agents pored through the books, letters, phone records, and belongings of apprehended individuals, while neighbors stood outside and watched. While the arrests were not in themselves marked by physical violence, the emotional toll was severe and profound. Recounting the arrest of her husband, political activist Osvaldo Alfonso Valdés, independent journalist Claudia Márquez Linares wrote, "An authoritative fist knocked on our apartment door. It was State Security with a search warrant to look for what they called, 'material proofs of an offense.'" After sparring with the head of the search so that she could be allowed to dress in privacy, she watched twelve officers search her home for a period of ten hours. They removed hundreds of articles and books, old love letters from her husband, cameras, an old laptop, thirty-six diskettes with testimonies from individuals who'd had their human rights violated by the Cuban government, and several CDs that held the materials of the underground magazine De Cuba. Before the search was even completed, Cuban television reporters began denouncing the arrested individuals as "traitors."[6]

Cuba's legal pretext for the arrests hinged on two measures that carry severe sentences. Article 91 of the penal code provides for a sentence of ten to twenty years, and possibly even death, for "acts against the independence or territorial integrity of the state" committed in the interest of a foreign government. Law 88, passed by the National Assembly in 1999, calls for seven to twenty years' imprisonment for passing information to the United States that could be used to bolster anti-Cuban measures such as the U.S. embargo. Created in response to the U.S. Helms-Burton Act of 1996, the measure also prohibits the possession or reproduction of "subversive materials" from the U.S. government and carries penalties for collaborating with Radio and TV Martí.

With enough planning, the Cuban government can carry out complicated logistical and administrative tasks with a great deal of competence and efficiency—something that the massive arrests of dissidents proved once again. The trials, by contrast, were a ramshackle and slipshod affair based on weak evidence, rendering verdicts riddled with factual and typographical errors, without even the slightest regard for legal jurisprudence—almost a textbook definition of a "kangaroo court." Prosecutors called witnesses who had difficulty identifying the accused, with much of the evidence resting on overheard English-language conversations and correspondence with visiting Americans that no one involved with the case—prosecutors, defendants, and witnesses—could even understand. Foreign observers were barred, and even families of the accused barely knew when and where the cases were to be tried. Moreover, many dissidents had been working to create an open and democratic debate in Cuba, which meant that the proof of their "crimes" was public in nature, such as published articles or radio interviews in which they criticized the government.

During the first week of April, the Cuban courts handed down harsh verdicts ranging from sixteen to twenty-eight years in prison to seventy-five accused dissidents. More than eighty people had been detained during the March sweep, and seventy-eight were ultimately arrested, but several cases were processed more slowly, while a number of previously detained people who had already languished in prison for months were tried concurrently with the newly arrested. The victims of the spring crackdown became collectively known as "the seventy-five," a number that was adopted and repeated by human rights groups and became a broader symbol of the latest repressive wave and Cuba's political prisoners more generally. Amnesty International took the dramatic step of naming all seventy-five convicted dissidents "prisoners of conscience," which raised the total number of prisoners of conscience in Cuba to ninety—far more than in any other country in the western hemisphere and more than on the entire continent of Africa.[7]

Nearly forty years in age separated the victims of the crackdown, who ranged from twenty-six-year-old Lester González Pentón, a member of the human rights movement from the central province of Santa Clara, to sixty-five-year-old Carmelo Agustín Díaz Fernández, the president of an unofficial independent press agency.[8] Two cases were followed especially closely by conservative Cuban American circles in Miami and Washington. They were those of free market economist Marta Beatriz Roque, the founder of the Assembly for the Promotion of Civil Society, and Oscar Elías Biscet, a deeply Catholic black Cuban physician and antiabortion activist. His prison sentence of twenty-five years for "serving as a mercenary to a foreign state" was among the harshest handed down, and he was denied any reprieve. In November 2007, President Bush awarded Biscet the Presidential Medal of Freedom—but the honoree himself remained behind bars.

On April 9, 2003, Cuban foreign minister Felipe Pérez Roque invited foreign journalists to a press conference in Havana to explain the outcome of the dissidents' trials. Pérez Roque opened the meeting by unleashing one of his trademark diatribes against the United States and restating the case against the dissidents: "After more than forty years of an ironclad economic, financial, and commercial blockade, of aggressions, terrorist acts, more than six hundred attempts on the life of the Cuban president . . . on top of all that, our people have had to contend with the obsession of U.S. governments to fabricate an opposition in Cuba, to fabricate an organized dissidence in Cuba, to foment in Cuba the emergence or strengthening of groups responding to their interests . . . in the supposed scenario of the defeat of the Cuban Revolution."[9] After spending time recapping Cuba's main arguments for the arrests, Pérez Roque displayed a number of videotapes, including one that revealed the Cuban regime's trump card.

The videotape showed the cross-examination of one trial witness, Odilia Collazo Valdés, the president of the Pro Human Rights Party of Cuba. Collazo Valdés, a middle-aged mother of two with long dark hair pulled back, described how her human rights work earned her frequent interaction with the U.S. Interests Section in Cuba. In addition to using the Internet, she testified, she had the office, home, and cell phone numbers of American diplomats in Havana, who would often ask her "what things were like for the population at that time. It was like a barometer of the situation. They wanted to see if there could be a social outburst here." After posing a few more questions, the prosecutor turned and asked with a dramatic flourish, "Witness, Odilia Collazo Valdés, are you really a dissident? Are you only and exclusively the president of the Cuban Party for Human Rights?" To which his star witness replied, "Well, I'm really not a dissident. Today, I have the privilege of telling you that I am one of the persons selected by the government of Cuba, by the Interior Ministry. Precisely today, I can openly show everyone that I am an agent, Agent Tania."[10]

At this point in the press conference, Anita Snow, a savvy Cuba hand and longtime Havana bureau chief for the Associated Press, burst into laughter, much to the irritation of the Cuban foreign minister. "What are you laughing at, Anita? Why are you laughing so?" Pérez Roque demanded. Even years later, Snow recalled her reaction vividly. "It was an only-in-Cuba moment: absurd, bizarre, absolutely surreal. I was surprised, and I suppose I was laughing ironically as much at myself for not knowing that she and several other people we long thought were dissidents were actually state security agents! Where else could a journalist go to a news conference to see a videotape of a person who had called their office just a few weeks before to issue an invitation to an opposition news conference, only to have the nation's foreign minister tell the international press corps that the person and others we thought were dissidents were actually undercover agents for the government?" Snow viewed the revelations as a reminder of the labyrinthine nature of Cuban politics. "We reporters had all dealt with these folks on a pretty regular basis and never had a clue about their real identities. I guess it was just more proof that you never *really* know who people are here, or who they work for, or what their agenda is—and absolutely everyone has an agenda of some kind. I never did respond to the foreign minister's question, but I definitely had the impression that he and some other serious-faced Cuban officials there and members of the official press were not amused by my sardonic outburst. I cannot recall how other international journalists responded, but I think I was the only one to actually laugh out loud."

Meanwhile, it quickly became clear that Agent Tania was not alone. During the trials, the Cuban government authorized a number of secret agents working among the ranks of the Cuban opposition to unveil their true identities. Marta Beatriz Roque discovered that her closest ally was an undercover agent. Her assistant, Aleida Godínez, a heavyset woman with a gap-toothed smile who had worked among the opposition since 1994, revealed herself to be Agent Vilma. After the trials, Agent Vilma crowed, "No, she never suspected. In fact, I can tell you that on March 11, she even gave me the password to her private e-mail, because she had total confidence in me."[11] Less than a month after that indiscretion, Marta Beatriz Roque was sentenced to twenty years in prison. Néstor Baguer, a tiny, beret-wearing man in his eighties who liked to call himself the "dean of Cuba's independent journalists," later revealed that he was Agent Octavio and had worked as a government informant since 1960. Another notable spy was independent journalist Manuel David Orrio, who had been the key organizer of a journalism training workshop in James Cason's official residence but later unmasked himself as Agent Miguel. Many in the dissident community had had long-standing concerns about Orrio even before he linked up with the U.S. Interests Section. One person cited how Orrio rode his bicycle to meetings in Havana, despite the fact that he walked with a pronounced limp and often used a cane. Something did not add up, this person surmised—correctly, as it turned out.

Most opposition figures were well aware that their phones were tapped, that the neighborhood CDRs were spying on them, and that some of their associates might be reporting on their activities to the government. Still, many of their activities consisted of planning in private for subsequent events in public, and the scope and depth of the Cuban government's penetration caught them off guard. Some of the recently unmasked Cuban agents had been members of the human rights community in good standing for decades, and officials made it clear that the identities of many others remained a secret. Fragile bonds of trust among the dissidents were shattered, and suddenly no possibility seemed too farfetched to consider. Were some of the imprisoned dissidents actually Cuban spies? Were some dissidents left untouched because they had bartered information with the Cuban government in exchange for their own protection? There was simply no way to know. One foreign diplomat in Havana outlined an informal rule of thumb for dealing with opposition figures seeking international support, saying that "about one third of the dissidents are real, another third are under-cover security agents, and the rest are just looking for free Internet access."

The strange case of Elizardo Sánchez only complicated matters further. Sánchez, the well-regarded head of the Cuban Commission for Human Rights and National Reconciliation, was among a handful of prominent dissidents who escaped the crackdown. Sánchez had been a government critic for more than three decades and had spent part of the 1980s in prison, and his group had become the go-to source for tracking the number of political prisoners in Cuba. Like many other dissidents, Sánchez dismissed accusations of being on the U.S. payroll. "That's a very old argument," he said. "I have personally never received a cent from Washington."[12] But Sánchez soon ran headlong into the opposite problem, when the Cuban regime claimed that he was working for it. In August 2003, Cuba's official press published a seventy-page book alleging that Sánchez had collaborated with Cuban security agents. Titled *El Camajan*—Cuban slang for "con artist"—the book featured a lizard on the cover (a play on the name Elizardo) perched on a stack of U.S. one-hundred-dollar bills. The inside was filled with photographs and photocopied letters and faxes documenting Sánchez's ties with the United States, other dissidents, and, most damagingly, Cuban undercover agents. A month later, a tape of a Cuban colonel pinning a medal on Sánchez's chest was played on national television. Sánchez later explained that he had met privately with Cuban officials to lobby for the rights of political prisoners in a "quasi-diplomatic" role, adding, "I had no hidden cameras or secret microphones. There are two things you can do. You can believe the Cuban government. Or you can believe me."[13] While these events were deeply embarrassing, Sánchez's long struggle in the human rights community had earned him greater benefit of the doubt than others accused of being spies, and he remained a prominent voice. But the message was clear: No one could truly be trusted.

Oswaldo Payá escaped the crackdown, likely because his recent visit with Jimmy Carter meant that the international outcry would have been especially strong. Most of his top lieutenants, however, faced severe penalties. Labor leader Pedro Pablo Álvarez, for example, was sentenced to twenty-five years and packed off to a prison halfway across the country. Payá lives in a modest house in the working-class neighborhood of El Cerro, a short drive from the scenic tourist district of Old Havana. Payá was barely in grade school when Castro took power; today he is in his mid-fifties, married with three children, and his tousled dark brown hair is just beginning to gray. He is also perhaps Cuba's most internationally recognized dissident, a perennial candidate for the Nobel Peace Prize who has outlined a vision for reconciliation in Cuba that has earned him much praise abroad, but also provoked criticism from Miami exiles who find him too moderate for their tastes. In December 2002, when Payá was awarded the European Parliament's Sakharov Prize for Freedom of Thought, the Cuban government inexplicably granted him permission to travel to Brussels to claim the prize. In his acceptance speech, Payá declared, "The citizens who sign the Varela Project are not carrying arms. We do not have a single weapon . . . The first victory we can claim is that we do not have hate in our hearts. We therefore say to those who persecute and try to dominate us: You are my brother, I do not hate you, but you are no longer going to dominate me through fear, I do not want to impose my truth, and I do not want you to impose yours, let us seek the truth together." Shortly after his return to Cuba, the government crackdown on dissent decimated Payá's Varela Project and imprisoned dozens of his closest associates. Payá went free, but his political movement had been temporarily neutralized.

A serious man driven by deep religious conviction, Payá also has a sly sense of humor. Once Cuban agents followed him on a beach trip and snapped several photos of him cavorting in the waves. The pictures later emerged in an officially sanctioned book called *Dissidents*, which became a hot item in the black market and featured accusations that Payá was taking luxurious vacations with his human rights prize money from abroad. He later ruefully chuckled over the photos of him in his bathing suit. "Look at my potbelly," he exclaimed. "This will be terrible for my public image!" On another occasion, Payá found a microphone that was placed in his bedroom by Cuban security agents seeking to listen in on his pillow talk. He reacted by picking it up and whispering, "One . . . two . . . testing the internal network of espionage!" During the U.S. presidential campaign in 2004, Payá asked pointed questions about comments by Senator John Kerry that referred to the Varela Project as a "counterproductive" effort. "Can't he afford better advisers?" he inquired. Still, the arrest of many of his closest allies left him deeply shaken. In his meetings with outside guests, Payá would always sit facing the door and watch warily for unwanted intruders. It was a vivid reminder that Cuba still remains a police state—and that waiting at the door for the knock that never comes is its own form of terror.

Following the setbacks of 2003, Payá and his Christian Liberation Movement persisted by organizing a National Dialogue project that entailed hundreds of small discussion groups among Cubans across the island and dozens more in exile. In all, Payá estimated that thousands of Cubans participated in this exercise, which was intended to allow Cuban citizens to freely discuss their future outside the boundaries placed on them by the Cuban government. Payá soon found that the National Dialogue process faced many of the same challenges that had previously hampered the Varela Project. Cuban state surveillance was often intense, and participants in the dialogue roundtables could later be vulnerable to persecution and harassment. Cuba's collapsing infrastructure posed its own set of challenges, as travel between towns was difficult, slow, and expensive. Phone lines often did not work, and Internet access was virtually nonexistent. Moreover, it was often a struggle to explain the National Dialogue concept to Cubans who were not already directly engaged in the dissident movement. Was it really worth the effort, many wondered, to risk one's livelihood or even freedom for the purpose of engaging in a political dialogue that the government openly viewed as a hostile act?

Payá remained committed to the project, however, and the National Dialogue continued over the course of several years. The work produced a draft document titled "Program for All Cubans," which he described as "a plan to bring about a nonviolent transition to a constitutional democracy." It called for greater economic reforms while maintaining Cuba's social safety net in health and education. Payá's group also took aim at the existing fusion between military and civilian control in Cuba and anticipated Raúl Castro's rise by arguing that "in order for a military citizen to run for election or occupy a cabinet post, he would have to renounce his military status." The working groups continued to meet, but there was no doubt that Payá's National Dialogue project was fighting an uphill battle in its effort to democratize the political culture of Cuba.

Moreover, Castro's treatment of the dissidents remained as capricious as ever. On the one hand, political activists remained under tight surveillance, and a number of significant new arrests were made in the years following the crackdown. On the other hand, the Cuban government began to grant provisional releases to many of the seventy-five who appeared to be suffering from severe health problems in prison. The first release was made to little fanfare in April 2004, just after the one-year anniversary of the trials. By the end of the year, fourteen people had been released, including Marta Beatriz Roque, the lone woman arrested; the economist Oscar Espinosa Chepe, whose wife, Miriam Leiva, campaigned tirelessly for his freedom; independent journalist Manuel Vásquez Portal; Miguel Valdés Tamayo, who died of a heart attack less than three years later; Osvaldo Alfonso Valdés, the only political party leader to actually break down on the stand and confess; and the poet Raúl Rivero. Several left the country soon thereafter. Two more were subsequently released, including, in December 2006, Héctor Palacios, whose wife, Gisela Delgado, runs the independent library movement in Cuba. In February 2008, the Cuban government set free four more dissidents, among them the labor activist Pedro Pablo Álvarez, a close ally of Oswaldo Payá, in exchange for their immediate exile to Spain. While "the seventy-five" remain a touchstone for the human rights community, twenty had been set free by the fifth anniversary of the arrests.

Manuel Vásquez Portal was among the first group of prisoners to be freed, in June 2004, and he later fled into exile in Miami. He is a wiry and energetic reporter with a full head of bushy white hair, but his upbeat manner turned somber when he reflected back on the tumultuous events of 2003: "The dissidents were gathering strength and gaining more international recognition than had ever been achieved before. Castro precisely chose the moment of the Iraq War to rid himself of the dissident problem, and it worked." Vásquez Portal's time in prison was one of the bleakest periods of his life. "Cuba's economic failure is so disastrous that the person on the street barely has liberty—he can't own a home, he can't buy the clothes he wants, he can't buy milk for his son, he can't get the medicines he needs," he said. "But when you are in prison, all of this economic misery is multiplied one hundred times over. It's like something out of Dante's Inferno."

As a journalist, Vásquez Portal continues to cover Cuba's political opposition from Miami, but he is pessimistic about its future prospects. "The internal dissidence is based on resistance, but it is basically cornered," he told me. "It doesn't have public spaces where it can demonstrate; it lacks freedom of expression and association. It has no representation in government and has no public voice. Economically, Cuba still doesn't have a middle or upper class that could help to support it with logistics or resources." He shook his head. "The reality is that the internal dissidence is ineffective and, from an operational perspective, impotent. It can't take power and won't be able to defeat the government."

Indeed, many of the dissident movement's greatest innovators continue to flee into exile. Ramon Colas is the founder of Cuba's independent library movement, and he fled to the United States in 2001. An Afro-Cuban psychologist with a large family still in Cuba, Colas eventually settled in Mississippi, where he works on civil rights issues, but he continues to travel frequently around the United States and internationally to promote awareness of Cuba's plight. Cuba's independent library movement was founded in 1998 and has since spread to more than 135 libraries with at least several hundred books each. During a conversation over breakfast on one of his trips to Washington, Colas told me that the purpose was to subvert the Cuban government's ban on certain books and make them available to people through a civil society organization. He recalled how the organization was founded. "It was a reaction to a statement that Fidel Castro made at Havana's international book fair in 1998. A reporter asked him if Cuba had any banned books, and Castro responded by placing his hand on his chest and saying, 'There are no banned books in Cuba, we only lack the resources to buy them.'" Colas was stunned by the answer. "That surprised me a lot, because I knew that we could not read Jorge Luis Borges or Octavio Paz. We couldn't read Aleksandr Solzhenitsyn or Milan Kundera or even Raúl Rivero." He organized the opening of the first library in March 1998, but the political pressure on his family grew so intense that he eventually felt forced to leave Cuba. "The regime is intelligent," he said. "It doesn't just attack the person who opposes it but also his entire environment. Eventually my family, my brothers, my daughter all started to say to me, 'We can't bear this anymore.'" Colas won a visa to bring his immediate family to the United States and handed the project over to Gisela Delgado and Héctor Palacios, two of his friends in the dissident movement.

"Cuba is a society of masks," Colas explained, "and Fidel Castro has very cleverly exploited the use of mass psychology and created a form of propaganda that encircles the individual and makes him a protagonist in the government's discourse." He saw the impact as being particularly profound on Afro-Cubans like himself, who are often told that they owe everything they have to the Cuban Revolution. Once a Cuban dissident, Colas is now part of a new profile of Cuban exile: a black man in his mid-forties who spent his formative years in communist Cuba and retains a deep network of relatives and contacts on the island. The transition has not been easy. "I cry for Cuba, I dream of Cuba, and I feel the pains of Cuba," he told me. "Recently I was on a flight to South America, and we flew over Cuba, and I saw this incredibly beautiful thing, with the deep blue waters changing into light blue as it reached the white sand, and suddenly I began to cry. The flight attendant asked me what was wrong, and I could only say, 'I'm flying over my country.'" His expression grew serious. "You have to remember that exile is not voluntary. The exiles are political refugees, and nobody wants to be in that category. I left Cuba to protect my family. I feel comfortable in this country and I often defend it. But Cuba is my preferred place to live and die. I will return."

Meanwhile, many of the top dissidents who remain in Cuba are attempting to put aside their old squabbles to unite together and push for greater freedom. In a remarkable statement during the first year of Castro's illness, a number of formerly warring opposition leaders—including Oswaldo Payá, Marta Beatriz Roque, Elizardo Sánchez, Oscar Espinosa Chepe, Vladimiro Roca, and the newly freed Héctor Palacios—joined together to promote a new platform titled "Unity for Freedom." But Afro-Cuban social democrat Manuel Cuesta Morúa, who offered a more moderate set of proposals, later cautioned, "The opposition is less divided than before, but it is still divided. Unity is not around the corner."[14] Indeed, the obstacles faced by Cuba's prodemocracy groups remain as formidable as ever, and the long-awaited transition from Fidel Castro to Raúl Castro has done little to alter Cuba's political equation in their favor. Even as Raúl has cultivated a more moderate image abroad, his government continues to employ tough tactics at home. In April 2008, the Damas de Blanco organized a small protest in front of his offices to call for the release of their loved ones in prison. The "ladies in white" were soon surrounded by a mob of dozens of Cuban government supporters, and then dragged away by about twenty female corrections officers. They were later released, but the incident showed that speaking out against the regime remained fraught with risk.

During the presidency of George W. Bush, the U.S. government increasingly staked its hopes on Cuba's dissident movement as the harbinger of a free and democratic society—and it is one of precious few areas of U.S. policy on Cuba that has been supported by more than just rhetoric. Under the 1992 Cuban Democracy Act and the 1996 Helms-Burton Act, the United States government is authorized to fund nonviolent civil society groups that support democratic change in Cuba. Relatively modest amounts were granted during the Clinton years, but the Bush administration was a particularly eager proponent of this program. A high-level commission on Cuba policy chaired by Secretary of State Colin Powell in 2004 recommended raising this amount to thirty-six million dollars. A follow-up report chaired by his successor Condoleezza Rice in 2006 upped the stakes to eighty million over two years and guaranteed minimum funding of twenty million annually until Castro's death. (Ricardo Alarcón gleefully described the proposal as a "politically delirious provocation," while opposition leader Manuel Cuesta Morúa fretted that the report had provided "80 million arguments for the Cuban government to make it seem all Cuban dissidents are financed by the United States.") Congress eventually appropriated forty-six million dollars for Cuban democracy programs during the 2008 fiscal year, a whopping amount by past standards. What was once a trickle of funding has swollen into a flood of cash for American and international groups who want to try their hand at fomenting democracy in Cuba.

Unfortunately, U.S. efforts to finance democracy in Cuba are not exactly building on a track record of success. The Castro government has arrested many opposition figures, claiming that they were conspiring with the United States, while the dissidents themselves have complained that they see little benefit from the programs. Meanwhile, the trials of 2003 revealed that many opposition groups who received support were thoroughly infiltrated by Cuban security agents, which meant that the United States was perversely buying such goods as laptop computers and digital cameras for the very government it was trying to undermine. In November 2006, an official U.S. audit found that 95 percent of the seventy-six million dollars disbursed between 1996 and 2005 had been distributed without competitive bids, and three of the ten recipient organizations lacked financial records. In addition, some of the expenses recorded by Miami-based grantees proved hard to explain, such as large payments to smuggle items into Cuba and expenditures for luxury goods like Godiva chocolates, cashmere sweaters, and Sony PlayStations.[15] Given that some of these items were likely handed over to Cuban officials posing as dissidents, one can easily envision Fidel Castro propped up in his hospital bed, popping Godiva chocolates and playing video games purchased at U.S. taxpayer expense.

Furthermore, the U.S. embargo remains a major barrier to working directly with Cuban groups, which means American organizations have to either master the intricacies of getting cash and resources into Cuba legally, operate in violation of U.S. law, or simply use the money for staffing and activities in the United States. Many dissidents (although by no means all) are extremely critical of the U.S. embargo and especially favor lifting travel restrictions, but their opinions do not count for much in Miami or Washington. The Bush administration's democracy-promotion programs were increasingly directed toward organizations in other countries, especially in Eastern Europe, which were generally all too happy to benefit from American largesse. A substantial portion, however, was directed to Cuban American groups with strong links to Miami power brokers who in turn support their backers in Washington.

Larry Wilkerson, the former top aide to Colin Powell, described U.S. programs to promote democracy in Cuba as "part of this incestuous relationship between Cuban Americans and politicians in Washington with money going back and forth owing to Florida's electoral votes." He added, "One wonders sometimes how many Cuban Americans actually believe this bull and how many just think, 'Hey, it's nice getting seventy-five million dollars in Miami-Dade County.'" This view is prevalent among embargo critics in Washington, and like many assessments of the role of the Cuban American community in U.S. policy, it both contains seeds of truth and is more than a little unfair. Many of the groups that receive U.S. funding serve as important resources for Cubans living on the island, and most have professional and serious-minded staff dedicated to the issue. But the skeptics have no shortage of evidence to which they can point. In March 2008, for example, a midlevel Bush administration official was felled by scandal stemming from the Cuba grants. Felipe Sixto, a special assistant to the White House on intergovernmental affairs, was found to have illicitly pocketed hundreds of thousands of dollars from his former employer, the Center for a Free Cuba, a prominent anti-Castro group headquartered in Washington. The center's outspoken director, Frank Calzon, described the discovery as a "personal betrayal" and promised a swift and thorough investigation. "I want the U.S. government to get to the very bottom of this," he said. "I am confident that nobody else in the Center is involved."[16] Meanwhile, the management of U.S. aid programs to Cuba even became a source of controversy within the Cuban American community, when the Cuban American National Foundation released a study that sharply criticized how the money for democracy assistance was being used. In a survey of the four major recipients of U.S. funds to "build solidarity with Cuba's human rights activists," the study reported that 83 percent of the funding was used for overhead, salaries, and local activities, while only 17 percent of U.S. assistance actually made it to the island.

As millions of dollars continue to flow into this sector, it is hard to escape the conclusion that U.S. federal programs to promote freedom in Cuba are, at best, providing high-priced and marginally useful support to worthy democratic causes on the island. At worst, they are fast becoming the equivalent of federal ethanol subsidies to Iowa farmers, a constituent payoff divorced from America's larger national interest. Either way, Cuba's long-suffering dissenters have become a focal point of U.S. policy, despite the fact that their political role in Cuba's future remains highly hypothetical. The most conscientious dissidents are torn between accepting U.S. resources that may taint their legitimacy as true proponents of change in Cuba and spurning offers of badly needed assistance at a time when they need all the allies they can get. In the United States, however, promoting democracy in Cuba will remain a growth industry.

Meanwhile, Cuba's top dissidents greeted Raúl Castro's ascension to the presidency with their characteristic stoicism. On February 24, 2008, Oswaldo Payá released a statement saying that "the succession of Fidel Castro does not in itself bring the changes the people want and need . . . This has never been and will never be an election." Payá added, "Raúl Castro, the new President of the Council of State, said in his inaugural address that antagonist contradictions do not exist [within Cuba]. But they do exist, because there is an essential antagonism between this system of no rights, restrictions imposed by law, arbitrariness and repressive practices on the one hand, and the legitimate rights and interests of the people on the other." The Varela Project, he wrote, demanded that political rights be restored to the island's citizens, "so that, by exercising these rights, Cubans themselves can decide what this new chapter in the life of our nation will look like."

While Raúl showed no sign of embracing democracy, his government did appear to be taking small steps toward political moderation. Over Fidel's objections, he authorized Foreign Minister Felipe Pérez Roque to sign two United Nations human rights treaties that guaranteed freedom of assembly and the right to form independent trade unions. Elizardo Sánchez of the Cuban Commission for Human Rights reported that the number of political prisoners in Cuba had dropped by 26 percent during the first nineteen months of Raúl's rule, from 316 in July 2006 to 234 by February 2008. Still, Sánchez attributed the decline to a new strategy toward the pro-democracy opposition that favored harassment and short-term detentions over long and politically costly prison sentences. "They have changed tactics," Sánchez mused, "but the repression is the same."[17]

CHAPTER 4

The Empire Strikes Back

Shortly before the U.S. invasion of Iraq, President Bush tapped retired army general Jay Garner to head up the reconstruction and humanitarian assistance effort, with the admonition that he "kick ass." Garner spent much of the initial ground war at a U.S. military base in Kuwait and finally entered Iraq on April 22, 2003. The specter of Garner, the presumed head of the newly conceived U.S. occupation of Iraq, strolling the country in a polo shirt and khakis and telling assembled Iraqi leaders, "You're in charge," deepened the sense of confusion and aimlessness in the crucial early weeks after the fall of Baghdad. Even Garner's few worthwhile ideas, such as preserving the Iraqi army as a force for stability, were quickly brushed aside by L. Paul Bremer, the freshly appointed head of the Coalition Provisional Authority. Upon his arrival in Baghdad in May, Bremer quickly moved to implement de-Baathification (as the process of jettisoning members of Saddam Hussein's Baath Party was called), disband the Iraqi army, and dismiss the ad hoc Iraqi leadership group that had been assembled. Garner soon packed his bags and headed back to the United States, with precious time in Iraq already wasted and worse decisions yet to come from his successors. On June 18, after lying low for several weeks in Washington, Garner went to see Defense Secretary Donald Rumsfeld and criticized the U.S. postwar planning, then met with Bush. The meeting was cordial and ended on a lighthearted note, when Bush praised Garner's work in Iraq and then playfully slapped the general on the back, asking, "Hey, Jay, you want to do Iran?"

Garner smiled. "Sir, the boys and I talked about that, and we want to hold out for Cuba. We think the rum and the cigars are a little better . . . The women are prettier."

President Bush laughed and replied, "You got it. You got Cuba."[1]

*   *   *

The reality, of course, was that neither Jay Garner nor any other U.S. military leader would be heading to Havana anytime soon. By the time this conversation occurred in the summer of 2003, the White House already had its hands full with Iraq and a number of other pressing foreign policy priorities in the Middle East. Cuba occupied its usual place on the fringes of U.S. policy, a nettlesome but marginal issue that barely merited more than glancing attention. What the White House failed to recognize, however, was the creeping sense of unease that Bush's lackadaisical approach to Cuba policy had begun to generate in South Florida's Cuban American community.

Several months had passed since Fidel Castro had shut down most major dissident groups on the island and carted their leaders off to jail, as well as executing three attempted boat hijackers. While American officials had protested the moves and the European Union had implemented mild punitive measures, the Cuban government had mostly gotten off scot-free with its worst wave of repression in recent history. But it was the mishandling of several high-profile immigration episodes that most set tongues wagging in Miami. In mid-July, Cuba reported that two boats had been hijacked in an attempt to reach the United States. The first boat's journey ended in bloodshed when three hijackers died in an apparent shoot-out, while the U.S. Coast Guard picked up twelve hijackers in the second boat and returned them to Cuba after negotiating a deal that ensured the perpetrators would serve prison terms of less than ten years and not face execution.

Cuban officials praised the U.S. action as a "valuable contribution . . . in the fight against those who use violence and force to hijack planes and boats."[2] But in Miami, U.S. authorities were sharply criticized for negotiating the fate of Cuban hijackers with Castro's regime. Even stalwart Bush supporters such as Florida congresswoman Ileana Ros-Lehtinen denounced the move: "To return individuals to Cuba is to hand their fate to the criminal, who is Castro."[3] Eventually Robert Novak, the conservative *Washington Post* columnist known as "the Prince of Darkness," weighed in on the furor, writing that "what inflamed pro-Bush Cuban-Americans in south Florida is that the United States negotiated with the communist dictator to impose 10-year prison sentences. This sudden agreement between Washington and Havana could cost George W. Bush a second term."[4]

The coup de grâce came at the end of July, when the U.S. Coast

Guard discovered twelve Cubans driving across the Straits of Florida on a 1951 Chevy truck outfitted with pontoons and a propeller. Photographs of the bright green truck plowing the Caribbean Sea were soon broadcast around the globe, but the would-be refugees earned no points for creativity. They were promptly apprehended and sent back to Cuba several days later—without the truck, which the coast guard deemed a navigational hazard and strafed with gunfire until it sank. When this latest episode of callous treatment of migrants scandalized Miami, the White House dispatched its special envoy for Latin America, Otto Reich, himself a member of the exile community, to soothe Cuban American outrage. But the strategy backfired when Reich used his interview on the Spanish-language channel Telemundo to ask, "What would Dade County do with a million more Cubans who don't speak English, who haven't been well educated, that have lived under a totalitarian government where values don't exist, moral or economic?"[5] Even his Cuban-born interviewer, the well-known Castro critic Juan Manuel Cao (who later would provoke Castro into a public tirade at a summit in Argentina), took offense, asking, "Are we really that bad?"

The Bush administration's successful effort to overthrow Saddam Hussein's government in Iraq paradoxically left a bitter aftertaste in the mouths of Miami's Cuban American community, where public opinion polls showed a clear majority favoring a U.S. invasion of Cuba.[6] The Iraq occupation had not yet metastasized into the bloody civil war it would become, and the euphoric scenes from a newly liberated Iraq contrasted sharply with Castro's unchallenged rule in Cuba. Many Cuban Americans questioned why the United States would spend billions to bring freedom and democracy to Iraq while mouthing only empty promises about toppling Castro in Cuba. Marco Rubio, who later became the first Cuban American Speaker of the Florida House of Representatives, was one of several members of the state legislature to acknowledge the frustration with Bush, saying, "There's growing sentiment by the rank-and-file voter that he's done little on the issue of Cuba." Interviewed by reporters while holding a sign saying PRESIDENT BUSH PUSH FREEDOM FOR CUBA NOW! WHY ONLY IRAQ?, sixty-two-year-old Miami resident Santiago Portal summed up the mood in Little Havana: "He can't ask Cubans for votes if he hasn't helped Cubans get freedom. He should ask Iraqis for votes, not Cubans, because he freed them."[7]

In mid-August, thirteen Republican Florida state legislators—including ten Cuban Americans—sent a letter to Bush in which they bluntly `threatened to withdraw their support unless a tougher Cuba policy was enacted. Citing "great disappointment and outrage," the state legislators warned of "a growing and alarming concern in the Cuban-American community regarding the Bush administration's current Cuba policy." This discontent carried a political cost: "We fear the historic and intense support from Cuban-American voters for Republican federal candidates, including yourself, will be jeopardized . . . We hope this matter can be resolved before Cuban-American support for Republican candidates is further damaged."[8]

The letter sounded a clarion call for the freedom of Cuba and urged the Bush administration to take four specific steps. Most important was the reversal of the "wet foot/dry foot" immigration policy implemented by Bill Clinton in 1994. This policy mandated that Cubans picked up at sea (with "wet feet") were to be repatriated to Cuba, while those who made it to U.S. soil (with "dry feet") were to be given permanent residence. Prior to the Clinton administration's ruling, Cubans found at sea were granted automatic asylum. The other demands included more funding for Cuban dissidents, improvements to Radio and TV Martí, and the indictment of Castro for the 1996 shoot-down of the Brothers to the Rescue planes. State representative David Rivera, one of the letter's principal authors, later emphasized, "As the summer has passed, there has been a snowball effect of frustration within the Cuban-American community. We want immediate, tangible, substantive action. If this is ignored, abstention or neutrality in federal races becomes a real possibility."[9] In short, without a more vigorous Cuba policy, Bush risked losing financial and political support in a crucial swing state for his 2004 election campaign. Given his razor-thin margin of victory in Florida of 537 votes in the 2000 election, it was a threat to be taken seriously.

On October 10, 2003, Bush delivered a major address on Cuba in the Rose Garden of the White House, flanked by Secretary of State Colin Powell and Secretary of Housing and Urban Development Mel Martinez. Bush declared that events of the past year showed "how the Castro regime answers diplomatic initiatives. The dictator has responded with defiance and contempt and a new round of brutal oppression that outraged the world's conscience. In April, seventy-five peaceful members of Cuban opposition were given harsh prison sentences, some as long as twenty years." He announced that the U.S. government would be embarking on a new wide-ranging policy review, chaired by Powell and Martinez, that would "plan for the happy day when Castro's regime is no more and democracy comes to the island." The new initiative, christened the Commission for Assistance to a Free Cuba, would seek to hasten the end of the Castro regime and usher Cuba into a new democratic era.

Bush's proposal soon snowballed into a sprawling federal exercise that absorbed thousands of man-hours and engaged more than one hundred U.S. government employees spread across seventeen agencies. On December 5, Powell and Martinez convened the first commission meeting and later released a public statement saying that the goals were "to identify additional means by which the United States can help the Cuban people bring about an expeditious end of the dictatorship, and to consider the requirements for United States assistance to a post-dictatorship Cuba." By then, however, the White House had already decided that Martinez should run for an open Senate seat in Florida, where his candidacy could help mobilize the support of the disgruntled Cuban American Republicans who had sent such a harsh warning in August. Martinez soon quit the cabinet to begin his Florida campaign, leaving Powell as the sole chairman of the commission.

In January 2004, the U.S. Agency for International Development (USAID) convened a special public seminar titled "Humanitarian Aid for a Cuba in Transition" on a freezing day in downtown Washington. The meeting was held in the ornate ballroom of the Ronald Reagan Building and International Trade Center on Pennsylvania Avenue, a handsome, sprawling complex that also houses USAID. Roger Noriega, the assistant secretary for western hemisphere affairs, began his remarks by asking, "After forty-five long years of dictatorship, how can we help the Cuban people out of this nightmare?" Next came Adolfo Franco, the Latin America point man for USAID, who introduced the head of USAID, Andrew Natsios, but not before declaring, "There will be change in Cuba, and it will come under George Bush!"

A veteran of U.S. development assistance, Natsios served as the head of USAID from May 2001 until 2006, and he presented a dire view of the situation that would confront the United States and Cuba after Castro. "The Cuban dictator has held the Cuban people in political bondage for more than four decades," he began. "As we know from experience, the pent-up expectations and frustrations of a long-oppressed people can sometimes boil over and lead to 'serious evil' . . . Given the island's proximity to the United States, there is a high risk of a rapid and chaotic out-migration from Cuba in the aftermath of Fidel Castro's departure. A very real possibility exists, therefore, that a failed Cuban transition could lead to a complex humanitarian emergency."

Natsios briefly sketched several scenarios of democratic transition, but lingered on the one that would require a massive humanitarian response from the United States: "An unstable democratic government takes over which dissolves into a failed state due to widespread violence from a national military divided into factions supporting various elements of the old regime. Under this scenario, we would expect widespread human rights abuses to occur and the political system and economy to collapse." The room was packed with a cross section of academics, policy analysts, and U.S. government officials, and several representatives from prominent Cuban American organizations listened attentively, nodding their heads. Natsios continued, "This third scenario is what we refer to as a complex humanitarian emergency. This is where a democratic transition unravels into chaos, leading to a food and health crisis or an economic crisis or both. Imagine, for example, what the collapse of Cuba's tourist industry might mean . . . In a true complex humanitarian emergency, supplies—such as food aid, medicine, computers, trucks, and other equipment—become targets for various armed factions to steal and use for their own purposes. So not only is there a likelihood that donated supplies will be stolen, but a very real threat that relief workers will become subject to violence and intimidation." Winding down his tour through the postapocalyptic landscape that would be facing Cubans after the death of Castro, Natsios concluded, "I want to thank you all for being here today and for keeping the hope of a free Cuba alive."[10]

As the Bush administration's top Latin America hands worked feverishly to prepare the commission's final report by the May deadline, the Commission for Assistance to a Free Cuba evolved into a government exercise with a unique pedigree. Chaired by Powell, the commission involved a core group of high-level officials including USAID head Natsios, Condoleezza Rice, Treasury Secretary John Snow, Homeland Security Secretary Tom Ridge, Commerce Secretary Don Evans, and

Alphonso Jackson, who replaced Mel Martinez at the head of Housing and Urban Development. More important, the top staff actually running the exercise included a number of people who had committed a large part of their professional lives to the cause of ousting Fidel Castro. The work was coordinated by Assistant Secretary Roger Noriega, and his deputy, Dan Fisk, chaired the crucial Working Group on Hastening Cuba's Transition. Both Noriega and Fisk were former aides to archconservative senator Jesse Helms, with a long history of advocating sanctions toward Cuba. José Cárdenas, a former staffer at the anti-Castro Cuban American National Foundation, edited the report in his capacity as adviser in the State Department, and at least a dozen other midlevel officials with ample Cuba experience participated. Many had battled for a tougher Cuba policy from their previous vantage points on Capitol Hill or in the advocacy community. Now they were in the heart of the executive branch leading a cabinet-level initiative that had been blessed by a still-popular president, with the purpose of bringing the Castro regime crashing down and creating a democracy in its place. Given the participants' desire to export Bush's "freedom agenda" to Cuba, they must have felt it was a dream opportunity.

That was certainly how it appeared to Otto Reich, one of the most indefatigable opponents of Castro during the last quarter century. Now in his early sixties, Reich fled Cuba as a teenager shortly after Castro came to power, and by his own admission, Cuba has been a focal point in both his professional career and his personal life. Among other positions, he served as U.S. ambassador to Venezuela in the 1980s and in the 1990s worked as a lobbyist for the Bacardi Corporation, where one of his key achievements was pushing for the 1996 passage of the Helms-Burton legislation that transformed the U.S. embargo into a congressional mandate. When Bush took office in early 2001, he tapped Reich to be U.S. assistant secretary of state for western hemisphere affairs—essentially the State Department's top Latin America policy post. But the Democratic-led Senate, principally spurred on by Senator Chris Dodd of Connecticut, blocked his ratification, forcing Bush to give Reich a recess appointment in early 2002. This lasted for a year, until he was transferred to the White House as special envoy to Latin America with the National Security Council. Reich left the government in June 2004, just after the release of the commission report, but when I met with him three years later, Cuba was still very much on his mind.

Reich told me that when he joined the National Security Council in early 2003, Cuba policy was his top priority. "One of the things that I did was convince my boss, Condi Rice, that the United States was not sufficiently well prepared for a change in Cuba, and we needed to organize the executive branch of the U.S. government to respond to a request from a future democratic government in Cuba. Because Cuba's needs are so enormous, anybody who has studied Cuba in the last forty-eight years, or the Cuba *of* the last forty-eight years, knows that the Castro regime has had the impact of a major war on the Cuban infrastructure." In Reich's view, the lasting achievement of his efforts was the Commission for Assistance to a Free Cuba. "This was my idea. As John Kennedy said after the Bay of Pigs, 'Victory has a thousand fathers, and defeat is an orphan.' Since the commission is seen as successful, I'm sure there are a thousand fathers out there, but I'm perfectly willing to submit to a paternity suit on the commission. And if anybody asks Condi Rice, she'll tell you."

At the National Security Council, Reich was unencumbered by issues like personnel and budget matters, congressional hearings, and other governmental busywork. "So," he said, "I decided I'm going to 'think big thoughts,' as we used to joke, and one of the big thoughts I brought with me was the need to prepare the United States to act. What will we do tomorrow if Fidel Castro dies and there's a change in Cuba? No matter what the change is, we need to be organized . . . Cuba is ninety miles away, and there's going to be a lot of suffering on that island, it's going to be shown on television in the United States, and whoever is in the White House is going to get blamed. And the answer I would get was, 'We're ready, we're ready.' OK, how are we ready? The coast guard is going to stop the boats—oh, that's great. What about feeding ten million people in Cuba? What about a distribution system that has two or three days of reserves of rice and beans and oil and things like that? What are we going to do when that falls apart? What about the one million weapons that are in Cuba in the hands of the militia and the military? What if they start firing at each other? Do we have any plans?"

Reich was skeptical about the State Department's rank and file, so he went directly to the top of the National Security Council. "I took the idea to Condi Rice in early 2003, and she said, 'You're right, we need to do this, but we may have to go to war over Iraq.'" Reich mentioned to her that he had already reached out to Mel Martinez, who was also excited about a commission. "And she said, 'Well, keep doing what you're doing and come back to me.' Right after the war, she said, 'Absolutely, we'll do it.'" Colin Powell, who eventually chaired the initiative, did not even know that the proposal existed until he was introduced to it by the National Security Council.

Now a private consultant based in Georgetown, Reich has lined his office wall with twelve framed photographs that portray his time working at the highest levels of the U.S. government. They include pictures with a range of top officials including three presidents, Ronald Reagan, George H. W. Bush, and George W. Bush, the latter signed "To Otto, All My Best Wishes." A cover photo of Reich in the international edition of *Newsweek* with the headline "Bush's Point Man" is framed off to one side next to a U.S. flag. Reich jumped up from the leather chair where he was sitting and walked over to the pictures. "In fact, this photograph right here was taken on that day, October 10, 2003." The picture, taken just before the commission was announced, showed Bush, Reich, and several other officials gathered in the Oval Office of the White House, with papers spread out on the president's desk. Reich recalled one moment with particular fondness. "'This is all well and good,' the president says, 'but what are we going to do to hasten the end of the dictatorship?' Just like that! I mean, that is a direct quote. And I'm standing there in the Oval Office, it was a beautiful day, sunshine streaming in through the windows. And I'm saying to myself, if the people of Cuba could only be here to hear this from the president of the United States!"

The Commission for Assistance to a Free Cuba eventually produced a thick document that covered everything from elections to privatization to restocking fisheries, but the first and most controversial chapter outlined a series of new sanctions against Cuba to hasten the end of Castro's rule. Reich declared, "That first chapter of the commission, that was George W. Bush. When he said, 'What are we going to do to hasten the end of the dictatorship?' we went back to the drawing board—and I was very happy, of course, to do it—and built a chapter around the president's six or seven words: hasten the end of the dictatorship."

Roger Noriega initially joined the Bush administration as the U.S. ambassador to the Organization of American States. He later became Reich's successor as assistant secretary for western hemisphere affairs before leaving government in 2005 to become a director in the Washington office of the Miami-based law firm Tew Cardenas and a visiting fellow at the American Enterprise Institute, a conservative think tank. (Due to his deep support for the U.S. embargo, he is often mistakenly believed to be Cuban American, to which he replies, "Well, I've been called worse." He is in fact of Mexican descent.) Noriega recalled the moment in the White House slightly differently. "I remember literally standing in the Oval Office when the president was going through his notes, and he and Martinez were the ones who said, 'Wait a minute, wait a minute—we need to say something more than just *planning for* the transition; we need to say *hasten* a transition.' Which is interesting . . . because Martinez can't pronounce 'hasten.' He pronounces the 't'—has*ten*—and the president's like, 'Am I getting this right?' It was kind of like one of those 'potato' moments." But Noriega agreed that "the hastening part was the first part of it, and it's what captured a lot of people's attention . . . Our attitude wasn't 'let's just find another way to make life a little bit more miserable for people over the long haul,' but in point of fact to have an impact on the ability of the regime to hang on."

The final report was delivered to Bush in early May 2004, and he publicly welcomed its findings following a meeting with Powell at the White House, saying, "It's a report from a commission that I have put together in my administration to hasten the day that Cuba will be a free country. We believe the people of Cuba should be free from tyranny. We believe the future of Cuba is a future of freedom." Issued under the signature of Colin Powell, the report quickly became known as the Powell Commission. The document itself was a doozy: a 423-page opus that outlined steps for accelerating the end of Castro's regime and facilitating the emergence of a democratic government on the island. It revealed a great deal about what the Bush administration perceived to be the best course for U.S.-Cuba policy, the preferred nature of transition, and the presumed role of the United States in a post-Castro Cuba—in areas such as meeting human needs, establishing democracy, free market reforms, modernizing infrastructure, and environmental protection. In addition, Cuba was repeatedly described as an imminent security threat to the United States, and the report asserted that Cuba is a "state sponsor of terrorism" and reaffirmed controversial claims that the island has "a limited, developmental offensive biological weapons research and development effort."

Most American presidents kowtow to Cuban exiles in South Florida during an election year, and Bush was no different in this regard. What made him unique was that he allowed the vagaries of Florida politics to prompt him to establish a high-level presidential commission in the heart of the executive branch, placed his respected secretary of state in charge of the effort, and rolled out a massive new U.S. government plan for the island in the middle of the presidential election. Bush's record on Cuba still remained imperfect in the view of Miami's anti-Castro activists, because the Clinton-era "wet foot/dry foot" immigration policy remained in force and Castro still had not been indicted for the 1996 Brothers to the Rescue shoot-down. (At the urging of the White House in August 2003, the U.S. attorney for South Florida unveiled indictments for the former head of the Cuban air force and the two Cuban MiG pilots involved in the shooting. Exile groups praised the move, which had no legal relevance in Cuba, but still wanted a separate U.S. indictment for Castro.) Few exiles expected Bush's new measures to bring democracy to Cuba, but he had once again earned their support by taking their demands seriously and showing that his heart was in the right place. Bush was a shrewd enough politician to know that when it came to formulating a Cuba policy to please his Miami-based supporters, it was the thought that counted.

In that spirit, the Powell Commission was an exercise in ratcheting up pressure on the Cuban government in an effort to provoke its demise. The United States made a fifty-nine-million-dollar grant to increase funding for anti-Castro broadcasts by Radio and TV Martí, aid dissidents on the island, and develop an international public diplomacy campaign to promote the U.S. view that Cuba was a dangerous rogue nation. New U.S. regulations limited Cuban American family visits to once every three years (instead of once annually), reduced the allowable spending per diem during visits to fifty dollars, and restricted remittances to direct family members who were not affiliated with the Communist Party. The White House fact sheet that accompanied the release of the report stated that the leading U.S. policy objective toward Cuba was to "bring an end to the ruthless and brutal dictatorship," and the "expeditious end of the Castro dictatorship" was repeatedly identified as the central goal of the U.S. government. Many sections of the report anticipated violence, warning that "the domestic Cuban food supply, transportation, infrastructure, and the storage base could be disrupted by turmoil that could follow a vacuum of authority." It recommended, among other things, that the United States should "prepare to keep all schools open during an emergency phase of the transition in order to keep children and teenagers off the streets and learning during this unstable period." The report also envisioned a long list of officials likely to be targeted for punishment, or "vengeance," including "prominent senior officials of the Communist Party, the government, the mass organizations, and especially the police and security services."

What was most striking about the Powell Commission, however, was that it was written during a period when the U.S. effort in Iraq was unraveling, yet it clearly promoted many of the same assumptions about Cuba that had proved so faulty in Iraq. The proposed dismantling of the Cuban Communist Party and related institutions appeared to be a tropical version of de-Baathification. Its recommendations for radically privatizing the Cuban economy were based on the principles of the market-oriented "Washington Consensus" that had proved extremely disruptive in Iraq and already had a long and checkered record in the former Soviet Union and many Latin American nations. Cuba was treated as a tabula rasa where new democratic institutions could quickly be built on the rubble of a collapsed authoritarian regime. Most dramatically, the Powell Commission anticipated a major role for the U.S. government in the political, economic, and social life of the country—in areas as diverse as property restoration to Cuban exiles, adoption and family services, and painting dilapidated schoolhouses. In the depth and scope of the presumed U.S. commitment, the report evoked Powell's "Pottery Barn rule" regarding Iraq: If you break it, you own it. The first section outlined the new sanctions and policies intended to end the Castro regime, while the subsequent chapters outlined major American involvement in rebuilding Cuba.

There was one crucial difference, however. By the summer of 2004, no one was pretending that U.S. military action against Cuba was on the table. Indeed, even the top U.S. officials who were leading proponents of a rapid democratic transition in Cuba strongly agreed that U.S. military intervention in Cuba would be bad for both countries. Asked if he believed there were prospects for U.S. military action in Cuba, Otto Reich replied, "No, I don't. Well, as we say in government, we can't rule anything in or anything out. But I don't foresee it unless there is complete chaos on the island, and the military factions start fighting each other. You'd have to have a protracted civil war in Cuba to even think about involving U.S. military forces . . . I cannot see that, and I say this here wearing a number of hats: former U.S. official, Cuban

American, hawk, every epithet you want to use. It would not be good for the United States of America. It would not be good for the people of Cuba, or even for the hemisphere. It's just not good and it's not necessary."

Reflecting on this question after his return to private life, Roger Noriega concurred that the U.S. military should have no role in Cuba's future: "I've said privately and publicly to my Cuban American friends, the toughest ones of the bunch among them, that it would be just a terrible tragedy if the United States had to intervene and do it for them." Noriega could envision, however, that "a bloodbath might provoke an international response that the U.S. could be a part of." In addition, he was not necessarily opposed to Cubans taking matters into their own hands. "First and foremost, it has to be what Cubans are prepared to sustain. I, for one, see no innate virtue in incrementalism or gradualism. I'll be very honest with you, I didn't even like the word 'peaceful,' because what's so cool about peaceful if you are being held hostage, you know what I mean? As a matter of fact, it had this sort of prejudicial ring to it, because the only people who have guns are the regime, so as long as the Cubans go along and allow themselves to be cowed by that force, then things are going to be peaceful. And maybe Cubans don't want it that way . . . What's so good about stability, for example, if you've had fifty years of stability in Cuba?"

Noriega dismissed any parallel between Cuba and Iraq: "I don't think anybody in their right mind would think that the United States should aspire to have a decision-making role of that nature in Cuba . . . I think the U.S. should run screaming in the other direction." But he identified another parallel that was much closer to home. In 2004, the government of poverty-stricken Haiti collapsed when an armed rebellion forced President Jean-Bertrand Aristide into exile, and Latin American nations deployed thousands of UN peacekeeping troops to the Caribbean country to prevent further bloodshed. "Quite frankly, I whispered to my staff that I saw Haiti as a dry run for Cuba. I said, 'For crying out loud, don't say that publicly.' But I really do." Noriega cited the wide range of Latin American countries involved, led by Brazil, "running an operation under the most difficult conditions perhaps in the world. You literally had a guy kill himself seeing that mess." (The Brazilian general commanding the UN forces in Haiti shot himself in the head in his hotel suite in January 2006 after less than six months on the job.) "Cuba is where you would have a more cultural affinity," he told me. "I certainly think that the Cuban military is far more capable than the Haitian national police . . . I don't think you are going to lack for a security apparatus in Cuba."

Regarding the Commission for Assistance to a Free Cuba, Noriega argued, "We wanted to make a transition in Cuba a national priority, and one which would engage the work of other departments to set the policy very clearly along the lines of what President Bush's vision was and give him something that would operationalize that transition and prepare us for the transition . . . but it isn't meant to be our blueprint for reinventing Cuba." He did concede, however, that "it's very, very easy to mistake it, absolutely."

In the final analysis, the Commission for Assistance to a Free Cuba resulted from a unique collision of politics and foreign policy that led the Bush administration to train its sights once more on Fidel Castro's government. Bush was a popular figure in Miami who won the presidency, in part, because of his anti-Castro positions, and he staffed his administration with strong embargo supporters. Once Otto Reich was transferred from the State Department to the National Security Council in early 2003, he enlisted the support of powerful administration figures like Mel Martinez and Condoleezza Rice in an initiative to step up U.S. efforts to promote democratic change in Cuba. When Cuban American representatives in Miami expressed discontent with Bush in August 2003, it created an opening that led the White House to embrace a far-reaching review of Cuba conducted at the highest levels of the U.S. government.

Since the deep-seated opposition to engaging with Castro was widely shared by Bush, his foreign policy team, and his Cuban American supporters in Washington and Miami, the policy decisions inevitably led toward tightening the sanctions even further. The possibility that the United States would eventually confront a post-Castro Cuba characterized by a gradual communist succession, rather than a rapid democratic transition, was ruled unacceptable and thus not considered. The resulting report therefore focused its planning on what the Bush administration viewed as its preferred scenario for Cuba: the rapid breakdown of the Castro regime and its replacement by a democratic, pro-U.S. government. But its efforts to "hasten" the transition relied on strengthening current policy tools, such as travel sanctions, Radio and TV Martí, and aid to Cuban dissidents, which had failed to achieve much progress in the past. The political imperatives of Florida, and the professional biases of the people involved, meant that an alternative strategy of greater dialogue, expanding people-to-people contact, and increasing trade was never even contemplated. Indeed, anyone who had argued for this approach would surely have been laughed out of the room. But Bush's new measures did carry a very human cost, as would become increasingly apparent in the days ahead.

Sergeant Carlos Lazo's life path had already taken him a long way from his childhood home in Havana by the time he arrived in Iraq as a U.S. Army medic in the spring of 2004. A naturalized U.S. citizen, Lazo had escaped from Cuba with five friends on a raft powered by a lawn mower engine in 1992. The motor eventually conked out, but the group was discovered adrift at sea by the U.S. Coast Guard. This was in the era before the 1994 migration accords required migrants picked up at sea to be returned to Cuba, and Lazo was brought ashore, processed, and released into Miami, where he lived for six years. He later moved to Seattle and worked as a state counselor for social and health services. When an earthquake struck the state in 2000, he became motivated to join the Washington National Guard and received training as a medic. Although he had lived in the United States for more than a decade, he remained in close contact with the two sons he had left behind in Cuba, visiting them as often as he was able. Lazo's last trip to Cuba was in April 2003. That November, his National Guard unit was mobilized to participate in Operation Iraqi Freedom, and he left for Iraq in March 2004 for a one-year deployment.

Lazo is in his early forties, but he has upbeat, almost boyish energy. A music lover, he taught himself to play guitar around the age of twelve while growing up in Havana. But like many young men in Cuba, he was frustrated with the limited opportunities under communism and dreamed of one day seeing the free world that he read about in old copies of *Reader's Digest* that belonged to a family friend. He first attempted to leave Cuba on a raft in 1988 while still in his early twenties, but the effort ended in failure when he was captured by the Cuban coast guard and sentenced to one year in a maximum security prison. Lazo earned a work pass to organize the library and then prolonged the job by arranging the books during the day and dismantling his handiwork at night, which allowed him to spend much of his prison sentence in the library reading. He especially related to the plight of Penelope, the faithful wife of Odysseus in Homer's *The Odyssey*, who kept her prospective suitors at bay by saying she needed more time to finish weaving a funeral shroud, which she painstakingly pulled apart each evening to delay the day of reckoning.

When Lazo was deployed to Iraq in 2004, he was based principally at Camp Anaconda, a logistics supply area located in the Sunni Triangle, about eighty miles north of Baghdad. His responsibility was to provide medical care to wounded insurgents and civilians, although he recalled, "Sometimes we didn't know if they were insurgents or civilians because there were prisoners denying any wrongdoing. But they were wounded, very badly wounded." Later during his deployment, Lazo volunteered to serve as a medic in Fallujah, the dusty Iraqi city that emerged as a major combat front following the gruesome ambush in the spring of 2004, when the badly burned remains of four U.S. military contractors were dragged through the streets and hung from a bridge. Lazo earned a bronze star for his performance under fire in Fallujah, where he joined up with two other Spanish-speaking medics to form a three-man "Latin Team" that provided primary care to U.S. soldiers wounded in battle. Lazo explained how they managed to stay calm during the heat of battle: "When we were out on missions, we'd sing together in Spanish. It kept our spirits up and helped us make sure the other one was alive when the bullets were flying past our heads."[11]

Lazo remembered his experience in Fallujah with both pride and melancholy. "We spent the whole month doing missions with the marines. I mean very hard missions, going inside the city where the combat was taking place with the marines there, and getting the wounded or the dead and taking those back to the battalion station, and going back to the front . . . The three of us, our ambulance was constantly attacked by mortars and direct fire from snipers. But by the grace of God, I was not killed. That was very, very tough." The Fallujah that Lazo encountered was a destroyed and ruined city. "The only word I have for Fallujah is 'sadness.' When we went inside the city, there was not a house that was not touched by bullets. Every house had a hole. Every house was blown out. Dead people in the streets. It was a very tough experience. Even when most of the people had left the city, still there were several thousand people, and they got trapped inside the city. It was very hard. I remember the smell of the dead, because there were no chances to recover dead people at the beginning . . . The city streets were full of dead people, and it was very sad."

As a native of Cuba, Lazo was among a small fraction of U.S. soldiers serving in Iraq who were born in a country deemed to be a state sponsor of terrorism by the United States. There are about sixty thousand immigrants in the U.S. military, representing about 2 percent of total active personnel. About half, like Lazo, are naturalized U.S. citizens, but they hail mainly from Mexico, Central American countries, and the Philippines. While there are more members of the U.S. military and National Guard who were born in Cuba than in the six other mainly African and Middle Eastern countries classified as terrorist states at the time of the Iraq War, this is one of the U.S. military's most unusual clubs. And as a member of this rarified group, Lazo could not help but see flickering images of his native Cuba as he attempted to rescue the dying in the shattered rubble of Iraq: "When I went inside that city to work as a medic, my mind always was thinking that was not what I wanted for Havana. I was looking at Fallujah, and what I was looking at was [the Havana neighborhoods of] Miramar, or Playa, or Vedado. I mean, sometimes tears came to my eyes because I was thinking always that I don't want to see this happening in the country where I was born. I always, especially after that, think that any solution or any change in Cuba has to be a peaceful one. Not one where the marines or the army or any country goes over there to bomb the country and kill innocent people, just for the sake of bringing a different system of government to the people living in Cuba."

Lazo had been in Iraq for only a few weeks when he learned that the U.S. government had formed a commission to create a tougher policy toward Cuba that would be unveiled in May 2004. His experience as a combat medic in Fallujah still lay several months in the future, and he was looking forward to visiting his two sons in Cuba during his scheduled R&R in June. He was too busy caring for the stream of wounded and dying Iraqis who passed through Camp Anaconda to spend much time thinking about what the new measures would entail, and besides, he did not see how the new restrictions would affect him. But he remained curious to see what Bush would announce: "I was wondering what else the president could do. I mean, there is an embargo—what else? And then I hear about this commission giving to the president some ideas about how to please the community and how to be tougher with Cuba." Then, in May or June, he heard that new restrictions would be implemented that would allow Cuban Americans to visit their family on the island only once every three years instead of annually and would instate a narrowly written definition of family (parents, children, and siblings would be OK— but aunts, uncles, cousins, and godchildren would not count). "And I thought at the beginning, 'That won't pass,' " Lazo recalled. " 'I don't think he's going to mess with our people not even going to funerals.' I mean, I never thought that would be in place—the possibility that if you went to Cuba in the last three years, and if your mother died, you wouldn't be able to visit again. But that was exactly what happened."

Castro responded to the new sanctions proposed by the Powell Commission with a dramatic flourish, declaring a state of emergency and closing the island's U.S. dollar stores. One week after the report was unveiled, Castro led a march of hundreds of thousands of Cubans before the U.S. Interests Section in Havana to denounce the latest maneuverings by the "American empire." Many carried signs printed with swastikas and showing Bush dressed in a Nazi uniform and with a Hitler mustache. Castro described the march as "an act of indignant protest and a denunciation of the brutal, merciless and cruel measures" and declared that Cuba will never fall into "the humiliating condition of a neo colony of the United States. I will be in the first line of defense, ready to die in defense of my people."[12]

The Castro government also recognized that the Powell Commission report was a propaganda tool of enormous value. High-level communist officials waved copies of it at public meetings, and the state television ran a series of nightly roundtable discussions denouncing the measures. Sections of the report were translated into Spanish and taught in local high schools. Government operatives scanned the report for particularly juicy lines they could exploit. Two of their favorites: the proposal for allowing Cuban exiles to reclaim expropriated properties and the call for "the immediate immunization of all children under five"—notwithstanding Cuba's already-high vaccination rate. Soon there were regular television cartoon programs that illustrated how Cuban Americans were going to seize back their properties and evict Cubans from their homes. Billboards sprouted across Havana showing smiling children playing together under the phrase THANK YOU, MR. BUSH, BUT WE'RE ALREADY VACCINATED!

In the United States, most of the Cuban American community's leading Republicans praised the Powell Commission as a welcome step in the right direction, even though the document said nothing about the controversial "wet foot/dry foot" immigration policy that had sparked such outrage in Miami in the summer of 2003. But the new sanctions were fiercely protested by some in the Cuban American community. The one Cuban American Democrat in Congress, Representative Robert Menendez from New Jersey, normally a strong supporter of the embargo, criticized Bush for "playing election-year politics with the lives of the Cuban people. The need and timing of a White House Cuba commission and its release of a report today is highly dubious and politically transparent."[13]

The tough new restrictions on Cuban American family travel and remittances cut especially close to the bone. More than 120,000 Cuban Americans in the United States traveled back to the island annually, but now they found their ability to legally return to Cuba reduced to once every three years. Many would be forced to either miss the important milestones that bring together scattered relatives—such as a new grandchild, a cousin's wedding, or a death in the family—or travel illegally to Cuba through third countries to maintain some semblance of family connectedness. Moreover, new regulations published on June 16 were extremely detailed and intrusive. The amount of money Cuban Americans were allowed to bring to Cuba was cut from $3,000 to $300, daily spending limits while in Cuba were slashed from $167 to $50 per day, and luggage was limited to forty-four pounds. Cuban Americans could now send gift parcels only to their grandparents, parents, children, siblings, and spouses in Cuba, and they were banned from shipping basic items like clothing, personal hygiene items, fishing rods, and soap-making equipment.

The Bush administration had taken months to formulate the new rules, but did not fully think through its strategy for implementation. The stricter regulations were scheduled to take effect on June 30, thus leaving thousands of American citizens and residents in Cuba in violation of U.S. law, even though they had departed for their trips with all the required permissions. Thus a special waiver hastily granted a one-month reprieve before legal penalties, including a hefty $7,500 fine, kicked in on August 1. But this applied only to travelers who departed prior to June 30, and the sudden surge in demand for last-minute tickets left charter plane companies scrambling to add new flights. As the deadline rapidly approached, the passenger gates at Miami International Airport quickly devolved into an angry and chaotic scene, with scores of people chanting in protest as planes were banned from bringing additional passengers to Havana.

On the final weekend before the new rules went into effect, hundreds of Cuban Americans lined up to try to get on the flights before June 30, but their attempts proved futile. The State Department ruled that the last-minute tickets were unauthorized, and eleven of the sixteen planes departing from Miami for Havana left empty, allowed only to pick up passengers in Havana who were returning to the United States. Some denied passengers vowed to vote against Bush as a result, such as one thirty-nine-year-old Cuban American woman who lost her chance to visit her aging parents: "This is very bad. A lot of things can happen in three days, let alone three years. You have to vote with your interests, and my interest is to be able to visit my family in Cuba." Another woman in her forties still supported Bush, even though the new policy left her outraged: "To prevent me from seeing my parents, it breaks every human rights rule that exists. I think Bush means well. He wants a free Cuba. He's just not thinking of the people who have family. It breaks my heart."[14]

Sergeant Carlos Lazo unexpectedly found himself among the angry passengers denied the right to board the final planes leaving for Havana. The U.S. combat medic had been granted two weeks of leave in the middle of June and immediately flew to Miami to arrange a visit to Cuba to see his teenage sons and his extended family before returning to the war zone in Iraq. The June 30 deadline had not yet arrived, but Lazo found that he was already too late. "That was three days before the restrictions took place, and at that time when I went to the Miami airport, I found out that they were not letting people get on the planes." He remembered the scene clearly. "There was a big huge scandal down at the terminal, and I was there. That was a moment in time when I get so mad. I have *everything*: the tickets, the things I bought for the kids—when you go to Cuba, you always buy things for the family, some clothing, chocolates, presents. And they were not letting people on." A group of local journalists were covering the scene at the airport, and Lazo was interviewed by a Miami television reporter. "I told her that I came from Iraq, and due to the restrictions imposed by this administration, I have to go back to Iraq without a chance of seeing my kids in Cuba. If I lost my life in Iraq, the irony would not be that I didn't get to see my kids because I was killed. I didn't get to see my kids because my commander in chief didn't allow me to go see them when I was able to."

The saga of a Cuban American veteran of the Iraq War prevented from visiting his sons in Cuba was soon picked up by the mainstream press, and Lazo's plight was highlighted by the *Miami Herald*, the *Washington Post*, and MSNBC. The unlikely confluence of events transformed Lazo into a symbol of a policy gone awry: an Iraq war hero honored by the U.S. military but punished by the tough ban on travel to Cuba. An accidental activist, Lazo would find himself lobbying regularly to change U.S. policy toward Cuba in the years ahead. But that day he was just another passenger rendered powerless by the U.S. bureaucracy as it shifted its Cuban embargo into a higher gear. Lazo shipped back to Iraq a week later without seeing his family in Cuba.

The snapping of the ties between the United States and Cuba that had relied on the existing routes of travel and communication echoed from Miami to Washington and back again. The only people to win a special reprieve were a group of eighty U.S. medical students, primarily from black and Latino families, who had won scholarships for a free medical education in Cuba at the Cuban government's expense. A provision allowing "fully-hosted" travel to Cuba was eliminated by the new sanctions, which meant the students would be breaking U.S. law and risking heavy fines if they remained on the island past July 31. When more than two dozen black and Latino members of Congress sent a strongly worded letter of complaint to Colin Powell, he intervened to allow the medical students to continue their studies. He won praise for his intervention, but it also gave the appearance that he had been caught off guard by the new set of policies that bore his imprimatur.

Massachusetts senator John Kerry, the Democratic presidential candidate in 2004, strongly criticized the harsh new measures, but the White House had a keen sense of the politics of Cuban Miami. A public backlash against the Bush administration's Cuba regulations reverberated during the November elections, but many of the Cubans who were most disenfranchised by the new policies were relatively recent arrivals to the United States who were less likely to vote. By contrast, the older and more powerful Cuban Americans supported the restrictions because they rarely if ever returned to Cuba, felt no personal costs, and strongly backed Bush. While Bush was unable to match his 80 percent Cuban American support in the 2000 election, his 70 percent vote haul still beat Kerry handily in this demographic. The popularity of Bush's brother Jeb as the governor of Florida helped the Bush-Cheney ticket win Florida's twenty-seven electoral votes by a comfortable 5 percent margin. Republican candidate Mel Martinez edged out his Democratic opponent to become the first Cuban American member of the U.S. Senate. The decision to create the Commission for Assistance to a Free Cuba may not have been the critical factor in Bush's convincing electoral victory, but it sure didn't hurt.

Larry Wilkerson is a retired army colonel who served as the right-hand man and top aide to Colin Powell for sixteen years, beginning in 1989 when Powell was named the commander of Fort McPherson, on the outskirts of Atlanta, Georgia. Soon thereafter, Powell began his meteoric rise, which included his promotion to four-star general, a memorable term as the chairman of the Joint Chiefs of Staff, and his emergence as such a popular public figure during the mid-1990s that a grassroots movement tried to draft him to run in the 1996 presidential elections. Throughout this period, Powell's relationship with Wilkerson—a Vietnam veteran, former Army Ranger, instructor at the Naval War College, and fellow Republican—proved so enduring that when Bush tapped Powell to be the sixty-fifth secretary of state, Powell asked Wilkerson to be his chief of staff. During the tumultuous years that followed, including the response to the September 11 terrorist attacks and the launching of the Iraq War, Wilkerson was a crucial behind-the-scenes player for the popular secretary of state, who found himself increasingly isolated and out of step with a Bush administration that would brook no dissenters in its decision to bring the war on terror to Iraq.

But while Powell opted for a quiet retirement at the beginning of Bush's second term, Wilkerson took a markedly different approach. In a landmark speech in October 2005, Wilkerson catapulted himself into the top ranks of harshly critical former Bush administration officials and made headlines around the world when he declared, "What I saw was a cabal between the vice-president of the United States, Richard Cheney, and the secretary of defense, Donald Rumsfeld, on critical issues that made decisions that the bureaucracy did not know were being made. Now it is paying the consequences of making those decisions in secret, but far more telling to me is America is paying the consequences."[15] Perhaps inevitably, Wilkerson's merciless criticism of Bush administration policies ranging from the Iraq War to North Korea to Guantánamo Bay created a split between the army veteran and his former friend and boss. While the two are no longer personally close, Powell later told the media, "I wouldn't characterize it the way Larry has, calling it a cabal. Now what Larry is suggesting in his comments is that very often maybe Mr. Rumsfeld and Vice President Cheney would take decisions in to the President that the rest of us weren't aware of. That did happen, on a number of occasions."[16] Wilkerson conceded, "He's not happy with my speaking out because, and I admire this in him, he is the world's most loyal soldier."[17]

The decision to tighten U.S. sanctions on Cuba in 2004 was one more area where Powell's views were discounted—even though he was nominally in charge of the effort. At that time, Wilkerson was quoted in GQ magazine as saying that the Cuba embargo was "the dumbest policy on the face of the earth." More than three years later, he stood by that quote. "I do still mean it and still believe it. And I meant it when I said it. Colin Powell and I talked about how stupid it was probably since he was chairman of the Joint Chiefs of Staff in the early 1990s . . . He thought that, for example, all you needed to do was lift the embargo, and within twenty-four months Castro would be gone, because of this sweep of information and the cultural impact and so forth across Cuba."

Indeed, Powell's prior public statements on Cuba had struck a moderate tone sharply at odds with the tough policies that were later implemented on his watch. At a congressional hearing in 2001, Powell testified that "Castro has done some good things for his people," adding that "he's no longer the threat that he once was." Powell never viewed Castro through rose-colored lenses, and he described Cuba's crackdown on dissidents as "despicable," but his instincts tended to favor diplomacy and multilateralism over sanctions and a go-it-alone approach. He nevertheless ended up being drawn into an ambitious effort to strengthen the U.S. embargo of Cuba. During an extended conversation after he left the State Department, Wilkerson told me that the decision to tighten the Cuba sanctions during the 2004 presidential elections marked the convergence of two separate foreign policy trends. The first was the dominant influence of Bush's Cuban American supporters in the Republican Party, including in the administration, in Congress, and more widely in Miami-Dade County, who were eager to have the United States turn up the heat on Castro's regime. The second trend was the broad foreign policy thrust promoted at the top levels of government that America's enemies should be answered by unilateral U.S. action. But while the Florida political component was as old as the Cuban Revolution itself, the emerging crusade to crush dictatorships through military might was a bracing reaction to the post-9/11 world.

Wilkerson credited the shift in U.S. policy toward Cuba to the "feeling within the Bush administration, at the center of which is Richard Cheney . . . about tyrants in general, about dictators in general, about people who have defied the United States in general, and teaching them a lesson and bringing them down and ultimately regime change, wherever they may be—whether they are in Pyongyang, Havana, Tehran, Baghdad, or Damascus. That's their mind-set. They don't believe in negotiations, they don't believe in talking, they don't believe in anything but raw military power. Or that being impossible . . . then every other means, clandestine and otherwise, should be used to bring those regimes down, to topple them. That's their belief, their fundamental belief." Wilkerson thought that the Bush administration's approach to Iraq was relevant to Cuba. "There is a parallel. They think the same thing about North Korea, they think the same thing about Syria, they think the same thing about Cuba. Cuba is a lesser thought because it's kind of there as a footnote . . . But if the truth were known and if the parallels were drawn, it would be the same idea." Then, in reference to the Cuban exiles in Florida, he added, "Plus, throw into it that we've got all these people down there who have been giving us money to get their property back."

When Cuban American political interests merged with the Bush administration's new focus on regime change, the Commission for Assistance to a Free Cuba was born. In Wilkerson's words, "So these two things come together, and they find great cohabitation, and I think that's what produced it. And if I have any objections to my time with Secretary Powell at the State Department with regard to a specific policy, it is that he ate that. He made the calculation, I think, that 'there are so many things I can extend my political capital on, and so many of them are more important than Cuba, that I can't afford to brook this administration to oppose it . . . I can't afford to extend my political capital on something as small as Cuba.' So he tried to attenuate some of this as much as he could, but by and large he wound up being the chairman."

Wilkerson recalled his dismay at receiving letters of complaint addressed to Colin Powell from academic and policy groups protesting the measures: "We just gave this standard State Department boilerplate back about ending tyranny, and democracy, and freedom, and liberty, and all this other stuff that we give all this mouth to. And now the whole world thinks we're the biggest hypocrites in the world about it. I can't say that I dwelt on it for very long, because, like him, I had bigger fish to fry too. But it was a low moment for the State Department and a low moment for Colin Powell—that we had to be part and party to this." The Commission for Assistance to a Free Cuba was one battle that Powell was unwilling to fight. "I used to put it this way: Powell used to walk into the Oval Office once a week and clean up all the dog poop off the floor," Wilkerson said, but Cuba policy wasn't worth the effort. "I think in his heart of hearts he understood instinctually, if not intellectually, even in the beginning, that this travel ban was going to hurt *everybody*. That eventually it was going to hurt even those people at that time who were vociferous about implementing it." Many of the Cuban American power brokers who backed the travel restrictions later discovered that their friends, neighbors, and constituents were suffering the effects of the new regulations. Wilkerson paused and then added, "But you can only fight so many battles."

Indeed, the new set of policies toward Cuba could have been far more aggressive. The effort to identify Cuba as a critical bio-weapons threat caused so much friction in the administration that one intelligence analyst complained to the Senate about being pressured, and the dispute eventually derailed John Bolton's confirmation as U.S. ambassador to the United Nations. But the Cuba allegations never gained enough political traction to put Castro directly in the crosshairs of the Bush administration's efforts to rid rogue states of dangerous weapons. (Indeed, by August 2005, the State Department had admitted that the evidence was "inconclusive," citing a "split view" between policy makers who believed the programs existed and the intelligence community, which was doubtful. Cuba remained one of five countries on the list of "state sponsors of terrorism," however, even as countries like Iraq and Libya were removed.) From his vantage point at the U.S. mission in Havana, James Cason interpreted the Cuban government's warnings of an American invasion as both a propaganda tool and the product of genuine fears. "They had it in mind that we wanted to have a migration crisis, which we said would be a hostile act, so that we would invade. They said we were looking for a pretext," Cason recalled. In his view, Castro "needed the pretext of invasion to be able to continue to keep the lid on, to keep the system together, so he constantly invents the imminent invasions. But there are also some of them that actually believe it."

While there is no evidence that a U.S. invasion of Cuba was ever seriously contemplated by the Bush administration, there are several reasons that such a premise would have appeared quite plausible in Havana. While more than forty years had passed since the last attempted U.S. invasion of Cuba, at the Bay of Pigs in 1961, the post–September 11 climate had definitively put the U.S. military into the business of toppling rogue governments through preemptive war. Cuba was designated a sponsor of terrorism by a U.S. government that had declared a global "war on terror" against its enemies. Allegations that Cuba possessed a biological weapons program were finding their way into major speeches by top administration officials like John Bolton. Miami's Spanish-language radio (which Havana listens to religiously) was abuzz with rumors and plans for a U.S. occupation of Cuba. The military population at the U.S. naval base at Guantánamo Bay had swollen to four times its normal size with the arrival of captured prisoners from Afghanistan.

Moreover, the Cubans knew that the United States had a long and rich history of intervening in the Caribbean as a means of flexing its muscles before the world, especially when it felt challenged. In 1983, Ronald Reagan invaded Grenada to quash a communist coup and demonstrate his seriousness to the Soviet Union. In 1994, Bill Clinton's intervention to restore democracy in Haiti was motivated, in part, by the desire to repair America's global standing following a series of embarrassing setbacks in third world hot spots like Somalia. Moreover, many of the top foreign policy officials appointed by George W. Bush had been involved in efforts in the 1980s to arm the contra rebels in Nicaragua to fight against the left-wing Sandinista government. While international attention was focused on Afghanistan in 2001 and Iraq in 2003, the Cuban government was keenly aware that the United States had participated in the removal of President Jean-Bertrand Aristide from Haiti in highly dubious circumstances in February 2004. Castro is a master tactician who has seen everything under the sun, and he may well have viewed the threat of a U.S. invasion to be at its highest point since the end of the cold war. In any case, Castro also knew that calling Cubans to unite against the external threat posed by the United States had the added benefit of consolidating his political power on the island.

However, one unintended effect of the Powell Commission in 2004 was that it made it crystal clear to Cubans and Cuban Americans alike that the Bush administration viewed Cuba as a political problem that could be handled with sanctions, rather than a security threat that required preemption. After his retirement from the State Department in 2005, Larry Wilkerson traveled to Cuba for his first trip to the island since he visited with his grandparents in 1958. He was surprised to learn how deeply the Cuban government had feared some type of military action by the United States. "They were really worried," he recalled. "They wanted me first of all to assure them that we weren't going to invade . . . They were truly worried about an invasion." Wilkerson laughed. "I said, 'Let me just tell you something right now: There aren't any soldiers or marines to invade you with!' "

By that time, despite frequent speculation in Cuba about a U.S. invasion, many Cuban officials had probably reached that conclusion on their own. However, in June 2004, Castro addressed a message to Bush: "You and your closest advisers have brazenly proclaimed your goal of forcibly imposing what you call 'political transition' on Cuba, if I die in office, a transition which you do not, of course, hesitate to confess you will try to hasten as much as possible . . . Since this you can only do by sending troops to occupy key positions in the country, you are announcing your intention of launching a military intervention of our homeland."[18] The Cuban government began organizing drills and refining its public service announcements for the expected U.S. invasion that never came. The U.S. "empire" had lashed out at Cuba in the frenzy of the 2004 presidential election, but the result mainly targeted Cuban families and allowed Castro's government to escape with little more than a glancing blow.

In January 2005, Colin Powell ended his government service widely viewed as a tragic figure for his inability to prevent Bush from pursuing a range of damaging foreign policies, from the Iraq War to the establishment of the Guantánamo Bay detention facilities. His role in tightening the U.S. embargo of Cuba, a policy that he privately disagreed with, was a little-known dimension of that legacy. Powell may well go down in history as the last secretary of state to increase the economic sanctions on Cuba. Meanwhile, the Commission for Assistance to a Free Cuba lived on, chaired by the new secretary of state, Condoleezza Rice, and Commerce Secretary Carlos Gutierrez, who replaced Mel Martinez as the top-ranking Cuban American in the Bush administration. In 2005, the State Department appointed Caleb McCarry as its Cuba transition coordinator and began to build a permanent bureaucratic infrastructure to prepare for the post-Castro transition. In July 2006, the commission released its second report, which declared, "Fidel Castro senses his own mortality and the mortality of the economically bankrupt regime he leads. He works relentlessly to hold it together through a mix of political alliances, bartering, and debt extensions, and savage denial of political and economic freedoms to the Cuban people. Today, he and his inner circle are implementing a succession strategy designed to ensure the survival of the regime beyond his own incapacitation, death, or ouster." In response, Rice pledged that the United States would continue its work "to hasten the end of the Castro dictatorship," by supporting civil society, undermining Cuba's succession strategy, and denying revenues to the Cuban regime. In Miami's Cuban American community, however, the public mood was changing in subtle but important ways. Signs were beginning to emerge that the White House's fulsome embrace of a hard-line approach toward Cuba was subject to the law of diminishing returns.

CHAPTER 5

The Community

The Miami neighborhood of Little Havana still pulses with the rhythms of the island where many of its residents were born. Though many members of its founding generation, who fled Cuba in the early 1960s, have long since moved into the city's wealthier suburbs or work in the tony neighborhoods of Coral Gables or Coconut Grove, Little Havana remains the spiritual and cultural epicenter of Cuban Miami. It is the place where new arrivals from Cuba can receive social services, find a job, drink *café cubano*, and eat *ropa vieja*, while the generations that preceded them nurse the sense of nostalgia and loss that ties them to the land of their birth. The main street that runs through Little Havana has many names. Approaching from the west, it appears as U.S. Route 41 or the Tamiami Trail, and on a Miami city map it often appears as Southwest Eighth Street, but locally it is always called by its Spanish name, Calle Ocho.

On the corner of Calle Ocho and Thirteenth Avenue, there is a modest park that commemorates the Cuban exile fighters who lost their lives when Fidel Castro's forces stamped out their effort to retake the island during the botched invasion at the Bay of Pigs in April 1961. Ninety-four Cuban exiles died in that ill-fated expedition, launched at the scenic cove on Cuba's southern flank, in an episode that badly embarrassed the still-green president John F. Kennedy just months after his inauguration. More than fifteen hundred troops were transported to the Bay of Pigs on chartered aircraft as part of Brigade 2506. But lack of sufficient air support from the U.S. military, poor coordination, and skillful fighting by Castro's troops—who apparently were forewarned about the invasion—doomed the effort to failure. Within days, twelve hundred exiles were captured, several were killed, and the rest were sentenced to decades in prison for treason—although the United States (in collaboration with Cuban exiles) negotiated their release from the Cuban government two years later. For most Americans, the Bay of Pigs fiasco is all but forgotten, an unpleasant foreign policy memory eclipsed by more recent traumas. But at this quiet corner in central Miami, an eternal flame burns in memory of the fallen. Quotes by Cuban poet José Martí are prominently displayed, such as "Liberty is not to be pleaded for, it is conquered at the point of a sword" and "The fatherland is agony and duty." Nearby, the Bay of Pigs Museum and Library, featuring artifacts and photographs from the invasion, has been run out of a small stucco house for twenty years.

The Cuban population in the United States is less than two million people, but it punches far above its weight in national affairs. This considerable influence emerged from a potent cocktail of factors that have shaped the Cuban exile experience: the relative affluence and superb human capital of the first wave of émigrés in the 1960s; the fast track to legal residency afforded to subsequent Cuban immigrants under the provisions of the 1966 Cuban Adjustment Act; their successful efforts at political organization beginning in the 1980s; and, of course, the fact that the hatred the founding generations had for Castro dovetailed with the top U.S. foreign policy goal of containing communism during the cold war. But perhaps none of this would have mattered so much, or proved so enduring, if the majority of the exiles had settled anywhere in the country besides Florida.

There is little question that the U.S. Electoral College has magnified the Cubans' influence far beyond what would have otherwise been possible. More than one million Cuban exiles have settled in South Florida. According to an analysis conducted by the Pew Hispanic Center in 2004, Florida had 540,000 citizens of Cuban origin who were eligible to vote, which would equal 5 percent of the state's total voting population of eleven million. (Some estimates put the Cuban American vote as high as 8 percent.) Florida's twenty-seven electoral votes make it the fourth-largest vote haul in U.S. presidential elections, behind only California, Texas, and New York. More important is the fact that Florida is the only state in the top four that remains competitive between Republicans and Democrats—demonstrated most famously in the 2000 election, when the standoff between George Bush and Al Gore resulted in a frantic recounting of hanging chads and butterfly ballots to determine the presidency. Bush's top political strategist, Karl Rove, has been reported to say: "When people ask me about Cuba, it makes me think of three things: Florida, Florida, and Florida." In that way, where candidates stand on Cuba policy is unlike any other niche ethnic issue, because it can make or break presidential campaigns.

But Cuban influence is felt far beyond the presidential elections. Cuban political organization has been a trailblazer for immigrant politics in the United States. In 1981, exile leader Jorge Mas Canosa formed the Cuban American National Foundation with the purpose of exercising greater influence on Washington, and he created strong ties with the administrations of Ronald Reagan and George H. W. Bush. In 1989, Florida Republican Ileana Ros-Lehtinen became the first Cuban American and the first Latina to be elected to Congress. In 1993, she was joined by fellow Republican Lincoln Diaz-Balart of Miami and Robert Menendez of New Jersey, a Democrat. These three remained the only Cuban American representatives in Congress for nearly a decade, but their numbers on Capitol Hill have doubled since 2002 with the addition of another Florida Republican, Mario Diaz-Balart, and New Jersey Democrat Albio Sires to the House, and Mel Martinez to the Senate (where Menendez joined him in 2006). Add to that the fact that the Bush administration consistently had at least one Cuban American in a powerful cabinet post, beginning with Martinez at the Department of Housing and Urban Development and then Carlos Gutierrez as commerce secretary, as well as the many Cubans appointed to mid- and senior-level staff positions or working on K Street, and it is clear that the distance between Little Havana and the Beltway narrowed considerably during the Bush presidency.

The internal dynamics of Florida's Cuban American population are rapidly evolving even though their dominance at the top of Miami's political and business communites remains unchallenged. The founding wave of exiles who arrived in the 1960s is undergoing a leadership transition as many of the dominant figures pass away. Cubans who escaped the island as children and teenagers are now in their fifties and sixties, and the younger generations are U.S. citizens with weaker ties to the island of their parents' youth. Successive waves of immigration have changed the community. In 1980, 125,000 Cubans arrived during an immigration crisis known as the Mariel Boatlift. In 1994, another 35,000 boat people came during the *balsero* crisis that prompted President Clinton to implement two huge changes in immigration policy: establishing the "wet foot/dry foot" rule that required Cubans picked up at sea to be returned to Cuba, and the signing of immigration accords with the Cuban government to provide twenty thousand U.S. immigrant visas to Cubans each year.

Cuba is, paradoxically, the only country in the world that has signed an immigration agreement with the United States, and since the mid-1990s about 250,000 Cubans have migrated legally to America. Recently, as many as 15,000 have been arriving each year without authorization, traveling on rustic rafts, smuggled on high-tech go-fast boats, or traveling to Mexico and then sneaking across the border into the United States. (There are no official statistics on how many Cubans have perished in the Straits of Florida while attempting to reach the United States, but the number of accidental drownings since 1959 likely reaches into the thousands.) Unlike the political exile forced on the founding generation of Cuban immigrants, the profile of these new arrivals corresponds more closely to that of other Latin American immigrants who leave their countries for economic reasons, in search of a better life. South Florida today is filled with Cubans who have grown up under communism and maintain deep links with their families back home, unlike the city's founding generation of exiles, who fled to the United States with most of their families and cut many of their ties to Cubans on the island.

In 1997, Jorge Mas Canosa died at the age of fifty-eight of complications from lung cancer. The loss of Mas Canosa, who was the most influential and creative anti-Castro leader in Miami, dealt a severe blow to efforts to present Cuban Americans as a united front, especially through his powerful lobbying group. Through the force of his personality, he made it possible for Cubans to speak with a single voice, but the competing factions that emerged in Miami after Mas Canosa called to mind Yugoslavia after Tito. The Elián González crisis in 2000 was the trigger event that caused deeper schisms to come to the surface. Even many of those who favored keeping Elián in the United States—which included the vast majority of Cuban Americans in South Florida—were deeply disturbed by the dominant impression in the media that Miami had become an out-of-control banana republic. When the Cuban American National Foundation responded by moderating its policy views, it provoked a leadership split.

In 2001, two dozen board members resigned en masse and promoted tighter sanctions on Cuba through a separate organization, christened the Cuban Liberty Council. Separately, a group of influential exile businessmen founded the Cuba Study Group and began to promote ideas to support limited engagement with Cuba. In 2004, the new travel restrictions imposed by the Bush administration at the behest of some Cuban exiles further divided South Florida. Soon the political debate on Cuba policy in Miami dissolved into a cacophony of competing voices, each claiming to represent the majority of exile opinion.

Even the question of whether Cuban Americans are divided on Cuba policy has become a major source of division. More than ten years after the passing of Mas Canosa, Miami's public voice on Cuba policy remains remarkably consistent in its support for the trade and investment embargo and, to a lesser degree, the travel ban, but a separate conversation is emerging among rank-and-file Cuban Americans who question the wisdom of this approach. Currents of dissent are becoming increasingly apparent in areas such as the new restrictions on Cuban American travel to Cuba, the harsher elements of the Cuban embargo in terms of medicine and humanitarian aid, and the deep resistance to initiating a dialogue with the Castro regime. Many hardliners have responded by insisting that Cuban exiles are as united as ever against Castro. Critics of U.S. policy are accused of "confusing the issue." And even today, local journalists seeking to expose some of the darker edges of Miami's Cuban politics are accused of being communists—a laughable charge in any other major American city but a damaging character smear in South Florida.

And yet, Cuban exile leaders who are harshly critical of each other's positions still warmly greet each other in common gathering spaces like the famed Cuban restaurant Versailles on Calle Ocho. Miami's Cuban American population today is a place where people who have not seen Havana in forty years mix regularly with those who were just there last week. It is a rich mix of bomb throwers and pacifists, *dialogueros* and hard-liners, truth tellers and keepers of secrets, the wealthy and the destitute, blacks and whites, the powerful and the voiceless, Republicans and Democrats—all fighting for the soul of what they call "the community."

The headquarters of the Cuban American National Foundation are located on the third floor of a light-colored office building in southwest Miami, where the organization rents office space from a local insurance company. It would be easy to drive past on the busy Miami street and never know it was there. Founded in 1981 by Jorge Mas Canosa and often referred to as the CANF or the Foundation, it racked up an impressive array of achievements during the two-decade height of its political influence. The CANF is credited with almost single-handedly persuading the U.S. government to establish the Office of Cuba Broadcasting to transmit pro-democracy and anti-Castro media to Cuba through Miami-based Radio and TV Martí. Its political action committee, the Free Cuba PAC, put more than $1.6 million into congressional and presidential races between 1982 and 2000, and it spearheaded legislative efforts to strengthen the embargo during the 1990s.

As the hub of anti-Castro political activity in Miami, the CANF has more than once been linked to covert operations against Cuba. In 2006, a former board member, seventy-five-year-old José Antonio Llama, claimed the CANF had formed a paramilitary group to destabilize Cuba in the 1990s, saying, "We were impatient with the survival of Castro's regime after the fall of the Soviet Union and the socialist camp. We wanted to accelerate the democratization of Cuba using any possible means to achieve it."[1] Llama was among several men arrested in 1997 for their engagement in an assassination plot against Castro, but he was later acquitted in Puerto Rico. Like similar claims that have been leveled at the CANF in the past, the charge was denounced as a defamation attempt by the organization's current leadership and sparked little interest in the U.S. law enforcement community.

Such accusations do not ruffle Dr. Francisco "Pepe" Hernández, the foundation's president since 1990 and a longtime stalwart of the Cuban exile community, as well as a former close associate of Mas Canosa. A founding board member of the CANF, Hernández is a veteran of the 1961 Bay of Pigs invasion. He was captured and spent two years in Castro's prisons before being released in 1963. He later earned a Ph.D. in economics at the University of Florida and entered into a successful business career, but the plight of Cuba always remained close to his heart. In a meeting in his office, he sat before a cartoon sketch on the wall that showed a knight on a white horse, representing the CANF, raising its spear toward Fidel Castro, depicted as a dragon. Wearing a crisp white guayabera, with his gray hair neatly combed, Hernández dismissed the more outlandish allegations of the

CANF's escapades with a wave of his hand. "I am reputed to be one of the main *terroristas* in the exile community and a good friend of Posada Carriles and all that stuff, which I don't deny. I mean being friends and having had participation in a number of what I perceived as opportunities to do away with Castro. But I have come to realize that, first, we are powerless, and second, it is not a solution that will actually resolve anything."

Speaking haltingly with a strong Cuban accent, Hernández explained that the idea for the Cuban American National Foundation emerged shortly after the 1980 Mariel Boatlift, when South Florida was flooded with more than 125,000 Cuban refugees who had fled the island at Castro's urging. At the same time, the newly ascendant conservative administration of President Ronald Reagan created an opportunity for Cuban exiles to capitalize on the new U.S. leader's anticommunist fervor to bolster their political power, counter the influence of the newly established Cuban diplomatic mission in Washington, and develop greater influence over U.S. policy toward Cuba. "The initial idea," Hernández told me, "was that we have got to go to Washington. We cannot continue to scream at each other here in Miami and expect that people are going to listen to what we are saying." Although Reagan was an important ally, the foundation was intended to be bipartisan in nature. "When we went to Washington, we realized that we had to seek the support of both sides of the political system," he said, especially given that Democrats were then dominant in Florida state politics. "This is something that our Jewish friends helped us understand at that time . . . If you don't work both sides of the aisle, you really don't go anywhere." In fact, Reagan's first national security adviser, Richard Allen, met with Mas Canosa shortly after taking office and urged him to set up a lobbying organization modeled after the American Israel Public Affairs Committee, which advocated on behalf of Israel. Over the years, this led to a mutually beneficial relationship between the pro-Israel and anti-Castro lobbies on Capitol Hill, where the groups trade votes in support of their respective causes.

In the twenty-five years since the CANF was founded, it has definitively shaped Washington's Cuba policy and helped to codify the U.S. embargo into law. But Hernández himself acknowledged that the hour was getting late. The generation of Cuban exiles that he represented still had no interest in engaging with Castro, but it was losing its fighting mood. Hernández ruefully recognized that it would be difficult to dispel the image that "the Cuban American exile community was maintained and controlled by a mafia of people that were totally and absolutely against the government, against Cuba, against the Cuban people." Among his peers, Hernández conceded, "it has been extremely difficult to adapt to the idea that the exile community cannot possibly continue to play the role of the driving force in whatever changes are going to occur in Cuba. Looking at the future, we have to recognize that the people who have more contacts and relatives and families in Cuba therefore are going to have more of an influence on what the future of Cuba will be." Besides, Hernández added, "People who are seventy or eighty years old do not, you know, happen to have a lot of mobility."

Hernández has had lifelong sympathies for armed interventions against Castro, but in recent years his political views have tilted toward engagement with Cuba, such as expanding the ability of Cubans living in the United States to visit their families on the island, easing restrictions on sending money, and even some level of dialogue between the United States and Cuba on the governmental or nongovernmental level. But he realized that many older Cuban exiles would perhaps never be ready to cross this Rubicon: "The wounds, the memories, the history of their experiences—it is extremely difficult for people who have lived the terrible experiences that we have gone through, especially for my generation," he said. "There is a total, absolute mistrust of Fidel Castro and those who are around him. The fact that these people have suffered in the experiences of believing, of trusting, because you have to understand that all these people . . . trusted completely what Fidel Castro was willing to give us." Hernández recalled that many Cubans of his generation initially hoped that Castro's revolution would save the country from the corruption and dictatorship of the Batista regime. In Havana, a popular sticker placed on the front doors of many houses read, FIDEL ESTA ES TU CASA (Fidel, this is your home). When Castro's rise to power brought only further dictatorship and economic ruin, many of the Cubans who initially supported him felt embarrassed and ashamed of their actions. "We, the Cuban people, have had a long history of frustration and misaccomplished expectations, expectations that have never been fulfilled. Looking at that situation, we saw ourselves as victims again of our own naïveté."

Hernández quoted the director of the Cuban magazine *Bohemia*, who later was driven into exile and committed suicide. "He said that Fidel Castro was the result of an explosion of demagoguery and senselessness. In Spanish, it's *insensatez*—it has a stronger connotation than in English. This is what has followed the Cuban people throughout the years. Our history, that senselessness, that incapacity to realize the complexity of the political system in which Latins live and the fact that you require a lot of *malicia* or malice in order to go about it." Then, in 1961, with the buildup to the Bay of Pigs invasion, the Cuban exiles believed that they had gained the support of President Kennedy in their efforts to regain control of the island. Instead, Kennedy failed to provide the necessary air support, and Castro's forces won a stirring victory that further strengthened his hand at home. For Hernández and his exiled countrymen, that series of events led to "the realization, coming to the United States, that we have been victims again, of our own senselessness." He paused and seemed to be grasping for words. "So to some extent, our generation has said, 'Never again. We are not going to be part of this again. We are not going to trust again. We are not going to believe.' That is why the only defense that you have in a situation like that is to say, 'I am not going to change. I am not going to accept anything from these people. There cannot be anything good coming from those people.'"

But Hernández no longer believed that armed struggle against Cuba held any hope, which meant that the challenge of Cuba now belonged to the heirs of the defeated generation that fled Cuba in the 1960s and never managed to get it back: "I come to the realization that the future does not belong to us anymore. We failed in our effort to find a solution for the problem, so the solution and the responsibility is in the hands of a new generation." He dismissed the once-tantalizing but now-dated idea of pushing for a U.S. invasion of Cuba. "If we were able to, by miracle—and it would certainly take a miracle—to convince the United States to invade Cuba or let us do it, we are only going to extend the suffering and create conditions in which the Cuban people would have to confront again armed groups, and it will never finish."

"We Cubans have to stop killing each other. If we do not stop killing each other, we will never be able to find a solution to our problems, because the heritage that we would pass on to our children would be just continuing to kill each other. So the overwhelming majority of the exile community has firmly renounced the armed struggle or any violence as a means of obtaining power in Cuba." Hernández gave me a rueful look. "Which, to a certain extent, leaves us very little to work with."

The CANF's gradual move toward moderation began when Jorge Mas Santos took over the organization following the death of his father, Mas Canosa. Then in his late thirties, Mas Santos initially got along well with many of the CANF board members who had been close associates of his father, and they were pleased that the younger generation was willing to step in and take a leadership role. But the relationship soon soured as Mas Santos attempted to moderate some of the group's policy positions. The straw that broke the camel's back was the CANF's decision to back Miami's hosting the Latin Grammy music awards show in 2001, even though Cuban musicians would be featured. In June 2001, the CANF lost one of its most prominent directors when media personality Ninoska Pérez Castellón quit the board. Two dozen other board members followed her lead, creating the most public rift in the Cuban exile community in decades. By the fall, the dissenting directors had set up their own organization, the Cuban Liberty Council, to advocate for continued sanctions against Castro and to lobby against any efforts by the United States to open up to Cuba.

Pérez Castellón serves as the Cuban Liberty Council's spokesperson and chief advocate. In her mid-fifties, Pérez Castellón is one of the most beloved and feared radio broadcasters in Miami, and she is famed for the sharp-tongued wit she deploys on her show on Radio Mambí. She is married to Roberto Martín Pérez, the son of a high-level Batista official, who spent twenty-eight years in a Cuban prison. Her bio on Univision's Web site lists Cuba and radio as her twin passions, and her professional career has combined them seamlessly. Her daily radio show is required listening for thousands of exiles in Miami, and a necessary pit stop for any political candidate seeking to win support from South Florida's anti-Castro constituency. Fox News commentator Bill O'Reilly frequently invites her on his show to discuss issues related to Cuba, and she is well known in conservative media circles.

In person, Pérez Castellón is forthright and charming, with short brown hair, dark brown eyes, and a definite point of view. She is a skilled communicator and polemicist who sharply criticizes any public figure who reaches out to the Cuban government. When President Bill Clinton spontaneously shook hands with Fidel Castro at a UN summit in New York in 2000, Pérez Castellón told the *New York Post* that the impromptu exchange reflected "the same stupidity which led him to have oral sex in the White House with Monica Lewinsky." Laughing about it later, she said, "What the hell, it's the *New York Post*!" When the quote was highlighted in *Newsweek*, she figured that it meant she was "never going to be able to step into the White House or talk to Hillary again." But her critiques are not limited to politicians. When the singer Carole King traveled to Cuba in 2002 and serenaded Castro with the song "You've Got a Friend," Pérez Castellón threw out her collection of King's music, declaring it to be "tainted with the blood on Castro's hands." Pérez Castellón described the moment when she left the CANF after fifteen years as "one of the saddest and most difficult times of my life," but said, "I couldn't be part of something that I don't agree with."

Speaking in the offices of the Cuban Liberty Council, located on top of a bank just off Calle Ocho in Little Havana, Pérez Castellón expressed regret over the more moderate path charted by the CANF. "To me, the foundation had been such a powerful adversary for Castro, and we had done so much, that every time that I was about to make the decision [to quit], I would think, 'Who would be happier with this decision: Havana or . . . ?' " Even as spokeswoman for the Cuban Liberty Council, she conceded that "you will never have another group like the foundation, which is no longer what it was." But she argued that the Cuban Liberty Council has "been effective, because what the CANF has tried to do is give this vision that the Cuban American community has changed in the younger generations." She dismissed recent polls in Miami that have suggested that the Cuban American community is ready for a more open policy toward Cuba. "Every time that they tell me that the community has changed, this is my response: Who is Lincoln Diaz-Balart? Who is Ileana Ros? Who is Mario Diaz-Balart? Who is Mel Martinez? Who is Bob Menendez? And what do they stand for? That is the poll! . . . They stand for sanctions, supporting the embargo. And why do they get elected overwhelmingly every time? They have support."

Referring to her radio show, she told me, "My listeners support the embargo. But you can argue, 'Well, you're a conservative radio show, and maybe people that listen to you are conservative.' That can be a point. But then I go to the final poll, which is the elections. Tell me an elected official in this community that thinks differently in any aspect from the position of the traditional exile. There isn't one." Of course, she added, "Anybody would be frustrated after forty-eight years. The U.S. could be doing more and implement the law to the maximum. In the end, it's not about the U.S., it's about the Cuban people, but obviously the U.S. is the only ally that we've had in that sense."

Pérez Castellón believes that the property claims of Cuban exiles will be a crucial issue in the future. More than five thousand property claims have been filed with the U.S. government by Cuban exiles seeking to regain properties that were expropriated in the Cuban Revolution—in addition to another nine hundred claims filed by U.S. companies. The total estimated value of these claims exceeds seven billion dollars—more than three times Cuba's annual exports. Pérez Castellón said, "I will tell you something: In all the countries in Eastern Europe, people have settled their claims, most of them, and the Cuban people should be no different. I'm not saying you should go in there and drag somebody out of a house that they have lived in for so long. But in the end, that house belonged to your family." She described the case of a friend who was born in a house built by her grandfather that was later turned into a school and rechristened with a communist name. The friend said that even if she could not reclaim the house, she would at least want the school to bear her grandfather's name. "There are many emotional issues. If you ask more than half of the people who had property in Cuba, they probably have better properties here than they ever had in Cuba, but it's the principle of the thing."

Pérez Castellón holds no hope for a dialogue between the United States and Cuba, especially with Fidel Castro severely weakened and Raúl Castro strengthening his grip on power. "If you tell me, 'Do you favor an invasion or a dialogue?' I will always favor a dialogue. But obviously a dialogue is not going to solve Cuba's problem because a lot of people have been dialoguing. I'm sorry." She expressed frustration with people who "want me to change my position and say that I support a dialogue. You don't need my support to dialogue with Castro." Even worse was what she viewed as a concerted effort to rehabilitate Raúl's reputation: "The sale of Raúl Castro started by Alcibíades Hidalgo, his former aide." (Hidalgo, who served as Raúl's chief of staff for twelve years and was a Cuban ambassador to the UN, defected to the United States in 2002. He is generally viewed as a credible source of information about the Cuban government, but some exiles have accused him of intentionally trying to improve Raúl's public image.) "Different groups of people started saying, 'Well, you know, Raúl Castro is an organized man.' As far as I know, everybody knows that he is an alcoholic, and I don't know how organized alcoholics can be," she laughed. "The worst part is, 'He's a sentimental man, he's a family man.' "

She recited an oft-told story of how, upon learning of their mother's death in the early 1960s, Fidel Castro was stern and hard but Raúl Castro wept. She laughed mockingly, saying, " 'Oh, my God, Raúl Castro cried, that's feeling!' For crying out loud, Hitler loved his dog! So they're trying to create this myth about Raúl Castro. Sorry, but if you have been for forty-eight years the second person in that regime, you are as guilty of everything, whether you cry or not! This is an effort to humanize people who have done so much harm. This is like humanizing the people who were tried at Nuremberg." Pérez Castellón was not optimistic for change to come from within Cuba. "They are not going to change, because they can't change. If tomorrow they were to change, they would lose what has kept them in power, which is absolute control." She firmly opposed any effort to lift the U.S. embargo or other efforts to engage with Cuba, because otherwise "you're only giving credit to Fidel Castro—international credit. That's all."

The Cuban Liberty Council is only seven years old, but it has already proved to be a powerful vehicle to advance its mission of opposing any attempt to strike an accord between the United States and the Castro government. Its membership boasts some of the most influential media figures and business leaders in Cuban Miami. During the 2008 presidential primaries, most of the leading Republican candidates sent representatives to speak on Pérez Castellón's radio show, and the core topic was always Cuba policy. She believes that radio holds the key to understanding the Cuban community today. "Radio is vital. Cubans have an attachment to radio because it's so motivating, and we are very passionate . . . you have passion, people cry on the air. So I think it's the passion that drives it."

In January 1998, Pope John Paul II made the first visit to Cuba by a top Vatican official since Castro took power in 1959. The meeting took on epic proportions as a historic encounter between two major figures of the cold war. The pope's forceful challenge of communism in his native Poland, which he first visited as pontiff in 1979, was viewed to have played a major role in moving the country toward democracy. As one of the world's longest-lived communist leaders, Castro had, by contrast, extirpated religion from Cuba and spent decades enforcing the dicta of an atheist state. By 1998, the two leaders were in their seventies and entering the long twilight of their extended public careers. The pope's visit to Cuba was motivated by his desire to secure greater recognition for Cuba's long-suppressed Catholic Church and to help end the international isolation of Cuba represented by the U.S. embargo. Castro was seeking both the international attention and the legitimacy that the meeting with the pope would represent. Perhaps more fundamentally, Pope John Paul II and Fidel Castro both held a great fascination with each other as world leaders who had shared the burdens of the cold war and somehow emerged from the experience intact, even if on opposite sides of the struggle. In January 1998, their very separate destinies would briefly intertwine.

In Miami, the pope's visit to Cuba was one of the first divisive events to shake the Cuban American community after the death of Jorge Mas Canosa. Many Cuban Catholics in Miami were aghast that the spiritual leader of their church would be standing shoulder to shoulder with Castro. Worse was the fact that Miami archbishop John Favalora had arranged for the *Norwegian Majesty* cruise ship, with a capacity of one thousand people, to travel from Miami to Havana for a four-day pilgrimage to support the pope and show solidarity with people of religious faith in Cuba. By the middle of December 1997, more than four hundred tickets had been sold, with Cuban American Catholics accounting for a third of the purchases. But the planned pilgrimage sparked outrage among those who were deeply opposed to Pope John Paul II's decision to meet with Castro, a man who had spent much of his rule stripping religion out of Cuban society and replacing it with communist atheism.

Carlos Saladrigas, a prominent Miami businessman active in the Catholic Church, was among the influential opponents of the pilgrimage. He joined a Hispanic business group that sent a letter criticizing the church's decision and was vocal in his opposition to the cruise. "As a Cuban Catholic, I am very hurt," he told the *Miami Herald*. "We cannot force the archbishop to do anything. But he has to accept the fact that this is going to create a significant rift in the community and he's going to live with the consequences of that rift for many years to come."[2] With Miami roiled in controversy, Archbishop Favalora pulled the plug on the cruise a few days before Christmas, explaining that the voyage had become "a serious source of tension in our community." The next month, when Pope John Paul II conducted his Holy Mass in Cuba, it marked the first time in decades that Cubans gathered in celebration of a leader who was not Fidel Castro. Speaking before tens of thousands of Cubans in Havana's Plaza of the Revolution, the pope described the Catholic Church as bringing a message of "love and solidarity" that offered a path of "authentic peace, justice, and freedom." In reply, many Cubans began to chant, "The pope wants us all to be free!"

A decade later, Saladrigas has become one of Miami's most high-profile voices arguing for the United States to open up to Cuba. Saladrigas came to the United States by himself at the age of twelve, as one of fourteen thousand children rescued from the Cuban Revolution by Operation Pedro Pan, organized through the Catholic Church. He worked odd jobs in Miami until he was joined by his parents, and he got his undergraduate degree in night school. At the suggestion of a supervisor, he applied and won admission to Harvard Business School, and he went on to a successful career as the founder of a human resources firm called the Vincam Group, which, when he sold it to a larger company in 1998, made him a millionaire many times over. At the age of sixty, Saladrigas now dedicates much of his time to the Cuba Study Group, an organization he cofounded in 2000. His conversion on Cuba policy began shortly after his successful bid to block the pilgrimage cruise: "When I saw the effect of the pope's visit, and when I saw the things that were said in Cuba for the first time, and the things that Cubans heard for the first time, I began to have second thoughts about the wisdom of my actions. And I kept saying to myself, 'You know, I think I made a huge mistake.' "

Saladrigas's second watershed moment came during the Elián González crisis two years later, when he joined a small group of community leaders to play a mediating role as the standoff was reaching its climax. The group was led by businessman Carlos M. de la Cruz, then chairman of the University of Miami board of trustees, and included Saladrigas and several others. In the early-morning hours of April 22, 2000, both de la Cruz and Saladrigas were in the home of

Elián's Miami relatives, negotiating on the phone with Attorney General Janet Reno, when U.S. authorities raided the house and snatched custody of the boy. Saladrigas recalled, "I was devastated. I mean, here we are believing that we have reached a solution, and under no circumstances would she invade the house while we were there. So we were shocked. There was a lot of bad blood."

Following the traumas of the Elián González raid, Saladrigas reflected on the lessons of that period. "Right after the Elián González crisis ended, it was the shock that many people in the community needed to say, 'You know what, we need a different approach to Cuba. We cannot swing the bat with Fidel Castro pitching the ball. We need a fresh approach that is more strategic, less reactive, more tactical.' " Saladrigas thought that the handling of the Elián episode demonstrated that Mas Canosa's death had left behind a void of meaningful leadership in the Cuban American community. "Elián, in my opinion, would have never happened if Mas Canosa had been alive, because he had the power and the stature to prevent it from getting to where it got. It was clearly the absence of that kind of leadership that led to the Elián González incident," compounded by "too many people coming to prominence, all working against each other."

Shortly thereafter, Saladrigas joined with other Miami business leaders to form the Cuba Study Group. The new organization is, in essence, a public policy start-up venture bankrolled by twenty of the most powerful Cuban American businessmen in Miami. It is cochaired by Saladrigas, who is the chairman of Premier American Bank, and Luis Perez, a mergers and acquisitions lawyer who is a partner at Hogan and Hartson, a top-thirty global law firm. De la Cruz, the chairman of Coca-Cola Puerto Rico Bottlers and Eagle Brands, cofounded the group and remains actively involved. During its early years, the Cuba Study Group commissioned a number of polls to find out where the Cuban American community actually stood on Cuba policy. More recently, it has unveiled new proposals to incentivize change in Cuba, including a Cuba Enterprise Fund, modeled on economic aid given to Eastern Europe after the fall of the Berlin Wall, and a plan to extend microcredit to Cuban entrepreneurs. It has supported efforts to promote dialogue and debate within the Cuban American community, including Consenso Cubano, a joint charter signed by twenty exile groups of diverse ideologies, and Raíces de Esperanza (Roots of Hope), a university-based group of young Cuban

Americans seeking to become engaged with the Cuba that their parents left behind.

The Cuba Study Group deliberately describes its goals in moderate language, saying that it seeks "to formulate effective, multilateral policy recommendations through thoughtful discussion and critical analysis of ideas." But its core objective is a good deal more radical, in that it seeks to rebrand the Cuban American community as a partner to change in Cuba and break the stranglehold that Miami's current political leadership has placed on Cuba policy. According to Saladrigas, the Cuban American community suffered from a major image problem that undercut its effectiveness at home and abroad. "The old image is one of exiles being monolithic, which in principle is an antidemocratic image." He listed several firmly entrenched perceptions: "The image of Miami as being vengeful and anxious to get back to establish the old order, as opposed to a new Cuba. The image of Miami as trying to go back to Cuba and control things, and reclaim property and all these things, which we believe was a contributor to the fear factor of change that paralyzes you. And last, but not least, the image of Miami being uncompromising in the position that the only solution for Cuba is the absolute, total, and immediate collapse of the communist system—and that therefore was not conducive to the change processes that we believe are inherently modular and inherently gradual."

To test their hypothesis that the Cuban American community was more politically diverse than was widely believed, the Cuba Study Group commissioned a series of polls of Miami's Cuban population. One survey, released in February 2003, found that a majority of Cuban Americans favored a dialogue with the Cuban government and believed that the future of Cuba rested with dissidents on the island, not exile leaders. A *Miami Herald* poll conducted around the same period revealed similar results. The findings were hotly disputed by Cuban American members of Congress like Republican Lincoln Diaz-Balart and the members of the Cuban Liberty Council, but Saladrigas stood by the results. In 2007, the Cuba Study Group and Florida International University collaborated on a new poll of one thousand randomly selected Cuban Americans from Miami-Dade County.[3] Two thirds of the people surveyed were U.S. citizens, while the others were permanent residents. The poll's findings further documented a shift toward moderation in Miami's Cuban community. More than 70 percent favored selling medicine to Cuba, and 60 percent backed food sales to Cuba. Establishing a national dialogue between the Cuban government and exiles had 65 percent support. About 65 percent also favored removing the new restrictions on travel and remittances that the Bush administration had implemented in 2004, and 55 percent backed lifting all travel restrictions between the United States and Cuba. Many analysts touted these results as a sign that Miami was undergoing a sea change in attitudes toward Cuba, but the poll also revealed the persistent popularity of a hard-line approach. A slight majority of respondents favored both a U.S. invasion of Cuba and a Cuban transition that was "sudden and violent" to one that was "peaceful and gradual." Only 24 percent thought the U.S. embargo had worked well, but nearly 58 percent favored continuing it. The greatest point of consensus was around the desire to support human rights groups in Cuba, which was backed by an impressive 96 percent of respondents.

Saladrigas viewed these polls as a crucial tool for giving voice to alternative views in the Miami community: "In the past, the exiles would only be heard through the voice of mostly self-appointed spokesmen. So what the Cuba Study Group did was to give a voice to the majority of the Cuban American community—the famous silent majority—and that's what we did through the polling." He acknowledged, "Of course, it generated a lot of controversy. It challenged the fundamental core of those that wanted to continue to give this impression that they are the only gatekeepers of Cuba policy . . . This is a big challenge to certain status quo individuals in the community, and their attacks have been virulent and vicious in many cases."

The Cuba Study Group's strong base in the business community has given it the economic resources to emerge as a major voice on Cuba policy in the space of just a few years. Saladrigas himself has created a well-tailored PowerPoint presentation that he has delivered to dozens of audiences in the manner of a CEO pitching an exciting new investment to a skeptical boardroom. The most compelling graphic illustrates the ability and willingness to change of a number of key actors, including the Cuban government, the exile community, the Cuban people, and the United States. His point is always that the United States and the exiles need to make change in Cuba easier, not harder, and that means starting with incremental steps. "Fidel Castro wanted to promote that image of exiles as the barbarians at the gate, because it is an image that reinforces the fears of change," he said, adding that "that image, apart from damaging the relationship of the exile community with other nations and the rest of the world, diminished our effectiveness as an opposition force and our effectiveness to bring about positive changes in Cuba."

Carlos Saladrigas now spends about half of his time working on Cuba issues through the Cuba Study Group, a decision that he credits in part to his Jesuit education and the desire to give back to the community after making his fortune. But like many exiles, he still views Cuba from a distance. Since leaving in 1961, he has traveled back only once, in the 1980s, when he was an executive based in Mexico. None of his four children have ever been to Cuba. "You know, I could have engaged on some philanthropic issue, but the subject of Cuba was close and dear to my heart. So this was an opportunity for me to take this time and try to do something meaningful." But unlike in the business world, the rewards for his efforts have been harder to perceive: "Trying to be a change agent on Cuba is incredibly frustrating."

Versailles restaurant is the famed home of Cuban cuisine in Miami, and it is located in the middle of a steamy strip of shops and restaurants along Calle Ocho in the city's Little Havana district. Versailles is a beloved community treasure in a neighborhood that remains a repository for nostalgia about life in Cuba before Fidel Castro and a hotbed of antagonism toward the current Cuban government. Cuban Spanish is the language that is heard from the busy streets to the office suites, although many denizens can switch fluently from Spanish to English and back again, and newer immigrants from Central America are increasingly common. Black-and-white photos of pre-Castro Cuba are sold on street corners, and the music of the late Cuban exile diva Celia Cruz provides the sound track to daily life. But anyone who has a kind word to say about Castro will face the wrath of a community that has flourished in exile but has not yet overcome the psychological and emotional scars of his rule. Respected world leaders like Nelson Mandela have learned this the hard way. He spent twenty-seven years in a South African jail, but local leaders protested his visit to Miami in 1990 because he had earlier praised Castro for his opposition to apartheid. Che Guevara's image may remain revered in parts of the world, but in the shops of Calle Ocho it is more likely to appear on novelty rolls of toilet paper than on a T-shirt. (Indeed, someone strolling through Little Havana in a Che Guevara T-shirt ten years ago risked having it ripped off him. Today, the rebuke is more likely to consist of dirty glares.) In Cuban Miami, the expansive, noisy, gilded dining room of Versailles is one of the hubs for reliving memories of the past and plotting strategies for the future.

It is also a great place to see people and be seen, and Joe Garcia is one of many politically oriented Cubans who likes to talk shop at Versailles. Garcia, a fixture of the Cuban American scene for more than a decade, understands the jagged political contours of Cuban Miami as well as anyone of his generation. He spent four years as the executive director of the Cuban American National Foundation, but dramatically resigned that post in 2004 to serve as a key adviser to John Kerry's presidential campaign in South Florida. After Kerry's defeat, Garcia directed the Hispanic Strategy Center at the New Democrat Network, an advocacy organization dedicated to promoting progressive politics. He has also positioned himself as a key adviser to Democratic presidential candidates trying to take the Miami community's temperature on Cuba policy. In the spring of 2007, Garcia won the chairmanship of the Miami-Dade Democratic Party, but he resigned this post in February 2008 to wage a long-shot bid to oust Mario Diaz-Balart, the Republican representative for the West Miami-Dade district, from his seat in Congress.

In his early forties, Garcia is a voluble talker and an experienced operator, advocate, and provocateur in the insular and often Byzantine world of Miami's exile politics. A brash presence with a thick head of curly brown hair, he greeted me for lunch at Versailles wearing jeans and a light blue navy shirt and never bothered to unclip his cell phone earpiece. The restaurant swirled with lunchtime activity, and Garcia nodded his head, as if confirming the centrality of Versailles in the universe of Miami: "It's what Cuzco was to the Incan empire. It's the belly button of the world." When I asked him to describe the politics of U.S.-Cuba policy in Miami today, he replied without hesitation. "Cuba policy is in a collapsed state. Right now you have a situation where we in the Cuban community are victims of our own success. We've created the politics of status quo, which finally American politicians have learned so well that they only do the rhetoric without the reality. If you look at the layout today, you are at this

point where there is a tremendous amount of frustration, and you are
at the beginning of the end of the first generation of Cuban exiles, and
you're at the very beginning of the next generation, which is made of
U.S. citizens. You are looking at a wave that's about to begin."

After hopping up to warmly greet several colleagues, Garcia sat
down and continued. "It takes immigrants about twenty years to assim-
ilate, to become citizens, start voting, that kind of thing. The first big
wave of Cuban Americans assimilated in the late 1970s and early '80s.
And with that you had the advent of Ronald Reagan, the last cold war
president, and Cuban Americans saw themselves as victims of communism. That was after Jimmy Carter's famous attempt to normalize relations with Cuba literally exploded in the face of the U.S. [with the 1980
Mariel Boatlift], embarrassed exiles, destroyed the Democratic Party's
base in South Florida, and began the ascension of the Republican Party
within the Cuban American community. It also marked the beginning
of the Cuban American National Foundation, which was quite literally
a different type of Cuban American politics."

What changed, Garcia said, was that Cuban exile leader Jorge Mas
Canosa convinced the Miami community that their ticket to success
would come from promoting their initiatives through the U.S. government, not from sporadic mischief-making missions to Cuba. "He
changed the debate by saying, 'Stop looking south. That's not going to
bring you to power. The road back to Cuba leads through Washington.'" Over time, that insight led to perhaps the most successful immigrant conquest of official influence in the United States since the
earliest days of the nation. "Whether by accident or by plan, the
Cuban American community changed the face of U.S. policy towards
Cuba, and also changed the face of immigrant politics in the United
States. They did in one generation something that no other immigrant
has been able to do, which is accumulate vast amounts of power."
According to Garcia, when the CANF was founded in 1981, there was
only one Cuban American in the Florida state legislature, none in Congress, and few in the U.S. bureaucracy. "Today we have four Cuban
American congressmen, dozens of state legislators, not only here but
all over the country. There are two U.S. senators from different parties,
something that no one would have ever dreamed, and members of the
United States Cabinet. Clearly if you had mapped it out back then, it
would have been impossible to envision that kind of success."

In Garcia's mind, however, those achievements came with costs.

"The method to achieve the policy created a whole series of unintended consequences of tremendous success. It created a series of legislation, which, by the way, is doing exactly what was originally intended . . . It made sure that the Cuban community is at the center of the policy. Some of our good friends say that this is the tail wagging the dog, but that is not a sin, by the way. This is how the U.S. government works: It is special interests politics. The reality is, as pissed off as some people are, tell me one area of American politics that works different than that. The only difference is that there are Hispanics doing it."

Indeed, no one can deny that Miami's Cuban American community has been wildly successful in driving U.S. policy. But now, with public sentiment in Miami turning, even gingerly, against the embargo, I asked if the exile community has almost created a kind of Frankenstein's monster that it can no longer control. Garcia took a bite of his meal and chewed for a moment. "Yes, of course it has. As someone who helped put the brain into the monster, we obviously got it from the abnormal jar. It's the nature of policy, when you try to do something in Washington, you run up against the law of unintended consequences. But what it does is put the Cuban American community at the front and center in finding a solution." In his view, the Cuban regime that lay across the Straits of Florida remained in denial of that basic truth. "The Cubans like to say that they will only deal with sovereign states. But the people of Cuba need to find a solution together. As I said to a Cuban diplomat when we were talking once, 'When a dog is chewing off your leg, you can try to reason with the dog or you can talk to the owner, and they can probably reason with the dog.' As far as U.S.-Cuba policy, the dog that is biting your leg is the U.S. government. And the ones that can control the bite of that dog is the Cuban American community."

Garcia believed that Miami's exile community had become too disconnected from life as it is experienced by Cubans on the island. "Seventy percent of Cubans on earth were not born when Fidel Castro came to power. Why is that significant? If you want to talk about the absurdities of Miami, I ran the largest Cuban organization in the world outside of Cuba, and I've never even been to Cuba! But in Miami, that can make sense because Cuba is an ideological issue. In fact, it's almost a quasi-religious issue. It is ephemeral like the concept of nationhood. You can talk about it, but you can't put it in a jar. The problem with that religious element is that it never has to be reality, and—particularly in Miami—it is far removed from reality. The concept of Cuba here can't be tested because it has no give-and-take. The policy is like a religion, where you go on faith. The embargo is more a religious creed than an effective U.S. policy. The good thing about a creed is that you don't have to prove it. The problem with a creed is, how do you change it?"

Indeed, ever since Castro took power, the Cuban exiles' experience has been inseparable from the assumption that they would somehow find a vehicle that would deliver them back to Cuba on their own terms—whether it be an exile-led invasion, the collapse of the regime through the U.S. embargo, an American military intervention, or even the White House–backed Commission for Assistance to a Free Cuba. This conviction, which has only a fragile basis in reality, means that Cuban exiles have never been forced to confront the reality of Cuba as it is today and engage with the flesh-and-blood country that continues to grow, change, and evolve just off the shores of their adopted home in Miami. CANF president Francisco Hernández once recalled, "I was told by a young, recent arrival from Cuba that after experiencing old people in Cuba and Miami, he was convinced that the Cuban problem would not be solved until 'all *históricos* on both sides were dead.'" He added, "Since I am a *histórico*, I hope he is not right." But the problem is more than just generational in nature. The conflict is so deeply embedded into the cultural identity of the political leaders of Miami and Havana that it has become a force with a life of its own.

Garcia framed his struggle with the embargo in personal terms. "If there is a religion of the embargo, then at the very least I am a bishop in that church, and more probably I am a cardinal. So we've got a problem. I've just found out that one of the saints of the church engages in fornication on a regular basis. So I'm wrestling with my faith. But the truth is that I'm not going to stand at the pulpit any given Sunday and say this is a false religion, because it is not a false religion. Nationhood is not a false concept. The embargo is simply a substitution of our vehicle to achieve nationhood. Like war, it is an extension of foreign policy. It's a horrible one, it's a failure of diplomacy, but it is what it is."

The problem of unreality, in his view, haunted the debate on Cuba in Miami and made it nearly impossible for many people to assess the costs of the policy. "Because there is no real war going on except ideologically, we begin arguing how many angels can dance on a pin-head. This is wonderful for a philosophical debate, but the problem is there are people who are being victimized by that policy. While you and I are debating ivory-tower politics, there are people in Cuba who are hungry and their families are being divided, in part because the first generation is so delinked from the reality of Cuba."

As an example, he cited a meeting that he helped arrange between a reporter writing on Miami politics and some self-identified "ultra-conservative" members of the founding generation of Cuban exiles. Afterward the reporter called Garcia to thank him for helping to set up the meeting and recounted a particular moment of the conversation. "During the interview, one old man leaned forward, tapped the table, and said, 'If there was a button on this table, and I pushed it, and it would wipe Havana off the face of the earth, but guarantee that Fidel Castro would be among the dead in the rubble'"—Garcia looked up wryly and emphasized that two million people live in Havana—"then the old man said, 'I'd be willing to press that button' . . . Again, we are talking about angels on a pinhead. Because there is no button, and no one would let this man near the button if it existed. But as my reporter friend put it so clearly, it's possible for this man to think this way because he has no son or daughter, mother or wife living in Havana."

Garcia scanned the dining room. "Take a look around the restaurant. The debate on Cuba is going on right here at these tables with these very conservative guys, and most of the staff here just arrived from Cuba. Every single one of these busboys sent money last month to their family on the island, while at the table is sitting a person in their sixties yelling, 'And not a dollar should go to Cuba!'" To prove his point, he pulled aside a busboy and started a conversation in Spanish, asking when the young man arrived from Cuba and when was the last time he sent money to his family in Cuba. The impromptu inter-viewee, Maykel, had arrived three years ago, and he initially blanched at the question about sending money back home and started reciting a timid answer as if by rote. (Later Garcia asked me, "Do you under-stand? He's learned the rhetoric, because he needs to know it in order to live here.") But then the young man pushed back, admitting that he sent back money several months ago and asking, "What is the fault of my mother, my brother, my blood, if Fidel Castro is in Cuba?" When the conversation finished, Garcia turned to me and shook his head. "And that's the problem with Cuba policy. It's collapsing because of this debate of angels on a pinhead or if there was a fucking button. And it's a joke."

Obviously frustrated with the current policy, Garcia wanted to see U.S.-Cuba relations evolve through relaxing restrictions for Cuban American family travel and allowing a greater flow of remittances back to the island. He was planning to put his money where his mouth was by running to become the first Cuban American Democrat from South Florida in Congress, by unseating the incumbent Mario Diaz-Balart. Many political handicappers thought that the odds were against him, but 2008 was already shaping up to be a highly volatile and surprising election year in the United States. Garcia fiddled with his cell phone and leaned back from the table. "I want people to be able to walk Havana and see the country for themselves. The U.S. should do calibrated responses to Cuba's reforms, with the goal of moving towards a democratic government." He nodded soberly. "But this is a long road, and we may not all make it to the end."

Miami's Cuban American community may be debating the broader effectiveness of the Cuba travel sanctions and efforts to isolate the island, but few are willing to pick a fight over Radio and TV Martí. These pro-democracy and anti-Castro broadcasts are beamed into Cuba from a U.S. government installation in South Florida, and to many they remain a sacred cow. The first Radio Martí programs were broadcast to Cuba in 1985, and TV Martí went on-air in 1990. Since its founding, the U.S. government has spent more than five hundred million dollars on programming to reach the Cuban people from the Office of Cuba Broadcasting, located in a nondescript office park off of the Palmetto Expressway in northwest Miami. The studios are housed in a pale tan, low-slung building with long narrow windows that, aside from the American flag flying outside, bears no external markings that reveal its relationship to either the U.S. government or the Cuban exile community.

While waiting in the building's lobby during a visit in December 2006, I noted the official photographs of George W. Bush and Dick Cheney hanging behind the security desk, opposite a silver-framed portrait of Jorge Mas Canosa, the godfather of Radio and TV Martí. The largest wall space was reserved, however, for the station's namesake and famed Cuban poet José Martí, whose mustachioed image stared forward with somber eyes. The Office of Cuba Broadcasting is a U.S. government agency that is almost entirely staffed by residents or citizens of the United States who are of Cuban descent, and Spanish is the station's operating language for both conversational and broadcasting purposes. At lunchtime, a combination of elderly and middle-aged Cuban Americans strolled through the lobby, including one gentleman dressed in a green military uniform who bore a striking resemblance to Raúl Castro.

My tour of Radio and TV Martí led to an open floor of reporters and editors working on media programming in a spacious cubicle setting. Behind a curtain on the far end of this work space, three actors and a producer were filming the latest episode of La Oficina del Jefe (The Office of the Chief), and the actors, playing Raúl Castro, his assistant, and his secretary, were rehearsing their lines. Armando Roblán, the man I had spotted in the lobby, is the seventy-five-year-old Coral Gables resident who plays Raúl on the show. He had already achieved minor celebrity in Miami circles for his satirical performances of Fidel Castro on stage and screen, which stretched back more than two decades. When TV Martí decided to develop a political satire on Fidel's rule, Roblán easily won the lead part. But when Raúl was elevated to the position of president, Roblán jettisoned the beard and revamped his performance for the new era. In his element, he looked like a slightly exaggerated version of Raúl in full military regalia sitting in the TV Martí studio, and the effect was both sobering and slightly surreal.

Radio and TV Martí are broadcast twenty-four hours a day, seven days a week, on a range of frequencies, and offer both new programming and repeats. The programs are broadcast on two shortwave transmitters based in Greenville, North Carolina, and a third one in Delano, California, as well as a medium-wave transmitter in Marathon, Florida. Often the signals are blocked from entering the island by the Cuban government once the transmitting frequency is identified, although sometimes nature lends a helping hand, such as when the record hurricane season of 2005 knocked out a blimp parked off the Florida Keys that was broadcasting the signal. But in 2006, the outlook for Radio and TV Martí radically improved when Congress appropriated an extra ten million dollars to obtain a Lockheed Martin G1 aircraft to beam the television broadcasts into Cuba. This augmented the weekly broadcasts transmitted from a Pennsylvania National Guard Commando Solo C-130 plane that had been broadcasting four hours of TV Martí to the island on weekends since 2004. "The new plane makes a tremendous difference," coordinator for special programs Álvaro Alba told me. "It has really helped us to expand our audience." In a Radio Martí studio, two newscasters behind a pane of glass were announcing the top news item of the day: the release of Héctor Palacios, the sixty-five-year-old opposition leader who had been imprisoned since the spring of 2003. The radio producer waved a copy of the brief story and smiled: "Finally some good news from Cuba!"

Upstairs an editing team was adding sound effects and a laugh track to *La Oficina del Jefe*, which played without sound on multiple screens. "We need about three more editing stations, but right now all we have is one," the chief digital editor told me as he bent over the video clips. It was a few weeks before Christmas, and graphics were being added to a number of man-on-the-street interviews of Miami residents who were conveying holiday wishes to people in Cuba. In one, a middle-aged man in a baseball hat with a Corona beer logo offered rambling but clearly sincere greetings to people in Cuba. The series was to be broadcast throughout December.

Pedro Roig has been the director of the Office of Cuba Broadcasting since 2003. He is a charismatic and physically imposing presence, tall and bald, with frequent flashes of good humor. He argued that the broadcasting network he oversees is prepared to make a major impact on Cuba during the transition. "This is the most important moment for us since our founding," he told me. "Fidel Castro is like Stalin, and when he is dead, it will be as significant for Cuba as it was for Russia when Stalin died." Roig, a lawyer and a Bay of Pigs veteran, bristled at the thought that Radio and TV Martí could be described as propaganda instead of journalism, insisting that all voices are welcome to debate and discuss issues on their programs. (Soon after my visit, I began receiving regular invitations to be interviewed for one of the radio shows.) Recently, the station had conducted focus groups with freshly arrived Cuban immigrants that suggested that Cubans were desperate to receive an alternative to screeching political discourse. These findings had given more weight to the decision to diversify programming by including political satires like *La Oficina* and broadcasting sports and culture. Roig flashed a radiant smile and leaned forward in his chair. "Cuba is not a nation, but a hallucination," he intoned. "We are trying to introduce the Cuban people to reality."

But the introduction has not gone smoothly. Despite more than one hundred employees and an annual price tag of $27 million, many Radio and TV Martí programs still do not reach the average Cuban. Indeed, the station's management has faced a steady stream of challenges regarding the objectivity and effectiveness of its broadcasts. Perhaps more controversially, in 2006 the Office of Cuba Broadcasting began paying more than $180,000 every six months to the conservative local station Radio Mambí to carry its programming, and TV Martí programs were carried on a local television station through a similar arrangement.[4] The result meant that the U.S. government was now subsidizing the dissemination of anti-Castro news and propaganda to local audiences, the latest twist in the decades-old, multimillion-dollar effort to break Cuba's information blockade. During our conversations, Roig projected a confident demeanor about his efforts to transform the station into a beacon of free thought that can influence Cuba's future. Still, in his spare time, he was working on a book about the Cuban people, which he simply described as "the history of a tragedy."

In the twilight of Fidel Castro's regime, Miami's Cuban community is caught between competing impulses that ultimately will not be easily reconciled. The splintering of the Cuban exile leadership in the aftermath of Jorge Mas Canosa's death and the Elián González standoff is beyond dispute. But Cuban American elected leadership in the United States remains strongly hostile to the idea of engaging in dialogue with the Castro brothers. The waves of newer arrivals from Cuba have changed the nature of political conversation in Miami, but they have also adapted to it. The positions of Miami's anti-Castro hard-liners may be gradually losing support, but the scales have not yet tipped toward a critical mass favoring dramatic policy changes. Even many leading Cuban American critics of U.S. policy shy away from the dismantlement of the U.S. embargo, instead focusing on issues like expanding Cuban American family travel, increasing aid to dissidents, and upgrading institutions like the Office of Cuba Broadcasting.

But many analysts of Miami's Cuban American community do see larger trends afoot. Among them is Marifeli Pérez-Stable, a professor of sociology at Florida International University and vice president of the Washington think tank Inter-American Dialogue, who is at the forefront of a generation of Cuban academics who left the island as children and then made it the focus of their professional lives. Pérez-Stable was a supporter of the Cuban Revolution in the early part of her career, but she became increasingly critical in the late 1980s, to the point that the government barred her from returning to the country. In 2003, she chaired a task force on Cuban national reconciliation, and she has authored or edited several books on Cuba. Her *Miami Herald* column on Latin American politics regularly returns to the island.

In her view, the highly polarized politics of Cuba in Miami have not prevented a reconciliation that has taken place in two areas: among Cuban families divided by the revolution and between Cuban exiles and the domestic opposition. "Before 1990, Cuban families were very much divided by politics," she told me, but the arrival of hundreds of thousands of new Cuban immigrants has helped to bridge the gap. "Miami used to see itself as the protagonist of Cuba's future, and there are outliers who still think that, but I don't think for the most part that is the case. And that has meant that between Cuban political Miami and the opposition in Cuba there are all sorts of connections, and that has been good." She saw the process of family reunification as being well under way. "The Cuban government politicized the family, and on the other side of the Florida Straits, the response was in kind. That's a failure, but progress has been made. Ordinary people whose names we don't know have said family is more important than politics. That's an important step moving forward."

Pérez-Stable did not foresee immediate change on the horizon, although she predicted that change would come eventually: "Sooner or later, things in Cuba will start changing, and once that happens, the hard-liners on both sides will just have to run and see how they can keep the polarization going." But she envisioned a fierce battle to preserve the status quo breaking out both in Miami and Havana. "The hard-liners in the Cuban government, they won't scream in public, but if things start rolling, then they will try, as Fidel has done many times in the past, to slow it down or abort it. But the Lincoln Diaz-Balarts and others will scream their heads off in Miami, because reasonable people will see that you have to take little steps before you can take big steps. Miami is moving, and Cuba is as well, except we don't know fully about it yet." She added, "I think that the hard-liners who retain the hard line may find the ground shifting from under them." Indeed, the political terrain on Cuba is already shifting under the shady palm fronds in Miami, and Fidel Castro's resignation will undoubtedly lead to further changes. For the moment, however, the fate of the U.S. embargo relies on the political muscle of those who defend it—and the degree to which they can retain their influence over Cuba policy in Washington remains a pivotal factor.

CHAPTER 6

Capitol Punishment

Lincoln Diaz-Balart was born in Havana but now spends his days shuttling between his adopted hometown of Miami and his Capitol Hill office in Washington, D.C. He was first elected to Congress in 1992, shortly after the fall of the Berlin Wall and the collapse of the Soviet Union heralded dramatic change in Cuba. A lawyer by training, Diaz-Balart has been a strong advocate for U.S. efforts to destabilize Fidel Castro, such as aid to dissidents and funding for Radio and TV Martí. He was a key author of legislation to codify the sanctions on Cuba into law, and he has kept constant vigil to squelch any potential thawing of relations between the U.S. and Cuban governments. Diaz-Balart has lost many battles over Cuba policy, including most notably the Clinton administration's decision to return Elián González to his father in Cuba in 2000. But he has arguably won more than he has lost, and he continues to win the biggest battle of all, which is maintaining the U.S. embargo of Cuba.

Of course, this has not been a single-handed effort. Diaz-Balart is one of six Cuban Americans serving in Congress, including five who were born in Cuba. He is not the longest-serving Cuban American (his House colleague Ileana Ros-Lehtinen was elected four years earlier) nor the highest-ranking (Florida's Mel Martinez won a Senate seat in 2004 and was joined by New Jersey's Robert Menendez two years later). Maintaining the pressure on Castro has been a bread-and-butter issue for this elite group of Cuban exiles. To achieve their goals, they have actively forged alliances with other members on Capitol Hill by appealing to their anticommunism, democratic idealism, political opportunism, or deep sympathy for the plight of Cuban exiles—or some combination of all of these. But Diaz-Balart has brought a single-minded passion to the issue of Cuba, and a vitriolic distaste for Castro, that even some of his fellow Cuban American colleagues have difficulty rivaling. Moreover, his support was crucial to his younger brother Mario's 2002 election to the House of Representatives, which made the Diaz-Balarts one of three pairs of siblings sitting in Congress today.

Although there is no mention of this in their official bios, journalistic accounts of the Diaz-Balart brothers unfailingly note that they hold an unlikely relation to Castro, as nephews by marriage. Their aunt, Mirta Díaz-Balart, was Castro's first wife, and Castro's eldest son, a Havana nuclear engineer named Fidel Castro Díaz-Balart, is their first cousin. Their father, Rafael Díaz-Balart, was a prominent politician in Cuba during the Batista era and remained a fierce opponent of Castro throughout his life. The family was visiting Paris when Castro first took power in January 1959, and they never returned to Cuba, instead settling in South Florida.

Lincoln Diaz-Balart is now in his mid-fifties, but his views on Cuba policy have not mellowed with age. In a conversation in his Capitol Hill office a year after Castro gave up power on a provisional basis, he described how his initial excitement about Castro's illness gave way to a reluctant acceptance that his ailing nemesis had managed to postpone his date with the grave. On July 31, 2006, Diaz-Balart was alerted by a member of his staff to watch the announcement about Castro's health on Cuban television. "Obviously, anytime you're dealing with such a closed state, it's not possible to know actually what the facts are," he told me. "But yes, there was a lot of hope at that time. Then we saw as the weeks progressed, and the months progressed, that the physical process that he was going through, while it had been very serious, it had not ended his life. Many of us had hoped that death was imminent. I think that we realize now that he apparently overcame the very severe crisis, and so death was not imminent." Despite that disappointment, however, Diaz-Balart did see a bright side: "Before that moment, many had thought that he could live for a long, long time—ten or twenty years, or more. After that incident, it is fairly evident that his death will not take that long."

Diaz-Balart fundamentally rejects the notion that Cuba's communist government can survive Castro's death. His father, Rafael, often said that after Castro's demise, "the Cuban regime would dissolve like a sugar cube in a glass of water." The congressman holds fast to this view. "This is the Fidel Castro regime, and it is absolutely personal," he argued. "It is impossible to transmit to others the kind of absolute personal power in the context of how he obtained it, and how he has exerted and executed that personal power. There has not been a decision in the last forty-eight years plus that has not been made by him. Now when he got very ill, he delegated some tasks and the daily maintenance of the repression to others, but the source of power for the regime, without any doubt, is the existence of Fidel Castro." Diaz-Balart quoted the Cuban dissident Héctor Palacios, who had just been released from prison, as saying that "neither Fidel Castro has left nor has Raúl Castro arrived," and then he leaned forward to emphasize the point. "I don't think Raúl Castro can arrive, because Raúl Castro as people think of Raúl Castro does not exist. People think of Raúl Castro as a continuation of his brother. That does not exist . . . That's not possible."

In Washington political circles, Diaz-Balart is known for his fire-breathing opposition to any loosening of U.S. sanctions on Cuba and his intense focus on undermining the Castro regime. He is a man whose reputation precedes him, and in person he is sharp-witted, courteous, and engaging—but also unyielding. In a wide-ranging conversation on Cuba, he dismissed concerns about violence in post-Castro Cuba: "The violence is now. There can be no more violence than the violence that is occurring daily against the Cuban people." He anticipated a bright future for the Cuban dissidents: "Their numbers will grow. They will join with people who return from exile and be a base from which political parties will come." He equated Castro with a mob boss: "He has the instincts of a gangster. Fidel Castro, remember, is an Al Caponist. That's his only ideology. He is a Mafia don who knows how to blackmail." Diaz-Balart described Castro's Cuba as an urgent asymmetrical threat to U.S. interests: "It's a terrorist state . . . He hates the United States, and he wants to hurt the United States. He serves really as a brain for the anti-American community. Yes, he's a dangerous person ninety miles away." And Diaz-Balart firmly supports the U.S. ban on travel to Cuba, including the new restrictions implemented in 2004, which he approvingly cited as reducing Cuban American travel by 70 percent: "It's not travel to and from Costa Rica. It's travel to an enemy, a totalitarian dictatorship, so we have to be very cognizant, and we have to make sure we inspect people coming and going very carefully."

In the waning days of the Bush administration, there was very little daylight between U.S. government policy toward Cuba and the beliefs espoused by Diaz-Balart and echoed by his other hard-line Cuban American colleagues in the halls of Congress. Most important, his presence in Congress refutes the argument that Miami's Cuban American community is beginning to tilt toward engagement with Cuba. Diaz-Balart represents Florida's 21st Congressional District, which winds through Miami-Dade County in the shape of a question mark. But he has no doubts about where the voters in his district stand on Cuba policy, including the new arrivals from Cuba whom others have identified as a potential voice for change: "Those are much stronger supporters and the people that I have the most affinity with. Polling reflects it." He cited a poll taken before his successful reelection campaign in the fall of 2006: "We found the more recent the arrival, the more support for Diaz-Balart. What it means is not for me personally, but what I stand for . . . I mean, they've been wonderful."

In 2008, however, Diaz-Balart was gearing up for his toughest reelection fight in the fifteen years since he arrived in Congress. His opponent would be Raul Martinez, a popular South Florida Democrat and former mayor of Hialeah, the state's fifth-largest city. The fifty-eight-year-old Martinez (no relation to Senator Mel Martinez) was himself a controversial figure. His background included a conviction on extortion charges in the early 1990s (later overturned on appeal).[1] He had a penchant for describing his opponents in vulgar terms, and he was once filmed beating a protester who was blocking a highway. But it was their differences on Cuba policy that seemed certain to generate the most heat. Martinez called for expanding Cuban American family travel, a move Diaz-Balart dismissed as "supporting unilateral concessions to the Cuban dictatorship." The competition was shaping up to be one of the most closely watched House races in the country. A triumph by Diaz-Balart would signal the continued dominance of the anti-Castro hard-liners, but a surprise victory by Martinez could dramatically shift the dynamic of Cuba policy on Capitol Hill.

The U.S. embargo began as a presidential directive issued by John F. Kennedy in 1962 in the wake of the Cuban Missile Crisis. Today, the power to repeal the embargo lies with Congress. Of course, the White House can still set the tone for the U.S.-Cuba relationship, issue or repeal certain trade and travel sanctions, and encourage or forbid U.S. diplomats from meeting with their Cuban counterparts. But in the

1990s, Congress launched a successful assault on the president's ability to reshape the Cuba sanctions and codified many of the embargo's provisions into U.S. law. The results of these efforts have transformed Cuba policy into a complicated legal thicket that neither isolates nor engages with the country effectively. In the process, Congress has put itself in the driver's seat of U.S.-Cuba policy and made Capitol Hill the place where most of the action is—or isn't.

When the collapse of the Soviet Union deprived Cuba of billions of dollars in annual subsidies, Cuba's teetering economy prompted congressional hard-liners—with support from Cuban Miami—to tighten the screws even further. Throughout much of the 1990s, congressional debate was polarized between anti-Castro hard-liners who advocated tightening sanctions to hasten the collapse of Cuban communism and "normalizers" who believed that establishing economic and diplomatic ties was the best way to bring about change in Cuba. At first, the hard-liners held sway, as illustrated by the two main pieces of legislation dealing with U.S.-Cuba policy enacted after the cold war: the Cuban Democracy Act of 1992 and the Helms-Burton Act of 1996. The latter bill was signed by President Bill Clinton, who certainly had no love for Castro, whom he partially blamed for his loss of the Arkansas governorship in 1980 after only one term in office. (The state reluctantly hosted thousands of Cuban refugees who later rioted and left Clinton with a political black eye.)

More than any other single legislator, it is the specter of the late Jesse Helms that continues to linger over U.S.-Cuban relations. Helms, the archconservative five-term senator from North Carolina, retired from the Senate in 2002 following six years as the chairman of the influential Senate Foreign Relations Committee. During his time in office, Helms was an unabashed supporter of sanctions toward Cuba, and in his memoir he describes the Helms-Burton Act as "tightening the noose around the neck of the last dictator in the Western Hemisphere—Fidel Castro" and cites it among his most important foreign policy accomplishments. Helms's ideas also took root in the executive branch when President George W. Bush came into office and recruited many of the senator's top aides to positions with authority over Cuba policy. When Fidel Castro oversaw the smooth transfer of power to his brother Raúl in early 2008, it became evident that Helms-Burton had had little impact on the Cuban succession but had indeed tightened the noose on the United States' ability to respond intelligently to change in Cuba.

At the time of its passage, the law was chiefly criticized for its extraterritorial provisions that allowed Cuban exiles to sue in U.S. courts for properties they had lost in Cuba, and measures that targeted European companies for "trafficking" in expropriated properties and denied U.S. visas to their executives. Today, it is perhaps more relevant that Helms-Burton says that ending the American embargo can only occur if there is a transitional government in Cuba that meets more than a dozen specific criteria, including legalizing political activity, releasing political prisoners, and organizing free elections. Most pertinently, the law mandates that the president can only consider a government in Cuba to be transitional if it "does not include Fidel Castro or Raúl Castro." When Fidel Castro officially retired on February 24, 2008, the occasion was highlighted by Jesse Helms's hometown newspaper. Noting that the eighty-one-year-old Castro was sidelined by intestinal illness and the eighty-six-year-old Helms was suffering from vascular dementia, an article in the *Charlotte Observer* ran with the headline "Old Foes Helms, Castro Are Out, but U.S.-Cuba Rancor Goes on Unabated." Helms later died on July 4, but the embargo he championed remained as immovable as ever.

Indeed, the consistent White House support for the Cuban embargo reflects the fact that Florida has emerged in recent years as a tightly contested swing state in presidential elections. Despite differing on the details, all major presidential candidates since 1992—George H. W. Bush, Bill Clinton, Bob Dole, Al Gore, John Kerry, George W. Bush, John McCain, Hillary Clinton, and Barack Obama—have supported continuing the sanctions against Cuba. But less than four years after the passage of the Helms-Burton Act, the specter of normalizing relations with Cuba began stalking the halls of Capitol Hill—under a Republican Congress, no less. This sudden flip-flop occurred when the Elián González crisis overlapped with a heated congressional vote on trade relations with the People's Republic of China in the spring of 2000. The juxtaposition highlighted the awkwardness of U.S.-Cuban relations at a moment when President Clinton and the Republican leadership were making an aggressive push to pass a bill to normalize trade relations with China. The arguments in favor of engaging with this communist state gave many congressional members ideological whiplash when juxtaposed with the U.S. policy of isolating Cuba.

Congress approved the China trade bill by 237–197, with support from 164 Republicans, after House majority leader Dick Armey made the impassioned plea that "information is the lifeblood of a market. It is also poison to dictators. If we vote no today, then we will condemn the people of China to a life of despair."[2] In the aftermath of Elián, many Republicans felt emboldened to apply that core political argument to Cuba policy, which split the caucus. The feud between anticommunists and free traders resulted in warring *New York Times* op-eds by Senator Jesse Helms and Representative George Nethercutt of Washington State, who proposed an amendment called the Trade Sanctions Reform Act of 2000 which would allow U.S. companies to make one-way, all-cash agricultural sales to Cuba. The bill passed overwhelmingly in a vote of 301–116, and Clinton signed it into law before leaving office.

When Bush came into office in 2001, the White House started to shut down any lingering avenues for engagement with Cuba at a time when the congressional debate was heating up. That November, the commencement of food trade with Cuba piqued the interests of business groups, while new Republican congressmen like Jeff Flake of Arizona led a charge against the travel ban. In three successive years, Flake succeeded in passing an amendment in the House of Representatives to halt enforcement of the travel ban. The Senate followed suit in October 2003 in a vote of 59–36, a surprise decision that indicated Jesse Helms's retirement might have opened the door for change. All provisions challenging the Cuban embargo were stripped out of the final legislation under the watchful eye of Texas Republican Tom DeLay, the House majority leader nicknamed "the Hammer," who sided wholeheartedly with Miami's Cuban American Republicans. To many observers, though, it seemed that Congress was coming tantalizingly close to lifting the travel ban—the step most likely to lead to unraveling the entire embargo.

In 2004, however, the air went out of the balloon. Bush was locked in a tight reelection race, and the administration put extreme pressure on the House to shelve the debate on Cuban travel. Anti-Castro hardliners in Congress formed a Cuba Democracy Caucus to beat back any proposals that emerged from the pro-engagement Cuba Working Group, chaired by Flake. Then the November elections ushered in one of the most conservative Congresses in recent memory, which included the first-ever Cuban American senator, Florida's Mel Martinez. The next two years were an unadulterated bloodbath for any attempts to loosen Cuba policy. In 2005 and 2006, the House rejected numerous proposals to moderate the Cuban embargo that would have easily passed during Bush's first term. Almost overnight, the House of Representatives had transformed from an incubator of moderate proposals on Cuba policy into a graveyard littered with rejected ideas. Only the distant dream of a Democratic Congress could put change back on the agenda.

In November 2006, the impossible happened: The Democrats seized control of both houses of Congress for the first time since 1994. The Republicans were severely punished at the ballot box, hampered by Bush's withering poll numbers, a series of corruption scandals, and the political implosion of Florida representative Mark Foley over his sexual advances toward underage male pages. The Democrats won an overwhelming 233–202 victory in the House of Representatives and elevated California representative Nancy Pelosi to the position of Speaker of the House. They also emerged with a one-seat margin of victory in the Senate and ratified Nevada's Harry Reid as Senate majority leader.

Even before the 110th U.S. Congress convened, the congressional opponents of the U.S. embargo swung into action. In January 2007, Jeff Flake, and his fellow representative Massachusetts Democrat Bill Delahunt, led a ten-member bipartisan delegation to Cuba to meet with top government officials and prepare a new legislative onslaught. New York Democrat Charles Rangel emerged from a long wilderness as the ignored ranking minority member on the House Ways and Means Committee to seize the chairmanship of one of the most powerful bodies on Capitol Hill. Within weeks, the newly Democratic Congress was abuzz with legislative proposals to dramatically reshape the U.S. relationship with Cuba: the Export Freedom to Cuba Act, the Cuban-American Family Rights Restoration Act, the Free Trade with Cuba Act, the Cuban Reconciliation Act, and the Agricultural Export Facilitation Act. But as the weeks dragged into months, and the months dragged into years, most of these bills remained bottled up in committees, unable to even reach a floor vote. Against great odds, the political circumstances in both the United States and Cuba had dramatically changed: The Democrats had taken over Congress, and

Fidel Castro had abdicated power in Cuba. But the U.S. embargo would not perish so easily.

Capitol Hill has long been divided over the U.S. embargo of Cuba, and these divisions have sharpened in recent years. When President Bill Clinton signed Helms-Burton into law in 1996, it was predicted that the bill would hasten the demise of Cuban communism. Its harsh provisions tightened the sanctions on Cuba and forbade the United States from recognizing a government led by either Fidel or Raúl Castro. Now that Fidel had let go of the reins of power, many in Congress were seriously questioning the wisdom of remaining on the current course of isolating the successor government. At the same time, embargo supporters had regrouped to fight their case effectively under Democratic leadership and had established important alliances with power brokers in both parties. While several senators remained active in trying to overhaul Cuba policy, especially with regard to expanding agricultural trade, the deepest and most significant clashes on the sanctions were occurring in the 435-member House of Representatives. This body contains the fiercest advocates on both sides of the Cuba issue and also wields power over the purse strings of the federal government, because it originates the appropriations bills that set out how billions of dollars in funds are spent each year.

In the year after Castro's initial illness, I set out to take the pulse of the U.S.-Cuba debate on Capitol Hill by meeting with a number of legislators deeply involved with Cuba. In addition to Lincoln Diaz-Balart, I met with Indiana Republican Dan Burton and Arizona Republican Jeff Flake, the conservative with a libertarian streak who was one of the embargo's most vocal opponents. On the Democratic side of the aisle, my conversations included Bill Delahunt of Massachusetts, the passionately liberal Maxine Waters of California, José Serrano of New York, and Debbie Wasserman Schultz of Florida, who had emerged as a key ally of the Cuban exile community. In these and other meetings, a portrait of Congress emerged that showed how far Capitol Hill remained from leading a major change in U.S. policy unless it faced a galvanizing external event that would force it into action.

Burton, who coauthored the Helms-Burton Act with Jesse Helms, still remains actively engaged in Latin American affairs through his position on the Foreign Affairs Committee. A deeply conservative Republican, Burton is a hale and hearty seventy-year-old who has represented Indiana's 5th Congressional District for more than a quarter century. In a conversation with me outside the Capitol's Rayburn Room between votes, Burton made it clear that he had no regrets about the 1996 bill that bears his name: "It was designed to put pressure, economic pressure, on Fidel Castro. I think it's had some effect. But he has such an iron grip on the island that anyone who takes issue with him ends up in a gulag, or worse. It has not had every desired result that I would have liked, which would have been the removal of Castro and a democracy formed there. But I think it was a positive step. I don't think you can bargain with Fidel Castro. I think what you do is just try to figure out every way you can to put pressure on them to bring about change. Anything more would require strong action, maybe military." Now that Castro had fallen ill, Burton sensed there might be change in the air. "The feeling among the Cuban Americans with whom I've talked about this issue is that Raúl Castro, by himself, can't keep power. He doesn't have the charisma or the support that Fidel does. Now that's what I've been told. Maybe that's wishful thinking on their part, but that's what they think."

Burton recognized that not everything had panned out the way he had anticipated following the passage of Helms-Burton. "There's some unforeseen things that have happened. First of all, I don't think anybody believed Castro would last this long. Second, we felt that if he left the scene, there would be movement towards democracy and that we would see a democratic and free Cuba. Third, I don't think anyone perceived that somebody like Hugo Chávez would take over in Venezuela, especially at a time when oil was so necessary." Burton saw the recent leftward tilt in Latin America as an extremely worrying trend. "We are in a battle with the leftists. Not only in Cuba, but throughout Central and South America. Nicaragua has gone back to the left with Daniel Ortega, [Evo] Morales has taken over in Bolivia, Castro is still in Cuba, and Hugo Chávez is the big, unforeseen element in Venezuela. I wouldn't want to change anything at this time, because it's a fluid situation." Indeed, Burton bristled at my suggestion that the United States should consider adopting a more flexible approach toward Cuba. "It sounds like to me that you think we should open up our policy with Cuba; at least that is the tone of your questions. Let me just say that I am not for changing anything right now. And neither is President Bush."

In recent years, however, many of the toughest challenges to the Cuban embargo have emerged from within the Republican Party itself. In particular, Congressman Jeff Flake's frontal attack on U.S. policy toward Cuba has earned him a strange breed of success that may only be possible in the halls of Congress. As a freshman member in 2001, he set his sights on lifting the travel ban and authored an amendment to prevent the U.S. government from penalizing any American citizen who traveled to Cuba. The Republican-controlled House of Representatives passed the measure overwhelmingly in a vote of 240–186, but the leadership of his own party blocked it from reaching the president's desk. The pattern repeated itself twice more in 2002 and 2003, but the growing support for the "Flake Amendment," as it was known, infuriated the Cuban American lobby and prompted a massive effort to counter Flake's growing influence in Congress. A fresh-faced Republican in his mid-forties who was raised on an Arizona ranch, Flake temporarily electrified the debate on U.S.-Cuba policy on Capitol Hill, but his early efforts to tear down the travel ban have become the legislative equivalent of tilting at windmills.

Jeff Flake's blond good looks and easygoing manner belie his penchant to taking on tough fights. His caustic criticism of the congressional tendency to earmark funds—often called "pork"—for pet projects in home districts has alienated many members of Congress and even gotten him kicked off key committee assignments. He clearly relishes challenging the anti-Castro lobby on Cuba policy, although he has taken steps to deflect their criticism. He has traveled to Cuba five times but never met with Castro, saying, "It's just too easy for those who are on the other side of me on this issue to say, 'Flake's down there, he's just wowed by Castro's star power.' I don't want to give them an easy thing there." A father of five who once served as a Mormon missionary in Africa, Flake has developed a series of ready responses to his opponents on Cuba policy. When accused of sipping *mojitos* on the beach, he replies, "Well, they'd better be virgin *mojitos*, since I don't drink alcohol." He often quotes former Polish labor leader Lech Walesa as saying that the United States keeps the embargo only to preserve the "museum of socialism" in its backyard. When asked how his Arizona constituents feel about his high-profile opposition to the embargo, he quips, "I've polled all three Cuban Americans in my district, and they're just fine with it."

Flake expressed his distaste for Cuba policy in clearly conservative terms: "It just always struck me as an inconsistency in Republican foreign policy. We're all about openness and contact and commerce and exchange, and yet when it comes to Cuba we've preached the opposite. I would argue that the embargo is not an anticommunist position. Ever since the Soviet Union pulled out, I don't know how with a straight face you can justify our policy there without simply conceding that it's a sop to politics in Florida." The policy of "regime change" toward Cuba, he said, was doomed to fail. "It's a policy to isolate and try to starve out the Cuban regime. The problem is, even if we succeeded in cutting off all revenue from travel and remittances, it is still insufficient to bring down the regime, particularly with the economy in Cuba humming along, according to their estimates at twelve percent [GDP growth] and according to our own at about seven percent. Either way, the notion that we're going to succeed in bringing them down economically is just farcical." He shook his head. "I always say that if somebody's going to restrict my travel, it should be a communist. It's not befitting our government."

Flake targeted the Colin Powell–chaired Commission for Assistance to a Free Cuba for particular scorn. "It would be easy to dismiss it as just irrelevant and a nuisance, but it's worse than that. It's an area where we've been very counterproductive. Fidel Castro is very adept at taking what we do here and distorting it, fashioning it to his own use. With that commission and the documents that it has produced, he doesn't have to. When you go to Cuba, you'll find billboards with exact quotes from the commission report, talking about property issues. Basically, he's been able to scare people to death about what will happen to the apartment that they've been in for the past twenty years. So the commission is not just irrelevant. It's really detrimental, because it plays so well into their propaganda." In fact, Flake said, he found a lot of support for his positions within the State Department even as it was tightening the screws on Cuba. "I'll be pulled aside quite often by career foreign service officers who agree with where I am trying to go on Cuba because they are frankly quite embarrassed. They won't say this publicly, they are good soldiers on this, but it does eat at them that the kind of diplomacy that we have with Cuba is really sophomoric."

In January 2007, when Flake and Bill Delahunt led their ten-member congressional delegation to the island in an effort to meet with Raúl Castro and other top Cuban officials, Raúl rebuffed the meeting, which Flake found to be significant: "The official government line was Fidel doesn't have cancer, his condition isn't terminal, and he will be back. They all said the same thing. I think a meeting with Raúl would have been contradictory to that by suggesting the Fidel era is gone, and they didn't want to go there yet. The meetings with the others, like Ricardo Alarcón and Felipe Pérez Roque, frankly they're always guarded. But they seemed more guarded than usual to me. It seemed almost as if they were auditioning for a role in the new regime. It's a sensitive time, so they were extra-cautious."

Flake expected that there would be change in Cuba, but that it would unfold very gradually. "I think change is going to be slower than most people think. We've been led to believe by those who favor the status quo that there will be one event—Fidel's death, really—that will trigger free and fair elections, the release of political prisoners, free markets. I think it's going to be slower than that." But he thought that the U.S. policy debate on Capitol Hill was likely to experience a rapid transition that would make it easier to lift the travel ban. "If something were to happen to Fidel, then certainly I think the momentum would shift quickly. There are so many members who have a voting record built over the last decade or two, that it would simply look inconsistent if they were to change course now. If we have an event like Fidel's passing, even though Raúl is pretty much in charge and little will have changed in Cuba, a lot of members will finally feel that albatross is no longer around their neck and say, 'Let's have a more rational policy.' They'll look for any excuse to have a more rational policy." Flake acknowledged that the Cuba lobby had proved far more resilient than he had anticipated when he first led the charge against the travel ban in 2001. "We had hoped to solve it by now," he said. "But they just don't want to see any camel's nose under the tent here. Any weakening, any softening for them is a big defeat."

Politics makes strange bedfellows, and Flake has partnered with unlikely allies in his effort to dislodge the Cuban embargo, working closely with liberal Democrats like Charles Rangel, and especially Bill Delahunt. A lanky former district attorney in his mid-sixties, Delahunt was first elected to Congress in 1997 and has since taken a wide-ranging interest in international affairs. Boasting a thick mop of white hair and armed with New England insouciance, Delahunt has cut an independent streak in Congress. He presided over a deal for

Venezuela's Hugo Chávez to donate subsidized heating oil to poor Boston neighborhoods and has been a frequent visitor to Cuba. When the Democrats seized control of the House, Delahunt teamed up with Republican Ray LaHood from Peoria, Illinois, to introduce a bill to allow Cuban Americans to travel back to the island as much as they want with all the money they wish to bring. Miami's political circles clucked at congressmen from Illinois and Massachusetts horning in on the issue of Cuban American family travel. Delahunt retorted that his Irish roots gave him special insight into separated families, but LaHood's rationale was more unique: As a Lebanese American, he understood firsthand the impact of travel bans, as the United States had imposed one on Lebanon from 1987 to 1997.

In his Capitol Hill office, which was adorned with nautical charts of Boston-area waterways, Delahunt stretched out with his feet up on his desk and explained his interest in Cuban American family travel. "This is obviously an intermediate step," he told me. "I find restrictions on travel by Americans really antidemocratic and offensive. Yet I think one has to be a pragmatist and examine what the reality is. The Cuba lobby has been very effective, even though all the polling data demonstrate that the Cuban American community is becoming less enamored of the embargo, trade restrictions, and impediments. I think what brought home the absurdity and the pain of this very harsh policy was the restriction of family travel. I think it's created a different dynamic within the Cuban American community . . . I think they know that the current policy has accomplished nothing. Zero. And the continuing direction that this current administration was going has not only accomplished nothing but it's been a negative and impacted people and families in a very cruel way."

When I asked if U.S.-Cuba relations would become more normal when Fidel Castro left the scene, Delahunt replied, "I think it will be less crazy when George Bush leaves the scene." He dismissed allegations about Cuba's bio-weapons programs as "bullshit" and part of the "neoconservative, John Bolton school of intelligence." Delahunt was critical of Castro, describing him as "antidemocratic, as we understand democracy," but he found U.S. policy unjustified. "You know, it has been a repressive regime. That cannot be denied. I have a number of friends within the dissident community. I saw what happened in the famous roundup of the seventy-five dissidents. I condemned that. But is it any better in Egypt? Is it any better in Saudi

Arabia? Is it any better in Azerbaijan, Equatorial Guinea, Ethiopia? Part of the problem with our Cuba policy is that it opens us up to this accusation of hypocrisy and diminishes our credibility."

Delahunt had focused on Cuban American family travel because it tapped into broader changes occurring in Miami, and he thought it was a strategy for building support for change in Congress. Flake thought that the death of Castro could open the door to new policy initiatives. But it soon became apparent that the obstacles to changing the policy had survived and even flourished during the transition to a Democratic Congress. The old bogeyman of Republican leadership had been replaced by people like Democratic Senate majority leader Harry Reid, a longtime embargo supporter, and liberal Democrat Nancy Pelosi, whose opposition to the embargo was dwarfed by her lack of interest in pushing for change. Most critically, hard-line Cuban Americans had been recruiting freshman legislators so aggressively that Flake had been unable to capture many new votes on the issue.

In fact, under the Democrats, the House Foreign Affairs Committee was too stacked with embargo supporters to approve any bold legislation to ease the sanctions in Cuba. Its chairman for Latin American issues, Eliot Engel of New York, regularly accepted campaign cash from the anti-Castro groups. Its top-ranking Republican member, Ileana Ros-Lehtinen of Miami, was the longest-serving Cuban American member of the House. In December 2006, she was featured in a video clip on YouTube declaring, "I welcome the opportunity of having anyone assassinate Fidel Castro and any leader who is oppressing the people." (She initially denied making the statement but later demurred while saying, "If someone were to do it, I wouldn't be crying.") Even Delahunt did not project confidence that his bill would get much traction. "The Cuba lobby has been very effective," he sighed as he stood up and prepared to head out for a vote. "It's all about money. Follow the money."

The Cuban American community's political clout is derived from a number of factors, including political organizations, personal relationships, and effective use of media. What few realize, however, is that the Cuban exiles' vaunted machinery for channeling political donations all but broke down in the early part of the Bush administration. In essence, the anti-Castro lobby was bereft of an effective political action committee (PAC), a vital tool for wielding influence on Capitol Hill. PACs are private groups that are organized to channel funds to political candidates they support or campaign against candidates they do not.

The Cuban American National Foundation had disbursed millions of dollars during its twenty years in existence, but by 2002, its Free Cuba PAC was putting less and less money out the door. Accustomed to spending more than $100,000 per election cycle in the 1990s, it had dropped its expenditures to $36,000 by 2002, then to $22,000 in 2004. By 2006, the Free Cuba PAC was basically inoperative. Meanwhile, the CANF's hard-line splinter faction, the Cuban Liberty Council, had created a Cuba Libre PAC, but it never had more than a few thousand dollars in the bank. By 2003, with support growing for Jeff Flake's travel amendment, leaders in the Miami community realized that it was time to get back in the business of political money.

Sitting in a quiet Chinese teahouse in the Washington neighborhood of Georgetown, Mauricio Claver-Carone outlined the steps the Cuban American community took to reverse its declining influence on Capitol Hill. Claver-Carone is a tall, square-jawed thirty-two-year-old lawyer who serves as the Washington director of the U.S.-Cuba Democracy PAC. Born in Miami and raised in Spain, he studied law in Washington and worked in the U.S. Treasury Department before leaving to help the Cuban exile community pull itself out of its political tailspin.

"It was just one thing after another," he told me. "Jorge Mas Canosa died, then there was this whole leadership battle in the foundation and it imploded, then Elián came. No one emerged as a leader after Elián. The vacuum just kept widening. Then in 2000, the Trade Sanctions Reform Act came, and a lot of our Republican allies started leaving. The vacuum just kept getting bigger. In 2001, Jeff Flake comes to Congress and really becomes obsessed with this issue and brings Republicans along with the libertarian end of this discussion." Claver-Carone paused to sip his tea. "The wave just kept growing and growing. By 2003, on travel issues they came very close to being veto-proof. It was just done. Every pundit and every expert was saying 'It's over.' The administration became completely reliant on the veto-threat strategy. It just paralyzed U.S. policy. It was bad." Worse, in his view, was the fact that new exile groups were promoting a new, more moderate image for the Cuban American community, something Claver-Carone described as "the unicorn that has never appeared."

The U.S.-Cuba Democracy PAC was set up by a group of influential Cuban American embargo supporters to focus exclusively on winning support for their positions in Congress. "We are great at preaching to ourselves," said Claver-Carone. "We sit there in Miami and we hover and we kind of work ourselves up. We wanted to take that message out of Miami—the whole focus was to be Washington." The U.S.-Cuba Democracy PAC would take direct aim at Capitol Hill. "All we care about is the United States Congress, which is where U.S. policy is dictated from, because it is codified into law. So we also needed to educate the community in that sense, because Cubans have this whole presidential thing where they think the president rules the world, right? No! Congress on this issue has, I would argue, greater power because of Helms-Burton. That was an education campaign, and now people realize that."

In the five years since its creation, the U.S.-Cuba Democracy PAC has succeeded by any measure. Between November 2003 and March 2008, the PAC raised $2.1 million and disbursed $1.8 million into hundreds of congressional races. Its collections average about $700,000 per congressional cycle and it was the largest single foreign policy PAC in the country during the 2004–06 cycle. (One obvious point of comparison, the American Israel Public Affairs Committee, or AIPAC, is a powerful lobbying group but not a political action committee that makes campaign donations.) With an estimated four thousand individual contributors donating a maximum of $5,000 each, the U.S.-Cuba Democracy PAC has achieved a broad base in the Cuban American community coupled with effective outreach to targeted members of Congress. The PAC can donate up to $10,000 to an individual candidate, $5,000 each for the primary and general election, and also has unlimited ability to fund issue ads against candidates who favor opening up to Cuba. Claver-Carone added, "We always keep about $200,000 on hand. The reason we keep that money around is that if anyone wants to become the new Jeff Flake, it's a very nice way of saying, 'Hey, there's $200,000 that will go towards commercials against you if you try to do that. So pick another issue.' "

The U.S.-Cuba Democracy PAC coincided with a wave of newly elected members of Congress who were major champions of the Cuba sanctions: Mario Diaz-Balart, the Miami Republican, in 2002; the Democrat Debbie Wasserman Schultz, from South Florida, in 2004; and Albio Sires, the New Jersey Democrat, in 2006. Starting in the 2004 congressional elections, the U.S.-Cuba Democracy PAC backed more than 110 House candidates and 12 Senate candidates, including

Senate Majority Leader Harry Reid. In 2006, it pushed over half a million dollars into more than 140 House races and backed 28 Senate candidates. By the spring of 2008, the PAC appeared to be on track for another record-setting cycle, having already given a total exceeding three quarters of a million dollars to 150 House races and 18 Senate races, even before the general election began in earnest. Sixty percent of those funds went to Democratic candidates. In particular, Claver-Carone believed it was crucial to win over congressional newcomers. "A lot of these people have not heard about Cuba before. It's basically about who gets to them first. It's really that simple: who explains it to them first and from what perspective. After 2000, it was Jeff Flake who got to them first. It obviously wasn't any of our guys." The PAC was important, Claver-Carone explained, because "it allows you to create the relationships before they get to Congress and then continue that relationship. Because if you are a candidate running for Congress, what do you care about? You care about your constituents, and you care about people who can help you raise money. That's just a political reality. We're not discovering the Mediterranean here, you know. Basically, if I'm a nonconstituent and a noncontributor, what the hell is it going to interest that candidate to sit down and talk with me about the issues I care about? Zero."

Mauricio Claver-Carone was confident that the U.S.-Cuba Democracy PAC had played a major role in neutralizing any momentum on Capitol Hill to lift the embargo or otherwise relax the sanctions on Cuba, and it is hard to argue the point. He outlined the PAC's goals in a few quick sentences. "We will not support any economic or political engagement with the Cuban dictatorship until: one, all the political prisoners are released; two, fundamental, basic, internationally recognized human rights are recognized and respected; and, three, until opposition parties are legalized. We're not asking for the world." Indeed, few in Washington would argue with the goals that the U.S.-Cuba Democracy PAC was promoting, but it was clearly asking for more than the new government of Raúl Castro was willing to give. By pressing its case so effectively before Congress, the group was giving new life to a nearly fifty-year-old standoff between the two countries that showed few signs of achieving the desired result of a return to democracy in Cuba.

The Democratic Party has long suffered from a mild form of schizophrenia when it comes to Cuba. Although the initial sanctions were first established by President Eisenhower in October 1960, it was one of the Democratic Party's greatest heroes, President John F. Kennedy, who broke off diplomatic relations with Cuba in 1961 and declared a total embargo in 1962. Fifteen years later, in 1977, President Jimmy Carter oversaw the first major thaw between the United States and Cuba, halting the travel ban, opening respective diplomatic missions in Havana and Washington, and negotiating the release of political prisoners. In the 1990s, President Bill Clinton adopted a tough Cuba policy when it was politically expedient but then opted to loosen the sanctions when he felt he could get away with it. Toward the end of his term, the Clinton administration dramatically expanded legal travel to Cuba, decided to return Elián González to the island, and signed a bill authorizing U.S. agricultural trade with Cuba.

By the end of the 1990s, most Democrats in Congress had adopted the view that the embargo was a failed policy that needed to be over-hauled, if not scrapped entirely. Thus, when Democrats won back con-trol of Congress in 2006, many observers expected Cuba policy to shift in a more moderate direction. But several new roadblocks had emerged on the Democratic side of the aisle. Two Cuban Americans from New Jersey, Senator Robert Menendez and Representative Albio Sires, won positions on their respective foreign affairs committees and used them as platforms from which to fight for the embargo. The U.S.-Cuba Democracy PAC excelled in winning allies among newly elected Demo-crats. Perhaps most critically, the old bulls who had long opposed the embargo, including senators like Chris Dodd of Connecticut and Max Baucus of Montana and representatives like Charles Rangel and José Serrano of New York, lacked a legislative strategy for over-coming opposition within their own party.

Today, strong support for lifting the Cuban embargo can still be found among the Democrats, especially those among the more than forty African American members of Congress. In 1999, when she was the chair of the Congressional Black Caucus, California representative Maxine Waters led a delegation to Cuba that solidified the support of caucus members for lifting the U.S. embargo. Now in her late sixties, Waters first came to Capitol Hill in 1990 and is consistently one of the most liberal members of Congress. In 2000, she became reviled in Miami when she weighed in on the Elián González crisis and actively supported his return to Cuba, a position that she acknowledged to me with a smile. "There was so much press attention to it. I just thought it was a basic issue about the right of parents to lay claim to their children." Waters has supported efforts to overturn the embargo, but she tips her hat to the effectiveness of the Cuba lobby. "The organized Cuban exiles have done a tremendous job in raising money and being involved in the political system. They have had a more consistent agenda, a more focused agenda, and they've spent more time on it."

Hardly a typical Democrat, Waters freely admits that she is a fan of Castro and a supporter of the Cuban Revolution. When I asked her how Congress is likely to respond to Castro's death, she looked pained. "To be honest, I am not psychologically prepared to think about it," she said. "I like Fidel Castro an awful lot, and I have gotten to know him well. I like him and consider him a friend." She viewed him as a capable and charismatic leader. "The first thing you notice about Fidel Castro when you meet him is his eyes. He literally can see, I think, what other people do not see when he's looking at someone. He seems to size people up, to almost get into your head. I think he gathers a rather quick understanding of who you are, and what you care about, and why you're there, and all of those things. It's very, very interesting."

Waters described herself as most interested in the plight of black people in the world and what can be done to give them a chance at a better future. "I think that black people all over the world are in positions of second-class citizenship, oftentimes, everywhere I look. There's so much in the American educational system that I, as a black person, never learned. Every day of my life, practically, I'm learning our history. It's mind-blowing." Waters was inclined to see Cuba as a positive model in some respects, despite all of its problems. "I think that what has always attracted me to Cuba is the struggle that the people of Cuba experienced with the revolution. I'm always interested in the history of countries that have fought off dictatorships of the rich and powerful, and hearing the voices of the people emerge, and how they do that."

She deflected criticisms of Cuba by raising a series of rhetorical questions. "Just as we are wishing for the people of Iraq a democracy, a lot of people are learning it's easier said than done. What do we know about Cuba? Was it supposed to be a transition over time? Was there ever a thought of moving to democracy? Or was the thought that communism works better than a democracy? Now, there's some things about what Fidel has done that you cannot help but admire: the idea of free health care and education that appears to work. I don't try to defend everything about Fidel, because I don't know all those answers. I do know what I like. I like seeing all these people of color who are from all over the Caribbean that are being trained as doctors. I like to see that happen." In Waters's view, "the overall public policy of the United States has just not been very kind to these small countries of the Caribbean. We just haven't thought much about them." Still, she held out hope for better days ahead. "I have been exploring what could be done to lift the embargo," she said. "We've got a lot of potential, a lot of interest, in Cuba that will be realized some time in the future."

Debbie Wasserman Schultz is the new face of the Cuban embargo on Capitol Hill, and her job is to make sure that does not happen. A Florida Democrat elected in 2004, Wasserman Schultz has been cele- brated as one of the few working mothers in Congress, with three children under the age of ten. In her early forties, she is her state's first Jewish member of Congress, and she often speaks about the impor- tance of her faith. During her short time on Capitol Hill, she has emerged as a forceful advocate for the sanctions on Cuba. During a conversation in her office, Wasserman Schultz described to me the epiphany she had when she first learned about Cuban history from her Cuban American colleagues in the Florida legislature. "I really kind of noticed that the plight of Cuban exiles was similar to what Jews went through in the Holocaust, in terms of property confiscation and the persecution of people on the island. And I subscribe to the concept of 'never again' when it comes to the Holocaust, and I believe that it doesn't just apply to Jews."

Wasserman Schultz believed it was a mistake to characterize the Democratic Party as opposed to the embargo. "You have to avoid mak- ing sweeping generalizations about the views of any particular party on our foreign policy approach to Cuba. The overwhelming majority of the Congress, Republicans and Democrats combined, support continu- ing the embargo. Before there is even any discussion about easing those sanctions, Cuba needs to make sure that they make concessions on democratic reform and improving their human rights record." Even with few Cuban exiles in her district, Wasserman Schultz has pledged allegiance to this cause. "You don't have to have a big population in your district in order to be able to empathize with the people who are going through strife like they are," she said.

Members of the Cuban American lobby have described Wasserman Schultz as "our hero," and it's easy to see why. In recent votes, she has lobbied relentlessly to oppose lifting the embargo and to win financial support for Cuban dissidents, sometimes riling her fellow Democrats on the House Appropriations Committee. When she learned that Representative José Serrano of New York was planning to submit an amendment lifting the Cuban travel ban, she lobbied other members of the subcommittee he chaired behind his back, sparking a public feud when Serrano was forced to abandon the idea. He later complained, "You wait years to chair a committee, and once you do, people should discuss things with you and not go around you in a confrontational way."[3] Still, despite all of her advocacy for the Cuban embargo, Wasserman Schultz admits that she doesn't think the policy has shown results. "It's not like I delude myself that the embargo works or that it's brought about tremendous reform on the island. A lot of my support for the embargo and for the sanctions is principle. A relationship with the United States is a privilege, and an economic relationship is especially a privilege. And it has to be earned."

Serrano is a native of Puerto Rico who has represented New York's Bronx borough in Congress since 1990. Now in his mid-sixties, he has been a fierce critic of the U.S. embargo ever since he arrived on Capitol Hill, and his views are emblematic of many senior Democrats who view the policy with scorn. "Democrats, I think, on the whole feel that it's a bad, failed policy that we should revisit," he told me when I stopped by his office. Serrano viewed aid to dissidents as counterproductive: "It's really outrageous that we continue to think that we can go into another country and upset their government." He was scandalized by how the United States has treated accused Cuban exile terrorist Luis Posada Carriles with kid gloves: "It's hypocritical and it's insane. It shows that sometimes our decisions are so bizarre that they destroy the whole notion we're doing the right thing." Despite their shared Latino heritage, Serrano felt little common cause with Cuban exiles: "The Cubans have amassed large amounts of power, economic and political, and they use it for one issue and one issue only, which is their fight against the Cuban Revolution. In the process, they will make life miserable for any other Latino that doesn't view the Cuba issue as they see it, exactly."

Serrano said he looked forward to the day when Americans citizens could travel freely to Cuba. He would like to see the two countries regularly engage in areas ranging from counter-narcotics efforts to baseball tournaments. As a cardinal, or subcommittee chairman, who oversees financial services on the powerful House Appropriations Committee, Serrano has significant clout in the new Democratic Congress, but he did not express much hope that any of these visions would come to pass. "The policy wears you down to where you see some things and you don't even comment on it," he told me. "I think there would have to be some sort of crisis to get people to focus in on Cuba again. Otherwise it will be just more of the same." He scoffed at the suggestion by some presidential candidates that Fidel or Raúl Castro would use any dialogue with the United States for propaganda in Cuba. "You're the U.S., you call the shots. Castro can't use you for propaganda. Not more than he's used you for forty-five years." In June 2008, Serrano won a small victory when he managed to wrestle the approval for a measure expanding Cuban American family travel and easing U.S. food sales to Cuba from the House appropriations panel he chaired. However, the White House was expected to quash the proposal.

Perhaps no member of the House of Representatives has been more frustrated by the inability of the Democratic Congress to change Cuba policy than Charles Rangel. A Korean War vet who has represented New York's Harlem neighborhood for nearly forty years, Rangel became the first African American chairman of the powerful House Ways and Means Committee in 2007. Since the Democrats' victory, he has been reveling in his new status as a power broker on Capitol Hill with oversight over all measures dealing with taxes and trade. As one of the old bulls of Congress, Rangel is a year older than Raúl Castro, and he takes umbrage at any approach toward Cuba that hinges on waiting for old people to die. He has no patience for the Cuban embargo, and he has submitted bills to lift the travel ban, ease restrictions on food trade with Cuba, and repeal the sanctions entirely.

At an event on Capitol Hill that occurred shortly after he became chairman, Rangel took the floor and told an anecdote about a young Cuban American man who stopped him in the hallway and thanked him for his great work. But then the young man added that he disagreed with Rangel on Cuba policy, "because Castro took all the property that my grandparents had." When Rangel asked what property belonged to his grandparents, the man thought for a moment and bashfully replied, "I don't know. And I don't want to talk with you anymore because you're talking me out of my inheritance . . . whatever it is!"

Rangel swept back his gray hair and waited for the chuckles to subside before continuing. "But there's no question that in the past there's been an emotional group of people who love Cuba, who love democracy, that would make the call in the Electoral College vote. Now that's the whole thing. You can hear a lot of verbiage, I can talk to you about all the reasons, but the real question that presidential candidates have is, which way will this community go, and which way will Florida go? Maybe there's going to be a dramatic change. The real question is, what can we do to show that it makes no sense at all, if you are really hurting those people that are for the embargo, as well as those people who truly believe, like I do, that the best way to sell America is to have Americans sell themselves."

Rangel's tone had been good-natured up to this point, but then his raspy voice deepened with real indignation. "*Who can really tell me or anyone else not to visit a communist country?* And here I am with a trade bill, dealing with a billion communists in China, dealing with communists in Vietnam, we've just got finished with the communists in the Soviet Union, so let's not talk about communism! There is so much hypocrisy that drips from this that we owe it to ourselves to try to find out what works. And what works is for Cubans to get to know us, for Castro not to be able to say that every problem that they have comes from the U.S. embargo. Americans should be able to go any damn place they want, any time they want, for any reason they want! And the Cubans still have great affection for Americans. It's amazing how much harm our government can do without shattering the love that other countries have for the American people." Indeed, despite the antagonism between the two governments, Cuban people have maintained an open attitude toward Americans that contrasts sharply with official rhetoric.

But even Rangel, addressing a group of supporters at the height of his powers, was not making any promises about repealing the Cuban embargo. "Passing bills in the House and Senate has never stopped Bush from killing them. It is surprising to me how much this is an emotional issue for him. It's a very emotional issue. It's about Castro. It's about stopping Chávez. Even though this policy has failure written all over it." One man in the audience stood up and puzzled over why Rangel was not convinced that his bills would succeed, telling the congressman, "You are so powerful." Rangel laughed and shot back, "I'm going to take you home with me so that you explain that to my wife. Listen, Cuba is a very emotional issue."

Time soon proved that Rangel's pessimism was well founded. His proposal to expand agricultural trade between the United States and Cuba went down to a crushing 182–245 defeat in the House later that year. Debbie Wasserman Schultz led the charge to coordinate opposition on the Democratic side of the aisle, and sixty-six Democrats voted against the measure, including fifty-two who had received contributions from the U.S.-Cuba Democracy PAC. "I was blindsided," Rangel said upon learning of the defeat. "I don't really think we put up much of a fight."[4] In fact, during the first year that Congress was under Democratic control, the pattern repeated itself in other matters related to Cuba policy. A bill to fund Cuban dissident groups received a fivefold increase to forty-six million dollars and sailed through the House in a vote of 254–170, while modest measures to ease the travel ban and expand trade died in committee or were defeated on the floor.

Even Fidel Castro's formal retirement in February 2008 was not enough to force much change in Congress, whose members responded by holding hearings, firing off letters to the Bush administration, and speaking to the press—but doing precious little in terms of new legislation. Representatives Jeff Flake and Bill Delahunt penned a bipartisan congressional letter to Secretary of State Condoleezza Rice that was signed by more than one hundred members, or nearly a quarter of the entire House of Representatives. Noting that "an orderly succession has occurred in Cuba," it called for an intensive review of a policy that "leaves us without much influence at this critical moment" and "serves neither the U.S. national interest nor average Cubans, the intended beneficiaries of our policy." In the Senate, Montana Democrat Max Baucus and Wyoming Republican Mike Enzi sent a similar letter to Rice, signed by twenty-four senators, that said, "Our policy of isolation and estrangement has failed," and called for a new approach that included greater American engagement with Cuba through trade, travel, and communication. Indeed, it is a safe bet that a solid majority of both houses of Congress quietly agrees with these views, but prefers to stay below the radar to avoid drawing the ire of anti-Castro activists.

In April, even Nancy Pelosi, the Speaker of the House of Representatives, weighed in on the debate, telling CNN, "For years I have opposed the embargo on Cuba. I don't think it's been successful, and I think we have to remove the travel bans and have more exchanges—people-to-people exchanges with Cuba." After the 1996 passage of Helms-Burton, however, the Cuban embargo is the law of the land, and it will be nearly impossible to remove barring a dramatic change in Cuba that forces Washington to embrace the political logic of normalizing relations. Indeed, Cuban American legislators in Congress dismissed any suggestion that Raúl Castro's rise to the presidency should signal a change in U.S. policy. "It's a good day for the Cuban people," said Florida senator Mel Martinez upon learning of Fidel's retirement. "We have one down, maybe one to go." Lincoln Diaz-Balart declared, "As of this time, there has been no change in totalitarian Cuba," and cautioned against changing course. With their continued support of the embargo, this widely maligned U.S. policy is shaping up to be one of Fidel Castro's most far-reaching and enduring legacies.

Besides, while the Cuban succession sparked a renewed debate on Capitol Hill about the embargo, there were other, more pressing factors. The intensifying 2008 presidential elections and the continued presence of Fidel—even if he was no longer formally in charge of Cuba—meant that the majority of Congress felt little urgency to change the policy. Notwithstanding some significant policy differences, especially over the travel restrictions on Cuban Americans, the top American presidential contenders—John McCain, Hillary Clinton, and Barack Obama—had all urged a wait-and-see approach to Raúl's leadership. This gradual approach made sense in the context of American politics, but it would also give the pro-embargo lobby an opportunity to shore up its support in Congress prior to the upcoming elections. Despite new challenges emerging from their Miami-area districts, fervent anti-Castro legislators like Lincoln and Mario Diaz-Balart and Ileana Ros-Lehtinen were all likely to retain their seats in the 2008 vote, although a potential upset, and the political earthquake that this would represent, remained very much on their minds. Still, after nearly fifty years at Cuba's helm, Fidel Castro had finally abdicated power, but the desire to punish the communist government that he left behind remained alive and well on Capitol Hill.

CHAPTER 7

Spy Versus Spy

In the summer of 2007, the Central Intelligence Agency, based in Langley, Virginia, released 693 pages of top-secret documents that detailed the activities of its undercover agents in the early 1970s. Dubbed "the family jewels," the files had remained hidden from public view for nearly thirty-five years, until new CIA director Michael Hayden decided to release the secret dossiers. Hayden, a four-star general in the air force who had taken over the agency in May 2006, described the papers as "reminders of some things the CIA should not have done."[1] But one tantalizing document captured most of the headlines: the description of a CIA plot to pay $150,000 to two Mafia bosses in exchange for killing Fidel Castro in 1960, during his first year in power. The plot began when the CIA recruited a former Federal Bureau of Investigation agent to pose as a representative of international corporations who had lost their gambling businesses in the aftermath of the Cuban Revolution. The ex-FBI agent contacted mob leader Johnny Roselli, who introduced him to two Mafia members who were on the list of "10 Most Wanted" criminals in the United States. The CIA then provided the two fugitives with six poison pills to be slipped into Castro's food. But when several attempts to get the pills into Castro's meals failed, the operation was called off. Not all was lost, however, as the agency did manage to recover the poison pills.[2]

In the context of documented assassination plots against Castro, the new revelations contained in the CIA's family jewels were relatively tame. In the 1960s, Castro was a regular target for elimination by the U.S. government and its allies. An avid scuba diver, the Cuban leader once received the anonymous gift of a poisoned scuba suit. On a different occasion, a plot to hide explosives in a seashell at Castro's favorite diving site was aborted when no shell that was large enough could be found. Indeed, Castro was somehow left untouched by the exploding cigars, poisoned pens, drugged milk shakes, and rocket launchers that were dispatched to hasten his removal from power.

By 2007, Castro was an ailing and enfeebled man who had virtually disappeared from public view, but the Cuban leaders still took umbrage at the latest reminders of U.S. attempts to accelerate his trip to the grave. Just days after the CIA released its family jewels, the Cuban National Assembly passed a resolution stating, "What the CIA recognizes is not old history. It is present-day reality and the facts show it. The CIA documents reveal part of the efforts to kill comrade Fidel Castro and bring death and pain to our people." The Cuban government asserted its conviction that the United States would "keep employing the worst possible tactics against Cuba."[3] In fact, the family jewels incident shed light on one small corner of an intricately layered web of espionage and intrigue that continues to plague both the United States and Cuba to this day. Perhaps a famous quote by the American novelist William Faulkner best captures why the CIA's disclosure of a nearly fifty-year-old assassination plot struck such a nerve in both countries. "The past," Faulkner wrote, "is not dead. In fact, it's not even past."

In December 1990, a thirty-four-year-old Cuban man named René González flew a small yellow plane to Key West, Florida and, upon landing, announced his defection to the United States. His story was barely distinguishable from those of the thousands of Cuban refugees who pour into South Florida each year, and González soon became smoothly integrated into Miami's exile community. By 1994, he was serving as a pilot with the Cuban exile search-and-rescue squad Brothers to the Rescue, which monitored the Straits of Florida for Cuban rafters who were caught adrift in the perilous waters. Unbeknownst to his exile colleagues, however, González also held down a second job, earning thirteen dollars a day for sending intelligence reports to the Cuban government about activities in the Cuban exile community and monitoring air traffic patterns at the Miami-based U.S. Southern Command.[4] In fact, González belonged to a vast network of spies sent to penetrate the inner workings of militant exile groups in Miami.

During the mid-1990s, a series of dramatic events shook Miami and Havana, but two were thrust to the center of an espionage thriller with far-reaching consequences. On February 24, 1996, Cuban MiG fighter jets shot down two Brothers to the Rescue planes that had entered Cuban airspace, killing the four men aboard. All of the dead were Cuban Americans with deep roots in the Miami community, which convulsed in outrage over the incident. The following year, Cuba suffered a series of hotel bombings that injured eleven people and left one dead. In the summer of 1998, the U.S. and Cuban intelligence services appeared to draw closer in an effort to solve that case, as Cuban investigators exchanged information about the bombings with FBI agents.[5] But the initial contacts soon turned sour when Cuba refused the FBI permission to interview witnesses or examine forensic evidence from the bombing sites, and the FBI intensified its investigation of Cuban operatives working in Miami.

The case of the "Wasp Network" broke publicly in the fall of 1998, when fourteen people were charged with spying in Miami on behalf of Castro's government. U.S. attorney Thomas E. Scott declared, "This spy ring was cast by the Cuban government to strike at the very heart of our national security system and our very democratic process."[6] By December 2000, when the trials against the alleged Cuban agents began, five members of the spy ring had entered into plea bargains requiring them to cooperate with prosecutors, while another four remained fugitives from justice. That left just five suspects to face trial. The pilot René González and Antonio Guerrero, a Miami-born janitor at Naval Air Station Key West, were both U.S. citizens. The other three suspects were born in Havana in the mid-1960s and later immigrated to South Florida. They were ringleader Gerardo Hernández, who took control of the spy ring in 1994, his right-hand man, Ramón Labañino, and Fernando González (no relation to the pilot), who operated under an alias. All three were later proved to be Cuban intelligence officers operating in Miami whose work was supported by the two U.S. nationals. During the six-month trial that followed, U.S. federal prosecutors disclosed surveillance data reaching back to 1995 that revealed how the five men used computer codes and high-frequency radio broadcasts to transmit the data that they collected back to Cuban authorities.

In a move that virtually guaranteed them the upper hand but later almost derailed the verdicts, U.S. prosecutors beat back a request to move the trial from the Miami-Dade jurisdiction. They successfully argued that the defendants could receive a fair trial in Miami, brushing aside concerns that the fierce standoff over Elián González had left behind a charged political environment. The eventual federal jury was composed of twelve Miami residents, including five Latinos but no Cuban Americans. In his opening statement, assistant U.S. attorney David Buckner argued that the operation that Cuba had code-named the Wasp Network represented "a sophisticated and highly motivated espionage cell operating in the midst of our community."[7] The most serious charge was leveled at Hernández, the ringleader, who was charged with conspiracy to commit murder for sharing information with the Cuban government about the 1996 Brothers to the Rescue flight that was later shot down. After more than one hundred days of testimony from over ninety witnesses, including FBI agents, U.S. intelligence and military officials, and members of the Cuban exile community, the jury began its deliberations on the complicated case. A *Miami Herald* article at the time predicted that "a quick verdict is not expected."[8] It proved to be a faulty assumption. The jury entered its quarters to consider the evidence on Monday, June 4. By Friday, after twenty-eight hours of deliberation, they had reached a unanimous verdict: guilty.

U.S. district attorney Guy Lewis declared the outcome to be "a sweeping win, a sweeping victory for the United States of America and these families standing behind me," gesturing to relatives of victims of the 1996 Brothers to the Rescue shoot-down.[9] The five Cuban agents were found guilty of twenty-three spying-related charges, and stiff punishment was imposed at their December 2001 sentencing hearings. Hernández, thirty-six, was found guilty of conspiracy to commit murder and espionage and sentenced to two concurrent life terms in prison. Guerrero, forty-three, the naval air station janitor who surreptitiously counted flights, and Labañino, thirty-seven, both received life sentences for conspiracy to commit espionage. Fernando González, thirty-eight, who was convicted of using a false identity, document fraud, and being an unregistered foreign agent, was handed a nineteen-year prison term. René González, the pilot who had cozied up to Cuban exile groups nearly a decade before and was now forty-five, was sentenced to fifteen years in prison on related charges.

In all, the outcome of the case was an unadulterated triumph for U.S. prosecutors and a rout for the Cuban defendants. Even in defeat, however, the convicted agents remained defiant, denouncing their trials as a "propaganda show" and protesting their verdicts as the fruits of "a jury incapable of handing down justice."[10] Their intransigence launched the beginning of a public relations campaign by the Cuban government to cast the men as victims of a judicial process in Miami plagued by an anti-Castro bias and protective of its own. In response, Fernando González justified his spying as part of Cuba's defense against terrorism, saying that "the truth is that Cuba has no other choice but to keep people here. I sincerely trust that someday Cuba will have no further need for people like me."[11]

Castro faced a choice between two courses of action following the verdicts: simply cut his losses and move on, or attempt to transform the case into a sweeping national cause. He chose the latter course, and virtually overnight the five men were recast as national heroes who had sacrificed nearly everything for the cause of defending the island against Cuban exile terrorism emanating from the U.S. mainland. Eighteen months had passed since the Elián González saga had ended with the boy's return to Cuba in June 2000, and Castro was casting about for a new cause that would rally the Cuban public to the side of the revolution. In the faces of the five "youths" given harsh sentences for their efforts to protect Cuba, Castro saw the potential for another public relations victory at home. After the last verdict was rendered, Castro convened a special Saturday session of the National Assembly on December 29, 2001, where he declared that "they have sentenced these extraordinary men who were completing an extraordinary and human mission." Castro intoned that "the political battle has just begun. I emphasize, I repeat: they will return."[12]

The Cuban government then declared 2002 to be the "Year of the Heroic Prisoners of the Empire" in honor of its convicted spies, who became known as the Cuban Five. Billboards were erected across Cuba showing the five men's faces superimposed in front of a Cuban flag, with the tagline VOLVERÁN! (They will return). Their portraits hung in virtually every hotel and government building, and were distributed among the party faithful to be prominently displayed in private homes. The legal intricacies of the case were dissected on Cuban television, and the families of the imprisoned men became national celebrities. The Cuban government published books featuring the men's life stories, and the prison verse of Antonio Guerrero, a manual laborer turned jailhouse poet, was stocked in every bookstore. Top Cuban official Ricardo Alarcón, who played a crucial role in the battle to regain control of little Elián, was tasked with bringing home the Cuban Five. Castro recognized the cause as a battle that the Cuban Revolution could not lose, whatever the outcome. If the men remained locked up in the United States, then it merely proved the nefariousness of the empire. And if they were released, it would represent a diplomatic triumph of stunning proportions.

Instead of galvanizing the Cuban public, however, the case sputtered. Many Cubans who had been genuinely transfixed by the Elián González drama were far less sympathetic to the cause of five mustachioed men, now well into middle age, who were arrested while living the good life in Miami. There were far more pressing concerns at home, such as how to feed the kids and get to work in the midst of Cuba's lingering economic crisis. Moreover, while the Elián González story had had a gripping narrative arc that unfolded over eight short months, the legal wrangling over the Cuban Five dragged on and on with no end in sight.

The fates of the Cuban Five will ultimately be decided by the U.S. Court of Appeals for the 11th Circuit in Atlanta, which itself appears split on the matter. In an unexpected turn of events in August 2005, a three-judge panel threw out the convictions based on the intense anti-Castro fervor that surrounded the trial in Miami. "Waves of public passion flooded Miami both before and during this trial," they wrote in a ninety-three-page decision that was the longest ever written by an American court on the issue of trial venue. Citing "a perfect storm" of "pervasive community prejudice," the panel ruled that Cuban exile groups may have intimidated jurors and that "the perception that these groups could harm jurors that rendered a verdict unfavorable to their views was palpable."[13] The possibility of a retrial outside of Miami electrified the Cuban government, and even drew some interest from a Cuban public otherwise bored with the case, but it infuriated many Cuban Americans. Then, in November, the full Atlanta court overruled this decision and reinstated the convictions. But in August 2007, the lawyers for the Cuban Five were back before the Atlanta judges to argue that their clients were victims of overzealous prosecutors armed with insufficient evidence, a charge that was strongly challenged by the U.S. district attorneys. Judge Stanley Birch, who had previously ruled in favor of the Cuban Five, acknowledged that "this is an emotional case for both sides. We will look at this and do the best we can."[14] Meanwhile, the Cuban government has attempted to publicize the case of the spies, encouraging the formation of more than 300 "Free the Five" groups in the United States, Latin America, and Europe, and attempting to build support for their cause through public events about the case. In February 2008, one such group even rented a billboard on Hollywood Boulevard in Los Angeles to install a sign calling for their release.

Given the fact that the Cuban Five were sentenced after 9/11 and their appeals process unfolded concurrently with the Iraq War, it is interesting to note that Fidel Castro's practice of recruiting agents to keep tabs on U.S.-based exiles is a technique that was also embraced by Saddam Hussein's Iraq. However, U.S. courts have given the Iraqi spies much lighter sentences than their Cuban counterparts. In the wake of the Iraq War, American authorities uncovered evidence that Hussein had sent a number of operatives abroad to gather intelligence on the inner workings of the Iraqi exile community in the United States. In two recent cases featuring Iraq-born U.S. citizens who spied for Hussein, the publisher of a Chicago community newspaper, Khaled Abdel-Latif Dumeisi, was sentenced to three years and ten months in prison in March 2004 for being an unregistered foreign agent, and Sami Khoshaba Latchin, a gate agent at Chicago's O'Hare International Airport, received four years for working as a sleeper agent of Iraqi intelligence when he was sentenced in November 2007. (In a third case, William Shaoul Benjamin was tried and acquitted in Los Angeles in February 2008 on charges of being an Iraqi informant, although convicted on two lesser charges of providing false information to immigration authorities.) With respect to the first two cases, neither of the punishments doled out to these Iraqi spies for Hussein have come close to the lengthy sentences that the Cuban Five received for spying on Miami exiles for Castro.

On September 12, 2007, the Howard University School of Law in Washington, D.C., hosted a speech by Leonard Weinglass, the attorney for the Cuban Five, on the date that marked the ninth anniversary of his clients' arrest. About one hundred people sat dispersed in a large lecture hall to learn about the case. In his seventies, Weinglass already had a long track record of defending liberal causes since graduating from Yale Law School in 1958, with past clients including the Chicago Seven in the 1960s, Daniel Ellsberg's codefendant Anthony Russo in the Pentagon Papers trial in the 1970s, presidential daughter and activist Amy Carter in the 1980s, and death row inmate and black activist Mumia Abu-Jamal in the 1990s. The Cuban Five had become his most celebrated case of the current decade.

Weinglass approached the microphone and flicked back his longish gray comb-over. "This case tells the untold story of the low-intensity war emanating from our shores against a country ninety miles away for more than forty years, about which the U.S. public knows virtually nothing," he began. He described the Cuban American community in Miami as running its own foreign policy in which Cuba was declared "a free-fire zone," and he accused the United States government of failing to quell the efforts at violence and intimidation. "When everything else failed, Cuba sent these five men to the United States to infiltrate exile groups and prevent attacks on civilian targets in Cuba," but, he said, when the United States became aware of these efforts, it resulted in "the first case in the history of espionage charges without a single page of classified documents." Weinglass also decried how the Cuban Five were treated in prison, noting that two of the convicts had not seen their wives in nine years, as their visas to the United States were denied. Weinglass spends a lot of time on the road these days. His clients are now scattered across the country at prisons located in Wisconsin, California, Colorado, Texas, and Florida, while the appeals are argued before the 11th Circuit Court in Atlanta.

Meanwhile, the Cuban government continues to press its case for the five "youths," admitted spies who are now in their forties and fifties, tried and convicted by an American jury. Castro initially sought to make the plight of the Cuban Five an issue so loaded with political meaning that it would rival the Elián González episode as a transformative incident in U.S.-Cuban relations, but it has instead evolved into an obscure case winding its way through the American court system. Today the Cuban Five are less of a national cause than a bargaining chip, as Cuba has repeatedly intimated to the U.S. government that it would consider releasing a large number of its political prisoners in exchange for an American decision to repatriate the five men to Cuba. Still, the case of the Cuban Five offers a potent reminder that the Castro government and the Miami-based exile community remain locked in a high-stakes contest of cloak-and-dagger gamesmanship that is all but invisible to the rest of the United States.

Ana Belen Montes is a slight woman with close-cropped dark hair who recently marked her fiftieth birthday at a federal penitentiary in southern Texas. An American citizen of Puerto Rican descent, Montes was born on a U.S. military base in Germany in 1957, the same year that the successful launch of the Soviet satellite Sputnik sparked fears that the United States was losing its technological edge in the cold war. Montes's family later moved to Baltimore, where she excelled in school and won admission to the prestigious University of Virginia. She later earned her master's at Johns Hopkins University's School of Advanced International Studies. In 1985, she won a coveted job as an analyst with the Defense Intelligence Agency (DIA), the military intelligence arm of the Pentagon, with headquarters at Bolling Air Force Base in Washington, D.C. Demonstrating a sharp mind, keen analytic skills, and an enormous appetite for work, Montes moved steadily up the hierarchy, winning frequent commendations and gaining greater and greater levels of access to the United States' most classified secrets. Initially focused on the Latin American region, Montes began to specialize in Cuban affairs. In 1992, she was detailed exclusively to Cuba, and by the end of the decade she was the DIA's most senior-level analyst for Cuba. In 2001, she won a highly competitive National Intelligence Council fellowship that would have cemented her status as the dominant Cuba analyst with the U.S. government and marked her as one of the brightest stars within the intelligence community.

But Montes never received her promised fellowship. In early 2001, her seemingly impeccable career started to unravel when an internal investigation about a possible Cuban spy in the U.S. security apparatus began to focus on Montes as the chief suspect. By May, the FBI was regularly tailing Montes, and it gathered enough information to file an indictment against her. When the September 11 terrorist attacks placed the United States on the highest possible level of alert, the decision was made that it was too risky to leave Montes at large, lest she pass sensitive information about the Bush administration's response to the Cuban government that could find its way to more dangerous rogue nations. On the morning of September 20, 2001, Montes was arrested, handcuffed, and taken into federal custody. On the day of her arrest, a spokesperson for the FBI's Washington field office declared, "This has been a very important investigation, because it does show our national defense information is still being targeted by the Cuban intelligence service."[15] In fact, Montes had been recruited as a Cuban spy even before she joined the Pentagon during the Reagan administration, and her espionage activities reached back sixteen years.

Former CIA analyst Brian Latell has described the Cuban intelligence services as "among the four or five best anywhere in the world."[16] But unlike other serious examples of espionage, the Ana Belen Montes case never made much of an impression on the American public. This is partly due to the timing of her arrest in the days following the September 11 attacks and her sentencing trial a year later, which was virtually eclipsed in the media by the sensational case of the Washington snipers who were terrorizing the mid-Atlantic region. But many intelligence experts rank her among an elite group of successful modern-day spies that includes former Soviet spies Aldrich Ames and Robert Hanssen, who was later the subject of the movie *Breach*. In some ways, Montes was even more exceptional than other known spies, because she was a woman, and she accepted almost no money for her work. Most dramatic, however, is the fact that she entered the most protected levels of access in the U.S. intelligence community as a recruited spy for the tropical island nation of Cuba.

Of course, Montes was hardly the only spy for Cuba. In June 2000, Mariano Faget, a fifty-five-year-old employee of the Immigration and Naturalization Service, where he worked for more than three decades, was sentenced to five years in prison for espionage. In February 2007, Carlos Alvarez, a sixty-one-year-old professor at Florida International University, and his wife, Elsa, were respectively sentenced to five- and three-year prison terms in a federal plea deal after being accused of spying on Miami's exile community for the Castro government. And there were, of course, the Cuban Five, whose lengthy prison sentences had emerged as a fierce point of contention between the United States and Cuba. But no other recent target of an espionage investigation had penetrated the innermost sanctum of the U.S. government as effectively as Ana Belen Montes.

Montes had been a busy woman since joining the DIA at the age of twenty-eight, because she was working for two very demanding organizations. Established in the early 1960s, and now operating with more than seven thousand military and civilian employees worldwide, the DIA is one of nearly a dozen U.S. agencies engaged in intelligence collection and analysis. The Cuban government's intelligence activities are directed through the Ministry of the Interior's General Intelligence Directorate, which was established in 1961. For most of her professional life, Montes reported to both. During the day she would write U.S. intelligence assessments on Cuba and enjoy virtually unfettered access to a massive intelligence community intranet that pooled data from the CIA, the DIA, the FBI, the National Security Agency, and the State Department's Bureau of Intelligence and Research. She even participated in an interagency group called the Hard Target Committee that discussed U.S. operations in countries such as China, Iran, and North Korea.[17] In the evenings, on weekends, and sometimes over lunch, she was in regular contact with Cuban operatives. The FBI investigation revealed that Montes met with her Cuban handlers more than one hundred times in public at various Washington restaurants. She broadcast signals to them from her apartment at home, from D.C.'s Rock Creek Park, and from outside the shops that line pedestrian malls in Chevy Chase and Bethesda, Maryland. She leaked the names of four undercover U.S. agents in Cuba to Havana, and the agents were fed false information for months before being removed from the island. None were harmed, but all were used to the Cubans' advantage.

Spying for Cuba was risky business. According to the FBI affidavit made public following her arrest, Cuban intelligence services contact their agents in the field by broadcasting encrypted messages at high frequencies that can be received via shortwave radio. The messages are then typed into a computer by the agent, who uses a decryption program on a diskette to convert the random numerical sequences into Spanish-language text. For someone like Montes, who held a senior-level position in a U.S. intelligence agency, this meant double duty. She avoided detection by the United States for years and passed several polygraphs. But she was careless in erasing the traces of these messages from her computer hard drive, and the FBI found messages that Montes had received from her Cuban contacts still on her computer. "You should go to the WIPE program and destroy that file according to the steps we discussed during the contact," read one. "This is a basic step to take every time you receive a radio message or some disk." Other messages gave Montes direction and feedback on her work. Referring to a U.S. undercover intelligence officer in Cuba, one of Montes's handlers congratulated her for "tremendously useful" information about him and wrote that "we were waiting here for him with open arms." Upon learning that Montes was participating in a U.S. military war games exercise in 1996, Cuban intelligence told her that "practically everything that takes place there will be of intelligence value. Let's see if it deals with contingency plans and specific targets in Cuba, which are prioritized interests for us."[18]

Scott Carmichael, an in-house spy chaser for the DIA, later wrote a chatty but vague account of his pursuit of Montes titled *True Believer: Inside the Investigation and Capture of Ana Montes, Cuba's Master Spy*. He first crossed paths with Montes in 1996 when she was noted behaving oddly in the days surrounding Castro's shootdown of the Brothers to the Rescue planes, which prompted a new chill in U.S.-Cuba relations. An initial interview turned up nothing, but Montes appeared back on his radar screen four years later when he learned that the FBI was hunting a Cuban spy within the U.S. government, and this time he did not let her slip through his fingers so easily. One revealing item discovered in Montes's immaculately organized workplace was a handwritten line from Shakespeare's *Henry V* that was pinned to the wall. The phrase read:

The king hath note of all that they intend
By interceptions which they dream not of.

For Montes, Fidel Castro was the king, overseeing interceptions that the Pentagon dreamt not of. Speaking at the American Enterprise Institute, a conservative Washington think tank, after the case became public, Carmichael said, "The Cuban intelligence service is among the most professional and capable in the world. We have to doff our hats at them. They are really good at what they do. They are highly motivated to penetrate the United States government. Why? Because they perceive us to be the greatest threat to their very existence. They have no choice. They have to penetrate the United States government to find out what we're doing, what we plan to do, and how we're going to do it so they can counter our efforts."[19]

Montes, a crucial part of that strategy, lived in an apartment complex near Washington's National Zoo, which was one of several sites where she visited local pay phones to broadcast encrypted messages to her Cuban handlers. Perhaps predictably, since her arrest many of Montes's colleagues in U.S. national security have said that they never liked or trusted her. Brian Latell, who worked closely with her when he served as national intelligence officer for Latin America in the early 1990s, wrote that she was "perhaps the most sour and unpleasant person I have ever worked with, but unfortunately it never occurred to me during the entire time I knew her that she was diligently working for Fidel."[20] Overall, she was better regarded by her neighbors. She had served as president of her building's co-op board and was known to leave her apartment key with hall mates when their own units were afflicted with plumbing problems.

In his investigation, Carmichael found that those around Montes offered sharply varying descriptions of her personality, ranging from cool and aloof to charming and pleasant to manipulative and venomous. At forty-three, she was dating a man in his mid-thirties (another defense analyst) who was known to be outgoing and fun loving, if utterly unaware of her activities. Her family background was upstanding by all accounts, with two siblings employed by the FBI, including a sister who worked in the Miami field office that broke the case of the Wasp Network, which led to the prosecution of the Cuban Five. Carmichael concluded that "Ana wasn't much different from many of the people that you know in your own life . . . Her personality was, like most people's, many-faceted and complex. But never, to my knowledge, did anyone describe her as happy, joyful, or fun. There is a saying in the counterintelligence business: There is no such thing as a happy spy. I believe that maxim applied to Ana Montes."[21]

After spending months in prison awaiting trial, Montes eventually agreed to cooperate with authorities and plead guilty to one count of conspiracy to commit espionage. More than a year after her arrest, on October 16, 2002, she entered the Washington district courthouse for her sentencing. At ten in the morning, she was wearing a long white T-shirt under a black-and-white-striped jumpsuit, but her manner was all business. At her side was her lawyer, Plato Cacheris, whose past clients included Soviet spies Ames and Hanssen, as well as former White House intern Monica Lewinsky. Montes made a brief, unrepentant statement before the presiding judge.[22] Speaking in a calm, clear voice, she began by citing the Italian proverb "All the world is one country" and then continued. "Your honor, I engaged in the activity that brought me before you because I obeyed my conscience rather than the law. I believe our government's policy towards Cuba is cruel and unfair, profoundly unneighborly, and I felt morally obligated to help the island defend itself from our effort to impose our values and our political system on it. We have displayed intolerance and contempt towards Cuba for most of the last four decades. We have never respected Cuba's right to make its own journey towards its own ideals of equality and justice. I do not understand why we must continue to dictate how the Cubans should select their leaders, who their leaders cannot be, and what laws are appropriate in their land. Why can't we let Cuba pursue its own internal journey, as the United States has been doing for over two centuries?" Montes acknowledged, "My way of responding to our Cuba policy may have been morally wrong. Perhaps Cuba's right to exist free of political and economic coercion did not justify giving the island classified information to help it defend itself. I can only say that I did what I thought right to counter a grave injustice."

The justice overseeing the sentencing, Judge Ricardo Urbina, responded by saying it was a sad day for everyone: "If you cannot love your country, at least you should do it no wrong. You decided to put the U.S. in harm's way. You must pay the penalty."[23] He then sentenced her to twenty-five years in prison, to be followed by five years' probation and five hundred hours of community service. Any fines were waived due to her inability to pay, other than a $100 administrative court fee.

Today, Montes still has a strong fan base in Cuba among top government officials. After her sentencing, Cuban foreign minister Felipe Pérez Roque expressed "profound respect and admiration for Ms. Ana Belen Montes," saying that "her actions were moved by ethics and by an admirable sense of justice."[24] The president of Cuba's National Assembly, Ricardo Alarcón, was even more adamant in presenting Montes's activities as a matter of self-defense: "Cuba has the right and the need to defend herself. As a matter of fact, the UN Security Council resolution against terrorism presented by the U.S. calls upon all member states who work against terrorism to share information, to find out about the activities that somebody may intend to do from one country to another."[25] Shortly after her sentencing, the U.S. State Department expelled four Cuban diplomats from the country's missions in New York and Washington in retaliation for the Montes case. More than seven years after her arrest as one of the highest-ranking spies ever to penetrate a U.S. intelligence agency, the conclusions of Ana Belen Montes remain the basis for U.S. threat assessments against Cuba. The full truth of her strange legacy will be kept shrouded in secrecy in the bowels of the U.S. and Cuban intelligence services, while the only person who knows the full story spends her days without apology in a drab federal prison on the outskirts of Fort Worth, Texas. Montes will first become eligible for parole some time after the year 2020, when both Fidel and Raúl Castro will have long since passed into the annals of history.

Even as he approached the ripe old age of eighty, Luis Posada Carriles still had the fire in the belly that fueled his long career of trying to kill Fidel Castro. As a CIA operative in the 1960s, he was among the most militant anti-Castro Cuban exiles, and his commitment to the violent overthrow of Cuban communism has been unwavering during the past five decades. In 1976, Posada Carriles was linked to the bombing of a Cuban commercial airplane that killed seventy-three people, including two dozen members of a young fencing team from Cuba that had just won an international competition. That crime held the record as the deadliest act of air piracy in the western hemisphere for more than a quarter century, until it was finally eclipsed by the September 11 terrorist attacks. The bombing led to Posada Carriles's arrest and conviction in Venezuela, his residence at the time, where he spent nine years in prison before escaping in the summer of 1985, disguised as a priest. In the late 1990s, Posada Carriles resurfaced as the mastermind of a series of hotel bombings in Havana, which injured eleven people and killed a thirty-two-year-old Italian businessman who was sipping a drink at a hotel bar when an explosive device detonated nearby and the shrapnel sliced an artery in his neck. In an interview given the following year, Posada Carriles described the hotel attacks as part of a strategy to disrupt Cuba's vital tourist trade. "I sleep like a baby," he said. "It is sad that someone is dead, but we can't stop. That Italian was sitting in the wrong place at the wrong time."[26]

In November 2000, Posada Carriles once again turned his attention to the task of assassinating Castro. He teamed up with three other Cuban exiles to smuggle thirty-three pounds of C-4 plastic explosives into Panama, apparently with the intention of trying to detonate them near the Cuban leader during a university speech following the Ibero-American summit meeting in Panama City. When Castro caught wind of the plot, he announced that Miami-based Cuban-exile groups had "sent people to Panama with the purpose of eliminating me physically. They are already in Panama and they have introduced weapons and explosives."[27] Prodded on by Castro, the Panamanian police force conducted a sweep to look for the perpetrators and found Posada Carriles and his henchmen holed up at a local hotel, having entered the country with false passports. The explosives were later discovered buried near the airport. This was not the first attempt by Cuban exiles to take down Castro at the Ibero-American summit. In 1997, the U.S. Coast Guard apprehended a yacht piloted by five exiles armed with rifles, night-vision goggles, and satellite navigation equipment who admitted they were planning to kill Castro at that year's summit in Venezuela. Castro was irate when the men were later acquitted by a grand jury in Puerto Rico.

At first, it seemed that Posada Carriles and his crew would not get off so lightly. Panamanian president Mireya Moscoso vowed that the latest band of would-be assassins would face justice in Panama. Rebuffing extradition requests from Cuba, Moscoso affirmed that "they entered our country to commit damage and they have to be judged by our laws. If there is a crime, we must put them on trial. It doesn't matter if they are the biggest of terrorists."[28] While Posada Carriles was by far the most notorious member of the group, the other three had also accumulated impressive rap sheets before their Panamanian adventure. Guillermo Novo Sampol had been tried but acquitted in the case of the 1976 car bomb assassination of socialist Chilean diplomat Orlando Letelier in Washington, D.C. A dozen years earlier he had been arrested by New York police for firing a bazooka shell at the United Nations while Che Guevara was delivering a speech to the world body (Guevara later commented that the attack on the UN meeting "has given the whole thing more flavor").[29] Pedro Remón had spent ten years in U.S. federal prison for a botched effort to kill Cuba's ambassador to the United Nations in 1980. Gaspar Jiménez had attempted to kidnap a Cuban diplomat in Mexico in the mid-1970s.[30] Now in their late fifties and early sixties, they had banded together with Posada Carriles in a final attempt to off Fidel Castro. For the next several years, the controversial case wound through the slow-grinding wheels of the Panamanian justice system. In April 2004, the four men were eventually convicted of endangering public safety and falsifying documents. Posada Carriles and one accomplice were sentenced to eight years in prison, while the other two were given seven-year prison terms. At the age of seventy-six, Luis Posada Carriles seemed likely to live out his last days in a Panamanian jail cell.

In fact, a new chapter in his saga was about to begin. In an abrupt about-face, Moscoso offered an unconditional pardon to Posada Carriles and the three other convicts during her final days in office. Moscoso issued the decision at the end of August 2004 and was immediately forced to dispel suspicions that she was acting at the behest of the Bush administration, saying, "No foreign government has pressured me to take the decision." She was guided, she said, by "humanitarian reasons." It later came to light, however, that three Cuban American members of Congress—Representatives Lincoln Diaz-Balart, Mario Diaz-Balart, and Ileana Ros-Lehtinen—had written Moscoso at least twice about the case in 2003, first asking her to expedite the trial, then reminding her that the Panamanian constitution authorizes presidential pardons. One letter concluded, "We ask respectfully that you pardon Luis Posada Carriles, Guillermo Novo Sampol, Pedro Crispin Remon and Gaspar Jimenez Escobedo."[31] When this letter came to light in 2005, the U.S. legislators explained that they were responding to constituents' concerns over the lack of due process in Panama.

The U.S. State Department downplayed any reaction to the decision, instead deferring questions to the Panamanian government. By contrast, the Cuban government instantly severed its diplomatic relations with Panama and issued a scathing statement, saying that the pardon decision "constitutes an affront to the victims of terrorism and their families, and transforms the President of Panama into an accomplice of terrorism and a responsible party in the impunity of the four assassins."[32] Three of the men were U.S. passport holders, and they promptly hopped on a private jet to Miami, where a hero's welcome awaited them as they flashed victory signs in front of cheering relatives and assorted Castro foes. Posada Carriles lacked a U.S. passport, however, and his travels had not ended quite yet. After disappearing into Honduras and then crossing into El Salvador, the aging terrorist embarked on a secretive journey to the one country where he could find safe haven. In the spring of 2005, Posada Carriles became the first known foreign terrorist to slip over the Mexican border into the United States. Soon thereafter, he could be seen walking the streets of Miami's Little Havana, where his presence was an ill-kept secret that eventually burst into public view.

In April 2005, Posada Carriles applied for asylum and permanent residence in the United States under the 1966 Cuban Adjustment Act, which extends special rights to political refugees from Castro's Cuba.

Fidel Castro waves a Cuban flag before addressing thousands of people at the 2006 May Day celebration in one of his last public appearances after forty-seven years in power. (Claudia Daut © Reuters)

Cuban Americans celebrate the news of Fidel Castro's illness in Miami's Little Havana neighborhood on August 1, 2006. (Joe Skipper © Reuters)

Raúl Castro, now the president of Cuba, looks at his brother's empty chair at a meeting of the National Assembly in December 2006. (Claudio Daut © Reuters)

Venezuelan president Hugo Chávez greets his friend and mentor Fidel in a photo released in January 2007, ending a swirl of rumors that the Cuban leader had died. (Ho New © Reuters)

Fidel Castro welcomes Pope John Paul II in Havana in January 1998 in a historic meeting between two cold war icons that roiled Miami's Catholic Church. (Paul Hanna © Reuters)

Six-year-old Elián González was seized from the home of his Miami relatives by U.S. federal agents on April 22, 2000, which left Cuban exiles infuriated with the Clinton administration and paved the way for George Bush to win Florida, and the White House, later that year. (Alan Diaz © Pool Image/Reuters)

Secretary of State Colin Powell looks on as President Bush announces the formation of the Commission for Assistance to a Free Cuba in October 2003. Powell's reluctant role in tightening the Cuban embargo is a little-known part of his legacy. (William Philpott © Reuters)

Oswaldo Payá, a noted Cuban dissident, holds a copy of his political reform petition known as the Varela Project outside of Cuba's National Assembly. Many of his top associates were among the seventy-five prisoners arrested in the 2003 crackdown. (Claudia Daut © Reuters)

This 1951 Chevrolet truck-raft carrying twelve Cubans was discovered by the U.S. Coast Guard in July 2003, and the decision to sink the truck and return the migrants to Cuba provoked a strong backlash in Miami. (Ho New © Reuters)

James Cason, the chief of the U.S. Interests Section in Havana from 2002 to 2005, fiercely promoted the cause of Cuban dissidents and antagonized the Castro government. (Rafael Perez © Reuters)

The legacy of Che Guevara, the icon of the Cuban Revolution, still sparks fascination and controversy more than forty years after his death. (Oswaldo Rivas © Reuters)

Photographs of the victims of the 1976 Cuban airplane bombing are shown during a protest in Havana after the United States set free Cuban exile militant Luis Posada Carriles in April 2007. (Enrique de la Osa © Reuters)

Cuban students wearing T-shirts with the phrase "Prisoners of the Empire" beneath pictures of the five men arrested for spying on exile groups in Miami. (Christian Veron © Reuters)

When the Bush administration accused Cuba of being a "tropical gulag," the Castro government merely pointed to the U.S. detention facility in Guantánamo Bay. (Joe Skipper © Reuters)

Venezuelan president Hugo Chávez calls President Bush "the devil," and seals his reputation as the chief opponent of U.S. power in Latin America at the United Nations summit in New York in September 2006. (Ray Stubblebine © Reuters)

Senator John McCain, the Republican presidential candidate, advocates a tough approach to Cuba while campaigning in Miami's Little Havana. (Carlos Barria © Reuters)

Democratic presidential nominee Barack Obama speaks to the Cuban American National Foundation in Miami in May 2008. He pledged to engage in dialogue with Cuba and allow greater U.S. travel to the island, but vowed, "I will maintain the embargo." (Carlos Barria © Reuters)

His lawyer said that the claim would be partially based on the fact that Posada Carriles had worked "directly and indirectly" with the CIA over several years to further U.S. interests.[33] Author and journalist Ann Louise Bardach, a longtime observer of Cuban exile politics, noted, "In any other American city, Posada, who is now 77, might have been met with a SWAT team, arrested and deported. But in the peculiar ecosystem of Miami, where hardline anti-Castro politicians control both the radio stations and the ballot boxes, the definition of terrorism is a pliable one: One man's terrorist is another's freedom fighter."[34] Posada Carriles's defenders included Miami real estate developer Santiago Alvarez, who has helped to pay his legal bills over the years. "Mr. Posada has never been convicted of any terrorist act," Alvarez stated. "He's been a fighter against Castro all his life. He advocates violence, but that does not mean that violence and terrorism is the same thing."[35] (Alvarez himself was arrested several months later and jailed for several years on illegal weapons charges.) However, some U.S. officials close to the case, such as retired FBI counterterrorism specialist Carter Cornick, were convinced that Posada Carriles played a key role in the 1976 airplane bombing. "The Cubana [Airlines] bomb went off, the people were killed, and there were tracks leading right back to Disip"—the Venezuelan intelligence agency where Posada Carriles served as a senior officer from 1969 to 1974. "The information was so strong that they locked up Posada as a preventative measure—to prevent him from talking or being killed. They knew that he had been involved. There was no doubt in anyone's mind, including mine, that he was up to his eyeballs."[36]

It had been evident that Posada Carriles was in the United States at least since the date he filed his application for political asylum in mid-April 2005. By May, the U.S. media had begun to latch onto the juicy story of the apparent hypocrisy of the Bush administration's allowing an avowed anti-Castro terrorist to wander the streets of Miami at the same time that it was continuing to trumpet its own war on terror. U.S. officials denied knowledge that Posada Carriles was even in the country and seemed to express little interest in finding out. On May 2, U.S. assistant secretary Roger Noriega said, "I don't even know if he is in the United States," and stated that the Posada Carriles case "may be a completely manufactured issue."[37] On May 17, after weeks of inaction by U.S. authorities, Posada Carriles felt emboldened enough to call a press conference at an abandoned warehouse in Miami,

where he donned a white suit and vigorously proclaimed his inno-
cence. Hours later, he was detained by U.S. immigration authorities at
his home and whisked away by helicopter to Texas to face further
questioning. Less than a year since leaving Panama, Posada Carriles
was about to embark on a new legal odyssey in the United States when
the Department of Homeland Security decided to charge him with
entering the country illegally. During the summer, he continued to
pursue his request for political asylum while battling efforts to extradite him to Venezuela.

In late August, he faced a U.S. immigration judge in El Paso, Texas,
to plead his case. He dropped his asylum claim but eventually won a
ruling that he would not be deported to Venezuela because he would
face a reasonable possibility of torture. But this left the United States
with the quandary of what exactly to do with a man considered to be
a radioactive leftover from the cold war. The governments of Cuba
and Venezuela kept pressing their extradition claims, but to no avail.
Meanwhile, virtually no other country in the hemisphere wanted anything to do with Posada Carriles, who had filed a suit against the U.S.
government demanding his release from indefinite detention. In
August 2006, a year after his initial arrest, Posada Carriles remained
in legal limbo, while the Bush administration's efforts to find him a
new home had turned up nothing. Not only had Canada and Mexico
rejected its requests, but so had Costa Rica, El Salvador, Honduras,
Nicaragua—and even Panama, whose previous government had par-
doned him a year earlier.

Posada Carriles's woes were further complicated by a separate legal
drama. In November 2005, his benefactor, Miami developer Santiago
Alvarez, and an associate of Alvarez's named Osvaldo Mitat were
arrested for having illegal weapons. In the spring of 2006, the two
cases intersected when the two men called on Posada Carriles to tes-
tify on their behalf. He refused and they were found guilty and sentenced to several years in prison. In June 2007, however, Alvarez and
Mitat, both sixty-five years old, won an important victory when they
convinced a federal judge to reduce their sentences after they played a
role in arranging for anonymous individuals in Miami to voluntarily
turn over a massive weapons cache to U.S. authorities. The surren-
dered matériel included two hundred pounds of dynamite, thirty
automatic or semiautomatic guns, fourteen pounds of C-4 plastic
explosives, a grenade launcher and assorted grenades, and four thou-

sand feet of detonator cord. The military hardware was believed to
have been stored in homes and garages across Miami to be used in a
future armed assault on the Castro government. Former U.S. attorney
Kendall Coffey, a lawyer for Alvarez, announced, "I seriously doubt
these were munitions in the hands of terrorists. More than likely, they
were in the hands of freedom fighters for a beautiful land 90 miles
away."[38] The two men were released several months later.

In the case of Posada Carriles, however, a decision to turn over
arms and matériel probably would not have been a smart move.
Moreover, since U.S. attorney general Alberto Gonzales declined to
designate Posada Carriles as a terrorist, his future would turn entirely
on immigration issues. And since the courts ruled that he would not
be deported to Venezuela or Cuba, and there was no other country
willing to accept him, it soon became clear that the case of Posada
Carriles was inexorably leading toward his release on U.S. soil, a path
paved by a 2001 Supreme Court ruling that bars indefinite detention
for foreign nationals who cannot face deportation. Characteristically,
Castro transformed the Posada Carriles case into a national obsession in Cuba, holding nightly television roundtables on the topic and
convening memorial ceremonies featuring relatives of victims from
the 1976 Cubana airliner bombing. The rhetoric surrounding the case
provoked inevitable comparisons between Luis Posada Carriles and
Osama bin Laden. National Assembly president Ricardo Alarcón,
who often serves as the point man on U.S.-Cuba controversies,
declared that "it's as if you were to say to the American people that
country X has found Osama bin Laden, who arrived without a passport or visa, and that he is being held as an illegal immigrant but will
not be sent back to the U.S."[39]

In April 2007, a U.S. district court ordered Posada Carriles's supervised release on a $350,000 bond to live with his family under house
arrest in Miami. In an interview with the *Miami Herald*, Camilo Rojo,
the son of a Cubana employee who died in the 1976 airliner bombing,
plaintively reflected on the outcome. "They freed my father's killer.
Imagine how that feels. We ask: How is it possible for the United States
to be in a global war against terrorism and free a terrorist? Do the
American people know this?"[40] The following month, the district
court judge in El Paso threw out the indictment of Posada Carriles for
deceiving U.S. immigration authorities, ruling that the U.S. officials
who questioned the Cuban militant had used "deceit and trickery" in

their efforts to elicit information from him. Already at home in Miami, Luis Posada Carriles was once again a free man.

When Posada Carriles initially surfaced in Miami in May 2005, Roger Noriega was serving as the U.S. State Department's top official for Latin America. When he initially expressed doubts that Posada Carriles was even in the United States, it prompted some observers to question whether the U.S. government was trying to shield the aging fugitive. When I asked him about the case two years later in the sleek office building in downtown Washington where he works as a lobbyist, Noriega made it clear that sheltering Posada Carriles was the furthest thing from his mind. Indeed, Noriega made the startling claim that Posada Carriles had crossed over to work for Castro. "I have my own suspicions about him, and I think he's been an agent working for the Cuban government for decades. At the very least, he's an opportunist, and the reason I know this is that I think that Castro knew more about where Posada Carriles was than our government did. They could have captured or killed him half a dozen times while he was overseas. They didn't want him. They didn't want to kill him or grab him in El Salvador. They wanted to get him to the United States to create the nightmare that it's created for our system . . . I don't have any sympathy for people that kill innocent people, and in my view a terrorist is a terrorist, and I have great, great suspicions. I think that the record will show, and you will live long enough to see it, that he was working for the Cuban government all along."

Noriega recognized that the Posada Carriles case had snowballed into a fiasco for the United States. "I mean, this has become a real headache for us. And then people being able to say we're sheltering a terrorist. As far as I'm concerned, we ought to put him on a plane to Caracas and let it become Chávez's nightmare." Referring to the 1997 bombings in Havana and Cuba's subsequent failure to catch Posada Carriles, Noriega said, "The whole damn thing was an operation. The whole thing from top to bottom was a Cuban operation." He continued, "Send the old bastard back to Venezuela. Do I care if they torture him? No, I don't. I don't care if they torture him. Or waterboard him. Or drop him in the ocean . . . He's a headache for us. He's a propaganda victory for Castro." While Noriega conceded that "those are just suspicions, and I may be terribly wrong," he avowed, "I have a pretty good gut for this kind of thing, and I have a pretty good idea of who he's working for."

Despite Noriega's striking allegation, the balance of evidence points to the conclusion that Posada Carriles is what he appears to be: a renegade Cuban exile militant engaged in a long, armed struggle against Fidel Castro's Cuba. But whatever the truth about him, he is unlikely to enjoy his quiet retirement for very long, if history is any guide. New legal cases against him stemming from the 1997 Havana bombings or other shadowy events may well surface, and the possibility of future deportation still lingers in the air. In the 1980s, a similar case involving accused exile terrorist Orlando Bosch eventually culminated in a presidential pardon from George H. W. Bush in 1990, due to the intervention of Miami power brokers who advocated on Bosch's behalf. But that is a hard act to follow in the post–September 11 era. In recent years, the conflict around Posada Carriles has surrounded the U.S. diplomatic mission in Havana. The Cuban government erected more than one hundred large black flags outside the mission to protest U.S. efforts to "terrorize" Cuba. (The flags also conveniently block an electronic scrolling billboard that broadcasts messages to the Cuban people through the windows of the U.S. Interests Section.) Outside the building, dozens of people have frequently marched holding large black-and-white photographs of victims from the 1976 airliner bombing, while billboards featuring Posada Carriles and photos of tortured Iraqi prisoners at Abu Ghraib are posted along the Havana seawall, blocking the U.S. diplomats' view of the ocean.

Still, despite his alleged crimes, Posada Carriles is no longer a man on the run. In his poem "The Death of the Hired Man," the American poet Robert Frost wrote, "Home is the place where, when you have to go there, / They have to take you in." Posada Carriles allegedly played a role in the deaths of seventy-three people in the 1976 plane bombing as well as the tourist killed in the 1997 hotel bombings in Havana. He is a wanted man in two countries and a persona non grata in several others. He is unrepentant about the blood on his hands. But this aging assassin has the good fortune to find his home in the United States of America, the country that sidestepped its own war on terror to make room for one last freedom fighter.

The governments of the United States and Cuba have an absolute distrust of each other that has fueled a heavy reliance on the dark arts of espionage and covert operations for the past half century. While the CIA's botched efforts to assassinate Fidel Castro in the 1960s have long since evolved into a source of humor in American popular culture, in Cuba they are still viewed through the prism of a country that sees the United States as a threat to its survival. In more recent decades, the tendency of some sectors of Miami's Cuban exile community to incubate half-baked plots against the Castro government, and then actively shelter the protagonists when the plans inevitably go awry, has added to the sense of crisis between the two countries. Indeed, Castro has gained the upper hand in almost every armed encounter with Cuban exiles from Miami, dating back to the Bay of Pigs invasion in 1961, which he successfully repelled in part because of his mastery of intelligence gathering, which has helped keep him in power for decades.

What makes the Posada Carriles case so exceptional, in that light, is the fact that he has been one of the exceptions: a militant Cuban exile who allegedly succeeded in carrying out at least two operations against Cuba—in 1976 and 1997—that inflicted real damage on the island's interests. This made him a beloved figure among Miami's anti-Castro hard-liners, even though many other moderate Cuban Americans were disgusted by the entire affair. As recently as May 2008, Posada Carriles was the guest of honor at a dinner organized by his supporters in a Cuban American group called the Municipalities of Cuba in Exile, which draws its members from former residents of municipal districts in Cuba. One of the group's leaders, Pedro Peñaranda, explained that the tribute was intended to "recognize Posada as a great Cuban, a man of dignity and decency and a great patriot who has suffered a lot." José Pertierra, a Washington attorney who represented the Venezuelan government in its efforts to extradite Posada Carriles, described the event as "outrageous" and said, "It would be like Osama bin Laden being honored by the Arab-American community."[41] Indeed, there is little question that the Posada Carriles case created a fiasco for the Bush administration. The White House ultimately decided that it would rather treat him with kid gloves and face the charge of hypocrisy than put him on trial in the United States (or more controversially allow him to be extradited to Venezuela) and risk embarrassing revelations and an explosion of outrage in Miami.

The case of the Cuban Five is similarly situated in this context of the low-grade war between Miami and Havana that continues to smolder to this day. Cuba dispatched the agents to keep an eye out for threats to the island that emanated from Cuban exiles in Florida, and when they were caught red-handed, they faced the full brunt of the American legal process, which found them guilty on all counts. Since taking office as president, Raúl Castro has continued to publicize the case of the Cuban Five at home. The call to release the men remains a top goal of Cuba's international diplomacy, but Havana appears to be waging a losing battle on most fronts. In June 2008, the U.S. Court of Appeals for the 11th Circuit in Atlanta affirmed the guilty verdicts of the Cuban Five, including the two life sentences awarded to the ringleader, Gerardo Hernández, and the fifteen-year sentence for René González, the pilot who had landed in Miami so unremarkably all those years earlier. But the court also vacated the sentences of the three other men because it "did not find that top secret information was gathered or transmitted," thus leaving them to await resentencing. Still, there is no sign that the Cuban Five will be released from prison any time soon, especially given the incendiary nature of the case in Miami.

By contrast, the tale of Ana Belen Montes has much wider significance for U.S. national security, because it reveals that even a small, poor country like Cuba can develop the capacity to penetrate the highest levels of the U.S. intelligence community. Moreover, not only was Montes well positioned to shape U.S. security judgments about the island, but she also had direct access to sensitive intelligence information with global significance that could be funneled directly to Cuba. Havana may well have passed on some of this intelligence to any one of a number of countries that are friendly with Cuba and hostile to the United States, potentially including China, Russia, Iran, and North Korea. This goes far beyond the Castro brothers playing footsie with Cuban exiles and reaches to the heart of U.S. national interests. Indeed, some U.S. intelligence analysts now argue that Cuba is building up its capacities in third countries that are crucial to American foreign policy in the Middle East and Asia. In recent years, a small band of Cuba-focused U.S. counterintelligence experts, prodded on by conservative Cuban Americans in Congress and elsewhere, have been advancing the case that the threat posed by Cuba's spying capabilities should be taken much more seriously by American officials. Still, since her arrest in 2001, Montes remains the high-water mark in Cuba's efforts to penetrate the inner sanctum of U.S. intelligence agencies, and her case will continue to fuel the "spy versus spy" mentality that has become a core element of the relationship between the two countries.

CHAPTER 8

The Least Worst Place

The international airport outside of Kandahar, Afghanistan, transformed into a beehive of activity during the hot days and chilly nights of January 2002. This dusty, decrepit city in the southern part of the country had been the last Taliban stronghold to fall to U.S. forces in the invasion that quickly followed the terrorist attacks of September 11, 2001. The United States and Great Britain dropped the first bombs on the country on October 7 in a sustained aerial campaign against Al Qaeda and Taliban targets. In Washington, fears swirled before the invasion that the United States would become mired in a distant, remote land known as the "graveyard of empires," which had a long history of defeating great powers, like the Soviet Union in its ill-fated 1979 invasion. But top Bush administration officials argued that this time was different, and they were right. Within days, U.S. military firepower simply overwhelmed the ragtag Afghan forces. More than 85 percent of the designated targets were destroyed by the third day of air strikes, and Defense Secretary Donald Rumsfeld pledged to continue the onslaught. "First, we're going to re-hit targets," he said, "and second, we're not running out of targets. Afghanistan is."

The Afghan capital of Kabul fell to allied forces on November 12, prompting Taliban fighters to flee in droves. Mullah Mohammed Omar, the country's secretive leader, retreated to Kandahar, which was the seat of the Taliban movement, but the Afghan government was clearly in tatters. On December 7, exactly two months after the United States initiated Operation Enduring Freedom, Mullah Omar fled Kandahar and melted into the ethnic Pashtun area between Afghanistan and Pakistan, where he still remains at large. Afghan tribal forces seized control of the city, while the United States took over the airport and established a military outpost. American soldiers and their allies began rounding up hundreds of Taliban fighters and other individuals believed to be linked to Al Qaeda and the global jihad. The Bush administration was eager to interrogate the new captives without being bound by the Geneva conventions that protect prisoners of war. Scanning the globe for a location where the U.S. military could hold the "enemy combatants" without being subject to either U.S. or foreign laws, the Pentagon quickly settled on an obscure military outpost the United States maintained on the tip of eastern Cuba: the Guantánamo Bay Naval Base.

The Kandahar airfield soon became the jumping-off point for detainees being shipped to Cuba. The runway was repaired and lengthened to a full mile, which enabled it to handle a C-141 U.S. Air Force plane. On January 6, Rumsfeld ordered the commanding officer at the Guantánamo Bay base to build a prison within ninety-six hours that was capable of holding the terrorist suspects sent to the island. The U.S. forces in charge of Guantánamo scrambled to prepare for the arrival of those deemed to be "the worst of the worst." Hastily erected open-air cells, christened Camp X-ray, were constructed with concrete slabs, chain-link fencing, and razor wire. By the second week in January, nearly four hundred prisoners from the Afghan conflict were being held at the Kandahar detention facility, and the improbable across-the-world flights from Kandahar, Afghanistan, to Guantánamo Bay, Cuba, were set into motion.

On January 11, the first twenty detainees from the war on terror arrived at Guantánamo, the founding members of a prison colony that eventually swelled to nearly eight hundred people. They were met by forty U.S. Marines wearing face masks and Kevlar vests, while additional troops with grenade launchers and machine guns cordoned off a security perimeter. The handcuffed captives from Afghanistan were dressed in neon orange jumpsuits and ski caps, with bright blue face masks. Some fell to their knees as they were being frisked, either making a futile attempt at resistance or merely overcome by exhaustion after being chained to their seats for the eight-thousand-mile trip. Already shaved from head to toe for hygiene purposes, the men were photographed, fingerprinted, and interrogated before entering the six-by-eight-foot holding cages that would serve as their new homes. General Richard Myers, chairman of the Joint Chiefs of Staff, fended off queries from the media and human rights groups about the extreme security precautions. "These are people that would gnaw through hydraulic lines in the back of a C-17 to bring it down. So these are very, very dangerous people, and that's how they're being treated."[1]

Rumsfeld first confirmed that the Afghan detainees would be held at the U.S. naval base in Cuba at a Pentagon briefing organized in the waning days of 2001. The hard-charging defense secretary was at the height of his powers, basking in the glow of the successful invasion of Afghanistan and not yet sullied by the mistakes of the Iraq War that was still just a twinkle in the Pentagon's eye. The journalists present reveled in Rumsfeld's deadpan wit, laughing when he sidestepped questions about Osama bin Laden's location by saying, "We do know, of certain knowledge, that he is either in Afghanistan or in some other country or dead." When one reporter pressed him to confirm that the United States would be shipping people from Afghanistan to Guantánamo Bay, Rumsfeld replied, "We are making preparations to hold detainees there. We have made no plans to hold any kind of tribunal there." Another reporter persisted. "Mr. Secretary, you've gotten into trouble every time you've tried to use Guantánamo Bay in the past to hold people for other reasons. Why use it? Why is it the best place? And aren't you concerned that we could have trouble with Castro if we did?" Rumsfeld squinted at the question. "We don't anticipate any trouble with Mr. Castro in that regard," he said. "I would characterize Guantánamo Bay, Cuba, as the least worst place we could have selected."

U.S. Naval Station Guantánamo Bay has been a land apart from Cuba for more than a century. Often referred to by its nickname, Gitmo, it is the United States' oldest overseas base and has been under unrivaled U.S. control since the Spanish-American War concluded in 1898. The current lease agreement dates back to 1903 and has given the notoriously profligate U.S. military one of its few great bargains. The yearly leasing fees for Guantánamo were initially set as two thousand gold coins and renegotiated in the 1930s at a nominal annual sum of $4,085. When Fidel Castro seized control of Cuba in 1959, he declared the base illegal and demanded that the United States leave the island. However, the lease stipulates that the agreement can be dissolved only if both parties concur or if the base is abandoned by the United States. Thus, Washington's continued interest in Guantánamo Bay has sustained the lease despite Castro's frequent denunciations. Each year, the U.S. Treasury Department cuts a check to the Cuban government that Castro has refused to cash since 1960. (He once rue-fully noted that his government deposited the first check it received, in 1959, which he attributed to "a mere confusion.") From time to time, Castro has been known to impress foreign guests by reaching into his desk drawer and rifling through the scores of uncashed checks, fuming with indignation.

Guantánamo Bay's unique legal status made it extremely appealing to the Bush administration as a place to hold captured Al Qaeda prisoners. It was a territory that was legally part of another country, but under full American control for the perpetual future. In their memo from December 28, 2001, two conservative legal stars in the Department of Justice, Patrick Philbin and John Yoo, wrote the justification for keeping the Guantánamo Bay detention facility outside the jurisdiction of U.S. federal courts. The lawyers cited a provision of the 1903 lease agreement that stated that the United States recognized the ultimate sovereignty of Cuba over the lands and waters of the base, but granted the U.S. the right to exercise complete jurisdiction and control over the leased property.[2] The core issue was whether U.S. courts could entertain a writ of habeas corpus, a legal term for an action for relief of unlawful imprisonment, if it came from a foreign national held in Guantánamo Bay. Their answer was no: Guantánamo Bay existed outside the boundaries of U.S. law. The irony, of course, is that the Bush administration could argue its case only by ratifying Castro's position that the naval base was located on land that was rightfully Cuban.

When President Bush came into office, the naval base was doing little more than keeping the lights on. The 2,300 people residing there consisted principally of foreign laborers and included only 500 U.S. military personnel. After the September 11 attacks, its population swelled to 9,500 (excluding the detainees imported from the Middle East) before dropping off again in the past couple of years to about 7,500 people. The sprawling base occupies an area about twice the size of the island of Manhattan or about two thirds the area of the District of Columbia, but its population was never meant to exceed 6,000 personnel, a fact that has led to housing shortages. Today, about one third of the base's current population is foreign workers, drawn principally from Jamaica and the Philippines, another third is civilian contractors and dependents, and close to 3,000 are U.S. military.

Joint Task Force–Guantánamo (or JTF for short) is the name of the military detention operation that began following the invasion of Afghanistan. It has given the naval base a second lease on life, but at enormous cost. Since the arrival of the first detainees in early 2002, the prison population of the base reached about 680 at its height, and about 270 still remained there by the summer of 2008. In all, 775 prisoners are known to have spent months or years of their lives trapped in the legal black hole of Guantánamo. The first images from Camp X-ray of shackled and caged Middle Eastern men in orange jumpsuits were irrevocably seared into the international consciousness. Among the first detainees to arrive in January 2002 was twenty-four-year-old Shafiq Rasul, a British citizen of Muslim descent who lived in the small town of Tipton in western England. Rasul and several ruffian friends described their journey to Afghanistan as a road trip gone wrong, and they have no proven links to Al Qaeda despite their thin alibis. Attorneys working to challenge the Guantánamo camp filed a case to represent Rasul in federal court in Washington, D.C., known as *Shafiq Rasul and others v. George W. Bush and others*. His case is believed to mark the first time in 150 years that the subjects of litigation were unaware of the case that was filed on their behalf. Rasul was imprisoned at Guantánamo for more than two years but released in 2004, along with four other British nationals who were never charged with any crime.[3]

Rasul clearly recalls the moment his flight from Kandahar landed in the remote corner of Cuba. Before boarding the plane, he endured an uncomfortable body cavity search followed by a round of photographs, and he was given an orange uniform. Then he was outfitted with a face mask, thick earmuffs, black thermal mittens, and ski goggles placed around his eyes with the eyepieces blacked out. He has described his arrival in Cuba in subsequent interviews. "We were taken off the plane and made to sit on the ground outside. I was still goggled and masked . . . We were then led onto a bus . . . The bus then went onto a ferry which went over to the camp. On our arrival at the camp, somebody lifted the earmuffs I was wearing and shouted into my ear, 'You are now the property of the U.S. Marine Corps.' We were told this was our final destination."

Now overgrown with weeds, Camp X-ray was in fact abandoned within a few months, as detainees were moved to an expanding detention complex known as Camp America, which included the prison enclave Camp Delta. The Bush administration had conceived of Joint Task Force–Guantánamo as a massive intelligence-gathering operation, but its effectiveness was undermined by the haphazard vetting process for prisoners. The United States had designed the perfect legal black hole and then transported hundreds of men from Afghanistan to Cuba, only to discover that at least half of the detainees had little or no intelligence value whatsoever.[4] The U.S. soldiers awarded nicknames to several especially pathetic characters. Half-Head Bob had been lobotomized by combat wounds. Al Qaeda Claus was a wizened tribal elder who seemed older than time. Wild Bill, who often snacked on his own feces, was so clearly out of any terrorist loop that he was quickly released in April. There were also several children held on the base. In January 2004, the Pentagon released three children believed to be ten, twelve, and thirteen when they were captured, and several more followed.[5] By 2007, all the remaining juvenile detainees had reached the age of eighteen. Now in their late teens and early twenties, they are paradoxically both Guantánamo's longest-serving and youngest prisoners.

General James Hill, the head of the Miami-based U.S. Southern Command from 2002 to 2004, recalled, "Guantánamo has been a backwater location for many years. Now all of a sudden, we were involved in strategic intelligence gathering from an enemy unlike any we've encountered on the battlefield before, in a Guantánamo environment that at the beginning was very austere."[6] In November 2002, the hard-nosed Major General Geoffrey Miller arrived at the base charged with increasing Guantánamo's intelligence output. Miller's core insight was that professional and humane detention practices undercut the effectiveness of aggressive interrogations, and he encouraged the guards in charge of the camp to "soften up" detainees for aggressive questioning. Sleep deprivation, blaring music (Eminem's rap lyrics were a favorite), and aggressive dogs were among the tactics reported by detainees. The U.S. military has rebuffed claims of beatings, but this became a more difficult case to make when a U.S. soldier accidentally found himself on the receiving end of the new detention techniques. In January 2003, Specialist Sean Baker of Kentucky dressed as a detainee in an orange jumpsuit for an exercise to practice the forced extraction of an inmate from a cell. Led to believe that Baker was a real detainee, the U.S. soldiers in the drill beat him so badly that he suffered a traumatic brain injury. The seizures still persisted when he was discharged from the military a year later.[7]

The U.S. invasion of Iraq in 2003 opened up a new front in the war on terror. The controlled interrogation techniques in Guantánamo Bay were soon exported to the new military detention facilities in U.S.-occupied Iraq. In August 2003, the Department of Defense sent Miller on a special visit to Iraq to offer advice on how U.S. forces could elicit more intelligence from Iraqi detainees. Miller recommended "Gitmo-ising" their approach by combining interrogation and detention operations in the manner that was being performed in Cuba. The goal was "setting the conditions for successful exploitation of the internees." The top U.S. intelligence officer at Iraq's Abu Ghraib prison later confirmed that Miller had inspired the use of dogs to scare prisoners into releasing information.[8] But once Miller returned to Guantánamo, even more aggressive interrogation tactics could not resolve the fundamental issue of an inadequate system for vetting the detainees in Afghanistan to determine their intelligence value. In a further twist, it was later revealed that the coercive tactics implemented at Gitmo had been adopted from a study of prisoner management techniques used by Chinese communists during the Korean War.

The blurring of roles between military police, army interrogators, and intelligence operatives had been held up as a model in Guantánamo Bay, but it soon led to systemic failures in the Baghdad prisons under U.S. control. In the spring of 2004, the Abu Ghraib scandal erupted with the publication of photos that showed U.S. soldiers placing Iraqi prisoners in sexually humiliating positions while hooded, leashed, or stacked in human pyramids. At the end of 2004, the new head of U.S. Southern Command, Bantz J. Craddock, appointed Lieutenant General Randall M. Schmidt of the Air Force to investigate charges of abuse in Guantánamo Bay during Miller's tenure. "I followed the bread crumb trail," Schmidt said later. "I found some things that didn't seem right. For lack of a camera, you could have seen in Guantánamo what was seen at Abu Ghraib."[9] Given Miller's role as an adviser, his recommendations to Gitmo-ise Abu Ghraib had arguably led to the scandalous abuse of its prisoners. But once the scandal broke, he was deployed to Iraq to run its detention operations. (Meanwhile, the export of U.S. interrogation tactics from Gitmo to Iraq later boomeranged back to haunt the American diplomats in Cuba, when the Castro government erected billboards with photographs from the Abu Ghraib abuse scandal in front of the U.S. Interest Section in Havana.)

In a landmark decision in June 2004, the U.S. Supreme Court ruled in the case of *Rasul v. Bush* that foreign nationals imprisoned without charges at the Guantánamo Bay interrogation camps were entitled to bring legal action challenging their captivity in U.S. federal courts. This ruling gave detainees the right to legal counsel and prompted the U.S. military to institute its own review procedures on whether detainees should be held or released. More than four hundred detainees have been set free in the first four years since that ruling, and many of the released prisoners have alleged that they suffered torture at the hands of the United States. Military officials both refute these claims and argue that the United States should be praised for taking the unprecedented step of releasing enemy combatants in the midst of ongoing hostilities in the war on terror. As many as thirty of the released detainees are believed to have rejoined the jihad against the United States. In May 2008, for example, one former Guantánamo detainee from Kuwait was reported to have carried out a suicide attack in the Iraqi city of Mosul.

Still, there is no hiding the U.S. government's knee-jerk disdain for many of the Guantánamo prisoners, given that many officials view an individual's presence in the camps as irrefutable proof of guilt. In June 2006, three men—two from Saudi Arabia and a third from Yemen—hanged themselves in their cells in Camp Delta. They suffocated in makeshift nooses made from their sheets and clothes, and they left behind suicide notes penned in Arabic. The commander of Guantánamo at that time, Rear Admiral Harry Harris, dismissed the deaths as an effort to smear the United States: "They have no regard for human life, either ours or their own. I believe this was not an act of desperation, but an act of asymmetrical warfare waged against us." Another top U.S. official charged with improving America's image in the Muslim world was even blunter: "Taking their own lives was not necessary, but it certainly is a good PR move."[10]

In May 2007, a fourth detainee from Saudi Arabia committed suicide, and that December an Algerian detainee attempted to kill himself by slashing his own throat with a sharpened fingernail. By the end of the year, at least twelve men were on hunger strikes so serious that they had to be put in restraints and fed through a tube up their nose. When I visited Guantánamo in the fall of 2007, the base staff explained that in two cases the hunger strikes had lasted longer than seven hundred days. Holding a thin yellow tube, the senior medical officer who supervised the force-feedings (called enteral feeding in medical jargon) described the procedure: "Basically, the detainee is restrained during this procedure. He is put into a feeding chair commercially available from the Federal Bureau of Prisons, and a lubricating numbing gel is put onto the end of this." He wiggled the tube. "It's passed through the nose, round the corner, and into the stomach. This is done twice a day. The whole procedure takes about thirty to forty-five minutes." The doctor believed that the hunger strikers were trying to make a political point. "They become celebrities, if you like, because they are hunger striking. They want to be fed. They often chat with each other, tell each other little jokes. They often laugh during this. I mean, it is not a dread procedure. This is the same procedure that would be used for you or I if you break your jaw and have your jaw wired shut." He added, "It's a bit like social hour."

The experience of Shafiq Rasul, the British man who spent two years in Cuba before being released in 2004, was later featured in a film called *The Road to Guantánamo*. (Rasul is part of a growing group of former Guantánamo detainees who have found stardom, or at least notoriety, in books, films, and artwork based on their experiences in America's most famous prison.) In June 2006, Rasul fielded questions from CNN anchor Wolf Blitzer about his experience at Camp Delta. When Blitzer asked, "What specifically happened to you at Guantánamo that was so bad?" Rasul replied, "Basically, we were tortured physically and mentally. We were beaten constantly, taken to interrogation, put in interrogation rooms for hours and hours and hours in positions that are very stressful, that cause a lot of pain and having been taken out of your cell on numerous occasions, getting beaten, put into isolation for months on end and constantly having this fear inside of you that you don't know on a daily basis what's going to happen to you and having our religious rights abused." The indomitable Blitzer closed in on the moral of the story: "If you had to do it over again, you wouldn't have gone to Afghanistan, is that right?" Rasul agreed: "No. I wouldn't even think about going there."[11]

Fidel Castro has long described Guantánamo Bay as a dagger pointed at the heart of Cuba, but at first he was uncharacteristically silent about the Bush administration's decision to establish a prison camp there for terrorist suspects from the Middle East. Virtually the only strong word of public dissent came from Cuban attorney general Juan Escalona, who said, "It's another provocation from the Americans. I hope 15 or 20 get out and kill them."[12] Other top officials issued more muted criticisms. General Ramón Espinosa, head of the Cuban army in the eastern provinces including Guantánamo, said, "Of course we don't agree with this, since even though it is occupied by the Americans, this is a Cuban territory." But he was anxious to dismiss any speculation that these concerns might somehow lead to a zone of instability around the base. "We hope to maintain that zone as it is today, pretty quiet on both sides." Minister of Higher Education Fernando Vecino Alegret told a reporter, "I think it would be yet another mistake by the Americans to use that usurped territory. I think there will be repudiation of that around the world."[13]

Before September 11, perhaps the most dramatic impression that most Americans had of the Guantánamo Bay Naval Base came from the 1992 movie *A Few Good Men*. The film stars Tom Cruise as a young navy lawyer, and Jack Nicholson plays the powerful and arrogant base commander, Colonel Nathan Jessep, suspected of giving a "Code Red" order to two marines who then kill a poorly performing fellow marine named William Santiago. In the dramatic courtroom climax, the navy prosecutor confronts Jessep, and Nicholson delivers his famously withering response: "*You want the truth? You can't handle the truth!*" He speaks with barely controlled fury. "Son, we live in a world that has walls. And those walls have to be guarded by men with guns. Who's gonna do it? You? . . . I have a greater responsibility than you can possibly fathom. You weep for Santiago and you curse the marines. You have that luxury. You have the luxury of not knowing what I know: that Santiago's death, while tragic, probably saved lives. And my existence, while grotesque and incomprehensible to you, saves lives. You don't want the truth. Because deep down, in places you don't talk about at parties, you want me on that wall. *You need me on that wall*." The spirit of Colonel Jessep's remarks remains alive and well at Gitmo, and most of the American soldiers working on the base believe their role is both necessary and just. However, at the real Guantánamo Bay, there is no wall separating the United States from Cuba. There is a fence.

"The fence line" is the catchall term for the perimeter of the U.S. naval base, which is surrounded by a no-man's-land that is technically under Cuban control. My visit to the northeast gate to Cuba revealed a sleepy, bucolic vista of green fields and sloping mountains marked by a simple metal fence. According to the serious young marine chaperone, Staff Sergeant Kaveh Wooley, the scene was not always so calm. In the 1950s, during the Cuban Revolution, Raúl Castro's forces captured a couple dozen U.S. soldiers and held them hostage for several weeks before returning them unharmed. Since then, Americans have been banned from leaving the base and entering Cuba, but the two sides continued sparring in the ensuing decades. About fifty marines used to bunk in a small guard shack, but Cuban soldiers would sneak close to the fence and toss rocks onto its tin roof to keep the soldiers up all night. The marines responded by elevating a portion of the fence line to a height of more than forty feet, but the Cubans scaled the fence to hang wind chimes that were even more annoying. When the Cubans shone a spotlight on the marine barracks to make it even harder to sleep, the soldiers painted a massive marine seal for the Cubans to light up each night. The Cubans stopped shining the spotlight, but the marines decided to illuminate the seal themselves. "Every night, we show the Cuban army that the marines will always be here to protect the base," Wooley boasted. Fierce competition then erupted over which side could fly its flag the highest. The United States won the battle by constructing the tallest flagpole, but the Cubans won the war. They erected their flag on a distant hill crest, where it fluttered triumphantly, barely distinguishable amid the trees.

The Cuban frontier brigade has 1,500 troops guarding their side of the line, matched by 150 marines who guard the base in shifts. Wooley pointed to a hill in the distance with a small wooden structure on top. "That used to be a Cuban observation post. The military could see eighty-five percent of the base from up there. It is even said that the first pictures of Camp X-ray were taken from that position." He noted that the new detention facility, Camp America, was constructed in an area that was more difficult to see from the Cuban side. During the cold war, both sides of the fence line were heavily land mined, but President Bill Clinton ordered the removal of sixty thousand land mines from the U.S. perimeter. Wooley warned that "the Cubans still have their land mines on their side, so every once in a while a land mine will explode. It's usually just a rock iguana or a banana rat having a really bad day." The Cuban mines detonate at least once a month, sometimes starting fires that sweep across the fence line. He described a fire that started the previous summer and turned into a "giant cook-off" with about thirty mines exploding. "We were in constant contact with the Cubans to see if they needed any assistance to control the fire. I mean, it was really bad out there with the smoke coming over all the way back. It was horrible." But there was a bright side. "The guys love it when a mine goes off, because it gives them something to do."

In 1994, a major rafter crisis resulted in tens of thousands of Cuban refugees being held by the U.S. military on the Guantánamo Bay Naval Base. The next year, monthly fence line meetings were established between the U.S. and Cuban military authorities in Guantánamo, to exchange information related to the management of the base. Fourteen years later, these meetings continue on a regular basis, adding up thus far to more than 150 joint encounters that occur in the old marine barracks or a weathered Cuban customshouse below a sign that reads FREE TERRITORY OF THE AMERICAS. The monthly meetings are used to brief Cuban officials on activities occurring on the American side of the base and coordinate responses to shared emergencies such as fires and hurricanes. In one of these meetings, Cuban officials became among the first in the world to learn that the United States would be transferring its Taliban prisoners to Guantánamo Bay, even before the knowledge reached the American public.

Captain Mark Leary began his tour as the commanding officer of the Guantánamo Bay Naval Base in September 2005. A Massachusetts native in his early fifties, Leary speaks with the precision typical of a naval helicopter pilot. Despite his lifelong career in the navy, Leary had been shocked to learn that the U.S. and Cuban military held monthly meetings on the perimeter of the naval base. Prior to his arrival in Guantánamo Bay, Leary had been puzzled by a request that he attend a briefing with U.S. diplomats: "Why would I need to go to a meeting at the State Department if we don't have formal diplomatic relations with the Cubans?" He recalled his briefing with the officials in charge of U.S. policy toward Cuba: "I met with the folks up there, and one of the men I met with says, 'OK, two weeks from today we go to the fence line meeting.' " The navy captain laughed at the memory. "I said, 'Stop right there. What do you mean *fence line meeting*, and what do you mean *we*?' Of course, I had no idea that there was a fence line meeting that went on, and no idea that I would be involved. There have certainly been surprises like that here, but mostly they've been good surprises."

Leary described the meetings: "They are very local, very military-to-military, and it's a very practiced, pragmatic relationship for us. We do cover the same four or five topics every month." They included issues like checking the radios for field communication, fire drills, and requesting special clearance over Cuban airspace in the event that a wounded individual needs to be medically evacuated from the base. U.S. forces also escort Cuba-bound craft through the outer bay, which is under American control, and into the inner bay, which still belongs to Cuba. The conversations also included topics sensitive for Cuba, like the holding facilities for immigrants. Leary said, "Even when we actually started rebuilding some of the facilities we had for mass migration, we called them and said, 'Hey, this is what we're doing. It's to duplicate capabilities that we already had. It hasn't always been Cubans. It's been Cubans, Haitians, whatever, so it's not directed at you.'" Cuban refugees still occasionally turn up on the base, generally by launching small crafts from nearby Guantánamo province and floating to the shoreline under U.S. military control. After Castro's illness prompted fears of an immigration crisis, a new camp to hold up to ten thousand refugees was built on the leeward side of the base by the airport.

Leary exchanged e-mail and phone calls regularly with his Cuban counterparts, and he conceded that the generally positive collaboration between the United States and Cuba around Guantánamo was unique. "It is a little bit of an exception, but it is really kind of local, practical, and military-to-military, and I think it works fairly well for us." Another senior U.S. government official familiar with Guantánamo told me, "The main objective of the talks is to make sure that the Cubans understand what they are seeing or hearing from the other side of the fence line. If the U.S. has a twenty-one-gun salute on the Fourth of July, for example, we want them to know we are not attacking. It's just a natural impulse, when you hear cannon fire, to want to know what it is." The direct bilateral talks cut through the bureaucracy of channeling local requests or complaints through diplomatic missions in Havana and Washington.

While a succession of U.S. naval base commanders have participated in the talks, there have been only three interlocutors in charge of the Cuban side: the one-star commander of the Guantánamo military district, one-star brigadier general José Solar Hernández, and currently navy captain Pedro Román Cisneros. Not counting interpreters, the meetings include three to four Cubans and four to five Americans, and the same participants meet over time. The U.S. official with knowledge of Guantánamo said, "I would not go so far as to describe the talks as friendly. They are professional, courteous, and businesslike, and after the formal agenda there is coffee and pastries and some small talk, such as baseball or the glories of eastern Cuba. We are dealing with the military representatives of a government with which we have quite a poor relationship, and everyone knows it. One has to be aware that anything could come up." Still, the talks sometimes include personal touches. When Solar Hernández retired in January 2006, Leary gave him an engraved cigar humidor as a farewell present. "He seemed genuinely pleased with it," Leary later reported.[14]

Many Cuban workers used to be employed by the Guantánamo base, but the practice largely ceased when Castro took power. At first the Cubans were allowed to keep their jobs, but by last fall only three Cuban workers continued to be employed by the U.S. military. At the respective ages of seventy-five, seventy-eight, and eighty-three, each was well beyond retirement age, but every morning they would catch a ride with Cuban soldiers to the base perimeter, walk through the northeast gate, and drive to their jobs. Two worked in the U.S. Army's Morale, Welfare, and Recreation programs, while the third worked directly for the naval base. Perhaps their most important function was to carry pensions into Cuba for three hundred retired Cubans who received about two hundred dollars each a month. Once a month, the U.S. military sent its three elderly workers across the fence line carrying close to sixty thousand dollars in cash for its former employees from Cuba.

Despite the deep political tensions between their governments, the American and Cuban soldiers on either side of the fence line have apparently concluded that good fences make good neighbors. Once a year, U.S. and Cuban forces even put together an exercise drill where 150 soldiers from each side practice responding to a major accident along the fence. At the conclusion of his tour of the fence line, Staff Sergeant Wooley pointed to an open area near the gate. "In between these two fences right here, we act as if a bus crashed and there's a whole bunch of casualties. Our corpsmen meet up with their corpsmen and prepare for it. It's all scripted, and everybody knows exactly what's going on. No surprises. The marines that participate in it told me that they just laid there. I mean, they do fake wounds and stuff like that. Then the Cuban corpsmen act together, and they pretty much fix whatever's going on." Even the U.S. Marines, it seems, get a taste of Cuban health care.

The Guantánamo Bay Naval Base is an island on an island. The rhythms of life on the base occur in a self-contained atmosphere that is disconnected from both the realities of Cuba and the domestic and global controversy generated by Guantánamo's detention operation. The proximity of Cuba introduces a whiff of the exotic—ROCKING IN FIDEL'S BACKYARD proclaims one local radio ad—but the glowing golden arches of the base's drive-through McDonald's are never far away. Spanish is mainly spoken among the Puerto Rican contingent of the National Guard, and most of the base's foreign workers converse in Filipino dialects or Jamaican Creole. "It's so isolated here that it's weird to imagine there's another country over there," reflected one U.S. soldier, nodding at the Sierra Maestra in the distance. "But sometimes you see lights flickering beyond the base perimeter, and you can pick up Cuban radio stations in Spanish. It fascinates me."

Camp America, the detention facility operated by Joint Task Force–Guantánamo, is tucked behind a hillcrest and nestled along Cuba's rocky eastern shoreline. After you pass through an initial checkpoint marked with the slogan HONOR BOUND TO DEFEND FREEDOM, the razor wire and chain-link fences of Camp Delta sparkle in front of the deep blue Caribbean Sea. The Camp Delta complex contains a set of four detention facilities: medium security Camp 1; Camps 2 and 3, which have been emptied of prisoners; and Camp 4, an open-air facility for compliant detainees. Two maximum security facilities were added later: Camp 5 opened its doors in May 2004, and Camp 6 followed in 2006. (In early 2008, the military revealed the existence of Camp 7, a top secret holding facility for fifteen high-value detainees that is strictly off-limits to the press.) Visitors to the other camps are urged to adhere to the military's preferred language. In the lingo of the base, Guantánamo has no "prisoners," only "detainees," and no one is ever "punished," but many are frequently "disciplined." Even Camp 4, which gives the most freedom and amenities to detainees, such as outdoor recreation areas and a small library, is extraordinarily bleak. The "detainee gardens" are parched blocks of earth. The average detainee in Guantánamo Bay is thirty-three years old, and several men who appeared close to that age paced the yard. All wore white cotton prison dress, and several sported long black beards and shaved heads. In a nod to cultural sensitivity, a small black arrow pointing toward Mecca is painted in each cell throughout all of the camps, and some even feature arrows in the common spaces. A list of seventeen camp rules is posted in several languages throughout the camps. Rule number one is "You will be disciplined if you do not comply with camp rules."

During my visit, a tall, handsome African American soldier intro-

duced himself as the lead naval petty officer for Camp 4, in charge of
supervising more than one hundred guards. He had been based at
Guantánamo Bay for two and a half years, and his historical memory
was virtually unrivaled among the guard staff, most of whom had
served for only several months. The petty officer had been on duty
during a camp uprising the previous year that posed the most dramatic
challenge mounted by inmates. "I was a sergeant in the guard that day,
May 18, 2006," he said. "These detainees will yell in their native
tongue. Of course, with a lot of the guards not knowing Arabic, there's
no way for us to intercept those messages unless we actually have an
interpreter right then and there. It was definitely a highly coordinated
effort. They attempted to lure the guard force into a physical confrontation . . . They had large work-center fans, and they took those
fans apart in a matter of seconds. They used the blades as machetes
against the guard force. They used the fan grates, the steel mesh, as
shields. They took the fan bases and used those as battering rams. So
when the guard force entered to try to quell the riot, we were met with
weaponry. They had slicked the floors of the bays up with urine, feces,
food products, anything that they could think of to make the floor slip-
pery so we could not maintain our footing. As soon as my guards
entered, they went straight to the floor, and now the detainees are
jumping on top of them." The dramatic showdown ended with no
injuries, he attested. But Rear Admiral Harry Harris described the
uprising as "probably the most violent outbreak" to occur at Guantánamo, and the U.S. military poured seven hundred thousand dollars
into upgrading and safety proofing the facilities in Camp 4.

The majority of the detainees were now housed in Camps 5 and 6,
the two new maximum security facilities, built for a combined cost of
fifty-four million dollars, that in the fall of 2007 together held about
220 of the 340 prisoners that remained at Guantánamo. Camp 5,
principally occupied by prisoners of greater intelligence value, had
special interrogation cells with fake Oriental carpets and puffy blue
reclining chairs positioned next to leg-shackle points. Camp 6 had the
largest population, 145 detainees, who spent twenty-two hours a day
in seven-by-twelve-foot cells. In Camp 6, the military officer in charge
pointed through the window into an open area patrolled by guards
with cells ringed around one corner of the room: "The reason it looks
dark in here is because this glass is shatter resistant, bulletproof, and
also mirrored. So they can't see us out here. We can see in, but they

can't see out. The detainees that are in their cells, if they look this way, they'll just see a reflection." The men warehoused just beyond could be seen only as faint shadows, pacing back and forth in their cells, locked away behind steel doors and bulletproof glass as the military guards watched them closely. The camp boasted its own medical and dental clinic. Several vials of blood spun lazily on a gyroscope in the corner of the room. A helpful reminder about weighing detainees was posted on the scale against the wall: MINUS 3 LBS FOR HAND CUFFS AND WAIST CHAINS. MINUS 3.5 LBS FOR LEG SHACKLES.

With prior permission, the U.S. military allows visiting journalists to tour the detention facilities and meet with camp staff for supervised interviews. I participated in one such exchange between a navy guard and several reporters that took place on the weather-beaten front porch of Club Survivor, a seaside watering hole for the American military forces working within the confines of Camp America. The young, pretty Camp 1 navy guard arrived in full uniform. While security regulations prevented her from saying her name, she did reveal that she was twenty years old and originally from Texas. Five months on the job and still less than halfway through her tour, she praised the training she received at a simulated prison camp in Fort Lewis, in Washington State, before arriving at Guantánamo: "The training was a lot worse in Fort Lewis. They exaggerate on everything to get you prepared for the worst."

The young guard said that her Muslim charges treated her no different as a woman, with one exception. "The only thing different that I've noticed is that they don't look me in the eye. If they need something, they'll ask you. They'll just look down as they're speaking to you." She didn't know any of the prisoners' names and only addressed them as "detainee," despite the fact that she had been waking before dawn each morning for five months to walk past their detention blocks for twelve hours a day. "I'm sure everybody's curious, but it's not our job to find out," she said. "We treat them with the respect they deserve. If they ask for something, we'll put in a request for it." No individual cell was left untended for more than a minute and a half without being checked on by a guard. "I prefer days because it goes by quicker," the guard said. "The nights just seem to drag out." Yellow traffic cones referred to as "prayer cones" were placed in the corridors five times a day to alert guards when the prisoners were praying to Mecca. Even so, interruptions of prayer time persisted, causing tempers to flare. In one incident during Ramadan, guards unwittingly offered dates and honey through the slit in the cell door—or "beanhole"—to a detainee in the midst of prayer. An internal memo noted that the detainee "spit at one of the guards, striking both of his eyes, mouth and throat." The guard was removed for medical inspection and then returned to duty.

By the fall of 2007, the CIA and other U.S. agencies were still conducting regular interrogations of detainees. The young soldiers patrolling the camps were not privy to the details, although they did notice that some detainees were periodically removed from the camps and returned with packets of coffee or other goods referred to as "incentive items." "We don't know where they go," the navy guard said. "If they need to go somewhere, they'll send a team. Sometimes they bring back incentive items, that's it." Pressed about whether she was curious to learn more about who the men were and why the U.S. military had brought them half a world away, she shrugged.

At this point, Lieutenant Colonel Ed Bush, the public affairs officer monitoring the interview, jumped into the conversation: "The position of the JTF is it's mostly for the protection of the detainees, that it's safer for the detainees as a whole if the guards don't know who's who." Nodding at the guard, he said, "It takes away the possibility of her treating someone different. A lot of what we do is about a conscious effort to treat everyone the same—in this case, all detainees. If I know which detainee is Khalid Sheikh Mohammed, the mastermind of 9/11 . . ."

A visiting European journalist cut him off: "Well, I think everyone knows who that is, no?" Bush quickly retorted, "I think not." The journalist persisted, "But there are pictures of him all over the place," to which Bush responded, "I think you'd be amazed." As if to confirm this statement, the navy guard shook her head. "I wouldn't recognize any of them."

Bush nodded in agreement and underlined his point. "She doesn't need to know who Khalid Sheikh Mohammed is to do her job. And it's probably better that she doesn't, because she's able to treat everyone across the board the same. And that's kind of the same general philosophy for the whole guard force. The guard force doesn't know who's who, by intent. It's the way I make sure you treat everybody the same. So that when you go to shackle Khalid Sheikh Mohammed, you give his shackles an extra-tight little snug, just 'cause he's the guy? Well, if you don't know who the guy is, you're not going to do that, so it's kind of fair across the board. It's also a very, very smart way of making sure that somebody doesn't go get a little overzealous and embarrass us and abuse somebody. Because abuse from a guard to detainees brings this whole thing to a screeching halt."

The Guantánamo Bay detention facility is both cursed and blessed by the short-term memory of the U.S. military officers who work there. Most of the soldiers who manned the base in its rough-and-tumble early days have since moved on to other postings, and the new arrivals have memories that stretch back months, not years. This makes it hard to get straight answers to difficult questions, but it also provides fascinating insights into how the Americans charged with running today's Guantánamo understand their roles. When I asked what she had learned on her deployment, the navy guard replied, "I didn't know of Guantánamo until I got here. I had never heard of it." A chorus of agreement erupted from the small group of soldiers observing the conversation. One retired U.S. soldier who had just arrived from a two-year defense contract in Iraq tried to explain: "There's this perception that the average American knows a lot about it, and to be honest with you, I've been here almost a month, and I really knew very, very little. Once in a while, you see a little article here or there, but I knew nothing about it. So I got online and started looking it up: What is the history of this place, and what's been going on? I really thought it had been a prison forever! I didn't know. I had no idea."

The European journalist was clearly stunned by the fact that Americans in the U.S. military could plead ignorance on Guantánamo Bay. "But it's a big issue of course, worldwide!" he protested. "This has grave consequences for the image of the United States all over the world!" Bush leaned forward and spoke with the passion of someone trying to convey a core truth. "That's kind of my point, and I need you to get that. It's a big issue because you say it is. It's a big issue worldwide as far as the treatment of detainees. It's a big issue in Washington. *But you know what this is to me? This is just another job!*" He pointed again to the young navy guard, who was now a spectator at her own interview. "This is her first duty deployment, and it's probably the most boring one she's ever gonna have, because she's stuck on an island with nothing to do. And we can talk about the historic mission and worldwide—and that's all true—but not to her. It's really not. So she just goes and takes care of a bunch of guys that don't look her in the eye. For most of us who come and leave here, that's what this is going to be."

Expecting U.S. soldiers to have any impression of Guantánamo, Bush said, is "like assuming that the guys who are going to Iraq understand all the politics of the Iraq War. They don't. We just got our mission. She can better do her job if she doesn't get bogged down with all of the political *'you got Khalid Sheikh Mohammed and 9/11, holy crap!'*" He gestured again to the twenty-year-old woman, who was just a high school freshman in Texas when many of the prisoners were swept up from Afghanistan and deposited on the eastern tip of Cuba. "You know what? Just go walk the tier and make sure these guys don't kill themselves. Keep it simple and focus on the task at hand."

Guantánamo Bay has released hundreds of prisoners over the past two years, but new detainees have been added. In September 2006, President Bush authorized the transfer of fourteen high-value detainees to the base from CIA black sites where they had been in secret detention. In announcing the move, Bush declared, "The CIA program has been, and remains, one of the most vital tools in our war against the terrorists." The transfer included Khalid Sheikh Mohammed, who had been captured in Pakistan three years earlier. In March 2007, Mohammed confessed to his crimes in a closed-door tribunal in Guantánamo Bay, saying, "I was responsible for the 9/11 operation, from A to Z." The confession was a breakthrough for CIA interrogators. Mohammed had previously impressed them by withstanding the practice of waterboarding for more than two minutes before cracking.[15] In April 2007, the base received another high-value detainee in the form of Abdul Hadi al-Iraqi, a forty-six-year-old Iraqi man believed to be one of Osama bin Laden's top global deputies. Even with Guantánamo Bay's legal and political fate hanging in the balance, the mission was shifting from a sprawling detention complex for hundreds of Al Qaeda foot soldiers to a highly sophisticated offshore intelligence operation increasingly focused on a narrow slice of high-value prisoners. But with the clock ticking on the Bush administration's time in power, prosecuting cases took on greater urgency. During the first six years of the Guantánamo camps, the only man to be tried and sentenced was David Hicks, a former kangaroo skinner and Muslim convert who joined the Taliban. He served out his nine-month term in his native Australia and was released at the end of 2007. In February 2008, U.S. military prosecutors charged six men, including Mohammed, for their involvement in the 9/11 attacks and announced that they would seek the death penalty in military commissions scheduled to be held later that year. During his first public appearance before a military commission in June, Khalid Sheikh Mohammed declared that he would welcome the martyrdom represented by capital punishment at the hands of the Americans: "Yes, this is what I wish, to be a martyr for a long time. I will, God willing, have this by you."[16]

Brigadier General Cameron A. Crawford arrived in Guantánamo Bay in January 2007 as the deputy commander of the Joint Task Force. In a meeting in the beige building surrounded by scrub brush that serves as the mission headquarters, Crawford described how he saw the balance between detention and intelligence-gathering objectives. "Our actual entire mission is the safe and humane custody of enemy combatants. A subset of that, of course, includes interrogation and assisting with gathering intelligence for strategic and tactical purposes, as well as for criminal prosecution," he said. "Roughly one third of our three hundred and thirty or so detainees are interrogated on a regular basis. By regular, I mean approximately a weekly basis. That is a little higher than six or twelve months ago with the recent resurgence of the Taliban in Afghanistan and some activities in East Africa." He argued that important improvements in the guard force had taken place. "If you think about it, in 2002 there wasn't a current base of knowledge about large-scale detainee operations in the U.S. military, nor about interrogation practices. It was something that we had to learn and develop as we went."

Crawford followed the policy debates in Washington but saw an ongoing role for the detention operations. "I can tell you that as long as there is a single detainee left to detain in Guantánamo, we will do it well," he said. While conceding regret about the terrorist actions that had led to the camp being created in the first place, Crawford declared, "Beyond that, I have absolutely no sadness it exists. Because as long as we are engaged in hostilities and there are extremists that are trying to harm our country's people and interests, I think Guantánamo is the perfect place for them to be safely detained and kept off the battlefield, and also for us to gather intelligence that may help our brethren downrange to engage in the fight."

When I asked him about the political significance of the U.S. detention facilities' location on the end of Fidel Castro's Cuba, Crawford underlined the logistical difficulties of being positioned at the end of a long supply chain. "But from a geopolitical perspective, I don't think it affects the troopers in their job," he told me. "Frankly, personally I would love nothing more than to get on a bicycle or on a motorcycle and just ride around. I mean, I speak Spanish. I have studied the Latin culture. I would love to go explore Cuba, and that is very sad for me on a personal level that I am not able to do that. That is sad. But it is what it is, and I don't think it affects the mission of the soldiers and sailors here."

Indeed, for most of the American soldiers serving at the Guantá-namo Bay Naval Base, the fact that this U.S. military outpost sits at the tip of the communist nation of Cuba is little more than an after-thought. Among the Cuban officials on the other side of the fence line, however, there is a penetrating sense that Gitmo has been unfairly wrested away from the island by a United States that remains, in many eyes, a heavy-handed imperial power. Most Cubans who live in the provincial villages just outside the base have only a vague idea what goes on inside its perimeter, and they are unable to distinguish between the global controversy currently surrounding Guantánamo and their government's long-standing enmity toward the American possession of the base. Still, the base continues to attract Cubans who try to enter it illegally in the hope of winning asylum and eventually reaching the United States. In fact, the communist nature of Cuba's government has made it easier for the United States to ignore its views. Had Cuba followed the course set by the rest of Latin America and embraced democracy in the 1990s, it is likely that the United States would even-tually have responded to public pressure to renegotiate the lease. Nev-ertheless, in recent years, the Cubans have benefited from the fact that President Bush's denunciations of Cuba as a "tropical gulag" carry far less power abroad at a time when the United States is running a prison camp in Guantánamo that it is desperately trying to keep far from the reach of American courts.

Furthermore, the Bush administration faced a series of Supreme Court decisions that steadily eroded the base's unique legal status. This began with the 2004 ruling in *Rasul v. Bush* that allowed detainees to challenge their captivity in U.S. federal courts. It was followed by the 2006 decision that the White House proposal to try "enemy combat-ants" before U.S. military commissions lacked a constitutional or legal basis, which prompted Congress to rush through a bill to authorize the commissions. In June 2008, the Supreme Court issued a 5–4 ruling that the foreign detainees held there had the constitutional right of habeas corpus, which allowed them to seek relief from imprisonment in U.S. civilian courts. This represented the final, crushing blow to the Bush administration's effort to shield Guantánamo Bay from American law. On behalf of the majority, Justice Anthony Kennedy wrote that, "The laws and Constitution are designed to survive, and remain in force, in extraordinary times." Guantánamo Bay was now expected to face an onslaught of legal challenges from the 270 remaining detainees, but the practical and logistical difficulties presented by closing the detention center were daunting. In the spring of 2008, the U.S. Congress asked Defense Secretary Robert Gates, who succeeded Rumsfeld, about the future of the detainees still at the base. He replied, "The brutally frank answer is that we're stuck . . . Either their home government won't accept them or we're concerned that the home government will let them loose once we return them."

Meanwhile, the Cuban government kept a close eye on this U.S. military outpost. During his long rule, Castro frequently fulminated against what he termed the "illegal occupation" of Guantánamo Bay by American forces. Even after he fell ill in July 2006, he turned to the subject of the base in the periodic "reflections" that he wrote on international topics during his convalescence. In an article penned in August 2007, Castro described the base as a "horrendous torture center" and denounced U.S. plans to build new holding facilities in case of a refugee crisis from Cuba as a "concentration camp for illegal migrants." He wrote, "The Base is needed to humiliate and to carry out the filthy deeds that take place there. If we must await the downfall of the system, we shall wait." At the same time, his brother Raúl, ever the army man, was praising the military-to-military cooperation between American and Cuban forces at the base and emphasizing the need to keep an orderly fence line. Fidel's broadsides appeared to be an effort to undercut Raúl, but the comments also reflected the different approaches of the two leaders. Meanwhile, as the calls to close down Guantánamo's detention facilities gathered strength among the American public, U.S. military leaders were far from alarmed. Most agreed that the Bush administration's decision to use Guantánamo for this purpose had tarnished America's image, and they would be ready to bid good-bye to this particular mission when the time was right. The Guantánamo Bay Naval Base was a different matter, however. It had been under American control for more than a century, and its lease on life showed few signs of running out.

CHAPTER 9

Through the Looking Glass

Michael Moore's documentary *Sicko* opened in U.S. movie theaters on June 22, 2007. The controversial movie by America's most outspoken left-wing filmmaker went on to earn twenty-five million dollars at the box office and become the third-highest-grossing documentary ever— surpassed only by *Fahrenheit 9/11* and *March of the Penguins* and ranking just ahead of Al Gore's *An Inconvenient Truth*. *Sicko* offered a scathing critique of the U.S. health care system and featured comparisons with those of other countries, including Canada, England, and France. The movie's running time was over two hours, but by far the most-talked-about scenes in the film came from a fifteen-minute segment toward the end. Moore charters a boat to bring a group of sick 9/11 rescue workers to the U.S. naval base at Guantánamo Bay, Cuba, where he has been told that Al Qaeda prisoners receive better treatment than do many U.S. citizens at home. Rebuffed at the base, he then ventures on to mainland Cuba, where the American patients are tended to by Cuban doctors and marvel at the treatment available from Cuba's health care system.

The ploy is classic Michael Moore: a clever but cheap shot that is designed to push people's buttons. After landing in Cuba, Moore creeps through the cacti and scrub brush to peer into the base. He then hires a fishing boat and sails into Guantánamo Bay, pleading through a megaphone: "Permission to enter. I have three 9/11 rescue workers. They just want some medical attention. The same kind that Al Qaeda is getting. They don't want any more than the evildoers— just the same! Hello?" When a U.S. guard tower starts blaring an alarm, they flee to Cuba, where Moore laments in a voice-over, "What was I supposed to do with all these sick people and no one to help them? I mean, here we were stuck in some godforsaken third-world country—and communist no less. When I was a kid, these people wanted to kill us!"

Lo and behold, Moore and his fellow travelers ask for directions to a pharmacy and are soon in Havana's topflight hospital, where they receive expert care from Cuban physicians, with no insurance required. Moore says, "I asked them to give us the exact same care they give their fellow Cuban citizens, no more and no less, and that's what they did." Still, any viewer familiar with Cuba will quickly note that the presence of cameras obviously helped. The visitors are receiving the best care available to important foreigners, and probably diverting resources away from poor Cubans in the process. One clue is that all the hospital beds have clean white sheets, whereas most Cuban patients have to provide their own bedding (and, in some cases, their own anesthesia). Moore introduces this segment with a backhand acknowledgment of American suspicions of Cuba: "OK, OK, I know what you're thinking: Cuba is where Lucifer lives." An image of Fidel Castro speaking in demonic tones and a map of Cuba with flames rising from the island appear on the screen. "You know that because that is what you have been told for over forty-five years."

Whatever its merits and flaws, Moore's foray into Cuba was a public relations coup. The scenes take up less than one eighth of the film but dominated its television and newspaper coverage and enhanced its watercooler appeal. The U.S. Treasury Department opened an inquiry into whether Moore had violated U.S. law by filming in Cuba. The filmmaker bragged that he had rushed the master copy of *Sicko* to Canada to protect it from being seized by the Bush administration. When former Tennessee senator Fred Thompson criticized Moore's trip to Cuba, the filmmaker challenged him to a debate. Thompson, then a dark horse candidate for the Republican presidential nomination, responded by posting a video on YouTube. Shown chomping on a Cuban cigar, Thompson told Moore, "The next time you're down in Cuba visiting your buddy Castro, you might ask him about another documentary filmmaker. His name is Nicolás Guillén. He did something Castro didn't like, and they put him in a mental institution for several years, giving him devastating electroshock treatments. A mental institution, Michael," Thompson repeated. "Might be something you ought to think about."

The bizarre skirmish between Moore and Thompson over Castro's health system was only the latest episode in the long-brewing culture war between the United States and Cuba, which has spilled into the arenas of film, religion, sports, academia, and literature. The recent effort in Miami to ban the thirty-two-page hardcover book *Vamos a Cuba* (Let's Go to Cuba) eventually moved into the legal arena. The book was written for children from kindergarten to second grade and was widely available at libraries in the Miami-Dade school system. In early April 2006, a complaint was filed by thirty-six-year-old Juan Amador Rodriguez challenging the book's presence in Miami's schools. Amador Rodriguez, the father of a ten-year-old daughter, was particularly aggrieved by the fact that the Cuban children were shown wearing the red bandannas affiliated with the children's communist group known as *los pioneros*. He also protested the overall portrayal of Cuba as a normal country where children play. "As a former political prisoner in Cuba, I find the material to be untruthful. It is a Cuba that does not exist."[1] The phrase "the people of Cuba eat, work and study just like you" generated the greatest controversy. "Nothing could be further from the truth!" railed one Cuban American member of the Miami-Dade school board, while another compared the book to "pornography" and "devil worship."[2]

In June, *Vamos a Cuba* became the first book to be banned from Miami schools, but a federal judge later ordered it back onto the shelves pending a decision by the U.S. Court of Appeals for the 11th Circuit in Atlanta. Undeterred, parents launched a civil disobedience movement to remove the books from the shelves, led by Dalia Rodriguez of the Concerned Cuban Parents Committee. "If you take it out and don't return it, no kid can read it. It's not censoring. It's protecting our children from lies," she said. "We're going to take the books and lock them in a box."[3] Soon a movement took root to purge other books from the Miami schools, including *Cuban Kids* and the Cuba volume of the Discovering Cultures series. Even Armando Valladares, the celebrated former political prisoner who spent twenty-two years in Cuban jails, got into the act. He penned an alternative children's book, titled *Niños de Cuba* (Children of Cuba), intended to rebut claims that children are happy in Cuba. The book describes children being sent to work camps and is illustrated with photographs of kids playing with broken toys, shoppers milling through dirty, run-down stores, and neglected elderly people covered in excrement.[4]

Even major U.S. corporations occasionally stumble into the political hornet's nest driven by Cuba's culture wars. Target Corporation is the fifth-largest American retailer by sales revenue and ranks thirty-third out of the *Fortune* 500, but the Minneapolis-based company was harshly rebuked for its foray into this hotly contested terrain. In December 2006, Target started selling a twenty-four-CD carrying case that featured Che Guevara's image. The reincarnation of Cuba's most famous revolutionary leader as a controversial pop culture icon has infuriated exiles who believe that his execution by U.S. forces in Bolivia in 1967 should be a source of celebration. Che Guevara T-shirts and posters can be found on almost any large college campus in the United States, and his portrait has found a second life on notebooks, screen savers, and mouse pads, not to mention the small library of books that have been written to build, explain, or destroy his legacy. In early December, Target introduced the Che Guevara CD case to its fifteen hundred stores in forty-seven states at a retail price of $4.99. Days later, an anti-Castro editorialist with *Investor's Business Daily* launched a full-throated attack on Target's business ethics, denouncing the Che CD case as "tyrant chic" that celebrated a "psychopath."[5] This opening salvo sent a wave of energy through anti-Castro activist groups, who fired off hundreds of letters protesting Target's new product.

Caught off guard in the middle of a political storm, Target's executives immediately started groping for the exits. One week after the backlash began, Guevara's image promptly vanished from the chain's fifteen hundred stores. Target's public relations department issued a meek apology, and Cuba activists from the right and left enjoyed a rare moment of holiday unity. The *Wall Street Journal* called the decision "admirable," while a spokeswoman from the progressive San Francisco–based advocacy group Global Exchange expressed no regret about the Cuban icon's abrupt departure from Target: "Che would just be rolling in his grave if he knew his face was making money for Target. Everyone who does support that legacy of social justice is certainly not going to be opposed to stopping Target from using that tool."[6] Meanwhile, millions of shoppers continued to pour into Target stores across America, blissfully unaware that the controversy had ever occurred in the first place.

The Internet is the new battleground for heated exchanges over Cuba. Recently, the debate on Cuba exploded in the virtual chat room of Wikipedia, the online encyclopedia with more than one million entries created and maintained by volunteers. Cursed by teachers and beloved by students, Wikipedia is one of the top ten most popular Web sites in the world, with more than forty million unique visitors each month. In the spring of 2006, an "edit war" broke out about whether Cuba should be described as a dictatorship or a democracy. Any sense of online decorum quickly evaporated as total strangers began hurling accusations at each other of payoffs, cover-ups, and biased reporting. When an online mediator tried to broker a truce by suggesting better citations, he was rebuffed by another user: "If we need a citation that Cuba is not a democracy, then maybe we need a citation that Cuba is in Latin America."[7]

Soon the Cuba definition was subject to hundreds of dueling edits, forcing Wikipedia to take drastic action. New users were prohibited from editing the Cuba site, at least one user was banned from the site for life after threatening another editor with libel, and shorter bans were imposed on other offenders. The Wikipedia administrators felt compelled to establish a special project to monitor the content of the Cuba entry. But nearly a year later, the online debate was still capable of inspiring rage. When a question arose about the role of ideology in the Cuban education system, one user exclaimed: "I get so upset at attempts to enforce conformity of ideological thought and impose the propaganda of the Cuban government on Wikipedia that it makes me lose any rationality mustered in calmer moments." In response, one editor wrote, "I sympathize with your rant. But having spent the last week simultaneously arguing against both a communist pro-Castro editor and an anti-Communist extremist about the neutrality of the same page, I feel another period of gloom approaching."[8] Later it emerged that even U.S. military staff at Guantánamo Bay were engaged in the mischief, when an entry stating, "Fidel Castro is an admitted transsexual," which had been added to the Cuban leader's profile, was traced back to the base.[9] There would be no truce in the Wiki-wars over Cuba.

The Cuban Revolution may be despised in Miami's Little Havana, but it is the American embargo that has been increasingly targeted by religious communities in the United States. The 1998 visit by Pope John Paul II led many American Catholics to oppose the embargo, and a variety of Christian, Jewish, and interfaith groups have strongly criticized the sanctions. Under the Bush administration, new restrictions on religious and humanitarian exchanges with Cuba provoked a strong reaction from American religious organizations like the Alliance of Baptists and the United Methodist Church. The World Council of Churches, a Protestant group, was especially saddened when its Cuban counterpart, the Cuban Council of Churches, was criticized by name in the Commission for Assistance to a Free Cuba report that Secretary of State Condoleezza Rice chaired in 2006. Its director promptly fired off a letter to President Bush, saying, "We strongly feel that it is completely inappropriate for the U.S. government, or any government, to determine who is and who is not a legitimate national council of churches and to restrict or deny Christian fellowship and humanitarian assistance to any particular national church council."[10] When Raúl Castro took power in February 2008, his first meeting with an overseas leader was with Cardinal Tarcisio Bertone, the Vatican's secretary of state and the number-two official in the Catholic Church after the pope. After the meeting, the Vatican official stressed, in reference to the U.S. embargo, that he "gave assurances that the Holy See would work to have these sanctions reduced, if not altogether eliminated."

While most religious organizations oppose the embargo, few have been as vociferous in their opposition as the group led by Reverend Lucius Walker, the executive director of the Harlem-based Inter-Faith Community Organization and one of the United States' most ardent activists for the normalization of U.S. relations with Cuba. Beginning in 1992, Walker has organized annual caravans to bring humanitarian aid to Cuba under the banner of Pastors for Peace, an interfaith effort that flaunts its defiance of the U.S. sanctions by hauling shipments of food, medical equipment, and other goods across the U.S.-Mexican border and onward to Cuba. While Walker's views are not emblematic of the U.S. religious mainstream—he is politically located at the far-left end of the progressive spectrum—his long-standing engagement with Cuba and his penchant for leading actions of civil disobedience against U.S. policy have imbued him with hard-earned experience on the front lines of the Cuba wars.

Pastors for Peace operates out of a modest office space adjacent to the Convent Avenue Baptist Church in West Harlem. When I visited in the snowy early months of 2007, its walls were adorned with photos of the Cuban Five, logos opposing the U.S. "blockade" of Cuba, and a poster calling for the return of Elián González. Nearby was a calendar memorializing Maurice Bishop, the Marxist leader of the

New Jewel Movement, who seized control of the Caribbean island of Grenada in a revolutionary coup in 1979—only to be executed in 1983, prior to the United States invasion. Together the wall hangings represented a collection of cultural touchstones for the leftist solidarity groups sympathetic to Cuba. Indeed, whatever criticisms Walker may have of Cuba he keeps strictly to himself, instead training his fire on the United States.

Over the years, the Pastors for Peace caravans to Cuba have evolved into a ritualized form of civil disobedience in protest of the U.S. embargo. The organizers' long-term goal is to normalize U.S. relations with Cuba, but their short-term objectives include bringing needed humanitarian aid into Cuba and making a political point about what they view as the mean-spiritedness of the embargo. The first part of their argument is simple. They believe that the U.S. sanctions needlessly punish poor people in Cuba in a way that is unjust and inhumane, and that the U.S. government has no right to separate families and religious communities. The second part is more controversial, in that they overtly praise Cuba as a model of social justice—particularly for its achievements in health and education—and declare themselves to be in solidarity with the Cuban people, including their revolutionary icon, Fidel Castro. In response to these positions, Walker himself and more broadly the interfaith partisans he leads are praised by the Cuban government as the essence of humanity and derided by Cuban exiles as apologists for the Castro regime. Each summer, Pastors for Peace coordinates a caravan of several hundred people who travel through the United States collecting donations and then converge on the U.S.-Mexican border and attempt to brazen their way past U.S. customs officials to transport their aid to Cuba.

Walker invited me to sit down in the common room of the church next to his offices; it was sparsely populated with volunteers and elderly people from the community watching television. "In the earlier years, there were a lot of detentions by the U.S. border patrol," he said. "They didn't want to say we were arrested, but we were held in the same place as the prisoners. It is unbelievable the depth of commitment that people feel to the cause. On two occasions, when our aid was seized, there were fasts for life in shame for what the government had done. Both times the government returned to us the aid that had been taken." According to Walker, the confrontations with American border agents sometimes verged on violence. "Once it took me nearly six months to recover from a restraining type of hold that they put on my hand. Today, the physicality of the conflict has declined, and they have chosen to go after us legally by sending threatening letters. But arrests won't stop us. We've been doing this for sixteen years, and we will continue."

Dressed in a brown blazer and maroon shirt, Walker is a slender African American man in his early fifties with close-cropped hair, a salt-and-pepper goatee, and a relaxed demeanor. When the subject comes to Cuba, however, his words carry a punch. "We feel that we are not just giving aid but energizing people and standing up for justice. While we have had a positive effect, I don't consider our work to be successful because the U.S. has become much more hostile and mean-spirited towards Cuba, rather than less. In the early years, Cuban American groups would come after us and throw rocks and eggs. Once they hit a minister. They would show up at our press conferences and try to disrupt it. We identified one group and filed suit against them—Alpha 66—and we secured an injunction, and they had to pay a fine." Walker has little sympathy for the Cuban exiles who weigh so heavily on U.S. policy. "It's a despicable display of what we call democracy. The Bush administration has tied its interests to the pathological obsession that the right-wing Cuban exiles have to punish Cuba. Their behavior is so irrational that I can't think of any other explanation except that they are so beholden to the Miami vote that they have sold their souls to the right-wing Cuban American community."

His voice had been barely audible above a radiator hissing loudly next to the table, but Walker leaned forward to make his points heard. "We started the Caravans in 1992, when Cuba was in the middle of its 'special period.' There were shortages of *everything*— electricity, food, fuel, medicine. I know people who died because they couldn't get the medicines they needed in time. People were physically changing from hunger, and I could see them shrinking from one trip to the next. I know fathers who would eat very little so their children could eat. I saw agony in Cuba's effort to overcome that crisis." Walker spoke with intensity. "At Cuba's point of greatest need and difficulty, it was very painful to me, as a U.S. citizen, that in that period of time the U.S. passed the Torricelli Act [the Cuban Democracy Act] and the Helms-Burton Act to tighten the blockade. I consider that period of U.S. response to Cuba as a low point in any sense of morality and any sense of humanity. If it were possible for our government to have any sense of shame, that would have been the time to show it. The U.S. government was shameless."

Walker praised what he viewed as Cuba's democratic features, but he grimaced when I asked if he considered Fidel Castro to be a democrat. "I'm not going to play that game. You would see a different political reality in Cuba if the U.S. was not trying to strangle it or kill it. Fidel Castro has demonstrated that you can be poor and still be sovereign. He is about the only head of state in the world who has not been bought by the CIA or U.S. interests. We have been fiercely uncivilized in our aggression towards Cuba. What people see in Fidel is integrity they can trust. They do not want to trade that integrity for the uncertainty of U.S. friendship. What is democracy? We don't have democracy in the true sense of the word in our own country. Some call it a plutocracy—a contest of who can bamboozle the U.S. public the best." By contrast, he said, "Cuba's electoral system should be studied by people like us. I view it as an electoral system that has many positive features. So if you ask me if I think it is a democracy, yes I do. If you ask me if it's a dictatorship, I would say that it has high levels of participation. It has democratic features. You can't buy an election in Cuba. You don't have to be a millionaire in the National Assembly."

Walker made it clear he was an admirer of Castro. "I think that he will go down in history as one of the most effective, creative, and intelligent leaders of our time. I see him as a person of great integrity. He has great warmth and caring and love for the people. I see no reason to deny what my eyes see and what my heart feels. I don't have to kowtow to the Miami Cubans who are frothing at the mouth to go back and be the new American puppets in Cuba. When Fidel Castro dies, there will be a lot of sadness and mourning, and a sense of loss. In Cuba, he's revered like a father figure and seen to have such wisdom and caring. People will miss that strength and leadership. He will be missed in a lot of places in the world—but not Miami."

Several months later, Walker successfully led more than 150 people driving ninety tons of aid across the U.S.-Mexican border in the Pastors for Peace 18th Friendshipment Caravan to Cuba. "Anything can happen at the border," Walker warned, but there was no physical altercation, and American border agents pored over the luggage without taking any aid from the group. The delegation continued on to Cuba, where its members attended the graduation of the first class of

U.S. medical students at the Latin American School of Medicine in
Havana—the same group of black and Latino students whom Colin
Powell had intervened to protect from tougher U.S. sanctions in the
summer of 2004. Following its custom, the Pastors for Peace activists
refused to apply for a travel license from the U.S. Treasury Department to make their trip to Cuba. "If there is a law against loving your
neighbor," Walker says, "then I want to break it."

While religious activists continue to challenge the embargo, American
fascination with Cuban society endures mainly through the shared
passions of music, sports, and Cuba's large role in the popular imagination of the United States. Martyred revolutionary leader Che Guevara became a pop culture icon, the Cuban rhythms of salsa and *son*
have enchanted American music lovers, and Cuban rum and cigars
remain sought-after luxury goods by U.S. consumers. Even after the
collapse of the Soviet Union, the United States and Cuba stayed
locked in the paradoxical relationship of diplomatic and economic
isolation fused with cultural attraction. In the late 1990s, the Cuban
music of the Buena Vista Social Club became a runaway sensation in
the United States even as legendary Cuban musicians like Ibrahim Ferrer were accused of being communist stooges and barred from performing in Miami.

    Since its conception in 2000, the Latin Grammys awards show has
teetered on the dangerous fault line between Cuban music and American politics. The Latin Academy of Recording Arts and Sciences, also
known as the Latin Recording Academy, was launched by the
National Academy of Recording Arts and Sciences in 1997. It was
headquartered in Miami, and its mission was to recognize and promote excellence in recorded music from the Spanish- and Portuguese-
speaking world. Three years later, it launched the Latin Grammys.
The international awards show had the potential to bring about forty
million dollars in business to South Florida, but many Cuban exile
groups would not stand for an event that included musicians from the
island. Indeed, arguments over whether the Latin Grammys should be
held in Miami created such a deep split in the Cuban American
National Foundation in the summer of 2001 that conservative activist
Ninoska Pérez Castellón resigned along with two dozen other board
members. The first awards show, in 2000, was held in Los Angeles
because the organizers did not want to risk the exile community's ire

so soon after the Elián González crisis. In 2001, initial plans to stage the event in Miami again fell victim to local politics. The Grammy organizers learned that more than one hundred anti-Castro groups had been given permission to protest outside the show, and other demonstrators had obtained tickets to protest inside the venue.[11] When local police said they could not guarantee the safety of the concertgoers, the organizers were forced to take the show back to Los Angeles.

Enrique Fernández was the senior vice president and executive director of the Latin Recording Academy in 2001. Now a features writer with the *Miami Herald*, Fernández reflected on his experiences with the Latin Grammys during that time. "Miami was always a natural place for it because the Latin American music industry has been based here," he told me, "but we always knew there was going to be a problem. On the one hand, we have an organization that is international, and its only interest is Latin music. On the other hand, we have an exile community where certain people disapproved of Cuban nationals performing in the U.S. because they argued that this enriched the coffers of Fidel Castro." Fernández recalled, "We felt that the track record here in Miami had been one of demonstrations turning ugly, and that we had to protect our membership from being in harm's way." The possibility of hosting Cuban musicians in Miami generated so much political tension that it became impossible to safely hold the event there. In Los Angeles, by contrast, Cuban participation was a nonissue. "We could have had Fidel Castro in L.A.," Fernández said. "He and Raúl could have sung a duet."

In the end, Cuban musicians, including jazz pianist Chucho Valdés, pop singer Andrés Alén, and salsa star Isaac Delgado (who defected to the United States six years later), were allowed to participate when the venue was switched to Los Angeles, but these performances were silenced by tragedy. The event was scheduled for September 11, 2001, and the sudden and catastrophic terrorist attacks on New York and Washington forced the organizers to cancel the show. The Cuban musicians donated blood for the victims and later performed at the Beverly Hills Hotel at the first fund-raising concert for those afflicted by the attacks. Fernández shook his head at the memory. "There are many things to despise Osama bin Laden for, but I have my own agenda. He ruined my show."

The experience of Cuban musicians has been mixed since that

star-crossed event. In 2002, Cuba had twenty-two artists nominated for Latin Grammys, including Valdés, who won the prize for top instrumental album, but none received visas to attend the L.A. awards ceremony. In 2003, the Latin Grammys were held in Miami for the first time since their inception, but the ten nominated musical acts from Cuba were denied entry to the United States. While Cuban exiles like Gloria Estefan performed, and the late Cuban exile crooner and previous Latin Grammy winner Celia Cruz was commemorated, winners from mainland Cuba like singer Ibrahim Ferrer of the Buena Vista Social Club and the Cuban rap group Orishas were barred. From 2003 to 2005, the U.S. government denied more than forty-eight visas to Cuban musicians hoping to attend the Latin Grammys, part of a wider crackdown on artistic exchanges. Several Cuban musicians were allowed to participate when New York hosted the awards show in 2006, but few attended Las Vegas in 2007. During the first seven years of the show's history, artists from Cuba won a total of twenty-five Latin Grammys, including some of the island's most celebrated musicians—putting Cuba in fifth place for overall awards by country, trailing music powerhouses like Mexico, Brazil, and Spain but well ahead of Argentina, Puerto Rico, and the United States.

According to Fernández, Cuba's strong showing was not surprising. "Cuba is a powerhouse in music. So you can pretty much bet that, any year, there will be Cuban nominees in the Latin Grammys," he said. "I think you could argue that Cuba is a country that has such a big tourist trade because music is one of the things that makes it very appealing. Music does in some way enrich Cuba's cultural cachet, but that's not its main function. The main function of Cuban dance music is to shake your booty in a fun kind of way. The relationship between art and politics is a complex one." When I asked what made Cuban music so powerful, Fernández laughed heartily. "I wish I could answer. I don't know. I just don't fucking know. Why? What happened on that island? Why is it so good?" He mused about the Spanish and European culture mixed with American and Caribbean musical influences. "When you get some of the deep African rhythms of Cuban music, particularly in the rumbas—that stuff can change a heartbeat because it is so moving. At first it might seem a little harsh, but when you kind of relax and get deep into it, that stuff will just take you out."

Baseball is another arena where Cuban and American passions collide. Even more than in the United States, baseball is a national obsession in Cuba, and its players rank among the best in the world. However, Castro banned professional sports in 1959, and Cuba's top players earn only twenty dollars a month plus perks like luxury housing and transportation. This grants them an elite status in Cuba but is a pittance compared with the multimillion-dollar contracts signed by their American counterparts. Not surprisingly, dozens of Cuban baseball players and other athletes have defected to the United States in search of wealth that is beyond their reach at home. Some have achieved wild success. Cuban baseball star Orlando "El Duque" Hernández escaped in 1997, signed a $6.6 million contract, and went on to win his first World Series in 1998. Other high-profile defectors have played with the San Francisco Giants and the Boston Red Sox, but the odds have been stacked against them. Only fourteen of the sixty Cuban baseball players who defected to the United States between 1991 and 2002 entered the major leagues, while others either played abroad or dropped out of the sport entirely.[12]

Given the strength of Cuban baseball, the United States' Major League Baseball thought it was a no-brainer to include a Cuban team in the first-ever World Baseball Classic, planned for the spring of 2006. The competition was to feature sixteen national teams from the strongest baseball countries, facing off against one another over eighteen days at American venues, with the finals played in San Diego. Major League Baseball officials modeled the event on soccer's World Cup, which ranks among the most-watched sporting events in the world.

At first, Cuba was coy about whether it would play. In the summer of 2005, Humberto Rodríguez, the president of Cuba's National Institute of Sports, dismissed the tournament as an effort at crass commercialization: "Cuba doubts it will participate . . . If it's about capitalizing baseball to show off economic power, we are not in agreement."[13] In December 2005, Castro gave a five-hour televised speech in Havana in which he indicated that Cuba would play in the World Baseball Classic. In his comments, Castro blasted Cuban players "who cannot resist the millions of the major leagues" and admitted that defections of prized athletes remained a major sore spot. He was consoled, however, by the fact that "when one leaves, another ten better players emerge."[14] Soon thereafter, Vice President José Ramón Fernández, who headed the island's Olympic Committee, green-lighted

Cuba's participation. And indeed, the Cuban players, normally confined to amateur tournaments, were eager to compete against professionals. Carlos Tabares, an Olympic veteran and captain of the island's powerful Industriales club, described Cuba's participation in the classic as "the best news ever, because it will destroy the myth that Cubans can't play against the professionals."[15]

Gene Orza, the chief operating officer and a twenty-year veteran of the Major League Baseball Players Association, explained to me why it was crucial to include Cuba. "Cubans routinely play in international tournaments and almost as routinely win them. They were a legitimizing force in terms of the integrity of the tournament. The Cubans are just great players." Indeed, the Cuban team won the Olympic gold medal in 1992, 1996, and 2004—taking the silver medal only in 2000 when it was bested by the United States in the finals. However, Major League Baseball's invitation to the Cubans soon set off a firestorm of protest led by U.S. congressman Lincoln Diaz-Balart, who sent off a searing letter to U.S. baseball commissioner Allan "Bud" Selig: "You have invited a totalitarian dictatorship which has murdered thousands and imprisoned hundreds of thousands for the 'crime' of supporting freedom and democracy."

Diaz-Balart wanted Cuba to be represented in the tournament by a team of Cuban exiles, selected from the twenty-two major-league players and sixty-two minor-league players of Cuban descent in the United States. "Many such players, I am certain, would be honored to represent Cuba, and not Cuba's oppressors, in the WBC."[16] Baseball officials like Orza dismissed the proposal: "We're running the World Baseball Classic. We're not running a pick-up team tournament. I could make a great team out of left-handers. I could make a great team out of exiles from other countries, but that's not the point. This is nation against nation and territory against territory. Cuba has the right to pick its team." Diaz-Balart also sent a letter to Treasury Secretary John Snow, urging him to reject a license for the Cubans, arguing that "this license would allow a State Sponsor of Terrorism to use U.S. currency to finance its machinery of oppression."[17] A day later, liberal New York representative José Serrano jumped into the fray, urging Secretary of State Condoleezza Rice to "avoid the politicization" and "put sportsmanship over politics," pointing out that Cuban teams had played in the United States in the past. "We raised hell about it," Serrano later asserted. "They knew that this was giving them incredibly bad press."

Still, on December 14, the Treasury Department slapped down Major League Baseball's request to include a team from Cuba. Over the years, thousands of Cubans have been denied visas to the United States for participation in sporting events, musical concerts, academic and professional conferences, and awards ceremonies. But this was Major League Baseball, and some major dollars and egos were on the line. Orza later recalled, "We were so dedicated to getting them in because the legitimacy of an international event is in doubt in baseball if you haven't got the Cubans playing."

Over the next few weeks, the consequences of rejecting the Cuban team began to reverberate far and wide. Puerto Rico had been selected to host the first two rounds of games in March, but on December 22, the president of the Puerto Rican Baseball Federation declared it would refuse to host the opening games if Cuba was barred from playing: "The reasons that have been given have nothing to do with sports and are counter to the Olympic spirit. If the United States wants to continue imposing an economic and political embargo, that is its prerogative, but that should not be mixed up with sports."[18] Venezuela plunged into the controversy by announcing that it would volunteer to host the round of games scheduled to be in Puerto Rico, thereby enabling Cuba to play in the opening competition, though it would still be banned from the final in the U.S. The International Baseball Federation threatened to withdraw its sanction from the event if Cuba was left out. The shock waves reached all the way up to the International Olympic Committee (IOC). On December 20, Peter Ueberroth, the United States Olympic Committee chairman, called on the Bush administration to reverse its decision to bar Cuba, saying, "It is important to any future bid city from the United States that this be reversed. It's disappointing. This will impact IOC members negatively."[19] In January, IOC president Jacques Rogge warned that how the Cuban situation was resolved could affect the American bid to host the Summer Olympics in 2016.

With millions of dollars at stake, Major League Baseball intensified its lobbying efforts to include Cuba in the World Baseball Classic. President Bush got directly involved. As the managing partner of the Texas Rangers from 1989 to 1994, Bush had strong ties to baseball that pre-dated his more recent embrace of Cuban exiles. Anti-Castro groups still had a lot of clout with the White House, but they had simply overreached by trying to take on Major League Baseball. On January 20, 2006, less than ten weeks before the opening pitch was to be thrown in Puerto Rico, the Treasury Department reversed its prior decision and issued a license allowing the Cuban team to play. White House press secretary Scott McClellan said, "Our concerns were centered on making sure that no money was going to the Castro regime and that the World Baseball Classic would not be misused by the regime for spying. We believe the concerns have been addressed."[20]

In order to ensure that the Cuban team would not profit from the classic, a side agreement was made that all Cuban proceeds would be donated to the victims of Hurricane Katrina. Diaz-Balart denounced the inclusion of Cuba and called on the Cuban players to defect. Reflecting back on the episode, he fumed that "Major League Baseball acted basically as advocates, agents if you will, for the Castro regime. They just didn't want anything to interrupt their whole business scheme." With the political question resolved, the Cuban team quickly focused on the technical issues they would confront. Retired shortstop and team captain Germán Mesa reassured the Cuban public that the synthetic turf in the San Juan stadium was manageable: "The bounce is different, the players have to position themselves a bit further back. The ball spins more, but the Cubans are fast and won't be surprised by a bad bounce." Denied the chance to practice with the tournament bats that were sent to the other fifteen teams, Cuba's star batter, twenty-one-year-old Yulieski Gourriel, still kept his cool: "This tournament is going to be unprecedented. I feel calm and relaxed, even though it is not easy to think about facing pitches of 95-miles plus . . . I change at the plate. I go out ready to hit the ball. I'm a slugger."[21]

Cuba performed well at the opening games in Puerto Rico in March 2006, fending off Panama and crushing the Netherlands 11–2, despite an incident sparked when a protester in the stadium started waving signs saying DOWN WITH FIDEL! and BASEBALL PLAYERS YES, TYRANTS NO! at Cuba's team doctor Tony Castro, who also happened to be Fidel Castro's son. The top Cuban official at the game stormed toward the man and nearly caused a brawl before Puerto Rican police intervened. The Cubans then embarked on a winning streak that led them, two weeks later, to the final against Japan in San Diego. By winning all but two of the games it played in the tournament, Cuba fended off fourteen professional teams with star rosters, including the Dominican Republic, the United States, and Venezuela. Ultimately, though, Cuba had to settle for second place when Japan won the championship game 10–6. After coming so close to victory and then seeing it slip through their hands, members of the Cuban team were somber but philosophical. Cuban outfielder Frederich Cepeda said, "I think this Classic is historic because it demonstrated that not only the players from the paid major leagues can carry the supremacy. We've demonstrated that what matters is sacrifice, human values, and the effort you give on the field. This is a well-deserved second place. We're not satisfied, but we're happy with our performance."[22]

Cuba has already been invited to the next World Baseball Classic, in 2009, and its officials will likely seize this opportunity to face off once again with top international competition on American soil. The country was bitterly disappointed when the baseball competition was dropped from the 2012 Olympics in London, which leaves it seeking new venues to conquer. Already, star batter Gourriel said, "I am thinking about the 2009 classic where our revenge will be pending. Just like the fans, we have only one objective: to win."[23] If it were not for the American trade sanctions, the Cuban team would have earned one million dollars for its performance in the first classic. As agreed, the money was instead donated to the victims of Hurricane Katrina, but this did not dull the Cuban players' enthusiasm for a rematch.

When the American film director Oliver Stone landed in Havana in February 2002, his goal was to film a documentary of Fidel Castro speaking about his life. Now in his early sixties, Stone is no stranger to controversial subjects. A New York native and Yale dropout who was twice wounded in action as an army infantryman in the Vietnam War in the late 1960s, Stone went on to become one of the most successful directors of his generation. He won Academy Awards for *Platoon* and *Born on the Fourth of July*, and his other films have tackled thorny political topics including the Kennedy assassination, Nixon's downfall, and the 9/11 attacks on the World Trade Center. Exploring how men serve and betray their countries has been a central theme in Stone's work, and it is at the core of his fascination with Castro in Cuba.

When Stone first arrived in Cuba, he was anxious to begin filming his conversations with Castro. The only problem was that the Cuban leader had not consented to the interview, leaving Stone and his film crew holed up at a local hotel for two days attempting to make contact with their star subject. "There were skeletons of reporters sitting there in hotel lobbies, literal skeletons that had been waiting there for years," Stone later quipped to me when I called him to ask about the film. As a last-ditch effort, he sent a four-page handwritten note to Castro that described his project in sweeping language. "I am a filmmaker, you are a head of state. I think this is an opportunity to create a new document," Stone wrote. "I am not looking for revelations, scoops, gossip, all that sick modern-world stuff. I am looking for that thing, I suppose, which is classic and eternal in you." Soon he received word that Castro wanted to meet with him. The film project was back on track.

Stone spent more than thirty hours with Castro over three days, speaking with him in his office, visiting local landmarks in Castro's trademark armored black Mercedes, and peppering the Cuban dictator with questions about his life. The resulting ninety-five-minute film initially premiered at the Sundance Film Festival in January 2003. Stone's respectful, even admiring, portrait of Castro won him both acclaim and fierce criticism among those who reviewed the film. Stone later explained his approach: "I wanted to make it an essay on life and his philosophy on life, his look back, his feelings on history as well as the future. I wanted to do a portrait of a man. It was not a journalistic interview at all, in my opinion." Stone also thinks he knows why Castro was so open to speaking with him. "He trusted me that I wouldn't fuck him in the editing."

HBO purchased the U.S. rights to show the final documentary, titled *Comandante*, and scheduled its premiere for May 25, 2003. By April, the channel was running promotional ads describing the film as an "unflinching portrait of the famous icon." Behind the scenes, however, pressure was growing on HBO to pull the plug. Simmering discontent about the movie among the Cuban American community suddenly boiled over when Castro's security forces implemented the crackdown on dissidents in March 2003. By the time Cuba summarily executed the three boat hijackers in early April, HBO had deemed that a relatively upbeat movie about Fidel Castro was unfit for public viewing.

On April 17, HBO yanked *Comandante* from its spring lineup with the explanation that "in light of recent alarming events in the country, the film seems somewhat dated or incomplete."[24] Stone was left hanging. "We had sold it to HBO. They loved it, they put it on the air, they promoted it," he recalled with frustration. "Then HBO said they couldn't air it as a result of this outrage." He learned that Cuban American community groups had mobilized heavily against the film. "I believe that there was a tremendous amount of pressure on HBO, because these people are very organized. They are a political lobby, and they are very powerful in Washington and with the right. They can deliver, I guess, a thousand e-mails to HBO at any point, and they would also go to the sponsors." Stone even heard that the White House had intervened to block HBO from showing the film, something the company denied. "They would never admit to that," he laughed. "Pressure from a sponsor? No, never! A call from the White House? Are you joking?!"

HBO then asked Stone to return to Cuba to interview Castro about the crackdown and speak with several dissidents who had been affected by the recent wave of repression. Well-known dissidents like Oswaldo Payá were unsparing in their criticism of the director: "I thought he was very misinformed about what is going on in Cuba. He was more interested in the love life of Fidel Castro than in what is happening to 11 million Cubans."[25] Nearly one year later, on April 14, 2004, HBO presented American viewers with Looking for Fidel, a very different film than the one that Stone had initially screened at Sundance under the title Comandante. Shorn down to fifty-three minutes, Looking for Fidel is a grimmer and more combative piece. Stone challenges Castro on Cuba's human rights record, interviews the island's beleaguered dissidents, and exchanges questions with several attempted hijackers sentenced to long prison terms in Cuba. Whereas Comandante looks back at the long sweep of Castro's rule, Looking for Fidel captures a particular moment in time when the Cuban leader was engaged in a war of nerves with the United States.

Stone realizes that his perspective on Castro goes against the American mainstream, which doomed his original picture portraying Fidel as an icon but made possible a revised version that casts Castro as a tyrant. When I asked him if it was fair to say he held "romantic notions of Fidel Castro," he defended his point of view. "It's inevitable, I suppose, because many film people are considered ditzy, I guess, by you Washington types. But I think a lot of us are also experienced in the world. We meet a lot of people," he said. "If Castro died tomorrow, the Cubans would be well prepared for it. They have a strong system in place. He was surrounded by sharp young aides, people who spoke excellent English and had a good grasp of concepts. I say this because I've been in African countries, Latin countries, Asian countries, where a lot of the aides are terrible, by comparison. Their suppleness of mind was what I appreciated. I met with many of the officers, many of the elite, so to speak, and I was impressed by their mind-set. They're smart, they're realistic. They know he's going to die, and they're going to move on." When I asked him how the United States should respond, Stone shot back, "I think we should repeal the embargo and act like civilized human beings."

After being yanked by HBO, which still owns the rights, *Comandante* never returned to the airwaves. Stone's subsequent trip to Cuba in search of additional footage for *Looking for Fidel* resulted in a multiyear Treasury Department inquiry into whether he violated the U.S. sanctions. Stone spent tens of thousands of dollars defending himself in the case, and his California-based production company, Ixtlan, was ultimately fined $6,322 in December 2006. " 'The Oliver Stone rule' is what my lawyer called it," he said. "It's like, 'We don't know what the hell you did wrong, but we sense you did something wrong, therefore we're not going to let this thing off the docket.' It's crazy."

Stone is proud of the two films, but even several years later, both weighed heavily on his mind. "I prefer *Comandante* because it is more of a movie, but I love *Looking for Fidel* as a rat-a-tat-tat straight-on interview. I got him on the edge of his anger several times, but he went through with it, and I think the result is astounding." The films also brought him tremendous heartache, because his constant battles with HBO, with his coproducers, with the U.S. government's endless red tape, and with the tormented politics of U.S.-Cuban relations eventually wore him down. "They were so painful to make. It's time out of my life. These are causes I believe in, and they have absolutely no resonance in this country," he told me. "I wouldn't go through that period again. I mean, I learned a lot, and maybe it was good for me, but my God, it really is a hard game." He is particularly anguished that the film that expressed his original vision, *Comandante*, has been bottled up since its premiere at Sundance in January 2003 and was never again shown to American audiences. In his three decades in the movie industry, Oliver Stone has written or directed nearly thirty films, but *Comandante* carries a special mark of distinction. "Jesus Christ," Stone exclaimed, "it's been the most censored film I've ever done!"

Stone is far from the only one to find that the cultural terrain between the United States and Cuba is pocked with obstacles and land mines. These typically divide into two categories: controversy over how the island is depicted in American film, art, and books and conflict that is generated over whether Cuba should be able to participate in high-profile events in the United States like the Latin Grammys or the World Baseball Classic. In addition, many religious groups have expressed their discomfort with the U.S. embargo, ranging from the quiet protests of the conservative Catholic Church to the vocal advocacy campaigns of the left-wing Pastors for Peace. In particular, the tough travel restrictions have cut back on a broad spectrum of cultural activities that the United States has often encouraged in its dealings with other authoritarian countries.

In this area, again, Cuba is the exception to the rule. The United States has long viewed cultural exchanges through religious contact, sports, arts, music, and film as a form of soft diplomacy that can be used to create bridges between people who are divided by their governments. In the 1970s, the Nixon administration famously encouraged "Ping-Pong diplomacy" to help thaw relations between the United States and China, and there are hundreds of other examples of soft diplomacy, even including members of the "axis of evil" during the administration of George W. Bush. In the fall of 2007, Iranian president Mahmoud Ahmadinejad was invited to give a speech at Columbia University in New York, and in February 2008, the New York Philharmonic orchestra performed in the North Korean capital of Pyongyang. It is striking that, given the current climate of U.S.-Cuba relations, it is all but impossible to imagine Raúl Castro being invited to speak at Georgetown University or the Chicago Symphony Orchestra performing at the Karl Marx Theater in Havana.

It is true that the U.S.-Cuba relationship has experienced occasional interludes of cultural diplomacy over the decades. The most sustained period occurred at the end of the Clinton administration, which opened up pathways for cultural, artistic, and religious exchanges that were later sewn shut by Bush. In 1999, a series of exhibition games were played between Cuba's national team and the Baltimore Orioles, and the Washington Ballet and its Cuban counterpart exchanged performances in the two countries' respective capitals. However, as Cuba experiences its transition to a new government, the strained bilateral relationship has squelched all but the most minimal contact between the artistic, cultural, and religious sectors of the United States and Cuba. Instead, the people on both sides of the Straits of Florida view each other through the distant looking glass that has become a poor substitute for actual contact that could be a source for mutual understanding.

CHAPTER 10

The Capitalist Temptation

Fidel Castro wore his arm in a sling when he appeared on Cuban television to announce his most important economic decision in years: the removal of the U.S. dollar from circulation in Cuba. It was late in October 2004, less than a week after he fell off a stage and shattered his arm and knee, and Castro was determined to show that he was still firmly in charge of the country. Castro's regime first legalized the U.S. dollar in 1993, shortly after the collapse of Soviet subsidies plunged the island into profound economic crisis. Permitting the greenback to circulate in Cuba had kept the country's economy from imploding, but tolerating the Yankee currency had been a bitter pill for Castro to swallow. It created a complicated three-tier currency system that included the U.S. dollar, a "convertible peso" that was equal in value to the dollar, and the Cuban peso, which was worth far less. It also carried real risks, as the Bush administration escalated efforts to prevent U.S. dollars from flowing into Cuba in the form of remittances from Cuban Americans and cash spent by U.S. travelers. In the summer of 2004, the U.S. Federal Reserve had even levied a one-hundred-million-dollar penalty on the Union Bank of Switzerland for providing fresh U.S. banknotes to Havana. Now Castro cited these acts of "external economic aggression" by the United States as the core rationale for ridding the island of the dollar.

The Cuban Central Bank first introduced the new policy on October 23, when it issued a resolution mandating that all dollar transactions now be performed using "convertible pesos," commonly referred to as *chavitos*. (The Cuban peso, which was valued at around twenty-five to the dollar, continued to be used for salaries and ration stores but was virtually useless in stores where quality goods were sold at dollar prices.) The Cuban people were given until November 8 to exchange their dollars for convertible pesos, after which they would face a 10 percent exchange tax, a move the bank justified because "the U.S. government has intensified its economic war on the people of Cuba." Cuba's Central Bank is located on a narrow side street in Old Havana, just a few blocks away from the constant hum of dollars and pesos being exchanged in one of Havana's busiest tourist districts. On a typical day, the local butcher can be found around the corner cutting meat in the humid mid-afternoon air, near a crisp red plastic sign denoting the Provincial Communist Committee of the Old Havana district. The headquarters of the Central Bank is distinguishable only by a small placard, the cool black marble that lines the entrance, and the armored vehicles that are frequently parked outside. The ramshackle block shows few signs of being home to one of the island's most important financial institutions, but the bank's de-dollarization campaign rippled through all aspects of Cuban life.

Cubans lined up in surprising numbers to trade in hard-earned dollars and cherished cash gifts from relatives in Miami. In the decade since its legalization, the U.S. currency had reshaped the economic and political life of the country, as the population pursued dollars to seek some relief from Cuba's crushing poverty. During this time, the average monthly wage remained about ten dollars, paid by the state in fraying Cuban pesos valued at less than a nickel each. To provide greater liquidity, *chavitos* were circulated on a one-to-one basis with the U.S. dollar, but the populace was wary of the colorful notes, and few stored their earnings in convertible pesos. Now faced with the November 8 deadline, the Cuban people dug deep into their dollar holdings to swap their bills before the steep exchange tax went into effect.

In just two weeks, an estimated half a billion dollars poured into the Cuban government's coffers, an amount so large that it prompted Central Bank president Francisco Soberón to confess, "We didn't know how much money people were saving under their mattresses." The smooth monetary swap was both a highly profitable currency grab and an impressive display of political strength. (Since *chavitos* have no value in world currency markets, the government had in essence exchanged bills with no internationally recognized worth for U.S. dollars that could be used for purchases outside of Cuba.) Even normally skeptical foreign diplomats in Havana privately conceded that the process was extraordinarily well run and left the regime temporarily cash-flush. The Cuban government took pains to avoid the widely feared devaluation of the convertible peso and has since even strengthened the national peso against the dollar. Soberón himself cautioned, "It would be extremely unwise to change the one-to-one exchange rate after the Cuban people have shown such confidence in the Cuban government."

Forcing the U.S. dollar out of circulation proved to be a masterstroke by Cuba's economic planners. It bolstered the government's hard-currency reserves while leaving the average citizen with convertible pesos that in fact had no value outside the country. The move also helped to strengthen the hand of the central government as it sought to better control the large amounts of U.S. dollars funneling through the island's more than four hundred state-owned enterprises. In recent years, Fidel Castro had become increasingly convinced that it was time to put the genie of the U.S. dollar back in the bottle. In 2001, he established an auditing ministry to keep better track of internal financial flows, and all dollar payments were later channeled into a single account in the Central Bank. Still, potentially destabilizing corruption scandals continued to unfold in the tourism sector, prompting Raúl Castro to declare that the tourism industry was like "a tree born twisted that must be uprooted and planted anew."

By evicting the U.S. dollar from the island, Castro was signaling that the heady days of wheeling and dealing in large dollar sums between Cuban enterprises had effectively ended. Now all significant transactions were to occur under his watchful eye. Euros and Canadian dollars were still welcome in Cuba and would not be subject to the high tax levied on U.S. dollars, but the convertible peso was now the currency of the land. Several years later, when the plunging value of the U.S. dollar prompted grave concerns worldwide, Cuba's preemptive dollar purge appeared almost prescient. At the time of the dollar switch, Castro declared that "the fate of the empire's currency is to devalue. The fate of the currency of Cuba, the blockaded country . . . is to gain in value." That prophecy proved to be only half true, but Castro had issued a powerful warning to the emerging capitalists in his own government: The Cuban Revolution will not be dollarized.

The Cuban economy is still crawling out of the crisis that engulfed the country following the collapse of the Soviet Union in 1991. Cuba's dependence on billions of dollars in annual subsidies from its cold war ally had left it extremely vulnerable to the changes that swept across Eastern Europe and the Soviet Union in the late 1980s and early 1990s. The Berlin Wall fell in 1989, and the following year Castro declared that the collapse of the socialist bloc meant that Cuba was entering "a Special Period in a Time of Peace" that would bring profound economic repercussions to the island. Still, Castro deeply distrusted the reforms of perestroika and glasnost advocated by Soviet premier Mikhail Gorbachev, which led him to misjudge the political situation in Russia by relying on intelligence provided by Soviet hard-liners. In June 1991, Castro invited KGB chairman Vladimir Kryuchkov to Havana. They signed a series of secret agreements to preserve Cuba's status in the Soviet sphere of influence just months before Kryuchkov joined the Gang of Eight, who briefly ousted Gorbachev in an August coup in a last-ditch effort to preserve the Soviet Union. Castro was one of three foreign leaders to immediately declare their support for the coup (the others were Iraq's Saddam Hussein and Libya's Muammar el-Qaddafi), but history was unfolding in another direction.[1] Boris Yeltsin famously climbed onto a tank to denounce the coup amid popular protest, and the takeover unraveled. On December 25, 1991, Gorbachev resigned as Soviet president, the Communist Party was disbanded, the red hammer-and-sickle flag was removed from the Kremlin, and the Soviet Union ceased to exist. It was one of the greatest historical events of the twentieth century, but Fidel Castro did not see it coming until it was too late.

Cut adrift from its main sponsor, Cuba descended into one of the most crippling economic crises experienced by any country in the modern era. During the "special period," its trading patterns collapsed, its gross domestic product plunged by a third between 1991 and 1994, the incidence of malnutrition and disease surged, and virtually all motorized transportation in the country ground to a halt. Francisco Soberón described the situation in the starkest possible terms: "It was as if we woke up one day and the sun did not come up. There was no light anywhere. All we could see was darkness and we were totally alone." Almost overnight, even members of the Cuban middle class were forced to confront the stark deprivations of poverty: persistent hunger and lack of electricity, clean water, and life-saving medicines. Cars virtually vanished from the streets as Cubans began to travel on thousands of bicycles purchased at discounted rates from China. Doctors' offices disposed of old height-weight charts used to measure a child's physical progress, because in this harsh new era, Cuban children could no longer be expected to grow as tall or weigh as much as their predecessors. The estimated number of calories from daily food consumption fell from three thousand to below two thousand for the average Cuban, and severe malnutrition led to on outbreak of blindness. While it is impossible to know how many people suffered premature death as a result of the hardship forced on them by the economic collapse, the human cost was significant.

In 1992, Congress tightened the embargo in an effort to provoke the demise of the Castro government—and two years later an estimated thirty-five thousand Cubans tried to escape the island's crushing poverty in a refugee wave called the *balsero* crisis. By the mid-1990s, however, the Cuban economy had begun to turn the corner. An early decision to allow foreign direct investment in the form of joint ventures was bearing fruit as investors from Canada, Spain, Mexico, and other European and Latin American countries established a foothold in the Cuban market. Long opposed to tourism, Castro pivoted to embrace the tourist trade, and hundreds of thousands of visitors from Canada and Europe were soon spending millions of dollars annually sunning themselves on Cuba's beaches or exploring historic Havana. The U.S. dollar was legalized and accepted for trade on a one-to-one basis with the convertible peso, although Cubans' state wages were still paid in Cuban pesos that traded at a fraction of that value. The first glimmers of legal private enterprise materialized when the Cuban government issued new regulations permitting a host of self-employment activities, including barbershops, auto-mechanic shops, bed-and-breakfasts, and the famous private restaurants known as *paladares*. The reforms went furthest in the agricultural sector, where semiprivate cooperatives and farmers' markets were allowed to take shape with minimum state intervention. Cuba's new capitalist class was small and weak, but for the first time a substantial number of Cubans could provide for themselves without depending solely on the government for their livelihoods. All this occurred while Cuba remained largely cut off from the international financial system and banned from membership (at Washington's behest) in important development institutions like the International Monetary Fund and the World Bank.

By the end of the decade, Cuba was experiencing sustained economic growth, but deep problems remained. Citizens still received ration cards for food, but the subsidies had been cut way back, so that it was impossible to feed a family solely with state provisions. The government had slashed defense spending and maintained spending in health and education, but the quality of these services had become increasingly threadbare. More crucially, the multiple-exchange-rate system generated by the U.S. dollar circulating next to the Cuban peso created enormous distortions. The average wage in Cuban pesos was equivalent to ten dollars a month, but basic items like soap, clothing, and food were mainly sold in dollar stores at prices that were close to their U.S. equivalent. Peso stores still existed, but they were poorly stocked and sold goods of extremely low quality. This meant that access to the U.S. dollar was now the single greatest factor in determining quality of life. The tips collected each month by busboys and taxi drivers working in the tourist sector could overwhelm the thirty-dollar monthly wage of a Cuban brain surgeon, or even a government minister. Virtually every strata of Cuban society now had to trade goods and services in the black market to survive. Cuba's historic urban middle class began to work as waiters, tour guides, taxi drivers, and even prostitutes, completely upending the socialist values of the Cuban Revolution. These were painful trade-offs for everyone to make.

Having survived the 1990s, Cuba entered the twentieth century facing a profoundly different set of circumstances both domestically and internationally. Tourism was now a mainstay of the country's economy, and small-scale private entrepreneurship was thriving on a limited basis. Hundreds of joint ventures had been signed with foreign companies in sectors including tourism, nickel mining, biotechnology, and petroleum. The 1998 election of Hugo Chávez in nearby Venezuela meant that Cuba once again had an oil-rich ally, a fact that proved especially crucial as petroleum prices began to surge. The United States had created several chinks in the armor of its embargo, allowing more legal visitors to Cuba, authorizing Cuban Americans to send remittances totaling nearly half a billion dollars annually, and even legalizing one-way agricultural sales to Cuba. Canadian and European investment remained stable, and China leapfrogged ahead to become Cuba's second-largest trading partner after Venezuela. With the economic winds at its back, Cuba posted official growth rates of

11.8 percent in 2005, 12.5 percent in 2006, and around 7.5 percent in 2007. While the accuracy of Cuba's data was clouded by a new formula that included the value of social services in its accounting, even the CIA grudgingly acknowledged that the island was growing by more than 7 percent annually. But the life of the average Cuban was still plagued by a level of scarcity and hardship that is difficult for most Americans to imagine. (In the summer of 2007, Associated Press reporter Anita Snow experimented with living for one month on nothing more than the Cuban food ration system and an estimated local salary of less than seventeen dollars. She lost nine pounds and found herself "obsessing about food.") Meanwhile, the Bush administration continued to hold fast to the embargo, and Cuba's robust trade with other international partners could not obscure how profound the crisis remained for most of its citizens.

Tom Donohue is the president of the U.S. Chamber of Commerce, a major lobbying organization based in Washington, D.C., that represents more than three million American businesses. In July 1999, he led a delegation of businesspeople to Cuba to learn about the island's economic conditions and think ahead to the day when U.S. firms could play a role in the country. While on the visit, he met with Fidel Castro. Donohue later recalled, "My impression at the time was that he had not softened his communist views in the least and that he retained an iron grip on the country. But during our meeting, he acknowledged that there are sectors of the economy that are better handled by the private sector." Donohue had little sympathy for Castro, but his criticism of U.S. policy toward the island was equally withering. "The U.S. embargo is one of the biggest foreign policy failures of the past half century," he argued. "No one should be surprised by this. Unilateral sanctions don't work, and Cuba is just one case in point. In fact, the embargo has only served to make a martyr out of a tyrant . . . The fact that U.S. companies are denied access to the Cuban market is a gift to firms from other countries. That bothers me a great deal, but what bothers me most is Washington's failure to recognize this obvious failure for what it is."

However, Donohue recognized that Fidel's illness had changed the political context on the island. "Raúl Castro has said he wants to open the economy to some degree, and he is clearly looking at what China and Vietnam have done. I'm skeptical about him becoming the next Deng Xiaoping, but there is change in the air, whether Raúl wants it or not." Still, Donohue viewed substantial political obstacles to changing U.S. policy, irrespective of what occurs in Cuba. "It doesn't take a political rocket scientist to see that the Cuba issue is so highly charged because of Florida politics, and Florida was the key to the election in 2000 and to some degree 2004," he said. "At the same time, we are going through the greatest global economic boom in history, and U.S. business has vast opportunities overseas . . . For most of the business community, it's been an easy choice to avoid the charged issue of Cuba and go get a piece of the action in giant markets like China, all the while making a nice profit."

Even as Cuba hovers on the verge of the post-Castro era, American businesses have been reluctant to abandon their traditional position on Cuba: missing in action. European and Canadian companies have been quietly expanding their investments in Cuba, while China and especially Venezuela have been galloping into the Cuban market. U.S. businesses, by contrast, have been content to sit on the sidelines, and few have actively pushed for a more flexible economic policy toward Cuba. The one exception is the multibillion-dollar U.S. agribusiness industry, which won an important concession in 2000 when its support helped to pass a bill legalizing U.S. food exports to Cuba. Known as the Nethercutt Amendment for its main sponsor, former Republican congressman George Nethercutt of Washington State, the bill authorized the sale of U.S. agricultural products to Cuba on an all-cash basis. (It also opened a loophole allowing the sale of certain medical exports to Cuba, but a complicated monitoring requirement scared off U.S. companies from using it.) President Bill Clinton signed the bill into law during his last few months in office, and Castro initially vowed that Cuba would not purchase "even a single grain of rice" under the new legislation.

The dam burst in November 2001, when central Cuba was devastated by Hurricane Michelle, the most powerful storm to strike the island since the 1950s. When the United States offered a token amount of food aid, Cuba responded by buying the products instead. Within a month, several American companies had consummated a deal with Cuba valued at nearly thirty million dollars—marking the first direct trade between the two countries in thirty-eight years. This new trading relationship suddenly gave Cuba political relevance that extended far beyond Miami and Washington, D.C., and turned it into a local bread-and-butter issue that has motivated seven sitting U.S. governors to travel to Cuba. Governor George Ryan of Illinois first broke the long-standing taboo in 1999, and Minnesota's Jesse Ventura was the star attraction at the first U.S.-Cuba trade fair in 2002. Top state officials from Idaho, Louisiana, Maine, Nebraska, and North Dakota all followed suit. Since 2001, more than two billion dollars in trade deals have been signed with American companies, enabling Cuba to leapfrog over nearly two hundred other countries to become the twenty-fifth-largest export market for U.S. agricultural products. Nebraska governor Dave Heineman made two trips to Cuba in 2007 to ink trade deals worth forty million dollars. Like most of the new Cuba traders, Heineman has shown little interest in opposing the embargo even as he helps Nebraska farmers sell truckloads of wheat through its loopholes. "Well, I try not to get into that, because that's up to the president and the Congress," he told the *New York Times* on his last visit to Havana, "but I will say expanding trade relationships is good for Nebraska and altogether good for America."[2]

Cuba's population of eleven million is equivalent in size to that of Ohio, the seventh-largest U.S. state, and thus is a significant market for American products. The agricultural trade has become an economic win-win for the United States and Cuba, but the jury is still out on whether Cuba has the capacity to emerge as a "Latin tiger" of substantial interest to U.S. companies. Those who believe that the island represents a diamond in the rough emphasize how its virgin beaches and rich cultural heritage could quickly catapult it into a prime tourist destination for American travelers, resulting in massive opportunities for hotel and infrastructure development.

Still, soaring American expectations may face a hard landing when U.S. investors confront Cuba's communist framework for foreign direct investment. The legal cornerstone is the Foreign Investment Law, known as Law 77, which was ratified by the National Assembly in 1995. Cuba requires foreign companies to hire employees through a state contracting agency that charges a high premium for low-wage workers. Cuba may charge five hundred dollars per month for skilled workers who actually receive only three hundred Cuban pesos per month—equivalent to about twelve dollars. American companies—already wary of sweatshop scandals in other parts of the developing world—may think twice about agreeing to such practices. Current major investors from the European Union, which exports about $1.2 billion and imports over $600 million in goods and services from Cuba, have complained about excessive overhead, lack of flexibility, and interference in hiring practices.

Nevertheless, the day when U.S. tourists are allowed to flock to Cuban beaches has the potential to revitalize the Cuban economy. Like its neighbors in the Caribbean, Cuba now views tourism as a central pillar in its economic strategy, and the number of foreign visitors to Cuba has grown steadily over the past decade. Today, Cuban tourism represents a two-billion-dollar-a-year industry that brings in about 40 percent of the island's hard currency reserves. Cuba now has eleven international airports and receives more than two million visitors annually. Sensing the economic potential, U.S. travel agents have begun to lobby more intensively for easing the travel ban. Cuba expects that American tourism, which currently sags below one hundred thousand visitors a year (mainly academics, church groups, and Cuban Americans traveling with U.S. government permission, along with several thousand adventure travelers in violation of the embargo), could surge to ten million visitors annually if the travel ban were lifted.

Cuba has also worked to cultivate a set of knowledge-intensive industries unique for a developing country. Over the past decade, investments totaling one billion dollars have helped to develop a surprisingly sophisticated biotechnology infrastructure. Cuba has developed the world's only vaccine against meningitis B, and Cuban medical products are exported to more than forty countries. The island's biotech industry employs approximately ten thousand Cuban scientists, and more than twelve hundred people are headquartered at the Center for Genetic Engineering and Biotechnology, outside Havana, the largest and most advanced of the fifty-three biotechnical facilities on the island. Cuban officials estimate that of eight hundred essential medicines, about 80 percent are developed domestically, while the remaining 20 percent, mainly cancer and diabetes drugs, are imported. Thus far, the United States has granted one license to a single Cuban product, when pharmaceutical giant GlaxoSmithKline persuaded the U.S. government to exempt the meningitis B vaccine. In 2004, a Cuban cancer drug sparked the interest of California-based Cancer-Vax Corporation, which sought to conduct joint research on cancer vaccines in Havana and signed letters of intent with Cuba's Center for Molecular Biology. U.S.-Cuba collaboration in the biotechnology field could be the surprise engine of the island's future economic growth.

Cuba's hunt for oil has the potential to dramatically reshape the Cuban economy and its relationship to the United States. With oil prices rising at a record-breaking pace in recent years, Cuba has intensified efforts to convert its oil deposits into a powerful source of income. It today produces about 60,000 barrels of oil per day from a geologic belt located about a mile off its northern coast. The island receives another 100,000 barrels daily from Venezuela, which helps it to fulfill its domestic energy needs, and the two countries have collaborated to build a major refinery in the Cuban province of Cienfuegos, which represents a major new strategic asset for the Castro government. The crucial future test lies thousands of feet below sea level off the Cuban coast, where, the U.S. Geological Survey has estimated, Cuba may possess 4.6 billion barrels of oil reserves.

If this figure proves correct and the reserves are commercially viable, then Cuba would surpass half a dozen countries to become the fourth-largest oil-producing nation in Latin America, behind only the three giants Venezuela, Brazil, and Mexico. Major companies from Spain, Norway, India, Malaysia, and Canada have purchased exploration rights for sections of this reserve, and China is in serious discussions with Cuba. A major oil find would electrify Texas-based U.S. oil companies and potentially transform the debate on the embargo in the United States. In December 2003, Cuba's official newspaper, *Granma*, published a statement encouraging U.S. oil firms to participate in offshore exploration: "The government of Cuba wishes to say it has no objection whatsoever to the involvement of American oil companies in exploration and drilling in our exclusive economic zone on mutually beneficial terms."

Jorge Piñon is the former president of Amoco's Latin American operations, with more than a quarter century's experience in the oil industry at companies including Shell and BP. Piñon is now a senior researcher at the University of Miami, and when I called him to discuss Cuba's oil prospects, he was bullish about the future but injected a note of caution. "Remember that oil underground has zero value. I don't care how much reserves you own. If you are not able to explore, transport it, and turn it into gas fuel, then it is worth nothing. That whole process of the monetization of Cuban oil, particularly its offshore reserves, will take anywhere from three to five years," he said. "There are three categories of reserves: proven, discovered, and undiscovered. Cuba's are not proven or discovered. Cuba's are undiscovered, because all they have done is geological studies. Nobody has gone out there and drilled a bunch of holes to turn those reserves into discovered reserves and then proven reserves, and that is what you can take to the bank and actually make a lot of money." The reason is that soaring oil prices have paradoxically slowed the pace of exploration in Cuban waters by creating a shortage of the deepwater submergible rigs needed to explore its potential oil fields.

Still, Piñon recognized that Cuba had generated a lot of interest by offering exploration rights at extremely commercial rates. In his view, the best evidence that Cuba had viable reserves emerged when the Spanish company Repsol drilled a well in the summer of 2004 that caught the attention of Norway's second-largest oil company, Norsk Hydro. "Trust me, the results were very good," Piñon told me. "They were so good that they showed it to the Norwegians, and they bought thirty percent equity in the production of the field. Listen, the Norwegians are experts at deepwater drilling. They are not going to buy a concession if it's not commercially viable. They don't have any political reason to make Fidel look good . . . When Norsk Hydro signed on the bottom line, that told me, 'Holy shit, there is something there!' " Still, Piñon saw the U.S. sanctions as having a major chilling effect. "The other issue that everybody has is: OK, I drill and find the oil. What the hell do I do with it? I can't take it to Cuba because the refining system is not there. The U.S. embargo prevents me from selling it to any U.S. oil-refining company. I can't take it to some of the refineries in the Caribbean because they themselves are owned by U.S. corporations. So what the hell am I going to do with the oil? I can't monetize it. That's why they are dragging their feet."

In early February 2006, representatives from American oil companies gathered to discuss the possibility of future engagement with Cuba at the Sheraton Maria Isabel Hotel in Mexico City. The gathering was the brainchild of Kirby Jones, a longtime Cuba watcher and consultant who heads the U.S.-Cuba Trade Association, based in Washington, D.C. Jones first traveled to Cuba as a journalist in the 1970s, and he is among a small but hardy band of optimists who have built consulting careers brokering business contacts between the United States and Cuba in the hopes that the parties involved will reap benefits when the trade embargo is lifted. Jones had organized nearly a dozen similar conferences in Mexico, but this was the first that focused on the prospects for American energy companies in Cuba. U.S. companies represented included Exxon Mobil Corporation and Valero Energy Corporation. Also present were officials from the Port of Corpus Christi in Texas, which was angling to become a preferred port for future trade with Cuba. The stately hotel was located just off of Mexico City's main thoroughfare, Paseo de la Reforma, and adjacent to the heavily fortified American embassy.

Jones was just wrapping up a successful first day of the conference when the long arm of the U.S. embargo pulled the rug out from under his feet. "We had an entire day Friday where every Cuban made all their presentations," he later recalled. At the end, "I walked out and a guy came up to me and said, 'The hotel manager needs to talk to you.' So I said OK and walked over. He looked like a deer in the headlights. He just looked scared to death. And he said to me, 'I'm sorry to inform you, but the Cubans have to leave the hotel.'" Jones was told that the Starwood Corporation, which is the corporate parent of the Sheraton in Mexico City, had been informed by the U.S. Treasury Department's Office of Foreign Assets Control (OFAC), which manages the sanctions program, that hosting the Cuban delegation placed it in violation of the trade embargo. Recounting the story to me in my office, Jones looked up wryly. "Keep in mind this is five thirty Mexico City time. It is six thirty on a Friday night in Washington when this is going on!" As a longtime observer of Washington, Jones doubted that someone in the federal bureaucracy had taken it upon themselves to open a new case late on a Friday afternoon unless there had been strong political pressure from above. "So sometime after business hours, there must have been some phone calls from somebody to OFAC, then OFAC to Starwood, on a Friday afternoon at six o'clock." Jones informed the Cuban delegation of what had occurred. They decided to call their embassy in Mexico City for advice and then appeared in the lobby fifteen minutes later with their bags packed. "The vice minister went up to the manager surrounded by Foreign Ministry people. It was great theater. Then he gave the outrage speech: '*This is outrageous, we've never been treated like this before, yadda, yadda, yadda* . . . but we will be leaving in the next hour.' "

The sixteen-member Cuban delegation, headed by vice minister Raúl Pérez del Prado, was temporarily put out on the street until they found lodging at a Mexican-owned hotel several blocks away. The Cuban mission's hotel deposit was confiscated and sent to OFAC. The Bush administration had scored a tactical victory but detonated a political bombshell in the middle of Mexico's hotly contested campaign to replace outgoing president Vicente Fox. Less than seventy-two hours after the Cubans were unceremoniously evicted from the Sheraton, Mexico launched an investigation into whether the hotel chain had violated Mexican law. The leftist opposition, the Party of the Democratic Revolution, immediately attacked Fox for allowing the "shameful" incident to occur, while a top congresswoman declared, "Imagine this, we have reached the state where a U.S. company can tell us who we can receive and who we can't."[3] Not to be outdone, representatives from the National Action Party and the Institutional Revolutionary Party, Mexico's two other main political parties, hopped into the fray, respectively calling this effort to enforce the U.S. embargo in Mexico "intolerable" and of "no judicial worth."[4]

Not surprisingly, the Cuban reaction was even more vitriolic. The Cuban newspaper *Granma* whipped itself into an editorial frenzy, declaring that "the tentacles of the blockade and the U.S. government's criminal economic war against Cuba are willing to reach beyond any boundary on the planet, even to the detriment of laws of other nations."[5] The U.S. State Department refused to back down and instead dispatched its spokesmen to argue that U.S. law applies to American corporations no matter where in the world they are located. In Mexico City, a small band of furious citizens held demonstrations across from the Sheraton and burned a U.S. flag in protest. The left-leaning officials of Mexico City, clearly irritated by the Fox government's reluctance to pursue the case, effectively threw the book at the hotel for code violations ranging from lacking braille menus to flaws in the stairwells. The hotel was ordered to comply within twenty-four hours or its more than five hundred guests would be dumped on the street. City officials later backed down, but the Mexican foreign ministry fined the Sheraton $112,000, which marked the first time that a company operating in Mexico had been punished for complying with Helms-Burton.[6]

The political ripple effect from the Sheraton incident extended far beyond Mexico. A bipartisan group of twenty-five U.S. congressional members wrote a letter to the U.S. treasury secretary that said, "We believe that this incident is an overreaching application of U.S. law that could have significant implications worldwide." They accused OFAC of setting an unwieldy new precedent, asking, "If a U.S. owned movie theater in a foreign country sold a ticket to a Cuban, is that company subject to penalty?" The chilling effect on the U.S. hotel industry proved to be enduring. In January 2007, nearly a year after the Sheraton incident, Norway's placid capital city, Oslo, became embroiled in a similar brouhaha when a hotel chain recently purchased by the Hilton Hotels Corporation refused to book rooms for a Cuban delegation attending an international travel fair. The incident unwittingly awakened Norway's nationalist sentiments, and the uproar resulted in protests by two powerful Norwegian unions with more than one million members and a police complaint filed against the hotel by an Oslo-based group that advocated against racism. The Cuban delegation found a new hotel, but they packed some extra warm clothes for the trip. In recent years, U.S. companies had been snapping up European hotel chains, and the middle of Norway's harsh winter is not a good time to get tossed out in the cold.

OFAC, a little-known agency of the U.S. Treasury Department, is at the heart of all controversies over enforcement of the embargo. It handles a wide range of sanctions programs, including those against Iran, North Korea, and international terrorist groups, but at least one sixth of its budget and staff is focused on Cuba. OFAC issues licenses, levies fines, and regulates all American trade with and travel to Cuba. Its enforcement of the embargo is far from comprehensive, and the officials in charge compare their role to that of a highway patrolman watching for speeders: You don't catch everyone who violates the law, but you do catch some and hopefully deter the others. OFAC is in principle an apolitical agency, but in practice it often responds to cases that catch the attention of policy makers in the State Department or Congress, which makes it a powerful but unpredictable factor in how the United States enforces its Cuba policy. In December 2007, a U.S. government review of OFAC found that more than 60 percent of its investigations focused on violations of the Cuban embargo, leading it to neglect other crucial priorities like fighting terrorist financing and drug trafficking. The findings infuriated New York Democrat Charles Rangel, who had requested the report. "This is not good policy," he said. "It's vindictive. It's stupid. It's costly. And now we find out it's a threat to our national security."[7]

Looking back on the uproar that followed his U.S.-Cuba trade conference in Mexico, Kirby Jones reflected on the strange implementation of the U.S. embargo. "I never heard anything from OFAC, which surprises me. I never heard a peep from them on that issue— either before, during, or since," he said. "I mean, it's funny, but it's not humorous. Because one hallmark of U.S.-Cuba policy is that you have what essentially has become a rogue operation within the U.S. administration that can do anything to anybody at any time with no accountability. That phone call cost Sheraton $112,000." He sighed. "When you talk about U.S.-Cuba relations, you can't really do it without going into the unique role and operation of OFAC that this policy has created. You have a group of people inventing regulations to stop people from doing something when there is nothing in writing. It's like an old western where there's a new sheriff in town, but you don't know *who* is in town. You don't know the rules from one day to the next. All of a sudden, what is legal one day is not legal the next for no other reason than somebody in OFAC said you can't do it—and the hotel is a perfect example."

Pedro Monreal sat down with me over a cup of coffee on a cool and wintry day in Buenos Aires, Argentina, where we were both attending an economics conference. The café was located just off the central downtown area where street vendors hawked shoes, scarves, and memorabilia, including photos and calendars featuring Argentine native Che Guevara, who served as the first president of Cuba's Central Bank in the early 1960s. Monreal was barely a toddler when Che was running the Cuban economy, but today he is among the most prominent of a group of reform-minded Cuban economists who are looking to the future. Now in his early fifties, Monreal first came to public notice in Cuba in the mid-1990s, when he was one of several leading academics affiliated with the Center for American Studies in Havana who were advocating for more ambitious reforms of Cuba's socialist system. In 1996, the government responded by purging the institution, and Monreal was driven out and left jobless. Most victims of the purge eventually left the country, but Monreal found work with a University of Havana–affiliated think tank called the Center for Research of the International Economy.

Monreal keenly follows the economic debates in Cuba and has clear ideas about where the Cuban economy should be heading. He is both a card-carrying member of the Communist Party and a vocal critic of the island's current development path. Shortly after Raúl Castro took power on a provisional basis and urged Cubans to debate the economy fearlessly, Monreal told the *Wall Street Journal* that the island was lacking in "calculation, motivation, and innovation" and described the current policy discussion as "kind of a black box process."[8]

In his view, Cuba's recovery from the collapse of the Soviet Union in the early 1990s remained incomplete, despite the fact that the official growth rate has exceeded 10 percent in recent years. "It is true that the country's economic indicators have more or less recuperated to their 1989 levels, especially if you look at exports, which have dramatically improved due to the trade relationship with Venezuela," he told me. "The social indicators are still good, depending on the quality of education and hospitals. But at the individual level, the standard of living is way, way down—probably half what it was before the crisis. A Cuban's wages allow him to buy certain products at low prices, but in the rest of the economy the prices are very high, and salaries lag far behind."

During his first year in power, Raúl Castro called for a dialogue on how to improve Cuba's efficiency within the confines of the socialist system. In particular, the younger Castro highlighted failings in areas such as public transportation and the persistence of low-level corruption. Moreover, his past experience supervising market-oriented reforms in the military-run enterprises had heightened speculation that the provisional government might embark on a China-style reform that would result in greater economic capitalism presided over by the Communist Party. However, Monreal felt that those expectations had little basis in fact. "An economic debate has opened under Raúl that did not exist under Fidel," he said, "but even those who think we should follow the China model would almost never say it quite that openly. The debate is rooted among the country's academics, and while the highest leaders and other government officials know about the debate, they barely participate. So what you have is a discussion that is not explicit, lacks clarity, and doesn't include the people who should be involved."

Still, Monreal discerned the outlines of a future economic debate in Cuba. "I believe that there are three major positions in the economic debate taking place in Cuba today. The first group believes that Cuba should maintain or recommit to a traditional, highly centralized socialist state. That is the frank minority, but it represents the consensus position that Fidel leaves behind, which gives it political force. This makes it very easy to discredit anyone who favors fewer state controls, because the discussion does not revolve around technical issues, but is based in politics. The second position basically has to do with embracing 'enterprise rectification,' which is the process led by the armed forces in the late 1990s to introduce reforms to state enterprises and make the system less centralized. This was something that the party initiated in 1997 but was halted in 2003. Now it is being revisited and discussed in a more aggressive way, especially in agriculture. This would introduce a much less centralized scheme where productive cooperatives could decide what to grow and how to grow it and set their own prices. It's essentially embracing the Chinese model in agriculture. Of course, no one says it this way, but in practice that's what it would mean—allowing the market to work. This option is popular among economists and is gaining momentum."

"Third," he continued, "now there is opening a debate about reforms that have a social democratic or liberal perspective that exists in Cuba, but it doesn't have strength yet. The question is whether positions that are marginal today could gain momentum in the future. Their weight ultimately won't depend on the value of the idea, but rather on the political juncture that may occur. I will tell you, quite sincerely, that if Cuba and the United States start to reconcile, it will create conditions favorable to ideas that today are thought but not said. I often argue that reforming the Cuban economy has to be based on pragmatism. There is no way to avoid change or the problems that will come with it. I don't believe the official argument that change can be controlled. People in the government like to use the word 'harmony' and talk about 'harmonious change.' I always say that harmony is something you find in music, or maybe in China, but you don't find it in the Cuban economy."

Outside the window, black-and-white photos of Che Guevara rustled steadily in the brisk South American winter wind that blew through the streets. Monreal sipped his coffee thoughtfully as he considered whether wide-sweeping, market-oriented change was a real if unspoken possibility. "I think that this idea can enter the debate much more forcefully than people expect today. You know why? Because, in my opinion, when people dismiss these ideas as worthless, what they really mean is that the time is not right. They are not ready to separate themselves from Fidel. But when the time is right, they may say, 'All right, let's go!' Frankly, I think the pro-capitalist option that is repudiated today could gain real force in the future, perhaps in the form of a European-style social democrat model. Truthfully, the liberal ideas of the European consensus carry tremendous weight in Cuba, and they could gather strength in a situation where Cuba makes an accord with the United States."

Monreal acknowledged that fears of change persisted in Cuba, but he held a more nuanced view. "There is real anxiety about economic change in Cuba, of course, but it depends on one's perspective. Now, this is a little subjective, but my impression is that people in Cuba are becoming more disposed to taking risks. The present situation, for so many people, is so uncertain that they think savage capitalism might be better. You know what the main indicator is for this in Cuba? The number of people who are willing to get to the United States by any means possible, including pushing off in a raft."

Monreal had traveled to China the year before and has spent a significant part of his career examining the economic trajectories of China and Vietnam. He was not convinced that Cuba would embrace the Chinese model of capitalism. "I have seen and read in many places outside of Cuba that Raúl is pro-China, or at least he would favor Chinese reforms. That is far from clear to me. His discourse does suggest he may move to the side of reform, but he has done nothing to demonstrate that . . . I defend the Chinese experience because there's a lot to learn from it. If Cuba wants to produce more food under a communist regime, it doesn't have many places to look besides China and Vietnam. In Cuba, though, it is not politically correct to talk about China's economic message and say it will produce more food, more productivity, and more exports. Instead, people will make the political argument that following China's path is the best way to keep the Communist Party in power. And you know, the people around Raúl Castro, and Raúl Castro himself, just won't buy it. Their view is 'That's China. The Communist Party here doesn't need to take that step to stay in power.' They think that losing control would be inevitable. They'll say, 'During the special period, we had to make concessions with foreign investment, allowing the dollar, industrialization, tourism, and look how hard it was to stay on top of everything. It was a nightmare.' Remember that foreign investment in Cuba is perceived as fundamentally corrupt. Sure, it brings technology, markets, capital, but it corrupts people's minds—it's like sulfuric acid. If China's reforms represent the top of a ten-point scale, then Cuba's reforms are between zero and one. We are a half step from the bottom and trying to climb down, not up."

Still, he thought that Cuba might be better positioned than some of its neighbors to compete in the knowledge economy after an initial adjustment period. "What exists in Cuba is human capital that has received a lot of instruction but is not necessarily well qualified. People have studied a lot and are very well specialized, but their professional experience lags behind international standards. They would have difficulty competing against Taiwan, South Korea, or the United States. On the positive side, however, Cubans have the ability to learn new standards and techniques very rapidly. Setting aside our medical education, which tends to be quite good, maybe twenty percent of most professionals are well qualified, while eighty percent have received plenty of instruction but lack true qualifications. But the eighty percent can learn extremely quickly." Monreal cited the foreign investment that poured into Cuba's oil sector in the 1990s. "There was not a single Cuban who worked on the platforms that were out in the ocean, because workers needed to have internationally certified training that was renewed every year. Most of the workers came from Central America, especially Salvadorans and Guatemalans. Today, almost all the platforms are manned by Cubans that have been internationally certified for this work." Similar examples had occurred in areas such as tourism and hotel management.

Like most of his colleagues, Monreal readily agreed that the United States was the unpredictable eight-hundred-pound gorilla with the potential to transform Cuba's future: "Lifting the embargo would be totally disruptive for Cuba. I don't know if the impact would be good or bad," he told me. "You know, it's a mistake to believe that the Cuban government would have the ability and the manpower to manage or control the events that would follow. That is false. Because if the embargo were lifted, it would have such a huge, rapid impact that Cuba—at least the Cuba I know—would not be prepared for the changes it would bring. If you imagine that this is a boxing match, then right now the Cuban boxer is in the ring with the United States, but he knows the other guy's moves and how to protect himself. But what if, all at once, the boxer is put in the ring against fifteen other guys? You'd leave the ring crying! And for better or worse, the ability of the Cuban government to control this fight is very limited."

Monreal deepened his voice in an effort to channel his inner Sicilian. "It would be like that scene in the movie *The Godfather*, when he says"—Monreal rasped—"*'I'm going to make you an offer that you can't refuse.'* Today we like to think that we can keep the United States on the margins, and that we can just focus on Venezuelans, the Spanish, the Chinese, the Europeans, the Koreans, whomever, and choose our partners. But without the embargo, the U.S. will make us a lot of offers that we can't refuse, with American companies offering fifty million dollars here, five hundred million dollars there to buy products or make investments." He offered the image of a horseshoe moving toward a powerful magnet and laughed. "Many of my friends tell me that Cuba has the manpower to control the effects of lifting the embargo, but I'm not so sure. If the U.S. offers business that is so big and so good, but the cost of the business requires the government to make concessions, then guess what? They are going to make concessions." Pedro Monreal seemed to me to be the type of economist who could play an important role in Cuba if Raúl Castro decided to embrace a path of reform. In the end, however, Monreal decided that the possibility of true change occurring in either the United States or Cuba was too remote to be worth waiting for. Several months after our conversation, he accepted a development position with the United Nations in Jamaica and left Cuba behind.

Will Cuba be able to resist the capitalist temptation? This will become much clearer as the trajectory of Raúl Castro's presidency takes shape in the coming years, but the answer is probably not. There is little question that Fidel Castro viewed capitalism with contempt for most of his rule, until the breakdown in Soviet subsidies forced him to embrace emergency measures to stabilize the economy in the 1990s. Rolling back those reforms became a focus of Cuba's policies as the island acquired new allies, especially Venezuela's Hugo Chávez, who contributed one hundred thousand barrels per day in subsidized oil, and China, which became its second-largest trading partner. Still, Cuba's tourist industry and the small-scale entrepreneurship practiced by restaurant owners and service providers seem likely to remain permanent features of the island's economic landscape. After Raúl first took power in July 2006, Cuba's official press openly acknowledged many of Cuba's economic failures that had previously been taboo subjects, including inefficiencies and corruption in the health and education sectors. He called on his countrymen to "debate fearlessly" the path to economic reform while cautioning that any changes would be made under the banner of the Communist Party. Few actual changes were implemented, but the ones that occurred were sensible, such as allowing for private farming on state lands, a moratorium on fines for unauthorized taxicab drivers, and allowing Cuban workers for foreign companies to be paid higher wages.

During his provisional presidency, Raúl's signaling about future economic changes raised the expectations of many Cuban economists that bigger changes would come once Fidel was no longer president. "Right now, Cuba is like a boat with a twenty-five-horsepower engine with the motor turned on, and the boat is pointed in the right direction," one University of Havana economist told me during the spring of 2007. "But the problem is that the boat is still tied to the dock, and the dock is Fidel." It was a typically elliptical Cuban metaphor, but the point was clear. Once Fidel was no longer president, the rope to the dock would be cut, freeing Raúl to steer the boat—that is, Cuba—in the direction of reform. On February 24, 2008, Raúl accepted the presidency of Cuba with a speech that focused on incremental reforms like increasing the country's food supply and improving its purchasing power. The comments were largely interpreted by international observers to mean that little would change in the days ahead, but Cubans had a different interpretation, as evidenced by a sudden surge in currency speculation as people traded their dollar-equivalent *chavitos* for the virtually worthless Cuban pesos that were expected to rise in value. In the months ahead, Raúl would unveil a series of new measures to increase wages, expand access to consumer goods, and stimulate agricultural production. The sudden wave of decisions fueled speculation about Cuba's future trajectory, but Raúl also vowed to continue consulting with Fidel every step of the way. The rope was fraying, and for the moment it still held the promise of truly ambitious reforms at bay, but Cubans' rising expectations had heightened the likelihood of future changes.

CHAPTER 11

Chasing Chávez

Hugo Chávez walked up to the podium with a swagger at the annual meeting in New York of the United Nations General Assembly in September 2006. Chávez had already been in power in Venezuela for seven years, and his international profile as a major antagonist of the United States had risen in tandem with the sky-high oil prices that strengthened his political hand at home. He was just months away from winning a crushing electoral victory that would guarantee him another six-year term as president. This would embolden him to accelerate his embrace of what he called "21st Century Socialism," an ambitious effort to remake Venezuelan society by concentrating power in his hands, channeling oil wealth toward social programs for the poor, and building alliances with like-minded countries in Latin America and across the world. President George W. Bush had addressed the United Nations a day earlier, challenging Iran on its nuclear ambitions and casting U.S. foreign policy as an agent of liberation. Chávez spotted a rare opportunity to seize global media attention by bashing the United States before the world leaders gathered there, and he was prepared to make the most of it.

Dressed sharply in a dark suit and a red tie, Chávez waved a copy of the book *Hegemony or Survival: America's Quest for Global Dominance*, by the leftist American intellectual Noam Chomsky. Flipping through the pages, the Venezuelan leader declared, "It's an excellent book to help us understand what has been happening in the world throughout the twentieth century, what's happening now, and the greatest threat looming over our planet." He set the book aside with a recommendation: "I think that the first people who should read this book are our own brothers and sisters in the United States, because the threat is right in their own house." And then Chávez began his diatribe against Bush that was heard around the world. "The devil, the devil himself, is right in the house. Yesterday the devil came here. Right here." He gestured to the podium, crossed himself, pressed his hands together, and looked skyward. "And it still smells of sulfur today."

A wave of laughter and giggles rippled through the assembly of presidents, foreign ministers, and ambassadors in the hall, but Chávez wanted to make sure nothing was lost in translation. "Yesterday, ladies and gentlemen, from this rostrum, the president of the United States, the gentleman to whom I refer as the devil, came here, talking as if he owned the world. Truly, as the owner of the world. I think we could call a psychiatrist to analyze yesterday's statement made by the president of the United States. As the spokesman of imperialism, he came to share his nostrums, to try to preserve the current pattern of domination, exploitation, and pillage of the peoples of the world. An Alfred Hitchcock movie could use it as a scenario. I would even propose a title: *The Devil's Recipe*." Chávez then launched into a lengthy discourse on the state of the world, criticizing U.S. actions in Lebanon, Palestine, and Iraq, dismissing the UN system as collapsed, complaining about CIA protection of Luis Posada Carriles, and proudly announcing that his idol Fidel Castro was "not only alive, he's back in his green fatigues." But the headline that would dominate the news was written even before the Venezuelan leader finished his speech: CHÁVEZ CALLS BUSH DEVIL.

Chávez's bold insult was a public relations masterstroke that firmly placed him on the world stage, especially in the United States, where he was transformed almost overnight from an obscure foreign leader to a household name. Strategically, his outlandish performance misfired by eventually dooming Venezuela's efforts to win a seat on the UN Security Council, but he briefly became an international media sensation. U.S. officials dismissed the comments as "not becoming of a head of state," and even liberal Democrats friendly with Chávez, like New York's Charles Rangel, angrily denounced his behavior. Many Venezuelans were badly embarrassed by their president's tirade, and some U.S. consumers launched a short-lived boycott against Venezuelan-owned CITGO gas stations. American efforts to portray Chávez as a deranged demagogue were briefly vindicated. The only clear winner was Chomsky, whose obscure book shot to the top of the Amazon.com bestseller list after receiving an endorsement whose power even Oprah Winfrey would envy. (Chávez later said that he deeply regretted not meeting Chomsky while he was alive, so he was delighted to learn that his favorite author was actually a spry seventy-seven-year-old professor at the Massachusetts Institute of Technology in Boston.) Bush studiously ignored the controversy, although some Latin American leaders could not resist piling on, such as Ecuador's successful left-wing presidential candidate Rafael Correa, who fretted that the comparison to Bush might have insulted the devil.

Chávez's New York adventure had taken him one step closer to filling the shoes that his close friend Castro was leaving behind. Already Castro's closest ally in the hemisphere, Chávez had visited the Cuban leader frequently in the three months since he had fallen ill and was an avid student of his leadership style. In November 1960, Castro seized upon a UN meeting in New York to blast his nemesis President John F. Kennedy as an "illiterate and ignorant millionaire." Forty-six years later, Chávez had lobbed a different rhetorical grenade against Bush, but the purpose was the same: to cement his leadership as the principal challenger to U.S. power in Latin America. Castro was surely watching this performance on television from his hospital bed in Havana, beaming with pride as the torch was passed to the next generation.

Chávez, a former army paratrooper and a fiery populist, won the presidency of Venezuela in 1998 with the overwhelming support of the country's poor. Chávez first struck up a friendship with Castro in 1995, when he was given a hero's welcome in Havana following his release from prison after serving time for a 1992 coup attempt. Castro had quickly identified Chávez as a man to watch, and he courted him with flattery, offered strategic advice, and in essence became his political mentor. Chávez's electoral victory was founded on the promise of a "Bolivarian revolution" couched in leftist terminology, and he traveled to Havana as Venezuela's president-elect in early 1999. His public embrace of Castro consummated an alliance between the two men that proved to have a wide-ranging impact on both of their countries. Castro's gamble on Chávez paid off in spades in October 2000, when the two leaders signed the Convenio Integral de Cooperación, which has formed the backbone of an "oil for doctors" swap that provided an economic lifeline to Cuba and laid the foundation of Chávez's strategy to win the allegiance of the Venezuelan poor.

Castro first sent doctors to Venezuela in 1999, when torrential rains caused massive mud slides that killed thousands of people in the poor barrios. The Cuban medical brigade assisted and stayed on a long-term basis. Chávez agreed to pay for these services with oil, which was worth less than twenty dollars a barrel at the time. Initially, Cuba received fifty-three thousand barrels of oil per day in exchange for placing about fifteen thousand doctors and medical workers in Venezuela. In 2004, the arrangement deepened in its scope and complexity, with Cuba stationing more than forty thousand doctors, teachers, and sports trainers in poor Venezuelan neighborhoods. Chávez doubled the oil payments to one hundred thousand barrels per day, and as oil prices surged, Cuba's windfall from the deal rose to two billion dollars a year. Total bilateral trade between the two countries reached seven billion dollars by 2007, cementing Venezuela's status as Cuba's most important trading partner and its most significant economic ally since the Soviet Union collapsed more than a decade earlier.

The Cuban medical missions in Venezuela became hotly controversial, angering many Venezuelan physicians and sparking accusations that Chávez wanted to turn the country into "another Cuba." Determined to keep the Cuban infusion as low profile as possible, the two countries established an air bridge that allowed the passengers arriving daily from Cuba to disembark onto buses and exit the airport without passing through customs. The medical program, known as Misión Barrio Adentro (Inside the Neighborhood), began with doctors, but it provided a gateway for Cuban advisers to become active at nearly all levels of Venezuelan government. Dr. Renato Gusmão, a Brazilian physician with the Pan-American Health Organization in Caracas who had closely watched the progress of Barrio Adentro, recalled that at first there was no infrastructure to support the thousands of Cuban doctors pouring into the Venezuelan slums. "What the Cuban physicians first faced was tremendous repressed demand for services, because it was extremely difficult for a poor person in the barrio to go to a walk-in clinic to see a doctor," he said. Moreover, their living arrangements were extremely difficult. "I saw Cuban doctors sleeping in the same quarters as dogs, on the dirt floor. I said, 'My God, this cannot last forever!'" The program was expanded to cover about 70 percent of all Venezuelans, and the Cuban doctors were well equipped to care for children and young adults, but surprised to confront the illnesses of elderly Venezuelans, such as diabetes and hypertension. Dr. Gusmão noted, "They are used to working in Africa, and they have long-standing work in Haiti, where people don't get old enough to develop those diseases. So it was a surprise for them here." Chávez won an early battle by insisting that the doctors receive the Venezuelan minimum wage; Castro thought they should earn nothing beyond their paltry Cuban salaries.

Castro and Chávez had hit on a winning formula for consolidating their political power at home and cultivating new allies in the region. Venezuela is the world's fifth-largest producer of oil, and its payments to Cuba cost less than 3 percent of the total production of its state-owned oil company Petróleos de Venezuela (PDVSA). Cuba has nearly seventy thousand doctors, a surplus for its population of eleven million, and is training more all the time. Thus each was exchanging a commodity that it had in abundance for another that it desperately needed. Cuba's long-standing medical diplomacy had already sent doctors to more than seventy countries, mainly in Latin America, Africa, and Asia, and Venezuela began to copy this pattern by providing discounted oil to poor nations to win their allegiance. At the end of 2004, the two nations launched the Bolivarian Alternative for the Americas (known as ALBA), a trade and social investment pact that soon drew in left-leaning leaders like Evo Morales in Bolivia and Daniel Ortega from Nicaragua. Venezuela and Cuba also initiated Misión Milagro (Miracle Mission), which has brought more than 750,000 poor Latin Americans to Cuba for much-needed eye surgeries. Their successful medical diplomacy unsettled the Bush administration and provoked several ad hoc responses. These included a U.S. effort dedicated to convincing Cuban doctors to defect, known as Barrio Afuera (Outside the Neighborhood), and the launch of the U.S. naval ship Comfort, which docked at ports in Latin America and the Caribbean for a week at a time to offer free medical care to the poor.

Chávez's outreach in Latin America was successful despite the domestic political firestorm unleashed by his erratic and increasingly authoritarian rule in Venezuela. First elected in December 1998, Chávez ushered in a new constitution in 1999 and won reelection to a six-year term under its rules in 2000. Two years later, opposition to his social and economic reforms led to weeks of protest in the streets of Caracas. Against this chaotic backdrop, Chávez was briefly deposed in a coup on April 11, 2002, only to return to power two days later when several bizarre decisions by the interim president, Pedro Carmona, prompted the military to reverse its support for the overthrow. In subsequent interviews, Castro revealed that he had maintained close contact with Chávez throughout the coup, even making arrangements for him to escape from the presidential palace to Cuba, so that he could "leave the country without resigning, in order to fight another day, which would have had a real chance of rapid success."[1] On April 12, Castro arranged for Chávez's daughter to speak with international media to announce that her father had not resigned and was being held as a "prisoner-president." By the next day, that news had galvanized support for Chávez in Venezuela, which played a crucial role in restoring him to power by April 13. The travails of the Venezuelan president had by no means ended: Chávez later withstood a crippling strike by workers at PDVSA that extended into 2003. But he triumphed in a recall referendum in 2004, and his political opposition, dispirited and disorganized after losing the recall vote, boycotted the 2005 parliamentary elections, leaving him firmly in control of all levers of government.

Chávez handily won a new six-year term in December 2006 and then moved quickly to nationalize the country's oil fields, attempted to establish a single political party known as the Unified Socialist Party of Venezuela, and shut down one of the main opposition television stations. As one Latin American ambassador in Caracas explained, "Chávez is like someone riding a bike—he needs to keep up the momentum or he risks falling off." In December 2007, he narrowly lost a constitutional referendum that would have enabled him to be reelected indefinitely, but he vowed not to give up on his reforms.

During this time, Chávez and the Bush administration became tangled in a web of mutual suspicion and animosity. On the one hand, the United States remained the top purchaser of Venezuelan oil, to the tune of 1.2 million barrels per day, or about 60 percent of Venezuela's supply. Chávez even sought to build a constituency within the American public by providing up to one hundred million gallons of discounted home-heating oil to poor communities, a program that started in Massachusetts and soon spread to a total of seventeen states. On the other hand, the official rhetoric was hostile and bitter. Chávez accused the United States of supporting the 2002 coup, which top administration officials like Otto Reich denied, though they clearly approved of the Venezuelan leader's ouster even if they were later forced to backtrack when he returned to power.

Initially, much of the criticism of Chávez focused on his links to Cuba, such as when Reich, in his capacity as NSC envoy, declared, "We certainly see a Venezuela-Cuba axis which is broadening and deepening and which is not conducive to the promotion of democracy and human rights."[2] At her secretary of state confirmation hearing in January 2005, Condoleezza Rice described Chávez as a "negative force" in the region. Later that year, State Department officials were forced to distance themselves from religious broadcaster Pat Robertson, who called for assassinating Chávez on his Christian Broadcasting Network show: "We have the ability to take him out, and I think the time has come that we exercise that ability. We don't need another $200 billion war to get rid of one, you know, strong-arm dictator. It's a whole lot easier to have some of the covert operatives do the job and then get it over with."[3] Soon thereafter, Defense Secretary Donald Rumsfeld compared the Venezuelan leader to the chancellor of Nazi Germany, saying, "We've got Chávez in Venezuela with a lot of oil money. He's a person who was elected legally—just as Adolf Hitler was elected legally—and then consolidated power."[4] Chávez responded by frequently proclaiming that the United States was trying to assassinate him and by referring to Bush as "Mr. Danger" and mocking his top cabinet officials as "the dogs of war."

Eventually, the United States decided that there was little to be gained from this war of words and began to scrupulously avoid getting provoked by Chávez's taunts. Still, the Venezuelan president's threats to cut off the flow of oil to the United States—accounting for 15 percent of daily imports—meant that he was a major wild card in a region of the world that was otherwise neglected. Under the guidance of Castro, Chávez's dramatic star turn as the populist rogue of the new era elevated Venezuela from an oil-rich political backwater into a central player in a complicated new geopolitical game in which the old rules no longer count and new rules are being formed.

Hugo Chávez is nearly thirty years younger than Fidel Castro, but the two leaders have much in common. Both were raised in the countryside and were initially looked down on by the urban elite. Their birthdays are two weeks apart, and astrologers have noted that they are both Leos, the most dominant, dramatic, and extroverted sign in the zodiac. Castro studied law at the University of Havana and was an impatient twenty-six-year-old when he first launched his rebellion against Fulgencio Batista in 1953. Chávez attended the Venezuelan Academy of Military Sciences and served in the army for nearly two decades before launching his coup attempt in 1992. Both spent two years in prison for their efforts, but brushed off their initial failures and won early release. (Upon being captured, Chávez said, "Our objectives have not been achieved—for now," while Castro declared, "History will absolve me.") Chávez links his revolution to the legend of South American liberator Simón Bolívar, while Castro claims his inspiration from the Cuban poet José Martí. Castro has relied heavily on his younger brother, Raúl, while Chávez favors his elder brother, Adán, who has served as his ambassador to Cuba, chief of staff, and secretary of education. Castro's ties to the Soviet Union provoked the Cuban Missile Crisis, which brought the world to the edge of nuclear war, while Chávez has stridently defended Iran's nuclear ambitions.

The two leaders do have important differences. Castro was by far the more precocious of the two, seizing power in his early thirties, while Chávez was well into his mid-forties when elected president of Venezuela. Castro fought his way into government and has never submitted himself to a popular vote, while Chávez came to power democratically, continues to allow elections, and even occasionally accepts defeat. Castro is much more sophisticated and worldly than Chávez, who still exhibits deeply immature behavior and is given to crass and outlandish statements. Chávez lacks his mentor's keen sense of strategy and tends to operate in an impulsive and tactical manner. But they share their most important characteristic: both have cast themselves as the opponents of the United States and claim to be defending the oppressed peoples of the world against "American empire"—even as their economies and societies remain inextricably linked to their greatest foe.

The Venezuelan capital, Caracas, lies on the northern coast of South America, and thousands of U.S. visitors arrive every week aboard direct flights from across the southern United States, especially Florida and Texas. The flights follow a southeastern path, over a string of Caribbean islands and the desiccated southern flank of Haiti, gradually turning more eastward as the South American coastline comes into view. Oil tankers churn across the sparkling green Caribbean Sea below the country's striking northern coast, where clusters of ramshackle homes dot the craggy mountainside. In the spring of 2006, the collapse of an important bridge along the airport road had been converted into an international symbol for the incompetence and disarray of Venezuela in general and the Chávez government in particular. When I traveled there a year later, the traffic now flowed smoothly past the site of the doomed bridge as construction crews swirled around its newer and more modern replacement. The road was in good condition, passing through tunnels and shantytowns, with black men in blue shirts along the side balancing trays of soda and plates of homemade candy on their heads, squinting into the midday sun, as the traffic wound into the heart of Caracas.

My first visit was to the offices of Teodoro Petkoff, the editor of the opposition newspaper *Tal Cual* and one of the shrewdest observers of the Chávez phenomenon in Venezuela. A former guerrilla and communist leader who participated in the country's Movement Toward Socialism in the 1970s, he was several times a presidential candidate for the left. However, he broke with much of the left in the early 1990s and has opposed Chávez since the beginning of his presidency. *Tal Cual*, published daily, has a circulation of only ten thousand, but during its seven years in operation it has evolved into one of the most sophisticated voices in opposition to Chávez. Its modest headquarters are located in the upscale Caracas neighborhood of Altamira, and Petkoff's office wall is adorned by a large black-and-white photo of a journalist falling backward after being shot in the cross fire during the Spanish civil war. I arrived on a spring day in 2007, and a copy of *Tal Cual* sat on his desk with a headline focusing on the issue of the moment: Chávez's decision to change the slogan of the Venezuelan armed forces to "Patria, Socialismo, o Muerte," or "Fatherland, Socialism, or Death." (The old slogan was "Forjador de Libertades," or "Forger of Liberties.") The paper showed a sketch of a soldier saluting the words "Fatherland, Socialism, *and* Death," next to an article penned by Petkoff that began with the line "Marx was right: when history repeats itself, the second time is a farce."

Petkoff has the pale blue eyes and droopy gray mustache of an Eastern European intellectual, but his conversational style is purely Venezuelan: open and witty, with a touch of the cerebral. "In my opinion, Chávez has been very explicit about how he wants to change the economy and the structure of this society. His political and institutional plan is based on authoritarianism, autocratism, militarism, and statism. The result will be the strengthening of the personal power of Hugo Chávez. Chávez is, temperamentally speaking, a caudillo"—or Latin American strongman—"perhaps the last one left on the continent of South America. And through his rhetoric regarding the socialism of the twenty-first century, he seeks to consolidate his personal power." Petkoff described three processes under way that would shape the country's future: new enabling laws expanding the power of the president, the creation of a single socialist party, and the constitutional reforms proposed by Chávez that would allow him to stay in office for life. He grimaced. "If all of this succeeds, what will we have as a result? A neo-totalitarian society—maybe without an Auschwitz, without the gulag, without Gestapo troops, without the KGB, but still oppressive."

Leaning back in his chair, he stroked his mustache as he pondered how to answer my question about the relevance of Fidel Castro to Chávez's political philosophy. "I would explain this in the following way. Chávez has strongly pathological characteristics—I'm going to offer my own psychoanalysis, but it's obvious to anyone that he is a psychopath. And one of the attributes of his pathology is immaturity—an emotional immaturity. In some ways, he is still that seventeen-year-old who entered the military academy in 1970, when Fidel Castro was viewed as the icon of revolution"—Petkoff smiled faintly—"and that was how we all saw him then. And twenty-five years later, when Chávez left the armed forces, it was clear that for him, he still saw Fidel Castro the same way. Chávez has a level of veneration—of personal idolatry—for Castro. You can see it in his body language, in his verbal style when he is speaking with Fidel. Hugo Chávez adores Fidel Castro. And for Fidel Castro, who truly cares for nobody, he saw Chávez as naive, and he threw a lasso around him and roped him in. He is a manipulator—you can see it clearly when Fidel is talking with Chávez how he has manipulated and utilized Chávez, drawing him in, getting more oil, replacing what he lost from the Soviet Union."

Petkoff predicted that the alliance between Cuba and Venezuela would survive the death of Fidel Castro. "It is true, or so it appears, that Raúl Castro does not have the same types of feelings for Chávez that Fidel has. And Chávez has no deep affection for Raúl. This is known. But evidently, Cuba depends too much on Venezuela and is not going to break away from Hugo Chávez. With the thousands of barrels of oil a day, and millions of dollars that support the doctors and sports trainers, and all the businesses that they are creating—Cuba cannot live without the charity of Venezuela. Raúl will need to sustain all this. And from the Venezuelan perspective, Chávez will need the warranty for the revolutionary cause that Cuba provides."

He thought for a moment and then continued: "What is true is that the death of Fidel Castro will leave Hugo Chávez without his political core—without his id, as Freud would say. Chávez does not have his own id, his own moral center, and he totally lacks the capacity for introspection or self-examination. He has absolutely no ability to see himself. The only id that Hugo Chávez has is Fidel Castro. And Fidel Castro has been, in various circumstances, a factor of moderation, of common sense. For example, he intervened in the Granda case, with the FARC, and calmed down Hugo Chávez." Petkoff was referring to a high-profile case in 2005 in which a Colombian guerrilla captured on Venezuelan territory almost brought the two neighboring countries to blows, and Castro had to step in and broker a solution between Chávez and Colombian president Álvaro Uribe. "At the least, he has supported serious analysis of the policy options available to Chávez. Without Fidel around, Chávez will be left on his own."

In Petkoff's view, Chávez had benefited from the strategic advice of Castro, but the cost to Venezuela had been enormous. "Of course, he has also influenced the political experiments that are being conducted in Venezuela, and bears some responsibility for the increasingly undemocratic nature of this regime. I believe that this whole path that the Venezuelan state is traveling—of being authoritarian, autocratic, and militaristic—comes from Fidel." The main difference between the two leaders was that Castro was a revolutionary in the guise of a caudillo, while Chávez was the reverse. Petkoff acknowledged that the large Cuban presence in Venezuela had benefited many people, but he argued that most Venezuelans had little interest in following the Cuban model. "Due to the relationship with Cuba, Chávez is perceived as being from the left. But the Chávez government has many more features of fascism than communism. Of course, fascism and communism also have a lot in common, but Venezuela is still very far from being Cuba. This is a democracy that is nothing like a Jeffersonian democracy, but it still is not a regime like Cuba's. You can call it an imperfect democracy or an imperfect dictatorship."

When I asked Petkoff to envision what Venezuela would look like when Chávez's current presidential term drew to a close in January 2013, the political provocateur turned journalist seemed at a loss for words. He met my gaze and then looked up at the photograph on his wall of the reporter falling in combat. "I have no idea," he finally answered. "Everything here has become so unpredictable, and there are many worrying trends. In this country, I can no longer see more than three months ahead."

Venezuela is justly famed for its commitment to conspicuous consumption, and the Caracas skyline testifies to the fact that capitalism remains alive and well in the land of Hugo Chávez. Three skyscrapers that dominate the downtown area are capped by the logos of Pepsi, Polar beer—the local Venezuelan brew—and Nescafé, represented by a large red coffee mug perched on top of a sleek office building. Other buildings are adorned with the logos of companies like Citibank and Hewlett-Packard, and American fast-food chains like McDonald's and Subway are rarely far from view. Below the cacophony of capitalist brands, however, a secondary political conversation plays out in the graffiti scrawled across bridges, walls, and office buildings. Slogans like "We are all with Che!" and "Viva Chávez" compete with warnings like "Fraud!" and "Bolívar was not a Communist." The words "Sí!" and "No!" are spray-painted throughout the city, invoking the many referenda that Chávez has organized, led, and mostly won since first taking power.

General Alberto Müller-Rojas lives in a modest bungalow in the hills that loom above Caracas, and he has been part of Hugo Chávez's inner circle since the beginning. Müller-Rojas served as Chávez's campaign manager in 1998 and was then appointed ambassador to Chile for several years. He stayed close to the Venezuelan president even as Chávez's relations with other loyalists cooled. A decade later, at the time of my visit, Müller-Rojas was helping to lead Chávez's effort to create the Unified Socialist Party of Venezuela. His home was staffed by a blond, gap-toothed lieutenant in a green Nautica T-shirt and two friendly, slobbering rottweilers that were practically overwhelmed with delight at the prospect of a visitor. As the sun slowly settled behind the hilltops outside his window, Müller-Rojas dragged on a cigarette and explained that Venezuela was in the process of defining a twenty-first-century socialism that emphasized state control over the productive sectors and the incorporation of the poor masses who had previously been excluded from Venezuelan society.

Müller-Rojas smoked steadily as he described the role that Cuba was playing in Venezuela's revolution through the educational and health missions that were operating throughout the country. "It results from an agreement where Cuba receives Venezuelan cooperation in the energy sector, and in exchange they assist us in certain areas, especially health and sports." This exchange had deepened in the context of ALBA, the trading bloc that the two countries inaugurated at the end of 2004, but he resisted the notion that Venezuela was incorporating Cuban ideas into its political project. "The Cuban reality has no relation to the societal structure and culture of Venezuela. Of course we share common features that all Latin American countries share in terms of manners, customs, and traditions, but each of these nations has peculiarities that emerged in isolation from each other for almost two centuries. I believe that the Cuban experience is not transferable to the Venezuelan case, just as it would be impossible to transfer the Venezuelan experience to Cuba."

Indeed, on television the evening before, Chávez had emphasized the improvisational nature of his revolution after quoting Castro's recent response to a foreign journalist who asked him to name an error that he had committed during his long rule. Chávez recounted that the Cuban leader reflected for a moment and then replied, "It was an error to have believed there was someone who knew how to construct socialism." To the outsider, it sounded like a word of caution, but Chávez interpreted Fidel's words to mean that Venezuela's efforts to establish a socialist state would necessarily entail a twisting path of self-discovery whose final destination would remain unknown. "There are no formulas!" Chávez cried. "There are no models! Socialism will be the heroic creation of an awakened people!"

Müller-Rojas contemplated the question of whether Venezuela should be concerned about what will happen to Cuba after the death of Castro. "No," he finally replied, "precisely because we don't see substantial changes. Maybe the process will open a little more, depending on the international circumstances. If Cuba remains blockaded, obviously they won't open up, especially to the United States." He commented on a recent news item reporting that the Washington-based multilateral group the Organization of American States (OAS) was considering starting a dialogue with the communist country. "Cuba has until now rejected the inter-American system because obviously, as Fidel Castro well knows, the OAS has been a colonial ministry of the United States. The U.S. only goes to the OAS when it satisfies other motivations in its foreign policy, and it uses it as an instrument at its service."

The general acknowledged that relations between the United States and Venezuela had become increasingly tense, but he placed this change in a regional context. "What has fundamentally broken is the relationship between the neoconservative forces in the U.S. and the socialist movement in Venezuela, as well as any ties between the American military-industrial complex and the armed forces of Venezuela." In 2005, Castro had warned Chávez that the Bush administration was trying to kill him, and the Venezuelan leader had incorporated those threats into his political rhetoric. Müller-Rojas thought that the threat had been real in the past but was now declining. "Look, there were worries because there were so many signs that this was true. This has a factual basis. It wasn't a dream. There were indications coming from radio stations in Miami, for example, that were openly planted by sectors extremely close to the governor of Florida—who was the brother, by the way, of President Bush. Similarly, there was a very worrying declaration by a powerful religious leader in the United States, who recommended the personal elimination of President Chávez." The general was referring to Pat Robertson's suggestion that the U.S. "take out" Chávez, which was widely ridiculed in the American media but taken seriously in Caracas. "Add to this the Colombian paramilitaries operating in this country, which are part of a structure created by the United States and therefore pose a concrete threat of U.S. intervention in the Venezuelan process." Müller-Rojas brushed cigarette ash off his shirt. "Now the worry has lessened. After seeing what has occurred in the Middle East, we sincerely doubt that the U.S. has the capability to embark upon another adventure in another part of the world."

Still, Müller-Rojas defended Chávez's decision to call Bush the devil at the United Nations meeting in New York. "This type of rhetoric just answers the rhetoric of Bush. He has suggested that the government of Iran was the devil. He has not called Venezuela the devil, but it has happened with North Korea. It is the rhetoric that the United States uses, and it expresses the desires of the State Department and of President Bush towards Venezuela. If you attack a regime rhetorically, you are going to receive a response. It is a classic strategy of international relations." He leaned forward to emphasize the point. "If you place the declarations of Hugo Chávez in the United Nations General Assembly last year like it's something that Chávez launched, and not related to the conduct of the United States, then that is simply a distortion. This has been mutual."

The sun had tucked away behind the hills, and dusk had settled over the mountaintops. A smattering of lights illuminated the valley below and the rhythmic sounds of crickets chirping gradually rose and fell in tempo. I suggested that even many of Chávez's most fervent supporters in Venezuela believed that their president was trying to implement too much, too quickly, and potentially jeopardizing the coalition that had brought him to power. Müller-Rojas disagreed: "Look, in politics, as in economics, you have to take risks. You have to take risks. Right now the dangers of facing serious disruptions to Venezuela's political dynamic are relatively low, from the internal perspective, and they have also been dramatically reduced from the international perspective. If we take advantage of this window of opportunity, we will be much closer to establishing a society that is more inclusive and more just, which is the goal we are pursuing. It is possible that we will lose some political support in the process, but our legitimacy will be less dependent on the origins of the regime and instead be reinforced by the results." Despite his spirited defense of Chávez's agenda, even the loyal general would prove unsettled by the pace of change. Several months later, the two men became embroiled in a public argument about the politicization of the Venezuelan armed forces, and Müller-Rojas would temporarily abandon his role as one of Chávez's top advisers before later returning to the inner circle.

The conversation was winding down, but Müller-Rojas had time to entertain one last question. I asked him whether Chávez had changed during his eight years in power. The general laughed at the thought. "No, no. Not as a leader and not as a person. I've known him since his youth, when he was a student of mine. I was his campaign manager in 1998. I have not seen any important changes in him. He's changed a little in his physical appearance. Now he's a bit fatter—he looks better, actually. The thing with most military people, here and around the world, even in the U.S., is that they tend to look awkward in civilian clothing. They don't know how to dress elegantly. When Chávez started to wear suits, he looked like he was in costume. In the beginning, he was not at all elegant, but today he is a well-dressed man, and the suits fit him very well indeed."

The stars had come out and darkness had fallen across the hills. The thick traffic that had accompanied the journey from Caracas had dwindled to a trickle as I headed back downtown, with most of the city dwellers presumably at home eating dinner with their families, and the vendors on the streets back in their shantytowns of squalor. My young driver had sat listening to most of the conversation, and he expressed surprise at how radical the general's views were and was especially skeptical about the health and education missions that were spreading across the country. "Some of the missions have done good things, like in primary education," he told me as the car rounded a curve, "but in some cases, you have Cuban doctors working in hospitals filled with new equipment, but nobody knows how to use it." He recounted a story about a woman friend who was suffering stomach pains and went to a new clinic staffed by Cuban physicians called the Salvador Allende hospital. "When she was examined by the Cuban doctors, they asked her if it hurt when she lifted her leg. She lifted her leg and answered, 'Yes, it hurts.' So they diagnosed her with appendicitis. She decided to go to a private hospital and get a second opinion. It turned out that she was pregnant." The fellow shook his head regretfully. "It's like an assembly line in these clinics." As the car descended into the heart of Caracas, it passed a small but raging fire below several houses. About a dozen people had gathered around and were watching its progress with a mixture of wonder and anxiety. It was hard to tell whether it was a friendly neighborhood bonfire or an out-of-control blaze.

Venezuela used to be an ordinary Latin American nation, remarkable only for its model two-party system that gradually fell prey to the petrodollar-fueled corruption of its political elite. Today it is impossible to visit the country without being confronted with the fact that it is in the middle of a highly combustible political experiment. The rule of Hugo Chávez has left no one untouched. Just months after Chávez's most recent reelection in 2006, the hardscrabble urban market in Plaza Bolívar, located in the gritty historic district of Caracas, was in full revolutionary fervor. Red inscription tents were filled with people signing up with the Unified Socialist Party of Venezuela, and large placards hanging from buildings and street signs magnified the

sense of a political movement unfolding. CHÁVEZ IS RIGHT: WE ONLY
NEED ONE PARTY IN VENEZUELA, read one, while another proclaimed,
UNITED IN SOCIALISM! A woman in her forties with long dark hair
pulled back eyed American visitors with suspicion. "I will be here
every day until the CIA and FBI come to kill me," she vowed. "I am
a Chavista. The CIA and FBI want to abuse our country. Chávez is
the only one protecting us, God bless him. Our Bolivarian revolution
values solidarity and humanity. We won't tolerate a United States
that is abusive." She pronounced the Spanish word for "abusive"—
abusivo—as abushivo, making it a play on words that conjured up
President Bush.

   Across town, the largest opposition protests in three years
unfolded as tens of thousands of demonstrators gathered to denounce
the government's decision to revoke the license of RCTV, the fifty-
year-old private television station that was deeply critical of the
Venezuelan president. "Hugo Chávez wants to impose a communist
government on us and take away our rights so that we become like
Cuba," fretted one soft-spoken female protester. "We don't want to
be in communist Cuba. We are Venezuelan and deserve to be free."
But many of the most passionate Chávez supporters were unconcerned about this apparent decision to suppress the media. When I
stopped in for a meeting at an embassy representing another South
American country, the ambassador nodded at the local staff member
who had served me the customary cup of tea. "You see that guy who
just prepared your drink? He loves Chávez. Last year, the government
flew him to Cuba for an eye surgery. You know, in my car I keep the
radio station tuned to opposition channels, just to learn about how
they are thinking. But every time I step out of the vehicle, my chauf-
feur turns it to the Chavista stations and government radio."

   In the basement of the Caracas-based School of Social Management, the institution's director showed me the room used for
Venezuela's massive literacy campaign, known as Misión Robinson.
Inside, two dozen people pored over Spanish-language texts with
large type, which listed ways to conjugate basic verbs. The instructor
looked barely twenty years old, less than half the age of most of the
students in the class, who appeared to range in age from late thirties
to mid-sixties. "I am a great-grandmother and never learned to read,"
said one woman with red-dyed hair swept off her forehead. "Now I
can read for the first time. My grandchildren still read better, but I am

catching up!" Afterward the director and I stood outside in the early evening as he enthusiastically explained how the literacy programs were changing people's lives. "Before, these people could not read or write anything. They couldn't take a bus because they could not read a map. They couldn't sign their names to a check. Earlier you asked if Venezuela's social progress had come at a political cost, but for them no high cost is too high to pay. If something happens to Chávez, then this country will explode." Later, over dinner, a wealthy young couple worried that the country's politics were leading to barely disguised class warfare. "This political rhetoric of the government has become so harsh, and I know so many people who are leaving," the wife told me. "My children are starting to complain that all their friends have left the country and they will soon be the only ones left." Venezuela later announced its plans to nationalize the assets of the company where the husband worked.

Chávez remains an intensely popular figure among the Venezuelan poor, but his efforts to further radicalize the country's development path faced increasing challenges during the first year of his new term in office. Brushing off weeks of opposition protests, he shut down RCTV and replaced it with a state-run public television channel. His Unified Socialist Party of Venezuela succeeded in registering millions of new members, but his constitutional reform proposals sparked protests among university students, who briefly emerged as the principal opposition to Chávez. In December 2007, he narrowly lost a referendum on constitutional reform that would have eliminated term limits, declared Venezuela to be a socialist state, and given him even more sweeping powers over the country's politics and economy. During my visit to the country, one foreign journalist had assessed, "The opposition is dead. It's just that the death certificate has not been issued yet." Now it is not so clear that Chávez will be able to impose the totality of his vision on the country without even more bitter fights to come.

Nor has his Bolivarian vision found widespread acceptance in Latin America. José Miguel Insulza is the secretary general of the OAS, the thirty-four-member political body based in Washington that is the main multilateral institution of the governments of the western hemisphere. Cuba has been suspended from the OAS since the 1960s, but Venezuela is still a member. A distinguished Chilean diplomat, Insulza has deep experience in Latin American politics and has been trying to reduce tensions between the United States and Latin America from his vantage point at the head of the OAS. Insulza told me that he recognized that recently elected left-leaning presidents in countries like Bolivia, Ecuador, and Nicaragua saw great appeal in the Chávez model, but he predicted that other leaders would find the Venezuelan president to be a hard act to follow. "Venezuela has more to do with the situation today in Latin America, which is not a revolutionary situation or a political revolution. We should remember what President Chávez said in his first speech when he took office for the first time. I was there. He said, 'Gentlemen, I am not the cause. I am the consequence.' Chávez is the result of a rich country with eighty percent poor."

In the past decade, Latin America has emerged as a relatively stable middle-income region, but one that continues to be plagued by deep poverty and high levels of inequality. Insulza believed that Venezuela's political experiment could only be understood against that backdrop, but he was skeptical that it would have wide-ranging repercussions. "That's the whole point: Is Chávez going to be able to solve that problem for Venezuela, and is he going to create a new model which is acceptable for other Latin Americans? The problem is that the countries that are attracted by the Venezuelan model don't have what Chávez has," he said, referring to oil, gas, and other natural resources. "I don't think that Venezuela will ignite a new flame in Latin America. If you want to be pessimistic and think they do get to ignite a new flame in some countries, it won't last for too long." Still, Insulza did not expect U.S. efforts to convince other Latin American countries to isolate Chávez to come to fruition, especially given that the United States remained heavily reliant on Venezuelan oil. "They get irritated when he does some things like the insults to President Bush, or like chasing President Bush around the hemisphere, but it's more irritation than division. They want to get along with Chávez."

Learning to live with Hugo Chávez is no easy task, however, as was proved once again during a summit of European and Latin American nations in the fall of 2007. During the meeting between eighteen heads of state, Chávez launched into a tirade against the former Spanish prime minister José María Aznar, repeatedly calling him a fascist and declaring, "Fascists are not human. A snake is more human." When Chávez overran his allotted time and interrupted Spain's current socialist prime minister, José Luis Rodríguez Zapatero, the seventy-year-old King Juan Carlos of Spain lost his temper and told Chávez, "Why don't you shut up?" The angry exchange marked a severe breakdown in diplomatic protocol, but the king's royal rebuke became an instant Internet classic. The catchphrase was downloaded by millions as a cell phone ring tone and showed up on T-shirts and placards at anti-Chávez protests in Venezuela. Chávez later mocked the king's words, saying, "They had to rein in the King and he got very mad, like a bull, but I'm a great bullfighter—olé!"

Many Latin American leaders were privately delighted that the king told Chávez to shut up, but the Venezuelan president still had an old fighter in his corner: Fidel Castro. The Cuban leader clucked that "hell broke loose" at the summit, but he praised Chávez for his "dignified response" and denounced the king's interjection as "an unambiguous display of the genocidal ways and methods of the empire." Still, Castro was undoubtedly disappointed when, several weeks later, Chávez lost the referendum to approve a socialist constitution for Venezuela on December 2. Chávez's graceful concession speech surprised many observers, but his moment of humility did not last long. Soon he was promising to continue pushing the country down the path to socialism. "You should administer your victory properly, but already you are covering it in shit," he warned his opponents who were celebrating their triumph. "Our defeat is one of courage, of valor, of dignity . . . We haven't moved a millimeter and we won't." Like Castro before him, Chávez was not planning to shut up any time soon.

Chávez was always a close ally of Castro, but he became an especially crucial supporter following Castro's health crisis in the summer of 2006. No other foreign leader visited Castro so frequently during his long months of convalescence, and Chávez was well aware of the gravity of his mentor's failing health. During some visits, Castro could barely get out of bed, and at all times he moved slowly and with considerable discomfort. Still, Chávez remained Castro's crucial connection to the outside world, the one leader who could be trusted above all others and who, it seemed, would be able to carry the mantle of socialist revolution forward in Latin America, although his model of participatory democracy was dramatically different from the communist revolution that had taken root in Cuba. Castro had described Chávez as "a child of that Venezuela that was a mixture of races, with all those

noble features and exceptional talent" and praised him as "an educated, intelligent man, very progressive, and an authentic Bolivarian."[5] Now Chávez returned the favor, frequently complimenting
Castro and sending him warm wishes for a speedy recovery. More
important, the Venezuelan oil subsidies to Cuba had become such a
crucial economic lifeline that the triumph of Castro's successors virtually depended on their continuation. This meant that Castro had to
be treated with great dignity and care during his illness, lest Chávez
catch wind of tricky business afoot and respond by threatening to disrupt oil supplies.

It also meant that Raúl Castro, a man with no special attachment
or affinity to Chávez, would need to remain in his good graces. Many
in Cuba's top leadership circle were conflicted by the vulnerability
that was inherent in the island's growing economic dependence on a
single, admittedly unpredictable partner, even though sky-high oil
prices meant that the Venezuelan alliance was too good a deal to pass
up. The Cubans remembered well how their overreliance on the Soviet
Union during the cold war had left them utterly exposed to the economic fallout that accompanied its subsequent collapse. "Never put
all of your eggs in a single basket" is a popular saying in Cuba, but it
also carried a warning in a country that had found itself unable to
resist its attraction to powerful overseas patrons. Still, Cuban nationalism remained a potent political force on the island, and the Venezuelan relationship was affecting it in ways large and small. Chávez's
calls for a "confederation of the republics" had raised eyebrows, as
had the penchant of ambitious Cuban leaders for playing up to the
Venezuelan president's ego. Carlos Lage, the influential vice president
who managed Cuba's energy programs and traveled frequently to
Venezuela, once proclaimed, "Cuba has two presidents: Fidel and
Chávez!" Statements like that probably contributed to the decision to
pass over Lage when selecting who would occupy the number-two
post under Raúl.

Moreover, the benefits of the Venezuelan-Cuban alliance were
largely lost on the Cuban public, who saw Chávez frequently touted
in the national press but experienced little positive impact on their
daily lives. Thousands of Venezuelans arrived in Cuba each year for
medical treatment and ideological training, but they were often kept
in special dormitories and did not mingle with the average citizen.
Cubans were simultaneously envious of the special treatment that vis-

iting Venezuelans received and contemptuous of the slovenly looks and poor Spanish of many of the visitors, who were brought to Cuba from indigent barrios or rural villages. Although the island's once-severe blackouts had lessened, owing to better oil supplies and an improved electrical infrastructure, most Cubans associated Venezuela with their reduced access to primary care physicians. Cuba's health care system had relied for decades on a system that placed a physician in nearly every neighborhood, but the escalation of the "oil for doctors" swap between the two countries meant that nearly one third of Cuba's estimated seventy thousand doctors was living overseas, with more than twenty thousand in Venezuela alone. While Cuba's health indicators had not yet shown a decline, the frequency of complaints spiked sharply upward. One popular joke that made the rounds in Havana told the story of a man who goes to see a travel agent and says, "I want to go to Venezuela." When the agent asks, "Why?" the fellow responds, "Because I want to see my doctor!" (Like many Cuban jokes, the humor cut at multiple levels, because most Cubans cannot afford to travel, and the government controls the exit visas of its citizens.) In 2006, a dark rumor circulated about Venezuelans falling ill while staying at a residence hall outside of Havana, only to discover that someone had spiked their drinking water with oil.

Managing the pivotal relationship with Venezuela had been one of Fidel Castro's greatest joys ever since Chávez had come to power. Now that responsibility had shifted to Raúl Castro, but he was more likely to view it as a burden. "No speech of mine lasts more than an hour," Raúl said shortly after his confirmation as president. He then noted cryptically, "That's because Fidel and the president of Venezuela are more intelligent than me and have more to say, not for any other reason."[6] Whatever tensions may lurk beneath the surface, Chávez did not miss a beat when Fidel finally retired from power in February 2008. After Raúl was formally appointed president of Cuba, Chávez spoke of him warmly on his weekly television show, calling him a "good friend" and vowing that "nothing is going to change at all. We will continue united." Still, some of Chávez's praise appeared less than effusive when he underlined the new Cuban leader's low profile. "He is more than Fidel's brother. He is the inseparable comrade," Chávez said. "Raúl has always been here. Always silent, always almost invisible, but always working, true to the revolution, true to the Cuban people, and true, to his core, to his big brother Fidel."[7] In any event, Chávez made it clear that he was not ready to bid good-bye to his hero and mentor quite yet. "Fidel is not giving up or abandoning anything," Chávez declared. "Fidel always was in the vanguard. Men like Fidel never retire." Several months later, the Cuban government took steps to reinforce the image of harmony among Fidel, Raúl, and Hugo Chávez by airing a television segment in June that showed the three men chatting merrily in a sun-dappled garden. It was the first public image of Fidel since Raúl took power, and the ailing Cuban leader appeared thin but vigorous as he gestured animatedly to his two colleagues. The scene appeared to be intended to show there was a united front between the Castro brothers and their Venezuelan ally, and put to rest any suspicions that Raul's relations with either Fidel or Hugo Chávez were anything but exemplary. But it was a bit difficult to judge the quality of the conversation, as the tape's audio was withheld for national security reasons.

Meanwhile, Chávez continued to make headlines. In March 2008, the Venezuelan president became embroiled in a high-stakes international dispute between Colombia and Ecuador that seemed to bring the three countries to the brink of war. The incident began when the Colombian military, which is a major recipient of American support, launched an incursion into Ecuador's territory to attack an encampment of Colombian guerrillas located across the border. Ecuador's president, Rafael Correa, reacted with fury and drew on the support of Hugo Chávez, a close ally, to ratchet up the pressure on Colombian president Álvaro Uribe. It was just weeks after Raúl Castro ascended to the presidency of Cuba, and he studiously avoided the controversy unfolding in South America, but his retired brother Fidel did not hesitate to wade into the fray, declaring that "imperialism has committed a monstrous crime in Ecuador." Chávez called the raid a "war crime," broke off diplomatic relations with Colombia, and deployed tanks to the border, creating a potentially explosive scenario that was defused only through mediation by other Latin American countries at a summit of the Río Group in the Dominican Republic. But the crisis with Colombia had barely ended before Chávez had returned to attacking the United States, declaring that "in this century we will bury the old empire of the USA." Fidel Castro might have retired, but Hugo Chávez was more than ready to play the role of regional provocateur and adversary of Washington. He had, after all, learned from the best.

CHAPTER 12

The Next Revolution

The young man stood before a microphone during a crowded town hall meeting at the University of Computer Science in Havana. His name was Eliécer Ávila, and he was a twenty-one-year-old university student who clutched a large notebook with a black cover in which he had written down his questions, in case he lost his train of thought—or his nerve. His blue T-shirt boasted a large white "@" symbol that celebrated the familiar punctuation mark found in the middle of every e-mail address in the world. It was January 19, 2008, the day before Cuba's National Assembly elections, and the university was hosting a forum led by assembly president Ricardo Alarcón. The mood in the auditorium was already showing signs of restlessness when a student sporting a Puma T-shirt and a wispy goatee questioned the government's call for a *voto unido*—a blanket endorsement of all candidates—in the upcoming elections. "I don't know who they are. I am simply reading the biographies with the supposed merits of these citizens, but I've never seen them before, and they never come by the university. I have no idea who these people are. Where'd they come from? People say, 'Oh, the *voto unido*,' well, how am I going to vote for each of these people if I don't know them at all?" Alarcón grimaced when the inquiry provoked a burst of applause from the audience. Others protested the lack of Internet access, a common complaint in Cuba but a particular irritant to the island's computer science students.

Ávila thought of himself as a revolutionary—or government supporter—but he also had some questions that he wanted answered. He was thin and square shouldered, with light brown skin and close-cropped dark hair, and he spoke with the staccato accent of his region, the rural eastern province of Las Tunas. Addressing Alarcón directly, he criticized the dual-currency system that had cut so deeply into Cuban life. "Why has the internal commerce of the country migrated to the convertible peso, when our laborers, workers, and peasants receive their salaries in national money that has twenty-five times less purchasing power—so that someone has to labor two or three working days to buy a toothbrush?" he asked. "Why don't the people of Cuba—and I'm not referring to just a small group of people but to the majority—have a viable possibility to stay in hotels or travel to other parts of the world? For example, I don't want to die before being able to see where Che fell in Bolivia."

Ávila was targeting two deeply resented prohibitions in Cuba: the rule banning Cubans, irrespective of their ability to pay, from staying in hotels that catered to foreigners, and the detested exit visa, known as the *carta blanca*, that citizens had to receive from the government in order to legally leave the country. He showed typical youthful impatience with the grindingly slow pace of change in Cuba, tartly telling Alarcón, "It seems to us that a revolution cannot advance without a plan. I am sure that a plan exists. We just want to know what it is!" In response to the unexpected interrogation, Alarcón, looking grumpy and slouched over in a rumpled oxford shirt, dodged the economic questions and offered only a lame reply to the student's concerns about seeing the world beyond Cuba. "I appreciate that the Cuban youth are concerned about visiting the Egyptian pyramids or traveling to Bolivia, but no one has a right to travel," he said, adding nonsensically, "If the entire world's six billion inhabitants could travel where they want, then the congestion in the planet's skies would be overwhelming."

The flare-up at the university suggested that the Cuban people were growing frustrated with their leadership, but the island's voters could find few options at the polls. The next day, the Communist Party's slate of candidates for the assembly resoundingly triumphed in non-competitive elections, including 99.4 percent of the vote for Raúl Castro to keep his seat, an even higher vote percentage than the 98.2 percent received by Fidel. The Cuban leadership extolled the elections as democracy at work, but most citizens saw them as a joke, and a tired one at that. But in early February, a videotape of Ávila's grilling of Alarcón was leaked to the BBC, and within hours the testy exchange between the two Cubans—separated by nearly fifty years in age and an even starker gap in power—became an Internet sensation that was posted on YouTube, rebroadcast on CNN, written up as a feature story in the *Miami Herald*, and referenced in dozens of news publications around the world, including the *Los Angeles Times* and *Time* magazine. It seemed to confirm that the Cuban youth were finally ready to challenge the old guard's firm grip on the country. Shortly thereafter, Ávila's mother told a local journalist that he had been detained by Cuban authorities who had fetched him from his house in Las Tunas, sparking widespread concern for the boy's whereabouts. Two days later, on February 11, he appeared as a guest on the island's talk show *Cuba Debate*, a program whose tagline was "Against Media Terrorism." This particular episode would run under the title "*Cuba Debate* Speaks with Student Victims of Manipulation," which was meant to refer to the international press but was just as easily applicable to its Cuban counterpart.

Ávila was now dressed in a green T-shirt with the image of Cuban national hero José Martí, and he denied that any officials had removed him from his home, attributing the misunderstanding to a medical visit related to his wisdom teeth. Asked by the show's host if he had been arrested, the young man dismissed the rumors, and he went on to describe his questioning of Alarcón as motivated by his desire to strengthen the Cuban Revolution. "I want to explain that though there are several students who got together to put forward some questions and polemics, it's to build a better socialism and not to destroy it. And there are things that have to be analyzed and changed and revised but always within the revolution." He denounced the videotape's circulation by the international media as "an effort to misuse my name and image," adding that "practically everything that they're saying is a total lie, and it completely detracts from the meaning of the opinions we gave." During the interview, Ávila spoke calmly and clearly, but in the opening shot his legs were shown twitching nervously. While an air of mystery lingered around his abrupt journey from his home in Las Tunas to a television studio in Havana, there was little doubt that his earlier grilling of Alarcón had laid bare the depth of the generational divide in Cuba. Raúl Castro's greatest challenge in the days ahead would be posed by the growing impatience of the island's restless youth that had crystallized, for a moment at least, around the pointed and fearless questions that a twenty-one-year-old student had wielded against one of Cuba's top officials.

On February 19, Fidel Castro formally announced his intent to resign as the president of Cuba. By that point, he had already been provisionally replaced as president by Raúl for nineteen months, and Fidel had dropped numerous hints in the weeks before an upcoming National Assembly meeting that he was considering retiring from the post. Still, after his forty-nine years at the helm of Cuba, it remained difficult for many to accept the idea that anything short of death would prompt Fidel to release his grip on power—an assumption that led his enemies to underestimate him once again. Moreover, as a shrewd manipulator of the same international media that the Cuban government frequently denounced, Fidel was sure to leverage the announcement of his retirement to maximum effect. In a "reflection" published on February 15, Fidel ended a five-part essay series on the U.S. election by dropping this subtle clue: "In my next reflection I will deal with a subject of interest to many compatriots, but I won't give any hints." Then, in the early-morning hours of Tuesday, February 19, following a sleepy three-day holiday weekend in the United States, Fidel's retirement letter was posted on the Web site of *Granma* under the title "Message from the Commander-in-Chief." A furious battle among the Havana-based international newswire services ensued, with Agence France-Presse breaking the news worldwide and Reuters and Associated Press racing to keep up. By the time television and newspaper editors were waking up in the United States, the revelation of Fidel Castro's decision was set to dominate the twenty-four-hour news cycle and remain a top story for the rest of the week.

Raúl Castro's ascension to Cuba's presidency occurred five days later, on February 24, at a long-scheduled meeting of the National Assembly. Rather than seizing on the opportunity to remake the country's top leadership group, however, Raúl instead focused merely on filling a pair of positions that his promotion would leave empty: first vice president of the Council of State and minister of defense. To the widespread disappointment of those who were hoping Raúl would elevate younger members of the Cuban government, he selected a man even older than himself to the number-two spot: José Ramón Machado Ventura, the seventy-seven-year-old top Communist Party official, known as a tough disciplinarian. The sudden elevation of Machadito, as the taciturn party apparatchik is nicknamed, seemed a slap in the face to Cuba's younger generations, although some surmised that perhaps Raúl was plotting to gain the hard-liners' support for needed reforms. The new minister of defense was seventy-two-year-old Julio Casas Regueiro, a former head of the Eastern Army who was principally known for his talents at managing a number of state-owned enterprises controlled by top generals of the fifty-five-thousand-troop-strong Revolutionary Armed Forces. Cuba's four other vice presidents were left unchanged: sixty-three-year-old Esteban Lazo, sixty-eight-year-old interior minister General Abelardo Colomé, eighty-year-old revolutionary leader Juan Almeida Bosque, and fifty-six-year-old Carlos Lage, the economic czar who also served as the executive secretary of the Council of Ministers. Rumors swirled before the meeting that the videotape of Ricardo Alarcón's unflattering encounter with the university students had been deliberately leaked to damage his standing, but the seventy-year-old president of the National Assembly retained his post.

Prior to Raúl's elevation to the presidency, his last major address before the Cuban public was his declaration on July 26, 2007, to mark the fifty-fourth anniversary of the attack on the Batista government that launched the Cuban Revolution. In that speech, Raúl commemorated the first year since Fidel became gravely ill, remarking that "we could barely even suspect what a hard blow was awaiting us." In addition, he signaled the two main shifts that would differentiate his government from that of his brother: an expressly stated desire to open a dialogue with the United States and a willingness to acknowledge Cuba's economic problems and encourage an internal debate about potential reforms. At that time, Raúl looked forward to November 2008, when "the elections will also have taken place in the United States and the mandate of the current president of that country will have concluded along with his erratic and dangerous administration." He reasserted the Cuban government's "willingness to discuss on equal footing the prolonged dispute with the government of the United States, convinced that this is the only way to solve the ever more complex and dangerous problems of this world."

What most caught the attention of Cubans, however, was Raúl's pledge to work on the chief economic problems facing the average citizen: paltry salaries totaling little more than a few dollars a month. "Wages today are clearly insufficient to satisfy all needs and have thus ceased to play a role in ensuring the socialist principle that each should contribute according to their capacity and receive according to their work," he declared. "I can responsibly assure you that the Party and government have been studying these and other complex and difficult problems in depth." Even before that announcement, Raúl had encouraged Cubans to debate the issue of economic reform "fearlessly," and in the fall of 2007 he initiated an island-wide process for Cubans to meet in neighborhoods and workplaces to air grievances and propose solutions to the economic problems facing the island. Each meeting was attended by a member of the Communist Party who took notes and filed reports back to the government, after pledging not to associate names with the complaints.

In December 2007, Raúl presented a report to the National Assembly stating that more than 3 million Cubans had participated in the discussions and shared more than 1.3 million complaints—a result that probably undercounted the true level of dissatisfaction in Cuba but was nevertheless shockingly high for a top official to admit, given that the process was so overtly led by the Communist Party. While Raúl warned that "nobody here is a magician or can pull resources out of a hat," the tenor of political debate on the island had shifted from terse and secretive to ever so slightly more open and flexible. By authorizing this process, Raúl had increased his political relevance and drawn the eyes of Cuban citizens away from the fading Fidel and toward their new leader. But by raising Cubans' hopes for substantial future change, he risked uncorking the genie of public opinion only to find that he was incapable of putting it back in the bottle. It was almost certainly this awakening political climate that led to the student outburst against Ricardo Alarcón at the University of Computer Science, a scene that would have been virtually unthinkable when Fidel was still in charge. The newspaper *Juventud Rebelde* called the sweeping economic debate a "revolution within the revolution," and signs were emerging that Raúl Castro had perhaps unintentionally sparked Cuba's next revolution. It would be a revolution of expectations.

Mindful of the cautiously stirring sentiments among deep swaths of the Cuban populace, Raúl knew he had to tread carefully when making his first public address as president before the six hundred members of the National Assembly on February 24, 2008. He began by paying homage to his brother: "Fidel is Fidel. We all know it very well. Fidel is irreplaceable, and the people should continue his work when he is no longer physically with us, although his ideas will always be with us." He then asked for permission to continue to consult Fidel on decisions related to "defense, foreign policy, and the socioeconomic development of the country," begging the question "What's left?" But Raúl justified the move by saying that "Fidel hears the grass growing and sees what is happening around the corner." He then praised the "debate and criticism within socialism" that had occurred in the preceding months and briefly referenced the stir that Eliécer Ávila's impertinent questions had created several weeks earlier. Warning in reference to the United States that "the enemy never sleeps," Raúl declared that nevertheless "we shall not avoid listening to everyone's honest opinion, which is very useful and necessary, simply because of the sometimes ridiculous noise made every time a citizen of our country says something that the noisemakers would pay no attention to if they heard it anywhere else on the planet." In this assessment, Raúl judged that the young student had committed no sin except for inadvertently providing fodder for the "ridiculous noisemakers" of the international media.

Once again it was his economic plans, not his exhortations concerning Fidel, that most sparked people's interest. Raúl outlined a plan for the Cuban government that sounded suspiciously like the American business practice of downsizing, calling for "a more compact and operational structure," "a lower number of institutions under the central administration of the state," and an effort "to reduce the enormous amount of meetings, coordination, permissions, conciliations, provisions, rules, and regulations," noting that "our government's work must be more efficient." Moreover, he explicitly emphasized, "The country's priority will be to meet the basic needs of the population . . . based on the sustained strengthening of the national economy and its productive basis, without which, I'll say it again, development would be impossible." Raúl used the speech to sketch his vision of a leaner Cuban government concerned with elevating production, and he even suggested that the Cuban peso would be reevaluated in the future to allow people to live on their legally earned incomes, rather than scraping to survive in the country's thriving black market.

Raúl ended his remarks on February 24 by reflecting on key moments in Cuban history and quoting from Fidel's writings, but it was a single bureaucratic phrase buried in the final third of the speech that most kindled popular imagination: "I referred to the excess of prohibitions and regulations, and in the next few weeks we shall start removing the most simple of them." This was the first time that the Cuban people had heard an estimated time frame for the implementation of reforms, and it was measured in weeks, not months or years. The island buzzed with rumors about the likely possibilities: eliminating the exit visa, allowing Cubans to stay in hotels with visiting family members, expanding Internet access, allowing foreign investment in agriculture, microcredit for the country's beleaguered entrepreneurs, maybe even legalizing cable television via satellite. In addition, some Cubans hopefully eyed the expansion of a public discussion on gay and transsexual rights in Cuba, promoted by Raúl's forty-six-year-old daughter Mariela Castro Espín, as a sign of increasing social space on the island. One political analyst surmised that Raúl might legalize private property and allow the Cuban people to buy and sell homes, on the theory that the government would buy crucial time if the people spent the next few years obsessed with real estate, rather than, say, democracy.

Raúl's first effort to deliver on the expectations he had raised came in mid-March, several weeks into his tenure as Cuba's new president. Citing the "improved availability of electricity," the government lifted a ban on ordinary Cubans' ability to buy consumer electronic goods like DVD players, computers, 24-inch televisions, and microwaves—all goods that were previously only legally available to foreigners and companies in Cuba. Soon thereafter, Cuba legalized the private use of cell phones and dropped the hated ban that prohibited Cubans from staying in the country's top tourist hotels. A flurry of new measures followed. In April, Raúl released a plan that would allow thousands of Cubans to receive titles to their homes, which had previously belonged to the state. The government then eliminated salary caps and increased pensions for the island's more than two million retirees to nearly twenty dollars a month. Government employees such as court officers saw their median monthly salaries jump by more than 50 percent, to twenty-seven dollars. While Cuban pensions and wages remained extremely low by international standards, they still put more money in the pockets of one fifth of the population. In June, Raúl introduced a new incentive system of performance-based salaries for most state workers. Meanwhile, a quiet revolution was unfolding in Cuban agriculture, as the state moved to eliminate bottlenecks and decentralize decision making to the farmers on issues like land use and crop selection. The long-standing practice of assigning all supplies from the central government was dropped, which was one sign that Cuba was starting to embrace market practices as part of its efforts to boost food production.

Political changes were also in the wind. Soon after taking office, Raúl Castro commuted the sentences of all Cubans who had been condemned to capital punishment. The decree excluded only three men who faced terrorism-related charges: Two men had been linked to the hotel bombings of the 1990s and a third, who was Cuban American, had been tried for a murder that occurred during his attempted armed infiltration of the island. Raúl also declared that he planned to hold the island's Sixth Party Congress in the second half of 2009, to plan for the day "when the historic generations are no longer around." It would be the first such gathering in twelve years to plot the future leadership and strategy of the Cuban Communist Party, and the announcement suggested that he planned to restart institutional processes that had long been neglected by Fidel.

In May, the first personal computers became available for purchase. One early customer remarked, "Hotels, cell phones, DVDs, Cuba is changing a lot. That's positive. But we want more."[1] The new rules marked an important step forward, but also reminded people how far they had to go and how tightly controlled the Cuban economy remained. Air conditioners, for example, were scheduled to remain restricted until 2009, and the private sale of toasters would only be legalized in 2010. As one University of Havana professor commented, "The ceiling for the maximum amount of change we can expect in Cuba under Raúl is beneath the floor of what the international community will even be able to perceive." Still, the possibility of Cuba embracing an Asian-style market reform process was becoming increasingly conceivable. Earlier Raúl had pledged to consult closely with Fidel, but the elder Castro dropped hints that he was displeased with the reforms being implemented by his successors. Writing in *Granma*, he warned, "Do not make shameful concessions to the Empire's ideology."

While many Cuban people began to look to Raúl Castro with a glimmer of hope, other Cubans beheld him with great skepticism. Dagoberto Valdés Hernández, the longtime director of both the bimonthly magazine *Vitral*, a publication of the Catholic Church in Cuba, and the Center for Civic and Religious Formation, also under the auspices of the church, counts himself among the skeptics. He lives in Pinar del

Río, the eponymous capital of the island's third-largest province, located 120 miles west of Havana. I went to visit him in February 2007, about six months after Raúl assumed Cuba's presidency on a provisional basis, and driving down Cuba's national highway brought the country's transportation crisis into sharp relief. The worn but smooth two-lane road that connects the two cities had only light traffic, consisting mainly of boxy Russian-made Ladas, sputtering 1950s-era Fords and Chevrolets, and the occasional smoke-belching bus moving at a crawl. The road was lined with hundreds of people waiting for rides from all walks of life—well dressed and threadbare, old and young, black and white, uniformed military and desultory civilians. Off to the north loomed the dramatic mountains and cliffs of Viñales, a popular destination for tourists and rock climbers. (The Cuban government considers the area to be militarily sensitive due to its vast network of underground caves, and actively discourages this recreation.) Horse-drawn carriages and bicycles dotted the highway, passing under faded signs that proclaimed Cuban revolutionary slogans like TRIUMPHANT ARE THOSE WHO STRUGGLE AND RESIST and HONOR AND ETERNAL GLORY FOR THE PEOPLE.

Settled in Cuba's richest tobacco-producing region, Pinar del Río is a quaint, rustic town with clean streets and colorful but faded neighborhoods. Dagoberto Valdés was waiting for me in front of a stately yellow building that served as the regional headquarters of the Catholic Church. I had caught a ride to Pinar del Río with a fellow named Vladimiro, a mechanic, chef, and illicit cabdriver, who was Old Havana's version of a good old boy, and Valdés looked surprised but delighted to see me arrive precisely at the appointed hour. "You are a very punctual man," he told me as he ushered me into a waiting vehicle. "Let's go somewhere we can talk." The car sped through the narrow city streets until it arrived at a modest blue and green two-story house nestled in a working-class neighborhood. The home belonged to Virgilio, a tall, cheerful man with salt-and-pepper hair who was the layout editor of *Vitral*, and we were soon joined by Carina Galvez, a pretty young woman in a flannel shirt and bright pink skirt who headed the Center for Civic and Religious Formation's economic programs. As we sat down to talk, a light breeze blew through the curtains, and the sounds of motor traffic, trotting horses, and the calls of the occasional vendor intermittently echoed through the house.

Valdés was a Catholic layman in his early fifties, and he had spent more than a decade as the director of the center and *Vitral*, its flagship publication. Since 1993, more than five thousand Cubans had passed through the center's hundreds of workshops on civic and social values that focused on themes such as personal freedom and spiritual independence. The first issue of *Vitral*, which translates as "stained glass window," had been published in 1994, and its subscriber base had gradually grown to ten thousand, with copies distributed throughout the island via the internal mail system of the church. It had flourished in part owing to the protection of the province's bishop, José Siro González, who strongly backed the magazine's mission. Photocopied and stapled together by volunteers, *Vitral* sold for about two pesos (or eight cents), and it stood virtually alone in Cuba as an example of the independent press that openly and sometimes fiercely challenged the official values of socialism, conformity, and sacrifice.

This independent profile came with a cost. During the early years, Valdés's involvement with *Vitral* resulted in a demotion from his supervisory job at a tobacco plant that left him doing menial tasks. Other members of the magazine's editorial board sometimes faced harassment or surveillance. But the Catholic bishop of Pinar del Río had provided a level of protection that enabled the magazine to survive. During a November 2006 press conference in Spain, Ricardo Alarcón was challenged on Cuba's restrictions on press freedom. Alarcón replied, "Read the magazine *Vitral* that has been published for years in Pinar del Río, that is quite well-known, and is directed by a personality from the Catholic sector who is not a priest but a layman. Its director, Dagoberto Valdés Hernández, unlike the moderate posture of the Catholic Church, forcefully criticizes the Revolution, and the state does not impede its circulation nor sanctions those who choose to subscribe . . . A publication like this is one thing, but the opposition fabricated by the United States is something else altogether."[2]

Valdés has a warm and open demeanor, and his eyes flashed from behind his round-rimmed glasses when our conversation turned to politics. "The Cuban government represents the last bastion of a failed ideology, and the people have suffered greatly for this," he told me. "Our spiritual life is moribund, and the country needs a spiritual and civic reawakening." Valdés recalled the optimism that had accompanied Pope John Paul II's historic visit to Havana in January 1998. "Then there was a religious opening in Cuba, but it lasted only a week. As soon as the government realized that the spiritual creativity of the people was not dead, the regime clamped down again in an effort to *despapizar*"—a uniquely Cuban slang term for the effort to rid the island of the effects of the pope's visit. "Today we have a new Soviet Union, but it's called Venezuela. It is providing oil to the regime as a pure, hard subsidy that has enabled the government to reassert control over the economy." The conversation turned to the state of Cuban politics in the months that had passed since Fidel Castro had provisionally relinquished power. "No one can doubt that we are living at the end of an exhausted political project. That is why the government is obsessed with disguising the real Cuba with a virtual reality."

Valdés clutched his coffee cup and leaned forward as he developed his argument. "Cuba's political screenplay today rests on five fictions. The first is that everything here is absolutely normal and that nothing has changed since Fidel Castro left power. The second is that the country is progressing economically. Where is this economic progress? No one can see it, no one can feel it, but the government states it like a fact. The third fiction is that a certain opening is occurring in the cultural and artistic sectors. The fourth is that Cuba is experiencing an opening toward the world and that we are riding high on a wave of international solidarity coming from Latin America, the Middle East, everywhere. Fifth and last, the Cuban government is acting as if there is a new revolution unfolding that will enable it to better challenge the United States, because a new consolidated government will not need the physical presence of Fidel Castro. These five points make up Cuba's virtual reality, and they are absolutely false."

A black tray and a green thermos rested on the coffee table between us, and Valdés stood the thermos in the center of the tray and then placed an empty white coffee cup in each of the four corners. "Think about it this way. Each of the four cups represents a different faction in the leadership: the military, the civilians, the historic generation, and the younger leaders. The green thermos in the middle is Fidel Castro." Upon hearing this, our host, Virgilio, smiled slyly at the thermos and then turned it on its side. "Now if Fidel is no longer there"—Virgilio picked up the thermos and motioned as if to throw it away—"then each of these groups will be vying to take over the center. There will not be consensus because the ties between them are too fragile. Raúl Castro will initially occupy the center, but he is an enigma and extremely unpopular with the people. His cup may have more coffee in it, but in the end he is just another cup. And the truth is that Raúl still doesn't know what he will do when Fidel dies. But for now he is still alive." Virgilio returned the thermos to the tray with obvious regret. We all stared at the prostrate object for a moment, each perhaps bemused by the fact that the country's greatest geopolitical moment in half a century could be sketched on the top of a coffee table. Raúl Castro's formal ascension to the presidency still lay more than a year into the future. Once that occurred, however, it would be difficult to argue that he was merely one cup arrayed among many on the coffee table of Cuban politics.

Valdés stood up. "We'd like to invite you to lunch," he said, and the two of us walked with his colleague Carina Galvez, who had been observing our conversation thoughtfully, through a part of town where the houses seemed worn but not in massive disrepair. We entered a basic but pleasant restaurant on the ground floor of Hotel Vueltabajo, and they shared anecdotes from their classes on civic formation. Galvez smiled wistfully. "People here have been living so long without making decisions for themselves that they have almost lost the ability to think independently. When we hold an event at the center, we try to force people to make choices, but it's not easy. For drinks we will offer soda and lemonade, but when we ask people what they want, they will say, 'I don't care. Whatever's available.' I have to tell them that 'whatever' is not an option, and if they do not choose soda or lemonade, then they will go thirsty. But it is hard to get people to shift their thinking from 'I will take what is offered' to 'I will seek what I want.'" As the meal drew to a close, Valdés leaned in and said, "Do you know that everyone in this restaurant thinks that we are hustling you? That is what Cuban people are trained to think when they see another Cuban with a foreigner. But we have invited you and we will pay." Galvez searched through her pockets for some folded pesos and rose to go to the counter. "We could leave the money here," she said apologetically, "but only if I pay at the counter will they know that you were our guest."

As we walked back through sprinkling rain to the church to find my ride back to Havana, my companions exchanged greetings with a trim-looking professional man dressed in a blue polo shirt and carrying an umbrella. Afterward Valdés confided to me, "You know that man we just saw? He is the top specialist in microbiology and a leading surgeon in Pinar del Río. He is the best medical mind in the province. But he cannot make ends meet on his state salary, so at night he tends to pigs which he sells on the market. He operates on people during the day and feeds animals at night." A look of disgust crossed his face. "And this is the medical system that we want to export to the rest of Latin America?" We eventually located the car, where Vladimiro was waiting patiently, and bid our farewells. As the car hit the open road back to Havana, I thought about how difficult it must be to carve out independent political and social space in a country like Cuba, where the government was so intrusive, the rewards were so uncertain, and the risks were so high. It also struck me how Galvez had gotten up to pay the bill at the end of our lunch. In my many trips to Cuba, watching an ordinary Cuban pay for a foreign guest was among the rarest sights I'd seen—and no one in the government was willing to take the bold steps necessary to change Cuba into the prosperous country it could become.

Several weeks after my visit, *Vitral* suffered a major upheaval with the retirement of Siro González, the bishop who had protected the magazine for so many years, when his successor in Pinar del Río closed down the Center for Civic and Religious Formation and dismissed Valdés. In April, the new bishop issued a statement: "I have asked that *Vitral* magazine keep to the truth based on the Gospel and the church's social doctrine, without falling into aggressive and argumentative expressions." *Vitral* remained in publication but was purged of all political content. One more voice in Cuba had been silenced, but not for long. Shortly after his separation from *Vitral*, Valdés joined with several others to found an online magazine titled *Convivencia*, which translates roughly as "coexistence." Valdés had found a way to resurrect his life's work through a virtual magazine designed to challenge what he viewed as Cuba's virtual reality. The dusty tobacco fields of Pinar del Río sit on the edge of western Cuba as if it were the end of the world, but even in this remote outpost, hope springs eternal.

Over the past few years, the savvy visitor to Havana has been able to evaluate the state of U.S.-Cuban relations merely by driving past the offices of the U.S. Interests Section, which houses the American diplomatic mission in Cuba. While Fidel Castro had long reveled in leading hundreds of thousands of Cubans in marches across from the tall, boxy building along Havana's seaside boulevard, known as the Malecón, it was only during the Elián González crisis, at the end of the Clinton administration, that the empty lot across from the Interests Section was transformed into a massive "anti-imperialist" tribunal. An amphitheater was constructed for Castro's rousing speeches, and a statue was erected portraying Cuban poet José Martí cradling little Elián in one arm and pointing an accusing finger at the American mission with the other. During the tenure of the pugnacious James Cason as chief of the Interests Section, the propaganda war surrounding the mission grew increasingly ostentatious. In December 2004, the United States erected a glowing sign with the number "75" to commemorate the dissidents who had been arrested in the Cuban government's crackdown the previous year. Cuba retaliated by erecting a gigantic billboard along the seawall that blocked the U.S. diplomats' view of the ocean with photographs of Iraqi prisoners being tortured by American forces in the infamous Abu Ghraib prison scandal. The United States later removed its "75" sign, but the Cubans refused to remove the grisly billboard.

Cason even redecorated his official residence in Havana as part of this contest of wills. In September 2004, he built a replica of the jail cell of Oscar Elías Biscet in his backyard. It was subsequently moved to the consular section of the American mission, on the notion that Cubans applying for U.S. visas would benefit from seeing firsthand how their country treats political prisoners. Later, on July 4, 2005, while hosting the annual Independence Day celebrations at his residence, Cason unveiled a three-story-high replica of the Statue of Liberty that held aloft a torch emblazoned with the number 75. "Nothing will be achieved, and in fact nothing has been achieved over the past forty-seven years, by being courteous with a dictator," he declared in reference to Castro. "And this person is on his last leg. Stay tuned: When this person is no longer there, the United States will be there to help you build a prosperous and democratic Cuba. Better days are ahead."[3] While some dismissed Cason's antics as foolish, he later explained to me that there was a method to his madness: His goal was to keep the plight of Cuba's political prisoners alive in the international press. "Journalists would say, 'Unless you give me a hook nobody will print anything . . . but if you give me a news event, our editor will publish it and then you'll get the message out.' So everything we did was designed to remind the world that it is a police state."

Cason soon left Cuba for a new appointment as ambassador to Paraguay, where he became a musical sensation after recording an album that featured him belting out folk songs in the local dialect of Guaraní. (Cason had hired a Paraguayan medical student to teach him the language during his last weeks in Cuba.) But he left behind a parting gift in Havana. In the months before his departure he oversaw an effort to smuggle in the pieces of a five-foot-tall scrolling electronic sign—basically a low-tech version of the ticker-tape-style signs seen on buildings in New York's Times Square—which entered Cuba through the U.S. diplomatic pouch. (When the Cubans inquired what the large shipments contained, the United States reportedly told them that it was building a gazebo.) The sign was secretly installed across twenty-five windows of the Interests Section and went live on January 16, 2006, broadcasting a quote from Dr. Martin Luther King Jr. that read, "I have a dream that one day this nation will rise up." Soon this and other human-rights-oriented messages were regularly scrolling across the face of the Interests Section in an effort to "break Castro's information blockade." Michael Parmly, who took over the U.S. mission in the fall of 2005, had inherited the sign project from his predecessor and green-lighted its eventual launch, which ensured that the cold war between the Interests Section and the Cuban government remained entrenched during his tenure. Parmly defended the move, saying that "the billboard is an effort to dialogue with the Cuban people. Only in totalitarian societies do governments talk and talk at their people and never listen."

Unfortunately, the sign's rusty technology and its awkward placement across the windows meant that curious Cubans found the scrolling messages to be about as exciting as watching paint dry. The sign's lack of Spanish accents also held the potential for embarrassing mishaps. For example, the word *año*, which means "year," appeared as *ano*, the Spanish word for "anus." Nevertheless, the Castro government was apoplectic about being caught off guard by the Americans, and it quickly mobilized hundreds of workers to erect a massive new monument of 138 black flags to commemorate Cuban victims of terrorist actions allegedly linked to the United States. Hanging from separate, tightly clustered flagpoles, the flags also had an important secondary function: to block the view of the Interests Section's "inflammatory" scrolling billboard. The propaganda war surrounding the U.S. mission then reached a standoff that endured for years, creating an overall effect that was creepy, comical, and slightly surreal. In the summer of 2008, Bush appointed Jonathan Farrar, the State Department's number-two official in the Bureau of Democracy, Human Rights, and Labor, to take over the Interests Section. With the United States setting aside massive new aid flows for Cuban opposition figures, the diplomatic fisticuffs seemed set to continue into the next presidential administration.

The sparring around the Interests Section underlined the degree to which American diplomacy in Cuba lay in tatters, but diplomacy was the furthest thing from the mind of George W. Bush when he stood before a packed audience at the State Department to deliver a stern message to the Castro brothers in the fall of 2007. Nearly fifteen months had passed since Raúl Castro had taken power on a provisional basis in Cuba. The initial anticipation of Fidel Castro's impending death had long since faded, and Bush was seeking to dispel the notion that U.S. policy toward Cuba was adrift. On October 10, at a Rose Garden reception celebrating Hispanic Heritage Month, Bush had pulled the wife of a Cuban dissident imprisoned during the 2003 crackdown onstage and called for the release of her husband: "One of the messages I have for the Cuban leaders: free this man and free other political prisoners. He's not a threat to you."[4] A month later, he would award the Presidential Medal of Freedom to Oscar Elías Biscet, the Afro-Cuban antiabortion activist who had lingered for years in Cuban jails. And on October 24, Bush delivered a major address on Cuba policy before assembled diplomats and activists to highlight the cause of human rights and assure Cuban exiles that his passion for ousting Castro had not been dulled.

Several relatives of jailed Cuban dissidents flanked the president on the stage as he began his remarks at the State Department. "Few issues have challenged this department—and our nation—longer than the situation in Cuba," Bush asserted. "In this building, President John F. Kennedy spoke about the U.S. economic embargo against Cuba's dictatorship. And it was here where he announced the end of the missile crisis that almost plunged the world into nuclear war. Today, another President comes with hope to discuss a new era for the United States and Cuba. The day is coming when the Cuban people will chart their own course for a better life. The day is coming when the Cuban people have the freedom they have awaited for so long." Claiming that "the socialist paradise is a tropical gulag," Bush declared that Cuban dissidents were coming together for democratic change and proposed new measures to expand Internet access on the island and introduce U.S. scholarships for Cuban students, but made both measures contingent on steps by the Cuban government. He also announced the creation of the multibillion-dollar Freedom Fund for Cuba. The concept was that the United States and its allies would place money in a fund that would assist Cuba's democratic transition. Of course, the proposal faced a few stumbling blocks. Outside of a few countries in Eastern Europe, the United States lacked the allies to underwrite the fund, and there was still no democratic government in Cuba to which the money could be given.

Bush had learned long ago, however, that Cuban exiles were willing to forgive a lack of substance if it was accompanied by tough rhetoric—and this he supplied in spades. Evoking the "dying gasps of a failed regime," Bush proclaimed that "as long as the regime maintains its monopoly over the political and economic life of the Cuban people, the United States will keep the embargo in place." He denounced the smooth transition that had occurred under the leadership of Raúl Castro, saying, "Life will not improve for Cubans under their current system of government. It will not improve by exchanging one dictator for another. It will not improve if we seek accommodation with a new tyranny in the interests of 'stability.'" The audience applauded wildly. "America will have no part in giving oxygen to a criminal regime victimizing its own people. We will not support the old way with new faces, the old system held together by new chains. The operative word in our future dealings with Cuba is not 'stability.' The operative word is 'freedom.'" The president concluded, "I leave you with a hope, a dream, and a mission: *Viva Cuba Libre.*"[5]

At several points in the speech, Bush directly addressed people in Cuba, challenging the police and military to embrace the population's desire for change, urging Cuban people to shape their own destinies, and admonishing Cuban schoolchildren to "not believe the tired lies you are told about America." The White House made special arrangements to have Bush's remarks beamed directly into Havana on Radio and TV Martí, but it need not have bothered. Raúl Castro quickly decided that the president's latest address was a useful propaganda tool for the government, but Cuba's policy of jamming Radio and TV Martí broadcasts would mean that few people would actually get to see or hear it. Thus, the following day the speech was aired on regular

Cuban television via a cable feed from CNN en Español, and a full page of excerpts was printed in *Granma*. The specific names of Cuban political prisoners were omitted, but the lion's share of the attacks on the Castro brothers, the scathing criticism of the island's human rights situation, and Bush's specific messages to different elements of Cuban society were all included.[6] Cuban foreign minister Felipe Pérez Roque described the speech as a "fantasy," but said it had been useful to "give an idea of the level of frustration, of desperation, and of personal hatred toward Cuba." Indeed, the Castro brothers probably would not have minded if the United States had scrolled the message on its electronic sign at the Interests Section in Havana, but the effort to dismantle Cuba's massive black flag monument would have been too much trouble. Nevertheless, Fidel Castro heartily agreed that Bush was "obsessed with Cuba."[7]

If so, this obsession was not shared by all of the president's staff. Shortly after Bush's remarks, White House press secretary Dana Perino was asked a question about the Cuban Missile Crisis. She managed to give a vague answer, but later confessed on National Public Radio that she had missed that history lesson. "I was panicked a bit because I really don't know about the Cuban Missile Crisis," admitted the thirty-five-year-old Perino. "It had to do with Cuba and missiles, I'm pretty sure." Several weeks later, Perino informed the White House press corps that "when Castro is no longer leading Cuba, the people there should be able to have a chance at freedom and democracy. That opportunity is coming." The White House might not remember the past, but it was confident in its predictions that the future of Cuba would be defined by a democratic revolution.

The most interesting element of Bush's speech on Cuba was the declaration that the United States favored freedom over stability. Even in the face of the managed transition to Raúl Castro, the hard-won lessons from pushing for democratic change in Iraq and elsewhere, and the clear desire of most American diplomats and military officials to prevent any type of refugee crisis emanating from Cuba, U.S. policy makers were still clinging to their preferred scenario of an uprising for freedom on the island after Fidel Castro's death. Harvard University professor Jorge I. Domínguez, who fled Cuba with his family in the summer of 1960 and went on to become one of the top U.S. scholars on Cuban affairs, had coined a term for just this scenario: "the poof moment." When I caught up with him it was on the margins of the annual meeting of the Latin American Studies Association, a U.S.-based academic group that had been forced to move its conference to Montreal, Canada, in order to include professors from Cuba who had been denied visas to the U.S. since 2004. I asked Domínguez why U.S. policy makers have become so enamored of thinking about Cuba's future in terms of waiting for Fidel's government to disappear in a "poof moment." He chuckled at the question. "Talk about a technical creation! I invented that term in the early 1990s while I was working on a research project housed at Florida International University funded by the U.S. government. The idea was to think about transition scenarios. Most transition discussions, I thought at the time, come in two big families: one where someone is figuring out how to get from point A to point B, and the other one, much more common in the United States, is to assume that the Cuban political regime goes 'poof!' Then you can fantasize about what can happen. That has some analytical utility. It is also slightly unreal."

As a professor of government, Domínguez favored examining the island's existing institutions—such as the Communist Party, the Council of State and the various ministries, and the social and popular organizations—as the most likely vehicles for political change in Cuba. The U.S. government planning assumes that Cuba after Castro would quickly yield a pro-U.S., democratic government that would actively seek Washington's help. "It would be nice if it were as simple as just 'poof,'" Domínguez told me, "but to get from A to B, you need the existing institutions. You have to think about the National Assembly, you have to think about the municipal assemblies, and you have to think about the Communist Party." Moreover, Domínguez anticipated that it would take the Cuban people many years to sort through the legacy of Fidel Castro. "This is the most important person in Cuban history," he said. "He is the person of most real impact on the country and will be one of the most significant figures in the history of Latin America. In terms of legacy, salience, and presence, he is a giant. His legacy will be contentious among politicians and historians, and some of the conflict will begin early on as people in the Cuban government and also Hugo Chávez will try to contest for that mantle of leadership." The path to democracy in Cuba, he predicted, was likely to be a long and tortured road with no instant gratification for believers in U.S.-style democracy. Indeed, Cuba has no shortage of power-brokers-in-waiting on the island, and this poses both a source of strength and a potential weakness in the near future. On the one hand, Cuba is equipped with a strong backbench of policy makers and administrators who can carry forth the banner of revolution once the Castro brothers have passed into history. On the other, fighting for power has been a national pastime since the country gained independence in 1902, and internal rivalries are likely to emerge in the post-Raúl moment.

Several individuals will bear particularly close watching, including José Ramón Machado Ventura, who is now the number-two man in government after Raúl. Ricardo Alarcón, who lived in New York City for a decade as an envoy to the United Nations, has long sought to parlay his deep knowledge of the U.S. power structure into a dominant role once Fidel left the stage. Economic czar Carlos Lage, one of the younger members of Fidel's inner circle, has fought off advances by the army to pare back his economic clout and is managing Cuba's crucial and potentially very profitable energy relationship with Venezuela. General Abelardo Colomé is a vice president and head of the powerful and feared Ministry of the Interior, which operates as Cuba's secret police. Foreign minister Felipe Pérez Roque has acquired more power than anyone else from his generation, and his hard-line attack-dog persona is matched by his skills as a tough political infighter. Ramiro Valdés is a veteran of Fidel's rebel army and a tough former interior minister who was elevated to run Cuba's Information and Communications Ministry. Julio Casas Regueiro, who replaced Raúl as minister of defense, is a senior general who made sweeping changes in state-owned enterprises and is well regarded in the army. Fernando Remírez is a former chief of the Cuban Interests Section in Washington who has taken on a powerful role in managing the Communist Party's international affairs. This leadership group will evolve further in the coming years, but it has already outlasted Fidel's presidency and shifted its allegiance to Raúl without missing a beat. The ease of this leadership transition suggests that Cuba's future economic reforms will unfold in slow motion and be managed by technocrats within the island's existing institutions. Cubans, exhausted by nearly fifty years of Fidel's charismatic politics, may greet this mellower approach as a revolution in itself.

Meanwhile, Thomas Shannon, who took over the top Latin America position at the State Department in 2005, roundly dismisses the idea that the United States should engage in dialogue with any members of this leadership group, although he insists that Washington has adjusted its diplomatic strategy to support democracy in Cuba, even if its commitment to the embargo remains airtight. In a conversation in his Foggy Bottom office, Shannon told me, "U.S. policy hasn't changed, but what has really changed is the level of U.S. diplomacy in support for a peaceful, democratic transition." He cited the two reports from the Commission for Assistance to a Free Cuba and other steps taken by the Bush administration. "The policy was well set in anticipation of some type of change in Cuba. It was clear that Fidel Castro was not getting any younger and that there would be a series of changes in the upper level of leadership—allowing his brother to step forward, and those around his brother." The decision was made to focus on international diplomacy, with special outreach to the Eastern European countries, like the Czech Republic, that were strongly opposed to the Castro government. "Fidel Castro's illness created expectations that change was imminent, which brought a sense of urgency to our diplomacy. We began our efforts to reach out to Europe, Latin America, trying to look for points of convergence and explore ways to work together to create democratic change in Cuba," Shannon said, noting that Caleb McCarry, the Cuba transition coordinator, was at that moment in Lithuania pressing the case for the United States. "Because of the changes in leadership, there was a lot of interest because everybody knew that this was no longer going to be symbolic, it was going to be real. We want a democratic transition, but one that is internally driven without imposing a solution."

Shannon emphasized U.S. efforts to build up civil society in Cuba through U.S. assistance programs, with funding channeled mostly through third countries. Millions of dollars had been funneled through these programs under the Bush administration, to little apparent effect. Still, Shannon thought this support played a crucial role. "All successful transitions have required interlocutors in civil society. Sometimes the interlocutor arrives naturally, like with Nelson Mandela in South Africa, and other times the interlocutor is forced on the government, such as the case in Poland. We want to build up the dissidents to be that interlocutor and help them to strengthen their capacity," he said.

In Shannon's view, the Cuban people were "a silent but important player" in a transition scenario. "Right now, the day-to-day life for most people in Cuba is one of subsistence or survival, and they see no better horizon under the Cuban government. Our assumption—and it might be wrong—is that once Fidel Castro dies, the demand for economic change, the demand for higher salaries and more options, will increase, and then we will have to see how the government manages these demands." Shannon disagreed with the perspective that the Cuban embargo was a relic of the past, instead recasting it as a tool for the future. "Whatever the history of the embargo or its effectiveness to date, it is clearly an important bargaining tool. It would be foolish to give it up without getting something in return."

Still, even Washington's closest allies on Cuba policy hesitate to embrace this view. Shortly before my visit with Shannon, I went to meet with Petr Kolar, the Czech Republic's ambassador to the United States, who represents one of the countries most critical of the Castro regime. "The view of Czechs about Cubans is very positive," he told me in a stately embassy conference room, seated below a picture of Václav Havel, the dissident who became president during Czechoslovakia's Velvet Revolution of 1989. "I am very sorry that this gifted nation—those people who are really skilled and who can create wealth and provide welfare—are prevented from doing that by this crazy communist regime. We know what this regime means, because we lived that. We know that we were cheated the whole time by our communist leaders and this is actually what Mr. Castro is doing." Kolar was proud of the Czech government's support for Cuban civil society groups, its strong criticism of the Castro government, and symbolic measures such as the Czech embassy's decision to adopt a Cuban crocodile at Washington's National Zoo to show its support for Cuban dissidents. "The United States is our strategic partner, but we don't work for democracy and freedom in Cuba because of the United States," he said. "We believe that if we have some friend and close ally, our duty is to be honest, frank, and speak openly about different views—not be an echo only."

Kolar believed that his country's recent political experience with communism showed that trade and commerce play a crucial role in the transition to democracy. "We know that it helped . . . The communists cut off the branch they were sitting on by opening the border," he explained. "We cooperate very closely with the U.S. on Cuba, but it doesn't mean that we do it always like some of our friends here in the State Department or Congress would like." Shortly after Bush's speech, the United Nations overwhelmingly passed for the sixteenth time a resolution condemning the U.S. embargo of Cuba. The Czech Republic joined the 184 nations that approved the measure, while the U.S. opposition was supported only by Israel, Palau, and the Marshall Islands. Several months after Raúl Castro became president, the European Union lifted diplomatic sanctions on Cuba that had been implemented several years earlier following the crackdown on dissidents. If the United States had indeed made inroads in getting other countries to support the principle of democracy in Cuba, world opinion against the embargo remained as fierce as ever.

On January 1, 2008, Fidel Castro marked his forty-ninth and final anniversary as the president of Cuba, one of the world's few remaining communist states. At eighty-one years old, he was the longest-serving head of government in the world, and only the queen of England and the king of Thailand could boast longer reigns as head of state. Until confronted with illness in July 2006, Fidel remained an active and visible leadership presence and faced no serious challenges as Cuba's chief decision maker. Now his long tenure in office has ended, and authority has been passed to Raúl Castro, provoking considerable interest in what will happen in the coming period. The crux of the question is whether Raúl will seek to maintain a hard-line communist government or instead embrace some form of economic opening. A crucial parallel question is whether steps can be taken to strengthen democratic elements in Cuba that will lead to the expansion of political freedoms. Admittedly, any effort to predict the politics of post-Fidel Cuba is akin to looking through a glass darkly. Yet there can be little doubt that the Cuban government and the Communist Party are preparing to weather his passing. For years, the death of Fidel was believed to pose the "biological solution" to Cuba's long hiatus from democratic rule. Now it is becoming apparent that the answers may not be so simple.

The future of the current Cuban government will depend, to a large extent, on whether it can find renewed support among the "bridge generation" of Cubans in their thirties, who were born in the late 1960s and early 1970s and came of age when the collapse of the Soviet Union plunged the island into the bleak crisis of the special period. They are old enough to remember the days when Cuba was an egalitarian society and lived through the harrowing period of economic decline that reshaped Cuban society in the 1990s. They will inherit the mantle of leadership in Cuba and hold the key to determining the future shape of the island's politics.

If things had turned out differently, Arturo Lopez-Levy might have been among them. Lopez-Levy cuts a slightly incongruous figure on the campus of the University of Denver, in the mountainous capital of Colorado, where he had invited me to be a guest speaker. In his late thirties, he is over six feet tall, with graying hair and a thick Cuban accent. He drives a red Subaru Legacy with a cracked windshield and a dashboard piled high with the books, notes, empty coffee cups, and fast-food wrappers of a Ph.D. student trying to complete his dissertation while simultaneously teaching four classes across three university campuses. "You know, I have this problem with my car," he joked as he tried to rearrange the piles to make room for me. "When I drive around town, people throw things in it." Lopez-Levy is a voracious reader and a devout Jew who departed Cuba for Israel in the summer of 2001 en route to a master's program at Columbia University in New York, and he has been in school in the United States ever since.

Back in Cuba, where he was born and raised, Lopez-Levy's first job was at the Ministry of the Interior, but he quickly discovered he was on the wrong career path. In 1991, as a junior analyst and army recruit, he recommended that Cuba improve its relations with the United States by sending troops to join in the coalition against Saddam Hussein that President George H. W. Bush had built for the first Gulf War. His superiors rewarded him for his suggestion by threatening to kick him out of training, and he was dispatched to eastern Cuba for a year to stand guard on the Cuban side of Guantánamo Bay Naval Base. ("It was boring. I read a lot of books," he recalled.) Upon his return to Havana, Lopez-Levy realized that he favored greater reforms than the Cuban leadership would allow, and he found that he lacked the enthusiasm for the Cuban Revolution that his highly competitive government job demanded from a young man in his early twenties. "It was very difficult for me to believe that the best way to promote changes was from the inside," he said. "And I was paying a very high price on a personal level, because I was not a communist, and they demand a lot of communist loyalty for this kind of job." So he quit in December 1994, but found it hard to get another job in line with his qualifications. "Interviewers would ask me, 'Why aren't you a member of the Young Communist League?' and I would reply, 'Because I am not a communist.' No one ever called back." Lopez-Levy ended up working odd jobs such as tour guide and DVD rental agent for the next seven years, until he finally got permission to leave Cuba on a religious trip to Israel in 2001 and used it as a springboard to realize his goal of studying in the United States.

Lopez-Levy was a respected member of Cuba's small Jewish community of less than two thousand people, but he embraced his faith more fully after coming to the United States. "I never felt attacked by the revolution because I was Jewish," he said, "but at the same time, I would say there are certain manifestations in the Cuban press, especially against Israel, or sometimes speaking about the Holocaust, that I found despicable." Still, the comparisons between Castro and Hitler that sometimes emerge in American rhetoric grated harshly on him. "I think this is totally wrong. Hitler is the incarnation of all evils, and it is difficult for me to find anything good he did for the German people. Fidel is a revolutionary leader who became a totalitarian leader, and there have been severe restrictions of civil liberties, but there has been progress in health and education and restoring the sense of dignity of the Cuban people in international terms. Cuba was able to achieve certain things under the revolution that were unthinkable in other contexts." He shook his head. "For me, historical analogies are an expression of intellectual laziness. If you want to analyze Castro, you analyze Castro in the context of his own unique features. He has his negative side and his positive side. It's wrong to compare him to Hitler or Stalin."

If he had stayed on his original career path in Cuba, Lopez-Levy would likely be serving as a high-level diplomat abroad or a senior-level official in the Cuban government. His thirtysomething generation is too young to remember the Cuban Revolution or the grim excesses of the 1960s, but old enough to have known life before the economic collapse of the 1990s plunged the island into crisis and upended the socialist order. Indeed, like many Cubans, Lopez-Levy viewed the bleak days of Cuba's special period as a wrenching experience, and the respective reactions of the Cuban government and the exile community at that time profoundly and permanently shaped his worldview. "Honestly, I was very affected by the special period in two senses. One is that it made clear to me that the exiles—or the right-wing exiles, to be more specific and accurate—they didn't have a solution for us at all," he said. "Because in the moment when we as a people were passing the worst crisis, they made this crisis worse . . . through things like increasing the embargo." He remarked that these moves came at a time of brutal scarcity on the island. "I saw people suffer. I was biking ten kilometers a day, more or less, and not because I was doing sports like I do here in Denver. It was because it was hard for me. My mother and father were spending all their savings to make their kids eat, only to make us eat. And then the Cuban government and the communists were so reluctant to reform. That was part of my departure from the communists, because I said, 'You don't see your own people here starving?' " He referred to cases where the hunger was so severe that people began to lose their eyesight, and recalled the plight of one family he knew. "I had a girlfriend at that time, and their breakfast was a glass of tea and a piece of bread, and they didn't have lunch, and for dinner, it was a cabbage soup. It was these experiences from the special period that will be remembered in Cuba forever and ever. I will talk about that to my grandkids."

As he spoke, Lopez-Levy's calm demeanor had hardened slightly, as if recalling that time had dusted off difficult memories. He had been thoroughly let down by a government that believed "it was more important to keep the communist ideas than to save these people. It was a major moment for me, because I said, 'I will break my ties. I will let these people know that I am not one of them. I will make them face the ethical dilemma of what they are doing, but at the same time I am clear that I need to preserve my independence.' " He voiced deep disappointment with the leaders in Miami and Havana whose decisions have heightened the pain for the average citizens caught in the middle of the Cuba wars. "I will not cooperate under any circumstances with the people that increased the embargo at the moment when my country was in the worst time of crisis, and I will never again be part of people that put their ideology before the practical situation in which my family was living . . . I can be a member of a party that is, say, a Revolutionary Cuban Party, a Cuban Social Democratic Party, but a party based on the communist ideology— never!"

Lopez-Levy's sense of betrayal extended to both sides of the Straits of Florida. "These people in both places put their interests before the pragmatic necessities of solving the problems of the country. And

I think the problems of the country are the problems of the Cuban people. I don't believe in these ideas in abstraction, of democracy and communism in abstraction." He added, "Don't tell me that people like Jorge Mas Canosa . . . didn't know that in Cuba there was a major crisis." Indeed, Lopez-Levy believed that the decisions made during this period laid bare the shortcomings of leaders on both sides of this bitter national divide. "I think, in this critical moment, that none of them measured up to the challenge."

When I asked him to describe what would happen to his former country now that its longtime ruler was passing from the scene, Lopez-Levy thought for a moment before replying. "Let me say a thing clearly about Fidel Castro," he said. "For the enemies of the Cuban Revolution, Castro is *Castro*. For the people that love him and have been his unconditional followers—and I broke with them—he's *Fidel*, and he's kind of a magical thing. But many people of my generation are looking to this guy like *Fidel Castro*." He expanded on why this distinction was important. "Fidel is the guy that some people love, and Castro is the guy that some people hate. My generation wants to find the balance, and some of us are at different points, but we are at the center of the spectrum that calls the guy Fidel Castro. We will not go to a demonstration and cry 'Fidel, Fidel,' and we will not fill our hearts with hate and call him 'Castro.' The sunset is happening now, and it's time to look at history with objective eyes."

In the thin air of Denver, Colorado, Lopez-Levy mused about the future of his distant homeland of Cuba. "They are nationalists. Something that is paradoxical is that Fidel failed to develop a socialist conscience, but they were successful, I think, in developing a nationalist conscience. It's very interesting." He believed that the Cuban nationalism that Fidel helped to shape would hold the country together during the difficult days to come. "Fidel is kind of a gigantic man," he said, "but Raúl is not stupid. I think that Raúl is a smart person, he's rational, he's surrounded by a group of collective leadership, and in the end, he will make some reforms." Indeed, Raúl has already inherited the authoritarian and centralized political system that his brother created, he enjoys the strong support and loyalty of top military officers, known as *Raúlistas*, and he remains deeply committed to the political primacy of the Communist Party. Equally important, Raúl has a streak of economic pragmatism that separates him from his elder brother and may pave the way for an extended period of rule. But it remains an open question whether Raúl can maintain the nationalist fervor in Cuba that was so crucial to Fidel's successful rule—or transcend it by delivering the concrete economic results that people on the island so desperately seek. If Cuba continues to lose talented individuals who could have formed the basis of the next generation of leadership, this challenge may well prove insurmountable even for Cuba's most powerful administrator.

Despite the doubts that lingered over Cuba's long-term political future, there was little question that the year 2008 had witnessed a smooth leadership transition on the island. By contrast, the outcome of the raucous and chaotic U.S. presidential election unfolding on the other side of the Straits of Florida was anything but certain. The intense competition for the White House had produced a remarkable comeback by Senator John McCain of Arizona, whose campaign overcame early financial troubles to rack up an impressive series of wins that transformed him into the presumptive nominee of the Republican Party. On the Democratic side of the aisle, Senator Hillary Clinton of New York and Senator Barack Obama of Illinois battled for primacy in the longest and most fiercely fought contest in decades. In the end, Obama seized the nomination in a victory powered by his shrewd campaign strategy, rousing oratory, and ability to tap into the hunger for change in the Democratic electorate. The looming general election battle between McCain, the maverick seventy-two-year-old Vietnam War hero, and Obama, the progressive forty-seven-year-old African American lawyer, marked the starkest contrast between any two presidential candidates in recent memory, if not ever.

Given the importance of winning Florida's twenty-seven electoral votes, Cuba emerged as an early campaign issue. While most of the main Republican candidates strongly backed the embargo (with the exception of the libertarian Ron Paul), the Democratic race had revealed deep differences on Cuba policy, particularly in the context of the overall foreign policy visions of the respective candidates. A seminal moment occurred during the first half of the CNN/YouTube debate in July 2007, when a man named Stephen posed the following query to the Democratic candidates: "In 1982, Anwar Sadat traveled to Israel, a trip that resulted in a peace agreement that has lasted ever since. In the spirit of that type of bold leadership, would you be willing to meet separately, without precondition, during the first year of your administration, in Washington or anywhere else, with the leaders of Iran, Syria, Venezuela, Cuba and North Korea, in order to bridge the gap that divides our countries?" The debate moderator, Anderson Cooper, directed the question to Obama, who responded: "I would. And the reason is this, that the notion that somehow not talking to countries is punishment to them—which has been the guiding diplomatic principle of this administration—is ridiculous." Hillary Clinton disagreed: "Well, I will not promise to meet with the leaders of these countries during my first year. I will promise a very vigorous diplomatic effort . . . and I will use a lot of high-level presidential envoys to test the waters, to feel the way. But certainly, we're not going to just have our president meet with Fidel Castro and Hugo Chávez and, you know, the president of North Korea, Iran and Syria until we know better what the way forward would be."[8] (Former senator John Edwards, the only other candidate to answer the question, expressed agreement with Clinton.) Following the debate, Clinton attacked Obama's newly formulated position, prompting him to adopt a two-track strategy of strongly defending diplomatic outreach to adversaries, while carefully adding calibrations and equivocations to defuse the alarm it had provoked among key constituencies, notably Jewish voters who were concerned by outreach to Iran and Cuban American voters made uneasy by the prospects of dialogue with Castro. In addition, Obama had to contend with the fact that, as a Senate candidate in 2004, he had declared that it was "time to end the embargo with Cuba" because it had "utterly failed in the effort to overthrow Castro."[9] In August 2007, Obama published an essay in the *Miami Herald* where he pledged to "grant Cuban Americans unrestricted rights to visit family and send remittances to the island" and to use "aggressive and principled diplomacy" through "bilateral talks" to promote democracy in Cuba. He stuck to these themes throughout the campaign, while affirming his support for the embargo.

John McCain had made a habit of flaunting his distaste for Fidel Castro during his quarter century on Capitol Hill, but it soon became clear that the Arizona senator also had some explaining to do. McCain had helped to lead the charge on normalization of relations between the U.S. and Vietnam in the 1990s, and he sometimes struggled to explain why an approach that he supported in the case of Vietnam, a communist country where fifty-eight thousand American soldiers died in combat, was inappropriate for Cuba, an island just off the Florida coastline. In 2000, McCain told CNN, "I'm not in favor of sticking my finger in the eye of Fidel Castro. In fact, I would favor a road map towards normalization of relations such as we presented to the Vietnamese and led to a normalization of relations between our two countries."[10] Such statements won him few fans among prominent Cuban Americans, who threw their support behind George W. Bush during the primary season that year. At a congressional hearing in 2002, however, McCain said he would "oppose increasing trade with this two-bit dictator," adding that, unlike some of his congressional colleagues, he had "never been subjected to a four, five, six hour dinner and lecture from Mr. Castro. And it must be a unique experience, but one that I am sure that I'll never have the privilege of having—listening to one of those lectures." Indeed, as it became clear that McCain would seek the presidency in February 2007, he quickly gained the support of prominent anti-Castro foes like the Florida legislators Lincoln and Mario Diaz-Balart and Ileana Ros-Lehtinen, who declared that "Senator McCain is a strong supporter of the U.S. embargo of Cuba and . . . has been working with us to help bring freedom and democracy to the enslaved island."[11] In January 2008, Florida senator Mel Martinez followed suit, praising McCain as someone with "firsthand knowledge of the evils of communism," and adding "I have total confidence that John McCain will be Fidel Castro's worst nightmare."[12]

By the summer of 2008, McCain and Obama had both traveled a similar path on Cuba policy, embracing the U.S. embargo more fully than their previous statements had suggested. Both candidates also chose to make their major Latin America policy speeches before Cuban American audiences in South Florida. Still, it was clear that stark differences remained between the cold war outlook promoted by McCain and the more flexible approach suggested by Obama. Their sharpest policy differences were in two areas: Obama called for dramatically expanding the ability of Cuban Americans to travel and send remittances to Cuba, and he pledged to engage in dialogue with the Castro government (although his earlier commitment to do so without preconditions during the first year of his presidency had been dropped). In May 2008, their nearly back-to-back speeches on the issue in Miami highlighted how they viewed the Cuba dilemma.

Whatever doubts McCain may have once harbored about the Cuban embargo had been fully purged from his political repertoire by the time that he addressed a Cuban American audience in Little Havana as the presumptive Republican presidential nominee. Describing Cuba as Fidel Castro's "personal fiefdom," McCain dismissed the reforms implemented by Raúl Castro as a "smattering of small changes" that were meaningless to "the political prisoners that fill Cuban jails, to the millions who suffer under poverty and repression, and to all those who wish to choose their leaders, not suffer under them." McCain pledged, "As President, I will not passively await the day when the Cuban people enjoy the blessings of freedom and democracy," but his proposed policies for change sounded eerily familiar. His administration would foreswear engaging with the Castro government, instead seeking to maintain the embargo until the day when Cuba released its political prisoners, legalized opposition parties, and held internationally monitored democratic elections. In addition, McCain vowed greater support for Radio and TV Martí and dissident groups, as well as stepped up efforts to convince European and Latin American allies of the wisdom of the U.S. approach. In short, when it came to Cuba policy, John McCain was promising to recommit to the set of policies that had won George Bush such deep support in the Cuban American community, and had yielded so little in the way of results.

Three days later, Obama elaborated on his views before a meeting organized by the Cuban American National Foundation, the exile group that had become alienated from Bush and was seeking to deepen its influence in the Democratic Party. "I know what the easy thing is to do for American politicians. Every four years, they come down to Miami, they talk tough, they go back to Washington and nothing changes in Cuba," Obama began. "My policy toward Cuba will be guided by one word: *libertad*. And the road to freedom for all Cubans must begin with justice for Cuba's political prisoners, the rights of free speech, a free press, freedom of assembly, and it must lead to elections that are free and fair." He dismissed McCain's criticisms. "Now let me be clear. John McCain's been going around the country talking about how much I want to meet with Raúl Castro, as if I'm looking for a social gathering. That's never what I said and John McCain knows it. After eight years of the disastrous policies of

George Bush, it is time to pursue direct diplomacy, with friend and foe alike, without preconditions. There will be careful preparation. We will set a clear agenda. And as President, I would be willing to lead that diplomacy at a time and place of my choosing, but only when we have an opportunity to advance the interests of the United States, and to advance the cause of freedom for the Cuban people."[13] Obama's call for diplomacy, together with his stated interest in removing barriers to Cuban American travel and exchange, suggested a dramatic change from the policies of isolation advocated by the Bush administration. Still, important questions remained about what type of diplomacy Obama envisioned. Furthermore, it was unclear how he planned to lift the travel prohibitions on Cuban Americans while still enforcing them for the rest of the American public, unless the plan was to create an environment where the broader travel ban was simply unenforceable. Still, Obama did have one important applause line tucked up his sleeve for his Miami audience. "I will maintain the embargo," he said, describing it as "leverage" over the Cuban regime.

In Cuba, Raúl Castro expressed little interest in the American elections, but Fidel watched the presidential race with fascination and wrote about it frequently in his periodic "reflections" that were published in *Granma*. Many Cuban Americans felt a special kinship with McCain because he had written in his bestselling memoir that Cuban agents had tortured some of his fellow American prisoners of war during his five years in captivity in Vietnam's infamous "Hanoi Hilton." Upon learning of these allegations, Fidel ordered to have the book translated into Spanish and then wrote a five-essay series about John McCain under the title, "The Republican Candidate." In it, he denounced the claims as "unethical" and wrote that America's "final pullout from Vietnam was disastrous . . . their only achievement was a Republican presidential candidate" more than three decades later. A bizarre public argument between Castro and McCain on the torture claims ensued. "For me to respond to Fidel Castro, who has oppressed and repressed his people and who is one of the most brutal dictators on Earth, for me to dignify any comments he might make is certainly beneath me," McCain said in response during a press conference in Maryland. "It's a matter of record and you can ask several of the POWs who had direct contact with some, some thug that came to Hanoi with an underling assistant."[14] Following McCain's tough speech on Cuba in Miami, Fidel Castro was nonplussed. "McCain, in his book *Faith of My Fathers*, admitted that he was among the last five students in his course in West Point," Fidel wrote. "He's showing it."[15] (Fidel apparently did not read the book too closely, since McCain actually attended the U.S. Naval Academy in Annapolis, Maryland, not West Point.) The Cuban leader also aimed his criticism at the Democratic nominee for vowing to maintain the embargo: "Obama's speech may be formulated as follows: hunger for the nation, remittances as charitable handouts and visits to Cuba as propaganda for consumerism and the unsustainable way of life behind it." Still, he praised Obama as "the most advanced candidate" and mused, "Were I to defend him, I would be doing his adversaries an enormous favor."[16]

Despite their significant policy differences on Cuba, both McCain and Obama had endorsed the embargo as a central tool in the effort to bring democracy to the island. In the process, they set aside more than forty years of evidence suggesting that U.S. efforts to isolate Cuba had, if anything, helped the Castro regime to stay in power. It represented a remarkable convergence for a maverick Republican who boasted of his "Straight Talk" and a liberal Democrat who advocated for "Change We Can Believe In." Still, there was little doubt that Obama's embrace of dialogue with Cuba placed him in a different category than his opponent, and his campaign had signaled a more flexible approach that could create new opportunities for change during the next U.S. administration. In the meantime, two certainties remained: After nearly fifty years, the future of the U.S.-Cuba relationship remained inextricably linked with South Florida politics, and the next occupant of the White House would again find himself inexorably drawn into the Cuba wars.

The United States, for its part, has tied itself into a Gordian knot that has left it ill prepared to do much except watch at a distance as the Cuban transition unfolds. George W. Bush's decisions on Cuba policy were motivated by an instinctive dislike of Fidel Castro, a deep friendship with many hard-line Cuban exiles, and the realities of Florida politics. In addition, the terrorist attacks of September 11, 2001, resulted in a dramatic hardening of U.S. policy toward all countries deemed by the Bush administration to be rogue states. Despite its location on the periphery of the U.S. war on terror, Cuba soon found itself at the crossroads of two competing thrusts in U.S.

foreign policy: the belligerent approach to nations perceived to be enemies of America and the Bush administration's sweeping calls to liberate the world from tyranny so that people could rise up and embrace democracy. During Bush's first term, Colin Powell was recruited into an effort to tighten the sanctions on Cuba prior to the 2004 election, while during his second term Condoleezza Rice declared Cuba to be an "outpost of tyranny" and presided over a near-total breakdown in official interaction between the U.S. and Cuban governments. The American diplomats who staff the U.S. Interests Section in Havana are almost totally cut off from their Cuban counterparts and are prohibited by Cuban regulations from traveling outside Havana, just as Cuban diplomats in Washington are stuck inside the Beltway. The minimal contact of counter-narcotics efforts in the Straits of Florida has all but ceased and the annual U.S.-Cuba migration talks broke down in 2004. Meanwhile, the United States has poured millions into democracy assistance programs that have little to show for their efforts.

Today, there are only three areas where regular official communication is sustained. The first and most important is the monthly meeting between the U.S. and Cuban military officers at the fence line of the Guantánamo Bay Naval Base, which is used to resolve local issues. The second is the occasional cooperation between the U.S. and Cuban coast guards to share information to help manage the flow of hundreds of refugees picked up at sea each year and to deter drug traffickers who are channeling shipments through the territorial waters of the two countries. Last, American and Cuban meteorologists remain in frequent contact for the purpose of tracking hurricanes in the Caribbean. Lixion Avila, a Cuban American who is the senior meteorologist with the National Hurricane Center in South Florida, shared with me his theory about why this cooperation is sustained, no matter how rough the official rhetoric gets on both sides: "I don't think that any Miami politician would be so stupid as to be happy that there are one thousand people killed in Cuba by a hurricane, because everybody has a relative down there." Indeed, the cooperation between American and Cuban authorities to protect their citizens from dangerous weather is one area where enlightened self-interest has taken precedence over political antagonisms.

The winds of change were clearly blowing through the U.S. electorate during the presidential election year of 2008, with the biggest divide opening up between Republican presidential nominee John McCain and Democratic challenger Barack Obama. McCain vowed to hold a tough line on Cuba policy. Obama signaled that he would consider engaging in dialogue with Raúl Castro and favored expanding travel to Cuba by Cuban Americans. Still, it is hard to envision that the next occupant of the White House will be able to broker a truce in the Cuba wars that began in 1959 and have ensnared the last ten U.S. presidents. Moreover, during its eight years in office, the Bush administration set in motion an important set of initiatives on Cuba that its successor will find hard to ignore. The U.S. embargo remains a contentious issue in both Miami and Washington, but the political shifts toward favoring greater engagement with Cuba are only beginning to manifest themselves at the political level in terms of candidates or fund-raising. On Capitol Hill, the Cuban Americans who support the sanctions have spent the past several years building a political firewall to prevent the embargo from being eroded. Despite momentous leadership changes in Cuba and the United States, the forces for continuity remain very strong on both sides of the Straits of Florida.

Still, Fidel Castro's Cuba is on the verge of one of the most anticipated and dramatic political transitions of our time. After nearly fifty years with Castro at the helm of Cuba, it is clear that the bearded leader's days are numbered—and his diminished health has paved the way for a political cliff-hanger of enormous magnitude. The future is awash in both possibility and risk. In the short term, Cuban communism appears likely to survive the death of its legendary leader. It has already withstood the forces that gathered in U.S. policy circles and the Cuban exile community, which reached their apex during the invasion of Iraq in 2003 and the presidential election of 2004, that intended to derail a leadership succession and push the country toward democracy. The Castro foes outside of Cuba who dreamed of bringing the regime crashing down have become increasingly aware that time is no longer on their side. Fewer and fewer Miami exiles envision a future in which they can return to Cuba and re-create the lives they fled after Castro came to power. In Cuba, domestic opposition leaders have tried to forge a common vision with sufficient international backing to force their government to accept democratic change. They, too, realize that their chances of success in promoting change from outside the system have diminished since the seamless transition from Fidel to Raúl.

The Castro brothers certainly have no shortage of friends, nor of foes, on the international stage. The U.S. government, which has spent decades trying to dispose of them through means both fair and foul, is increasingly anxious to avoid a Cuban adventure that could lead to a refugee crisis or even involve peacekeeping responsibilities. Stability, not democracy, is the watchword in the Pentagon and the Miami-based U.S. Southern Command, despite the White House rhetoric that preaches the reverse. Western nations like Canada and the member countries of the European Union have significant economic investments that dampen any enthusiasm for risking the destabilization of Cuba in the name of greater political freedom. Meanwhile, in addition to Venezuelan president Hugo Chávez, other rising powers, like Chinese premier Hu Jintao, have become major financial and political backers of communist Cuba. The cauldron of powerful interests engaged in the Cuban struggle raises the possibility that the island's political future risks becoming a proxy battleground for foreign influence with unpredictable consequences.

The U.S.-Cuba relationship remains filled with both longing and loathing, and the decades of official hostility between the two countries cannot be easily erased. On the verge of the fiftieth anniversary of the Cuban Revolution, Cuba remains caught in the viselike grip of the regime that Fidel Castro left behind and faced with the relentless antagonism and casual indifference of the United States. The fates of eleven million diverse and divided people hang in the balance, but their future will depend on whether they are given the chance to shape their own political destiny. In the meantime, the Cuba wars will continue to rage in Havana, Miami, and Washington. One hopes that a moment will come when the forces for peaceful reconciliation gather critical mass, but such a vision still remains on the distant horizon.

During his many years at the helm in Cuba, Fidel Castro used the United States as a foil to help maintain his power. Now Raúl Castro is pursuing a path of limited economic opening that may give new life to the Cuban Revolution or sow the seeds for Cuba to evolve into a different kind of society entirely. By instinct or design, the United States continues to perceive itself as having a major role in Cuba's future, but Cuba's fate will ultimately be left with the people who remain on the island. Yet even though Fidel rallied the populace behind his vision of a nation that must band together to repel the imperialist threat, he admitted that the United States does not pose the only challenge. "The Yankees cannot destroy the revolutionary process," Castro mused in an interview not long ago. But if Cubans turn away from socialism, then "this country can self-destruct. We ourselves could destroy it, and it would be our fault." Fifty years after the Cuban Revolution of 1959, Cuba is torn between socialism and capitalism, hovering on the verge of ending its isolation from the United States, and showing glimmers of openness that could lead to market reform and perhaps even a future path toward democracy. The United States did not recognize the significance of the first Cuban Revolution until it was too late to shape its course. Today, as new forces for change continue to gather within Cuba, it will be the responsibility of the next American president to avoid repeating this mistake.

Now the island is caught up in the midst of its next revolution: a revolution of expectations in Havana, Miami, and Washington about the steps that the United States and Cuba can take to plot a better future for the citizens of both countries. It represents a challenge that the two nations should embrace, because the Cuba wars have endured far too long, damaged the lives of too many people, and achieved far too little to justify making this conflict the inheritance of future generations.

Acknowledgments

This book took a long time to come to fruition, and many people contributed both to this specific work and to my knowledge of Cuba along the way. Harvard's John F. Kennedy School of Government facilitated my first trip to Cuba, at the height of the Elián González crisis in 2000, which whetted my appetite for trying to unravel the mystery of this island and its unique role in U.S. foreign policy. When I moved to Washington, D.C., in 2001, the Inter-American Dialogue proved to be an exemplary professional home for work on Cuba and broader Latin American issues. I am especially indebted to Peter Hakim and Michael Shifter for their support and guidance over the years, as well as to my other esteemed colleagues at the Dialogue. I am also grateful to the Swedish International Development and Cooperation Agency for its support of the Dialogue's work on the Cuban economy, and I thank the wide range of U.S. and international partners who have contributed to our analysis of Cuba. This book has benefited from the hard work of several talented program assistants who contributed to my research on Cuba, including Adam Minson, Jillian Blake, and Paul Wander, who was an excellent wingman in managing the interview process and helping to bring the manuscript to completion. My interns, Chris Gaspar, Kate Neeper, Joyce Lawrence, Antonio Martínez, and Gladis Sánchez, also played an important role in keeping this project moving forward. More than fifty people agreed to be interviewed for this book, but the work has also benefited from the insights of many, many more with whom I have talked, argued, and commiserated about Cuban affairs. In particular, I want to thank those Cubans and Americans who are pushing their countries, in ways large and small, toward a future that is more free, fair, and just than the reality that exists today.

My agent, Will Lippincott, rescued this book idea from the edge of the abyss and has been a steady source of advice and counsel. At Bloomsbury Press, my editor, Peter Ginna, has been a pleasure to work with, and Katie Henderson's keen eye helped to hone the final manuscript. I also thank my friends and colleagues who graciously agreed to review draft chapters or the manuscript as a whole, including Laura Bures, Peter Carry, Jorge I. Domínguez, Katrin Hansing, Jeff Metzler, Marifeli Pérez-Stable, and Michael Shifter. Catherine Wiesner's shrewd comments contributed importantly to the initial book proposal.

I am lucky to have an extremely supportive family, including my parents, Donna and Eric Erikson, my sister, Abby, and my grandparents, especially my grandfather Gordon I. Erikson Sr., who still tells stories from his visit to Cuba in 1958, before the curtain came falling down. My mother-in-law, Elizabeth Winthrop, was generous with her knowledge of publishing and my other in-laws, Jason Bosseau, Peter Mahony, Andrew Mahony, and Patricia Alsop, have provided constant encouragement.

Beginning with a long, moonlit walk in Havana, my wife, Eliza, has been the key to turning our dreams into reality, and this one is for her!

A Note on Sources

This book combines political analysis and firsthand reporting. Between March 2000 and March 2008, I traveled to Cuba on fourteen occasions (all fully licensed by the U.S. government) for the purposes of research on the island's political and economic situation, participating in international conferences, and, on one occasion, bringing a small delegation of U.S. congressmen to Havana. These trips enabled me to develop a keen sense of Cuban politics and society and follow the events that unfolded in recent years. My work also brought me frequently to Miami and gave me the opportunity to interact with many policy makers in Washington and travel widely throughout Europe and Latin America, including Venezuela, a country that features heavily in this book. In October 2007, the public relations team at Joint Task Force–Guantánamo hosted me for a four-day visit to the military base as part of a media tour, which gave me a much deeper understanding of this little-known dimension of the U.S.-Cuba relationship.

Any analyst of Cuba who is based in the United States relies heavily on the enterprising journalists who cover Cuba from the island. In that sense, this book builds on the excellent reporting conducted by many of the first-rate journalists who cover this sensitive topic. In order to give credit where credit is due, I have cited news articles and wire stories where appropriate in the endnotes. However, I would like to give particular thanks to my many friends and colleagues at the Associated Press, the BBC, the *Chicago Tribune*, CNN, the *Economist*, the *Sun-Sentinel*, the *Miami Herald*, and Reuters as well as the Cuban independent journalists who do their best to cover what other media may miss. This book benefited from the many stories that they

brought to light. I also took full advantage of the possibilities provided by YouTube to witness and review video footage of some of the
critical events referenced in this book.

More than fifty people agreed to be interviewed for this book, and
the vast majority of them spoke to me on the record. Many of the
individuals that I interviewed are identified in the text and I extend
my appreciation and gratitude for their willingness to speak with me
and the dedication they bring to the issue of Cuba.

The people who contributed to this book through on-the-record
interviews include:

Raúl Rivero (Madrid, Spain, November 15, 2006)

Pedro Roig (Miami, Florida, December 6, 2006; July 26, 2007)

Dagoberto Valdés Hernández (Pinar del Río, Cuba, February 10,
2007)

Ambassador Vicki Huddleston (Washington, D.C., February 22,
2007)

Alberto Ibargüen (Miami, Florida, March 9, 2007)

Dr. Francisco Hernández (Miami, Florida, March 9, 2007)

Joe Garcia (Miami, Florida, March 9, 2007)

Reverend Lucius Walker (New York, New York, March 19, 2007)

Ambassador Otto Reich (Washington, D.C., March 27, 2007)

Ramon Colas (Washington, D.C., April 3, 2007)

Carlos Saladrigas (Washington, D.C., April 3, 2007)

Caleb McCarry (Washington, D.C., April 12, 2007)

Colonel Larry Wilkerson (Washington, D.C., April 13, 2007)

Representative Jeff Flake (Washington, D.C., April 24, 2007)

Arturo Lopez-Levy (Denver, Colorado, April 26, 2007)

Representative Dan Burton (Washington, D.C., May 8, 2007)

Teodoro Petkoff (Caracas, Venezuela, May 16, 2007)

General Alberto Müller-Rojas (Caracas, Venezuela, May 16, 2007)

Dr. Renato Gusmão (Caracas, Venezuela, May 17, 2007)

Ambassador Roger Noriega (Washington, D.C., May 22, 2007)

Representative Bill Delahunt (Washington, D.C., May 24, 2007)

Ambassador James Cason (Falls Church, Virginia, June 6, 2007)

Representative Maxine Waters (Washington, D.C., June 21, 2007)

Sergeant Carlos Lazo (via telephone from Seattle, Washington, June
26, 2007)

Kirby Jones (Washington, D.C., June 27, 2007)

Mauricio Claver-Carone (Washington, D.C., July 5, 2007)

Oliver Stone (via telephone from Los Angeles, California, July 9, 2007)

Representative Lincoln Diaz-Balart (Washington, D.C., July 11, 2007)

Dr. Marifeli Pérez-Stable (Washington, D.C., July 11, 2007)

Representative José Serrano (Washington, D.C., July 24, 2007)

Representative Debbie Wasserman Schultz (Washington, D.C., July 24, 2007)

Manuel Vásquez Portal (Miami, Florida, July 26, 2007)

Enrique Fernández (Miami, Florida, July 26, 2007)

Ninoska Pérez Castellón (Miami, Florida, July 27, 2007)

Captain Edwin H. Daniels Jr. (Miami, Florida, July 27, 2007)

Lixion Avila (Miami, Florida, July 27, 2007)

Secretary General José Miguel Insulza (Washington, D.C., August 15, 2007)

Gene Orza (via telephone from New York, New York, August 16, 2007)

Pedro Monreal (Buenos Aires, Argentina, August 23, 2007)

Dr. Jorge I. Domínguez (Montreal, Canada, September 8, 2007)

Ambassador Petr Kolar (Washington, D.C., October 4, 2007)

Thomas Shannon (Washington, D.C., October 16, 2007)

Captain Mark Leary (Guantánamo Bay, Cuba, October 24, 2007)

Brigadier General Cameron A. Crawford (Guantánamo Bay, Cuba, October 24, 2007)

Jorge Piñon (via telephone from Miami, Florida, November 5, 2007)

Sergio Bendixen (Miami, Florida, December 5, 2007)

Tom Donohue (written interview, Washington, D.C., December 13, 2007)

Anita Snow (via email from Havana, Cuba, February 1, 2008)

This list does not include several current and former U.S. officials who asked not to be identified, and it omits the names of the staff at the Guantánamo Bay Naval Base other than the commanding officers.

Notes

Chapter 1: Die Another Day

1. Will Weissert, "Raul Castro Seeks Support for Fidel Bid," Associated Press, December 25, 2007.
2. "Fidel Refutes Forbes," *Granma*, May 16, 2006.
3. "Castro, Chavez Tour Che Guevara's Boyhood Home," Associated Press, July 22, 2006.
4. "Cuban TV: Castro Says Health 'Stable,'" CNN.com, August 1, 2006, http://edition.cnn.com/2006/WORLD/americas/08/01/cuba.castro/index.html.
5. "U.S. Has Plan to Aid Post-Castro Cuba," Associated Press, August 1, 2006.
6. "U.S.: No Plan to Reach Out to Raul Castro," CNN.com, August 2, 2006, http://www.cnn.com/2006/POLITICS/08/01/lawmakers.castro/index.html.
7. Tamara Lush, "Cuba Refugee Policy in the Works," *St. Petersburg Times*, August 3, 2006.
8. *Commission for Assistance to a Free Cuba: Report to the President*, Commission for Assistance to a Free Cuba, July 2006, www.cafc.gov.
9. "Cuban TV."
10. Bill Brubaker, "Cubans Suggest Castro Is Doing Well," *Washington Post*, August 2, 2006.
11. Larry Luxner, "An Exclusive Cuba News Interview with Ricardo Alarcón," *Cuba News*, May 2004.
12. *FOCAL'S Chronicle on Cuba: Domestic Affairs*, Cubasource, May 2006, www.cubasource.org.
13. "Speech by Raúl Castro on the 45th Anniversary of the Founding of

the Western Army," June 14, 2006, http://www.granma.cubaweb
.cu/secciones/raul-45ejercito/raul03.html.

14. "CIA: Fidel Castro Has Parkinson's," *Miami Herald*, November
16, 2005.

15. James C. McKinley Jr., "Castro 'Stable,' but His Illness Presents
Puzzle," *New York Times*, August 2, 2006.

16. The most detailed report on Castro's illness was written by Oriol
Güell and Ana Alfageme, "Una cadena de actuaciones médicas fal-
lidas agravó el estado de castro," *El País*, January 16, 2007.

17. "Castro Has Post-surgery Problems: Diplomat," Reuters, January
15, 2007.

18. "Castro no tiene cáncer, dice cirujano español," Associated Press,
December 26, 2006.

19. Secretary of State Condoleezza Rice, "Announcement of Cuba
Transition Coordinator Caleb McCarry," Washington, D.C., July
28, 2005, http://www.state.gov/secretary/rm/2005/50346.htm.

20. Darlene Superville, "Bush Point Man Has No Love for Castro,"
Associated Press, August 4, 2006.

21. Isabel Sanchez, "Cuban Dissidents and Regime Agree in Rejecting
New U.S. Official," Agence France-Presse, August 1, 2005.

22. Karen DeYoung, "Castro Near Death, Intelligence Chief Says,"
Washington Post, December 15, 2006.

23. Mike McConnell, "Annual Threat Assessment," testimony before
the Senate Armed Services Committee, February 27, 2007, http://
www.dni.gov/testimonies/20070227_testimony.pdf.

Chapter 2: War of Nerves

1. "Bill Clinton on Sanctions Against Cuba," *Democracy Now!*,
November 8, 2000, http://globalpolicy.igc.org/security/sanction/
cuba/00clintn.htm.

2. Speech by Fidel Castro, Havana, Cuba, September 22, 2001, http://
www.cuba.cu/gobierno/discursos/2001/ing/f220901i.html.

3. John R. Bolton, "Beyond the Axis of Evil: Additional Threats from
Weapons of Mass Destruction," speech delivered to the Heritage
Foundation, Washington, D.C., May 6, 2002, http://www.state
.gov/t/us/rm/9962.htm.

4. Tim Johnson, "Talk of Germ Weapons Jolts Congress," *Miami Herald*, May 8, 2002.

5. Judith Miller, "Washington Accuses Cuba of Germ-Warfare Research," *New York Times*, May 7, 2002.

6. "Report on the U.S. Intelligence Community's Prewar Intelligence Assessments on Iraq," Select Committee on Intelligence, Senate, 108th Congress, July 7, 2004, http://www.gpoaccess.gov/serialset/creports/Iraq.html.

7. Fidel Castro and Ignacio Ramonet, *Fidel Castro: My Life: A Spoken Autobiography*, translated by Andrew Hurley (New York: Scribner, 2008), 432, 444.

8. "Cubans Await Release After Flight to Key West on Crop-Dusting Plane," Associated Press, November 13, 2002.

9. Jennifer Babson, "Auction Could Bring Windfall to Duped Wife," *Miami Herald*, January 13, 2003.

10. "Carter Questions Timing of U.S. Accusations Against Cuba," CNN.com, May 14, 2002, http://archives.cnn.com/2002/WORLD/americas/05/14/carter./visit/index.html.

11. "Cuba's One-Party, One-Candidate 'Elections,'" *Cuba Transition Project Staff Report*, issue 36, January 21, 2003.

12. Jaime Ortega Alamino, "There Is No Homeland Without Virtue," excerpts from the pastoral letter of February 24, 2003, reprinted in the *Miami Herald*, March 3, 2003.

13. "Speech Made by Dr. Fidel Castro on the Current World Crisis on the Occasion of His Inauguration as President of the Republic of Cuba," Havana, Cuba, March 6, 2003, http://www.cubaminrex.cu.

14. David González, "A Cuban Dissident Is Defiant After Crackdown Nets Dozens," *New York Times*, March 26, 2003.

15. Jennifer Babson and Oscar Corral, "Hijacked Plane from Cuba 2nd in Two Weeks," *Miami Herald*, April 2, 2003.

16. "Sentencing Documents: Havana 2003, Case 11," accessed in Florida State University's Rule of Law and Cuba database, http://www.ruleoflawandcuba.fsu.edu/documents-havana.cfm. Translation by author.

17. Alfonso Chardy, "Quick Trial, Firing Squad for Three Men Provoke Fury," *Miami Herald*, April 12, 2003.

18. "Speech Made by Dr. Fidel Castro."

Chapter 3: The Dissenters

1. Human Rights Watch, *Cuba's Repressive Machinery: Human Rights Forty Years After the Revolution* (New York: Human Rights Watch, 1999), 1.
2. *FOCAL'S Chronicle on Cuba: Domestic Affairs*, Cubasource, January 2003, www.cubasource.org.
3. "Congressmen Meet Cuban Dissident Leader," Associated Press, March 3, 2003. This section is augmented by notes from the author, who accompanied the congressmen on this trip.
4. Notes taken by the author during the congressional visit of Representative Jim Davis and Representative Jim Kolbe to Havana, Cuba, from February 27 to March 4, 2003.
5. "Congressmen Meet Cuban Dissident Leader."
6. Claudia Márquez Linares, "Scenes from the Cuban Crackdown," *Christian Science Monitor*, April 16, 2003.
7. Nancy San Martin, "Cuba Gains a Dishonor for Jailing 75 Dissidents," *Miami Herald*, July 16, 2003.
8. San Martin, "Cuba Gains."
9. Press conference by Cuban foreign minister Felipe Pérez Roque, April 9, 2003.
10. Press conference.
11. Lucia Newman, "Cuba's Climate of Paranoia," CNN.com, May 8, 2003, http://www.cnn.com/2003/WORLD/americas/05/08/cuba.dissidents/index.html.
12. Matthew Hay Brown, "Crackdown on Dissidents Shows Cuba's Leniency Over," *Orlando Sentinel*, April 21, 2003.
13. "A Tale of Two Dissidents," *Toronto Star*, October 5, 2003.
14. Anthony Boadle, "Cuban Dissidents Seek Unity in Castro's Absence," Reuters, September 5, 2007.
15. United States Government Accountability Office, *Foreign Assistance: U.S. Democracy Assistance for Cuba Needs Better Management and Oversight*, GAO 07-147, November 2006.
16. Alfonso Chardy and Pablo Bachelet, "Fraud Charges Stun Cuban Exile Activist," *Miami Herald*, April 24, 2008.
17. Will Weissert, "Raul Takes Small Steps on Human Rights," Associated Press, March 1, 2008.

Chapter 4: The Empire Strikes Back

1. Bob Woodward, *State of Denial: Bush at War, Part III* (New York: Simon & Schuster, 2006), 224.

2. Tracey Eaton, "U.S. Reaches Deal on Cuba Hijackers," *Dallas Morning News*, July 22, 2003.

3. Anita Snow, "U.S. Returns 12 Cubans Picked Up at Sea," Associated Press, July 22, 2003.

4. Robert Novak, "Appeasing Castro," CNSNews.com, July 31, 2003, http://www.cnsnews.com/viewcommentary.asp?page=%5 ccommentary%5carchive%5c200307%5ccom20030731a.html.

5. "Trouble in Florida," *Washington Times*, August 12, 2003.

6. In 2004, a poll of eighteen hundred Cuban Americans by Florida International University found that fully 60 percent either strongly favored or mostly favored "direct U.S. military action to overthrow the Cuban government." The option of "military action by the exile community to overthrow the Cuban government" received equally strong support. FIU's previous poll in 2000 found similar support for U.S. military action and even greater backing for an exile assault against Cuba. By 2007, however, support for a U.S. invasion had fallen to 51 percent, while the backing for an exile invasion had soared to 70.7 percent, the highest level in a decade. "Comparisons among FIU Cuba Polls 1991–2007," http://www .fiu.edu/orgs/ipor/cuba8/cubacomp.htm.

7. John Pain, "Cuban-Americans Hit Bush Policies," Associated Press, August 15, 2003.

8. "A Letter to the President," *Miami Herald*, August 12, 2003.

9. Oscar Corral, "State GOP Legislators Urge Action on Cuba," *Miami Herald*, August 11, 2003.

10. Andrew S. Natsios, administrator, U.S. Agency for International Development, remarks at Cuban Transition Conference, January 16, 2004, http://www.usaid.gov/press/speeches/2004/sp040116.html.

11. Specialist Kathryn Spurrell, "Soldiers Participate in Fallujah Operations," *Desert Raven: 81st Brigade Combat Team Newsletter*, vol. 2, issue 1, January 1, 2005.

12. Vanessa Arrington, "Castro Leads Protest Against U.S. Embargo," *Newsday*, May 14, 2004.

13. Peter Slevin, "White House Moves to Tighten Cuba Travel, Money Restrictions," *Washington Post*, May 7, 2004.

14. Richard Brand, "Deadline Stirs Rush in Travel to Cuba," *Miami Herald*, June 28, 2004.
15. Edward Alden, "Cheney Cabal Hijacked US Foreign Policy," *Financial Times*, October 20, 2005.
16. Richard Leiby, "Breaking Ranks," *Washington Post*, January 19, 2006.
17. Alden, "Cheney Cabal."
18. "Second Epistle," message from Fidel Castro to George W. Bush, June 21, 2004.

Chapter 5: The Community

1. Wilfredo Cancio Isla, "Former CANF Board Member Admits to Planning Terrorist Attack Against Cuba," *El Nuevo Herald*, June 25, 2006.
2. April Witt, "Catholics Ask Archbishop to Cancel Cuba Cruise," *Miami Herald*, December 18, 1997.
3. "The 2007 FIU Cuba Poll," Institute for Public Opinion Research, Florida International University, 2007, http://www.fiu.edu/orgs/ipor/cuba8/index.html.
4. Vanessa Bauzá, "Radio, TV Martí Seal Deal in South Florida," *Sun-Sentinel*, December 20, 2006.

Chapter 6: Capitol Punishment

1. José De Córdoba, "Democrats Woo Cuban-American Voters," *Wall Street Journal,* April 15, 2008.
2. Ian Christopher McCaleb, "House Approves China Trade Pact," CNN .com, May 24, 2000, http://archives.cnn.com/2000/ALLPOLITICS/stories/05/24/china.trade/index.html.
3. Josephine Hearn, "Members Squabble over Cuba Travel Ban," Politico.com, June 12, 2002, http://www.politico.com/news/stories/0607/4469.html.
4. Ian Swanson, "Money Talks on Cuba Votes," the *Hill*, September 18, 2007.

Chapter 7: Spy Versus Spy

1. Karen DeYoung and Walter Pincus, "CIA Releases Files on Past Misdeeds," *Washington Post*, June 27, 2007.
2. Anita Snow, "CIA Plot to Kill Castro Detailed," Associated Press, June 27, 2007.
3. Will Weissert, "Cuba Hits Newly Released CIA Documents," Associated Press, June 29, 2007.
4. Carol Rosenberg, "Federal Jurors to Begin Deliberations in Cuban Spy Trial," *Miami Herald*, June 4, 2001.
5. Alfonso Chardy and Jay Weaver, "Posada a New Target of Federal Probes," *Miami Herald*, November 12, 2006.
6. "10 Accused of Spying for Cuba," *New York Times*, September 14, 1998.
7. Catherine Wilson, "Cuban Spy Trial Opens in Miami," Associated Press, December 6, 2000.
8. Rosenberg, "Federal Jurors."
9. Gail Epstein Nieves and Alfonso Chardy, "Federal Jury Finds Five Cuban Agents Guilty of Spying," *Miami Herald*, June 9, 2001.
10. Catherine Wilson, "Miami Judge Sentences Cuban Agent to Life in Prison," Associated Press, December 27, 2001; Wilson, "Cuban Spy Ringleader Denounces Trial at Sentencing Hearing," Associated Press, December 12, 2001.
11. Catherine Wilson, "Cuban Agent Sentenced to 19 Years in Prison," Associated Press, December 18, 2001.
12. "Cuban Parliament Honors Five Men Convicted in Florida for Spying," Associated Press, December 29, 2001.
13. Josh Gerstein, "Court Orders New Trial for Cuban Five," *New York Sun*, August 10, 2005.
14. Jonathan Springston, "U.S./Cuba: Appeals Court Reviews Case of Cuban Five," Inter Press Service, August 21, 2007.
15. Bill Miller and Walter Pincus, "Defense Analyst Accused of Spying for Cuba," *Washington Post*, September 22, 2001.
16. Manuel Roig-Franzia, "Cubans Jailed in U.S. as Spies Are Hailed at Home as Heroes," *Washington Post*, June 3, 2006.
17. Pablo Bachelet, "Turncoat Analyst an Effective Spy for Cuba, Book Says," *Miami Herald*, October 14, 2006.
18. "Affidavit in Support of Criminal Complaint, Arrest Warrant, and

Search Warrants," filed by FBI special agent Stephen A. McCoy, September 2001, http://www.fbi.gov/pressrel/pressrel01/092101.pdf.

19. American Enterprise Institute transcript, May 16, 2007, http://www.aei.org/events/eventID.1521,filter.all/event_detail.asp

20. Brian Latell, *After Fidel: The Inside Story of Castro's Regime and Cuba's Next Leader* (New York: Palgrave Macmillan, 2005), 191.

21. Scott W. Carmichael, *True Believer: Inside the Investigation and Capture of Ana Montes, Cuba's Master Spy* (Annapolis, MD: Naval Institute Press, 2007), 59.

22. Ana Belen Montes statement at sentencing, CI Centre, October 16, 2002, http://www.cicentre.com/Documents/DOC_Montes_3.htm.

23. "Ana Montes Espionage Case: An Unrepentant Montes Sentenced to 25 Years," Centre for Counterintelligence and Security Studies, October 16, 2002, http://cicentre.com/Documents/DOC_Montes_2.htm.

24. Anita Snow, "Cuban Praises Jailed Spy," *Miami Herald*, October 19, 2002.

25. "Analysis: Cuba Spies in the U.S.," National Public Radio, *Morning Edition*, November 18, 2002.

26. Ann Louise Bardach and Larry Rohter, "A Bomber's Tale: Taking Aim at Castro. Key Cuba Foe Claims Exiles' Backing," *New York Times*, July 12, 1988.

27. John Rice, "Cuba's Castro Cites Plot to Kill Him, Panama Detains Four," Associated Press, November 17, 2000.

28. "Panama Says It Will Try Cuban Exiles in Castro Murder Plot," Associated Press, November 24, 2000.

29. Peter Kihss, "Three Held in Bazooka Firing at the U.N.," *New York Times*, December 23, 1964.

30. Kathia Martinez, "Panama Rejects Extradition of Alleged Anti-Castro Plotters," Associated Press, April 17, 2001.

31. Oscar Corral and Alfonso Chardy, "Diaz Balart and Ros-Lehtinen Sought Freedom for Terrorist Luis Posada Carriles," *Miami Herald*, July 3, 2005.

32. Reed Lindsay, "Cuba Breaks Panama Links over Death Plot," *Independent*, August 28, 2004.

33. "Bomb-Plot Cuban Crosses into US," BBC online, April 12, 2005, http://news.bbc.co.uk/2/hi/americas/4436079.stm.

34. Ann Louise Bardach, "Our Man in Miami: Patriot or Terrorist?" *Washington Post*, April 17, 2005.

35. Michael A. Fletcher, "U.S. Asylum Sought by Cuban Tied to Terror Cases," *Washington Post*, April 13, 2005.
36. Tim Weiner, "Case of Cuban Exile Could Test the U.S. Definition of Terrorist," *New York Times*, May 9, 2005.
37. "U.S. Not 'Aiding Bomb-Plot Cuban,'" BBC online, May 4, 2005, http://news.bbc.co.uk/2/hi/americas/4513713.stm.
38. Curt Anderson, "Sentence Cut for Cuban-American in Illegal Weapons Case," *Miami Herald*, June 6, 2007.
39. Manuel Roig-Franzia, "In 30-Year-Old Terror Case, a Test for the U.S.: Decision Due on Cuban Exile Suspected in Airliner Blast," *Washington Post*, October 5, 2006.
40. Frances Robles, "Cuba, Venezuela Incensed at Posada's Release," *Miami Herald*, April 19, 2007.
41. Alfonso Chardy, "Militant Cuban Exile Honored," *Miami Herald*, May 2, 2008.

Chapter 8: The Least Worst Place

1. "Shackled Detainees Arrive in Guantanamo," CNN.com, January 11, 2002, http://archives.cnn.com/2002/WORLD/asiapcf/central/01/11/ret.detainee.transfer/index.html.
2. Patrick F. Philbin and John C. Yoo, "Memorandum for William J. Haynes, General Counsel of the Department of Defense," Department of Justice, December 28, 2001.
3. Joseph Margulies, *Guantánamo and the Abuse of Presidential Power* (New York: Simon & Schuster, 2006), 70–71, 145.
4. Tim Golden, "Administration Officials Split over Stalled Military Tribunals," *New York Times*, October 25, 2004.
5. Margulies, 66–67.
6. Golden, "Administration."
7. Nicholas D. Kristof, "Beating Specialist Baker," *New York Times*, June 5, 2004.
8. R. Jeffrey Smith, "General Is Said to Have Urged Use of Dogs," *Washington Post*, May 26, 2004.
9. Seymour M. Hersh, "The General's Report," *New Yorker*, June 25, 2007.
10. "Guantanamo Suicides a 'PR Move,'" BBC online, June 11, 2006, http://news.bbc.co.uk/2/hi/americas/5069230.stm.

11. "Bush Makes Surprise Visit to Baghdad; Interview with Joe Biden; Interview with Shafiq Rasul," *The Situation Room*, CNN, June 13, 2006, http://transcripts.cnn.com/transcripts/0606/13/sitroom.02.html.

12. "A Nation Challenged: Cuba Criticizes Plan," *New York Times*, December 30, 2001.

13. "Cubans Oppose US Plans," Reuters, December 31, 2001.

14. Carol Rosenberg, "Cuba Names New Guantánamo Boss," *Miami Herald*, January 27, 2006.

15. Brian Ross and Richard Esposito, "CIA's Harsh Interrogation Techniques Described," *ABC News*, November 18, 2005, http://abcnews.go.com/wnt/investigation/story?id=1322866.

16. "Alleged 9/11 Planner Wants Death Penalty," MSNBC News Service, June 5, 2008.

Chapter 9: Through the Looking Glass

1. "School Library Pulls Books About Cuba After Parent's Complaint," Associated Press, April 5, 2006.

2. Matthew I. Pinzur, "Book on Cuba to Stay for Now," *Miami Herald*, April 19, 2006.

3. Tania deLuzuriaga, "Cuban Mom Raids School Library," *Miami Herald*, February 22, 2007.

4. Tania deLuzuriaga, "Ex-Political Prisoner Pens Book About Cuba's 'Reality,'" *Miami Herald*, December 13, 2006.

5. "Targeting Che," *Investor's Business Daily*, December 14, 2006.

6. "Cries of 'Tyrant Chic' Spur Target to Pull Che Item," *Globe and Mail*, December 23, 2006.

7. Pablo Bachelet, "Cuba Entry in Wikipedia Stirs Controversy," *Miami Herald*, May 2, 2006.

8. "Talk: Cuba," Wikipedia, http://en.wikipedia.org/wiki/Talk:Cuba, March–April 2007.

9. James Gordon Meek, "U.S. Military Command Hacks Wikipedia," *New York Daily News*, December 13, 2007.

10. "Churches Challenge Plan to Limit Religious Assistance to Cuba," *Christian Century*, August 8, 2006.

11. "Protest Fears Force Latin Grammy Move," BBC online, August 21, 2001, http://news.bbc.co.uk/2/hi/entertainment/1502511.stm.

12. Kevin Baxter, "For Cuban Athletes Who Defect, Success in Sports Is Elusive," *Miami Herald*, June 2, 2002.

13. "Cuba Doubts It Will Participate in Next Year's World Baseball Classic," Associated Press, July 13, 2005.

14. Meghan Clyne, "Baseball Is Eyed by Congress over Plan to Let Cuba Play," *New York Sun*, December 12, 2005.

15. Omar Marrero, "Puerto Rico Says if Cuba Doesn't Play, it Won't Host Ball Fest," EFE News Service, December 22, 2005.

16. Clyne, "Baseball."

17. Clyne, "Baseball."

18. Marrero, "Puerto Rico."

19. Ronald Blum, "Ueberroth Wants Cuba in Baseball Classic," Associated Press, December 19, 2005.

20. "Bush Administration Allows Cuba Baseball Team to Join World Classic," Dow Jones Newswire, January 20, 2006.

21. Anne-Marie Garcia, "World Classic: 'Tremendous' Challenge for Cuba," *Granma International*, March 2, 2006.

22. Janie McCauley, "Cuba Loses World Baseball Classic Final but Still Makes Big Statement," Associated Press, March 21, 2006.

23. "Cuba Tight-Lipped on WBC Plans," Associated Press, October 30, 2007.

24. Frazier Moore, "HBO Postpones Airing of Castro Documentary After Recent Crackdown," Associated Press, April 17, 2003.

25. Anthony Boadle, "Stone Puts Cuban Dissidents in the Film Pulled by HBO," Reuters, May 16, 2003.

Chapter 10: The Capitalist Temptation

1. David Remnick, *Lenin's Tomb: The Last Days of the Soviet Empire* (New York: Vintage Books, 1994), 448, 477.

2. James C. McKinley Jr., "For U.S. Exporters in Cuba, Business Trumps Politics," *New York Times*, November 12, 2007.

3. Lisa J. Adams, "Mexico Says It Will Investigate Sanctions Against a U.S. Owned Hotel That Expelled Cubans," Associated Press, February 7, 2006.

4. "PAN, PRI Condemn Cuba Hotel Incident," *Latinnews Daily*, February 13, 2006.

5. Adams, "Mexico."

6. "Mexico-U.S.: Sheraton Incident Closed with a Fine," *Latin American Weekly Report*, March 28, 2006.
7. Marc Lacey, "Report Finds U.S. Agencies Distracted by Focus on Cuba," *New York Times*, December 19, 2007.
8. Bob Davis, "Cuban Economists Envision Role for Markets in Post-Castro Era," *Wall Street Journal*, January 10, 2007.

Chapter 11: Chasing Chávez

1. Fidel Castro and Ignacio Ramonet, *Fidel Castro: My Life* (New York: Scribner, 2008).
2. Alexei Barrionuevo and José de Córdoba, "For Aging Castro, Chávez Emerges as Vital Crutch," *Wall Street Journal*, February 2, 2004.
3. "Pat Robertson Calls for Assassination of Hugo Chavez," Associated Press, August 22, 2005.
4. "Rumsfeld Likens Venezuela's Chavez to Hitler," Associated Press, February 3, 2006.
5. Castro and Ramonet, 524.
6. Frank Jack Daniel, "Chavez Jokes with New Cuban Leader, Promises Help," Reuters, February 25, 2008.
7. Jens Erik Gould, "Raul Castro Will Succeed Brother as President of Cuba," Bloomberg.com, February 24, 2008, http://www.bloomberg.com/apps/news?pid=20601087&sid=aglux7mt76GU&refer-home.

Chapter 12: The Next Revolution

1. Will Weissert, "Cuba Puts First Computers on Sale to the Public," Associated Press, May 2, 2008.
2. "Entrevista con Ricardo Alarcón, presidente de la Asamblea Nacional Popular de Cuba," *El Mundo*, November 3, 2006. Quotes translated by author.
3. Isabel Sanchez, "Top U.S. Diplomat Unveils Statue of Liberty in Cuba," Agence France Presse, July 5, 2005.
4. "Bush Calls for Release of Cuban Political Prisoner," Reuters, October 10, 2007.
5. "President Bush Discusses Cuba Policy," U.S. Department of State,

Washington, D.C. October 24, 2007, http://www.whitehouse.gov/news/releases/2007/10/20071024-6.html.

6.   Pablo Bachelet and Frances Robles, "Surprise! Cuba Shows Bush Speech on TV," *Miami Herald*, October 26, 2007.

7.   "Castro, Cuba Defiant in Face of Bush Speech," Associated Press, October 24, 2007.

8.   "Part 1: CNN/YouTube Democratic Presidential Debate Transcript," CNN.com, July 24, 2007, http://www.cnn.com/2007/POLITICS/07/23/debate.transcript/.

9.   "Top Obama Flip-Flops," *The Washington Post*, February 25, 2008.

10.   "Elián González Takes Center Stage," *CNN Late Edition*, April 9, 2000, http://transcripts.cnn.com/Transcripts/0004/09/le.00.html.

11.   "Cuban-American Representatives Join Supporters of McCain," press release from John McCain 2008, February 1, 2007.

12.   "Senator Mel Martinez Endorses John McCain for President," press release from John McCain 2008, January 25, 2008.

13.   "Remarks of Senator Barack Obama: Renewing U.S. Leadership in the Americas," Miami, Florida, May 23, 2008.

14.   "Castro, McCain Spar Over Cuban Torture in Vietnam," Reuters, February 11, 2008.

15.   "Fidel Castro Attacks McCain and Bush in Column," Reuters, May 23, 2008.

16.   "Reflections by Comrade Fidel: The Empire's Hypocritical Politics," *Granma*, May 25, 2008.

Selected Bibliography

Anderson, Jon Lee. *Che Guevara: A Revolutionary Life*. New York: Grove Press, 1997.

Bardach, Ann Louise. *Cuba Confidential: Love and Vengeance in Miami and Havana*. New York: Vintage Books, 2003.

Burki, Shahid Javed, and Daniel P. Erikson, eds. *Transforming Socialist Economies: Lessons for Cuba and Beyond*. New York: Palgrave Macmillan, 2005.

Carmichael, Scott W. *True Believer: Inside the Investigation and Capture of Ana Montes, Cuba's Master Spy*. Annapolis, MD: Naval Institute Press, 2007.

Castro, Fidel, and Ignacio Ramonet. *Fidel Castro: My Life: A Spoken Autobiography*. Translated by Andrew Hurley. New York: Scribner, 2008.

Coltman, Leycester. *The Real Fidel Castro*. New Haven, CT: Yale University Press, 2003.

Corbett, Ben. *This Is Cuba: An Outlaw Culture Survives*. Cambridge, MA: Westview, 2004.

DePalma, Anthony. *The Man Who Invented Fidel: Cuba, Castro, and Herbert L. Matthews of the* New York Times. New York: Public Affairs, 2006.

Domínguez, Jorge I., Omar Everleny, Pérez Villanueva, and Lorena Barberia, eds. *The Cuban Economy at the Start of the Twenty-first Century*. Cambridge, MA: Harvard University, David Rockefeller Center for Latin American Studies, distributed by Harvard University Press, 2004.

Falcoff, Mark. *Cuba the Morning After: Confronting Castro's Legacy*. Washington, DC: AEI Press, 2003.

Gonzalez, Edward, and Kevin F. McCarthy. *Cuba After Castro: Legacies,*

Challenges, and Impediments. Santa Monica, CA: RAND Corporation, 2004.

Gott, Richard. *Hugo Chávez and the Bolivarian Revolution*. New York: Verso, 2005.

Helms, Jesse. *Here's Where I Stand: A Memoir*. New York: Random House, 2005.

Horowitz, Irving Louis, and Jaime Suchlicki, eds. *Cuban Communism*, 11th ed. New Brunswick, NJ: Transaction Publishers, 2003.

Klepak, H. P. *Cuba's Military 1990–2005: Revolutionary Soldiers During Counter-Revolutionary Times*. New York: Palgrave Macmillan, 2005.

Latell, Brian. *After Fidel: The Inside Story of Castro's Regime and Cuba's Next Leader*. New York: Palgrave Macmillan, 2005.

Margulies, Joseph. *Guantánamo and the Abuse of Presidential Power*. New York: Simon & Schuster, 2006.

Ojito, Mirta. *Finding Mañana: A Memoir of a Cuban Exodus*. New York: Penguin Press, 2005.

Oppenheimer, Andres. *Castro's Final Hour: The Secret Story Behind the Coming Downfall of Communist Cuba*. New York: Simon & Schuster, 1993.

Pérez-Stable, Marifeli, ed. *Looking Forward: Comparative Perspectives on Cuba's Transition*. Notre Dame, IN: University of Notre Dame Press, 2007.

Quirk, Robert E. *Fidel Castro*. New York: Norton, 1993.

Remnick, David. *Lenin's Tomb: The Last Days of the Soviet Empire*. New York: Vintage Books, 1994.

Robinson, Eugene. *Last Dance in Havana: The Final Days of Fidel and the Start of the New Cuban Revolution*. New York: Free Press, 2004.

Saar, Erik, and Viveca Novak. *Inside the Wire: A Military Intelligence Soldier's Eyewitness Account of Life at Guantanamo*. New York: Penguin Press, 2005.

Smith, Wayne S. *The Closest of Enemies: A Personal and Diplomatic Account of U.S.-Cuban Relations Since 1957*. New York: W. W. Norton and Company, 1987.

Sweig, Julia E. *Inside the Cuban Revolution: Fidel Castro and the Urban Underground*. Cambridge, MA: Harvard University Press, 2002.

Symmes, Patrick. *The Boys from Dolores: Fidel Castro's Schoolmates from Revolution to Exile*. New York: Pantheon Books, 2007.

United States Government Accountability Office. Report to Congressional Requesters. *Economic Sanctions: Agencies Face Competing Priorities in Enforcing the U.S. Embargo on Cuba.* Washington, DC: U.S. Government Printing Office, November 2007.

United States Government Accountability Office. Report to Congressional Requesters. *Foreign Assistance: U.S. Democracy Assistance for Cuba Needs Better Management and Oversight.* Washington, DC: U.S. Government Printing Office, November 2006.

Valladares, Armando. *Against All Hope: A Memoir of Life in Castro's Gulag.* Translated by Andrew Hurley. San Francisco: Encounter Books, 2001.

Woodward, Bob. *State of Denial: Bush at War, Part III.* New York: Simon & Schuster, 2006.

Ziegler, Melanie M. *U.S.-Cuban Cooperation Past, Present, and Future.* Gainesville, FL: University Press of Florida, 2007.

Index

A Note on the Author

Daniel P. Erikson is the senior associate for U.S. policy at the Inter-American Dialogue think tank in Washington, D.C. He has published more than fifty opinion pieces and scholarly articles in publications including the *Washington Post*, the *Los Angeles Times*, and the *Miami Herald*. He is the coeditor of *Transforming Socialist Economies: Lessons for Cuba and Beyond* and received a Fulbright scholarship in Mexico.